PRAISE FOR *THE LAST FRONTIER*

"Julia Assante's *The Last Frontier* presents a brilliant combination of three categories of evidence for survival of consciousness after death — the science, the history, and personal experience. Written from the unique perspective of an Ivy League scholar and a talented psychic, it is exceptionally well grounded and accessible. Assante's book offers an important contribution to our understanding of death, dying, and beyond."

— Dean Radin, author of
The Conscious Universe and *Entangled Minds*

"In *The Last Frontier*, Julia Assante helps us approach death in ways that enlarge life, and to grow our ability to step between worlds and have timely and helpful contact with those who are living on the other side. Writing with passion and eloquence, deftly mixing the data of science and history with firsthand experience, she succeeds magnificently in a venture that is of urgent and essential relevance to all of us, because when we make death our ally, we find the courage and clarity to remake our lives and our world."

— Robert Moss, author of *Dreamgates*,
The Dreamer's Book of the Dead,
and *Dreaming the Soul Back Home*

"Come along as Julia Assante guides you through a magnificent exploration of that uncharted, simply-out-of-this-world terrain we encounter when we die. With an eloquent balance of science and soul, she shows us that by beginning to grasp the miracle that is death we can transform guilt and grief as well as our relationships with loved ones on this side and the next, and in the process, create healing and peace in our troubled world. She unveils the afterlife as a realm of unlimited possibility, expanded awareness, and ineffable love."

— Dianne Arcangel, author of *Afterlife Encounters* and coauthor
(with Raymond Moody) of *Life After Loss*

the LAST FRONTIER

the LAST FRONTIER

Exploring the Afterlife and Transforming Our Fear of Death

JULIA ASSANTE, PhD

Foreword by LARRY DOSSEY, MD

New World Library
Novato, California

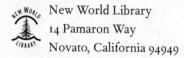

New World Library
14 Pamaron Way
Novato, California 94949

Text design by Tona Pearce Myers

Library of Congress Cataloging-in-Publication Data
Assante, Julia, date.
 The last frontier : exploring the afterlife and transforming our fear of death / Julia Assante, PhD ; foreword by Larry Dossey, MD.
    p.   cm.
Includes bibliographical references and index.
ISBN 978-1-60868-160-0 (pbk. : alk. paper)
1. Future life. 2. Near-death experiences. 3. Spiritualism. I. Title.
BF1311.F8A87 2012
129—dc23   2012026240

First printing, November 2012
ISBN 978-1-60868-160-0
Printed in the USA on 100% postconsumer-waste recycled paper

New World Library is proud to be a Gold Certified Environmentally Responsible Publisher. Publisher certification awarded by Green Press Initiative. www.greenpressinitiative.org

10 9 8 7 6 5 4 3 2

To my husband, Walter

✌❖✌

Contents

PART III: DYING, DEATH, AND BEYOND

PART IV: ALL ABOUT CONTACT

FOREWORD

oward the end of a life spent trying to see truly, novelist Arthur
Koestler said, "[We are] Peeping Toms at the keyhole of eternity.
But at least we can try to take the stuffing out of the keyhole, which
blocks even our limited view."[1] In *The Last Frontier*, Dr. Julia Assante
not only removes the stuffing from the keyhole but demolishes the keyhole altogether, along with the door containing it. Assante leaves us
standing blissfully awestruck, face-to-face with unsuspected splendor.

If *The Last Frontier* does not take your breath away, it should, for it
upends nearly all the assumptions in life that we unconsciously accept
as hard facts. Assante shows that the two major signposts we erect in
life — birth at one end, death at the other — are not absolute, one-
time events but transitions in states of being. The in-between duration
spanning the crib and the crematorium is not the one-way, flowing time
we take it to be but a nondurational expression of eternity. Assante
reveals the futility of striving for immortality; she shows that we are
already immortal, even if we are too blinkered to notice. Immortality is
our birthright, she says. It comes factory installed, part of our original
equipment. We do not need to acquire or develop it. We don't live *into*
eternity; we're up to our neck in it *now*.

The natural result of this realization is the diminution or eradication of the fear of death, which throughout human history has caused more suffering than all the physical diseases combined. That is why this book is an exercise in *fearolysis* — the dissolution or lysis of the death fear, that dark dread and weariness that are part of the human condition.

Many wisdom traditions have recognized the comic relief that can result when a death-haunted human suddenly realizes that the finality of death has been misconstrued all along — the Zen adept who erupts into laughter at the moment of enlightenment. The realization that the infinitude of life does not need to be developed, but has only to be realized, has burst upon the poets and mystics of all eras. Thus Emily Dickinson's exultation: "So instead of getting to Heaven, at last — / I'm going, all along."[2] Or St. Teresa of Avila's sixteenth-century statement: "The path to heaven is heaven."[3]

For those who believe we are blighted from birth with original sin, this is radical stuff. Assante confronts this dismal view firmly. She is uniquely qualified to do so, from her academic background as a scholar in ancient Near East cultures and beliefs. Her work points to intrinsic worthiness, not inherent sinfulness, as a hallmark of humanity. She would agree with Henry David Thoreau, an American original, when, on his deathbed in Concord, Massachusetts, in 1862, his aunt Louisa wondered aloud whether he had made his peace with God. Thoreau replied, "I did not know we had ever quarreled."[4]

Those individuals who have learned to sneer at "medium" and "psychic" should realize that Assante, who is both, has science on her side. *The Last Frontier*, in essence, is an exploration of the *nonlocal* manifestations of consciousness, for which there is overwhelming evidence.[5] Nonlocality is a startling concept that we twenty-first-century citizens might as well get used to. As Henry P. Stapp, the dean of quantum theorists at the University of California–Berkeley, says, nonlocality could be the "most profound discovery in all of science."[6] Nonlocality reveals an inherent connectivity, an unbroken wholeness, that is a fundamental aspect of the universe. This wholeness not only exists between subatomic particles but involves minds as well. As the prominent physicist Menas Kafatos and his coauthor, Robert Nadeau, write, "When nonlocality is factored into our understanding of the relationship between parts and wholes in physics and biology, then mind, or human consciousness, must be viewed as [a]...phenomenon in a seamlessly interconnected whole called the cosmos....[The] implications... are quite staggering...a new view of the relationship between mind and world."[7] Assante is at home with nonlocality, and the "seamlessly interconnected whole called the cosmos" is the canvas on which she paints.

For nonphysicists, *nonlocal* can be generally equated with *infinite*. If something is nonlocal or infinite in space, it is omnipresent. If something is nonlocal or infinite in time, it is eternal or immortal. Nonlocal mind, therefore, is infinite, eternal, and one — one, because there can be no separation between minds that have no boundaries in space and time. This astonishing realization has been embraced by some of the greatest physicists, including Nobelist Erwin Schrödinger, who proclaimed, "The overall number of minds is just one....In truth there is only one mind,"[8] and the distinguished physicist David Bohm, who asserted, "Deep down the consciousness of mankind is one. This is a virtual certainty...and if we don't see this it's because we are blinding ourselves to it."[9] With immortality and oneness in place, Assante's treatise begins to seem not radical but conservative.

One of the perennial objections to the phenomena Assante discusses is that they cannot possibly be true because they violate the laws of nature. If noncorporal spirits, telepathy, clairvoyance, and precognition exist, it is said that we would have to discard all of science and begin anew. This is an overheated objection for which there is no basis. The plain fact is that there are no known laws of consciousness that *could* be violated if consciousness survives bodily death or if these so-called paranormal phenomena are real. As cognitive scientist Donald Hoffman, of the University of California–Irvine, reminds us, "The scientific study of consciousness is in the embarrassing position of having no scientific theory of consciousness."[10] And as the eminent physicist

Gerald Feinberg said, "If such [nonlocal mental] phenomena indeed occur, no change in the fundamental equations of physics would be needed to describe them."[11] Physicist O. Costa de Beauregard goes further, saying, "Far from being 'irrational,' *the paranormal is postulated by today's physics*,"[12] and "Today's physics allows for the existence of the so-called 'paranormal' phenomena of telepathy, precognition, and psychokinesis.... The whole concept of 'nonlocality' in contemporary physics requires this possibility."[13] In other words, modern physics does not *prohibit* the events Assante examines, but it *permits* them. This permission is hugely important, because it encourages an openness toward human experiences that have too often been dismissed as the wild imaginings of sick brains.

And then there is the bugaboo of time. In *The Last Frontier*, we see time expanded, compressed, looped, reversed, and stilled. Surely these temporal antics violate the laws of physics and show that Assante is playing fast and loose with how the world works. But no. As with consciousness, the world of physics is in a muddle about time.[14] When asked what time is, the celebrated Nobel physicist Richard Feynman replied, "What is time? We physicists work with it every day, but don't ask me what it is. It's just too difficult to think about."[15] Physicist and author Paul Davies, too, describes this uncertainty: "In the emerging picture of mankind in the universe, the future (if it exists) will surely entail discoveries about space and time which will open up whole new perspectives in the relationship between mankind, mind, and the universe.... Notions such as 'the past,' 'the present' and 'the future' seem to be more linguistic than physical. There is none of this in physics.... No physical experiment has ever been performed to detect the passage of time."[16]

Readers should know that Assante is not a rogue voice. She has numerous allies in the "hard" sciences who also argue for an expanded view of consciousness. Consider the view of Robert G. Jahn, former dean of engineering at Princeton University, and his colleague Brenda

J. Dunne, who have researched the nonlocal behaviors of consciousness for three decades: "[An individual] may report that his consciousness seems to have been totally liberated from its center to roam freely in space and time....[R]ather than forming its experiences in the 'here and now,' consciousness may choose to sample the 'there and then.'"[17] Again, quantum theorist Henry P. Stapp: "The new physics presents prima facie evidence that our human thoughts are linked to nature by nonlocal connections: what a person chooses to do in one region seems immediately to effect what is true elsewhere in the universe....[O]ur thoughts...DO something."[18] And astrophysicist David Darling presents this view of what happens following death: "What was us will have merged again with the unbroken ocean of consciousness. We shall have returned to the place from which we came. We shall be home again — and free."[19] And not just free but, Assante assures us, ecstatic and loving as well.

I've peppered my observations with comments from authorities in science, which for three centuries has been considered the enemy of beyond-the-body expressions of mind, to show that science is cautiously tiptoeing toward a nonlocal view of consciousness. In science, it is no longer business as usual where consciousness is concerned. Brains are local entities; they stay put in the here and now. Consciousness does not — it behaves nonlocally; it can do things brains can't do.[20] To anyone paying attention, it is clear that the materialistic habit of equating consciousness with the brain is as dead as a doornail. It is a walking, desiccated zombie devoid of vital signs that thinks it is still alive. As Assante shows, these new views of the nature of space, time, and matter allow us to recalibrate our concept of the possible to include the likelihood of surviving bodily death. The entire idea ceases to seem outlandish. We may find ourselves agreeing with Voltaire: "It is not more surprising to be born twice than once."[21]

The barriers between science and a nonlocal view of consciousness, while they have not disappeared, are crumbling. *The Last Frontier* shows why. Just as the old foundations of earlier civilizations that Dr. Assante has excavated in her career as an archaeologist have had new structures built over them, she is building a new edifice atop the rubble of our primitive ideas of death. She has made a majestic contribution to human welfare by exposing the fallacy of the annihilation of consciousness with bodily death, in favor of immortality, joy, and love. I know of no greater achievement.

— Larry Dossey, MD,
author of *The One Mind* and *The Science of Premonitions*

INTRODUCTION

It's Simply Out of This World!

A nyone who has picked up this book probably has some belief in life after death or is at least open to the possibility. If so, you belong to a vast and age-old majority. For tens of thousands of years, humans have left signs in the archaeological remains of burials and art of their faith in an adjacent universe that receives them in spirit after the body's demise. For at least the past five thousand years, priests and priestesses, poets, prophets, and mystics have attempted to describe this universe in writing according to the knowledge of their times. In the modern era, the exact nature of the afterlife stands on rapidly shifting sands, with individuals harboring widely divergent opinions. And it is only recently that the very existence of an afterlife has come under fire. Whether or not any portion of the personality survives is now a topic of ardent debate. Between the believers and the debunkers are the fence-sitters who are leaving it to science to settle the question.

Yet for the first time in history, the voices of personal experience are being heard more loudly than the official ones of religions or science. Collectively, those who have had contact with deceased family and friends or who have themselves been clinically dead and returned to life speak powerfully and persuasively of a life to come. In these pages we will hear their stories. From several different vantage points, we will look closely at what is experienced before, during, and after passing. And we will explore the ever-flexible nature of the afterlife, largely from the perspective of the dead who are living it. They alone have the authority to answer what is perhaps life's most fundamental question: What happens after we die? From what they have told us so far, we have learned that where they are now is bursting with dazzling possibilities and freedoms undreamed of before. It's simply "out of this world"! And because it is also larger than life in every way, contact with it expands us in every conceivable direction.

The overall aim is to normalize communication between this world and the next, the necessary next step in humanity's development, a step, it seems, we are ready to take. Contrary to popular belief, contact with the departed brings immeasurable benefit to the living, the least of which is the alleviation of grief. The greatest good lies in the ability of the dead to reset our values, values that we need to build a better world. At the same time, contact also benefits the dead in many important ways.

It is astonishing that although every one of us will cross that threshold, we know close to nothing about what really happens on the other side. And it is downright tragic how few of us will consider communicating with the dead to find out. Whenever death is near, we pay for that ignorance. Questions so long avoided flood up: What's happening to me? Is there anything after I die or is this it? Will I feel anything? Will I be alone? Will someone come for me? Do I deserve to go to heaven? To hell? Is there a heaven or hell? Is there a God? All too often, these urgent questions are never seriously posed, because who "on earth" can we turn to for honest answers? Promises we hardly dare to believe in are made, to try to find a way to communicate, to send a sign, and to meet again in the hereafter. But we can know what happens. And communication is not only possible; it is also normal. Furthermore, you don't have to be a saint, shaman, or medium to do it, since the tools you need are already hardwired in your makeup. The fact is, you are already using them every day.

The reason we don't know more about the afterlife and how to make contact is simple: we are scared to death about death. Although the strongest force on earth is love, I have no doubt that the second strongest is the fear of death. Expectations of what is to come affect every private moment, shaping what we think and do, what we hope for, and what we hold as the meaning of life and reality in general. Poor attitudes about death and the afterlife lie at the core of our society's institutions; nearly anything you can name — law, religion, science, education, the arts, even economics — is structured around them. Whether you have a firm trust in survival, take a wait-and-see position, or think that "from dust to dust" is the literal end, you cannot escape these attitudes. The social fear of death traps us in a playing-it-safe existence in which we no longer actualize our inborn audacity to live up to our own ideals.

Pause for a moment and think about your own reactions when I use the term *the dead*. We can gauge how bleak our social attitudes are when we recognize the gap between a phrase like "talking to the dead" and the personal act of talking to your late Auntie Jean. Communication with the deceased eliminates the fear of death. So does encountering death directly, as near-death experiencers testify. In fact, any significant experience that brings you face-to-face with the true nature of your immortality will dramatically reduce this fear and enrich your life.

While working on this book, I was constantly exposed to alarming attitudes about death and the afterlife. Because people know me as an academic of the ancient Near East, they comfortably assumed I was writing a research book on death in extreme antiquity. If I explained what this book is really about, especially "the communication with the dead" part, the silence that followed was deafening. Once people recovered their composure, they quickly changed the subject. Occasionally, a person feels a duty to warn me, with grave authority, about the harm that comes from thinking about death, such as depression and suicidal longing. Nothing could be further from the truth. The irony is, if I had told them I was writing a novel in which half the earth's population was wiped out by weapons of mass destruction or a comet hit, they would have been enthralled.

But then, in private moments, the stories gradually come out, some of them remembered from childhood. I hear about visitations or sensed presences, strange dreams, intuitions, odd occurrences before and after the passing of someone close. I also hear point by point what happened when a person went to a professional medium and got messages from late relatives and friends. All these events reach deep into the human heart and mind. When people reveal them, their demeanor transforms. They move closer to me, their voices drop nearly to a whisper, and there is an urgency in the telling. These intimate moments are clearly unforgettable, sacrosanct, and very, very real.

I am also privy to confessions of secretly talking to the dead, most often silently and sometimes within the context of prayer. I have met more than one atheist who claim not a shred of belief in survival yet still mentally chatter away at their lost loved ones. How much communication with the dead really goes on is surprising, though it is generally denied. As it stands now, it takes real strength to withstand the onslaught of doubt and foreboding about "conjuring up the dead" deliberately. The notion that anything having to do with death somehow invites the Grim Reaper into our homes is just plain poppycock. Instead of feeling helplessly attracted to death, those who have met it directly in near-death experiences, *even if they were negative experiences*, as well as those who have been visited by the dead feel a renewed love of life and a profound sense of purpose.

Although this book is written for anyone with an interest in the afterlife, and especially for the bereaved, it is written just as much for the untold numbers already living on the other side. Some have been waiting for decades to tell you of their undying love, to inspire, encourage, reassure, counsel, and warn. To assuage your grief and bring solace and comfort. To seek forgiveness or to forgive.

Between a Rock and a Hard Place

The percentage of people reporting contact with the dead in surveys ranges anywhere from 42 to 72 percent. Widows having contact with their deceased husbands can go as high as 92 percent.[1] If the surveys had included children and deathbed encounters, which are extremely common, the percentages would have been even heftier. A whopping 75 percent of parents who lost a child had an encounter within a year of the child's death.[2] But a sad 75 percent of all those who had encounters reported not mentioning them to anyone for fear of ridicule.[3] It's hard to believe that a society can deny the validity of an experience shared by so large a proportion of its population. But we do. Many organized and not-so-organized religions go so far as to condemn communication with the dead, a position that at least admits contact is possible. Until recently, near-death experiencers have suffered great distress from disbelief and derision, silenced by those they were expected to trust most, their families and physicians. The same holds for people on the verge of death, since the phenomena they typically experience, such as visits from the dead and visions of the other side, are treated as symptoms of dementia. All these people are between a rock and a hard place.

I know what it's like to be between a rock and a hard place, as does anyone who regularly witnesses psychic phenomena. While I was in graduate school, I had to conceal my background as a practicing psychic of over thirty years in order to get my doctorate. Even today, very few of my academic colleagues know. Most people think of me as clearheaded and realistic, until I bring up something about the paranormal. Their discomfort, the prickling effect of their confusion, anger, and impatience, still takes me aback. Some of you readers might have similar reactions as you read through these pages — an "Oh, come on!" reaction — for I have risked my own credibility by drawing on personal and professional experiences to illustrate certain themes.

I am telling you this as a way of preparing you. As *you* become more familiar with the phenomenal world, you are bound to notice more within your own circle of family and friends, dead or alive. Then you too will be faced with risking your credibility if you dare to speak out about your experiences. The more of us who openly pioneer the last frontier and take that risk, the more we, together, add to the sum total of knowledge of the afterlife and of the nature of reality itself. When that total grows large enough, it will cause an unprecedented sea change in our collective worldview.

Psychic perception challenges and expands rationality. Yet critical thinking is equally important, because it disciplines psychic activity of any variety. Objectivity matters too, because it helps us avoid the problem of turning the unfamiliar into the familiar. For example, say you were born a long, long time ago into a religion whose chief divinity was a legendary holy man we'll call here Akhemotep. Let's suppose that in life Akhemotep had close followers. Over time he and his followers came to be regarded as celestial beings — he, equated with the sun, and his followers, with the planets. And then you had a near-death experience (NDE). When you were revivified, instead of telling people what you really saw, a being of light as well as dead friends and relatives, you unwittingly transformed your experience into the familiar and the acceptable. You told people that you had met Akhemotep and his planetary saints. How would we understand NDEs if you were the only person known to have had one? Your interpretation of what happened not only would be misleading, if not distasteful for people who don't believe in Akhemotep, but also would bury the existence of a being of light, a being independent of personal religion. It would furthermore preclude investigation of survival of the dead. Your genuine after-death experience would eventually be discarded as mythological twaddle. So, a lot can be lost when the unfamiliar is covered over with the familiar.

Knowledge is also buried when we ignore differences. Recently I read a book in which the authors survey afterlife beliefs within various traditions (Christian, Muslim, Jewish, Hindu, Native American, etc.) to come to the bafflingly and untenable conclusion that they are all fundamentally the same. This kind of uncritical thinking may be comforting, but it blocks avenues of new inquiry that could lead to a great deal of valuable information.

Just as versions of the hereafter are endlessly diverse, the multifaceted experience of dying differs for each person as well, despite its biological component. Each death is unique. Overall children die differently from adults, animals from humans, the long-ill from the accident victim. In the same way, afterlife experiences are highly divergent, shaped by an individual's beliefs, culture, and personal wants. The more we know about those differences, the more we discover new directions and broaden possibilities.

My goal is for you to become an independent thinker when it comes to the dead and the sphere they inhabit, basing your conclusions on your own intuitions and experiences while keeping them open to evaluation and change. Therefore, much of what is contained in these pages is hard at work challenging beliefs that impede independent awareness. This book is meant not only to stimulate your critical thinking but also to expand the range of questions you ask about the nature of the afterlife and, hence, of reality itself. Additional motives are at work here too. In chapter 12, you will learn that independent thinkers have more encounters with the deceased than others have. A third motive comes from my own work as a medium and from studies of positive and not-so-positive near-death experiences. Both show that if a person dies, clinically or permanently, with a fistful of unexamined, dogmatic assumptions, it can cause an array of complications in the immediate afterlife, whereas just a jot of open-mindedness leads to experiences that are full, deep, and transcendent.

WHY EXPLORE THE AFTERLIFE?

You might be wondering, why waste time exploring the afterlife if you are going there anyway? There are so many reasons I hardly know where to begin. First of all, the living receive outstanding boons from direct experience with the afterlife, the greatest of which is losing the fear of death. We will briefly go through all of this here and cover it in detail in later chapters. People have spontaneously achieved direct experience in many ways. It may come in the form of an NDE, obviously. It very frequently occurs to the dying when they are in the state newly coined nearing-death awareness (explained below). One-to-one encounters with the dead are another common way direct experience occurs. Lastly, the afterlife has been revealed to people in dreams, reveries, meditations, trances, hypnotic regressions, and revelations and while out walking the dog.

Direct experience of any kind will also bring you into contact with your immortal self. That alone will lessen, if not eradicate, the fear of death. The ancient notion that through progeny we perpetuate ourselves, achieving a kind of genetic immortality on earth, is perhaps the main reason we are now facing a population crisis. If it were common knowledge that the true self, the immortal self, transcends all lineages, familial, national, and racial, as well as the boundaries of time and place, global population would quickly come under control. Furthermore, if we were to truly understand the afterlife, our fear of death would vanish. We would then be able to let go of the chronic mistrust we currently have of our own bodies. Instead of regarding them as time bombs, we would recover a childlike faith in the body's capacity for health and healing, which would lead to longer, healthier lives.

Individually, afterlife experiences produce changes that are often radical, from the physiological to the intellectual, psychological, and spiritual, from winning the lottery to spectacular shifts in personal worldviews. Generally, people are no longer blind to what really matters. Petty fears pale in the light of the miraculous. Countless struggles that once seemed so important are suddenly seen as misspent energy, like Don Quixote's attacks on windmills. The desire for material gain gives way to a new desire for knowledge, to provoke fresh thought and deeper reflection, to develop spiritually. The need to compete against others gives way to the self-discovery of one's own authenticity. Space in the psyche is freed up, allowing emotional reserves once wasted on fear-based self-interest to turn toward creativity and service. Compassion replaces prejudice. And love, hate. Unbearable sorrow swings to joy.[4] Some NDEs have worked spontaneous cures, wiping out end-stage diseases without medical intervention. Imagine a whole world populated by people like this, people who know who they are and are clear about what really matters!

More specifically, communication with the departed not only helps rid us of the fear of death but can also end just about any emotional difficulty you might have after the demise of a loved one — grief, anxiety about what happens to the departed, feelings of abandonment, loneliness, regret, anger, and guilt. When contact is made, these feelings have a way of mutating with amazing speed into joy, relief, gratitude, and wonder. In cases where death is sudden and unexpected or where you could not or would not say all those words you meant to say before it was too late, the good news is, it's never too late.

Relationships don't stop at death; hopes and concerns for the living and, above all, love, are some of the things that you can and do take with you beyond the grave. A common impetus for communicating on both sides of the veil is to ask for forgiveness. Reconciliation is not only possible but practically inevitable, even if you do nothing from your end to achieve it. The tremendous therapeutic value of contact with the dead is now beginning to get the recognition it deserves with the recent birth of induced after-death communication therapy.[5] We'll look at some of those astounding cures in chapter 12. We are also beginning to learn that interaction with the afterlife greatly benefits the dying and eases their passage. It comes naturally to those who are weeks, days, or hours from death. As the final moment draws nearer, insights arrive with increasing frequency and depth, dreams and deathbed visions with brilliant lucidity. Glimpses of otherworldly landscapes of superenergized, radiance-filled vitality have such indescribable splendor that they transfix the beholder. It must have been just such a landscape that Steve Jobs saw when he uttered his last words: "Oh, wow! Oh, wow! Oh, wow!" More common are the vivid appearances of deceased family members who come to assist the dying, to escort their passage and bring comfort. These extraordinary deathbed features are so commonplace they have acquired a name, nearing-death awareness.[6]

When we disregard the paranormal events that surround the deathbed, we also miss a great deal of essential information about the death process and the afterlife itself, as well as messages about what the dying need, what they want for us, and, sometimes, what day or hour they will draw their final breath. Nearing-death awareness seems to arise when people make peace with death. It is most noticeable in those whose bodies are gradually shutting down. In situations where mortality is sudden, victims of accidents, crimes, and war are still lovingly assisted.

Sadly, even when it is medically evident that the end is imminent, any direct mention of death to the dying is avoided as a rule. We unconsciously believe that talking about death draws the moment nearer. In many areas of the world, doctors go so far as to promise terminally ill patients an improvement in health. If anyone is going to talk about death to the dying, let the experts take the risk, the pastors, priests, and rabbis, who have in stock ready-made descriptions of what awaits us. The painful irony is, when the dying have reached the acceptance stage, they generally want the fact of their demise to come out into the open. Only then can they be sure that their loved ones are prepared. If they don't speak of death, nine times out of ten it is because they are protecting the people around them.

Not all will admit they are dying, not even to themselves. Unbelievable as it may seem, some people go through the dying process with such denial that they realize their condition is irreversible only *after* death. Several dead I have worked with took days to fully come to terms with their new situation. A few were still blaming family and friends months after passing for evading the obvious and avoiding discussion about life plans in their absence. False expectations and unchallenged fears also get in the way of a smooth passage. A minority might be overcome by confusion, anger, and occasionally disappointment directly after death when confronted with something other than they expected. In a handful of cases, those with deep self-doubts might hallucinate scenarios that conform to their worst fears. Difficult adjustments are usually short-term, lasting no more than a few days from our standpoint. And someone is always on the other side ready to assist. If the dying were to explore the afterlife as it is actually lived, postmortem turmoil would all but cease. As it stands now, we expect them to head out into uncharted territories, alone and unprepared, unsure of even survival itself.

Although everyone will eventually enter this last frontier, we have made little attempt to chart it as a culture. Instead, we spend billions exploring outer space. Honestly! Who do you know who will ever go there? The traditional maps of the afterworld relied on in the past are not much more than fantasies. New maps of the utmost importance are now being drawn from composite studies of near-death experiences (see chapter 3); still they depict only specific sections of the coastline. The rest and the regions deeper inland remain to be explored. I cannot imagine how much it would ease all of us to know more about where we are going, not to a place of judgment, but to a place of compassion, a place of humor-filled self-discovery, unbridled creativity, and utter enchantment.

Because there is little reason as yet to invest hope in communication between the living and the dead, death is all the more despairing and frighteningly final. This too can change. Learning to make contact with the departed would dissipate the deathbed gloom of being condemned to unbridgeable separation and enduring silence. It would lift a now-unbearable sorrow while dramatically transforming the way we die.

Communication is good not just for the living but also for the dead. Contrary to absurd notions that we should not bother the deceased, not try to bring them "down" to our level, most of our loved ones want to make contact for all the reasons we do. Besides, it's harder to push the dead around than the living. So, if they don't want contact, it won't happen. From what I have seen, once they realize they have achieved two-way communication, they are overcome by relief. Instead of feeling bothered, they feel exhilarated and deeply grateful. Over the decades

I have watched them show up — at home, in my office, on the streets, and during all types of social events, from quiet telephone conversations to boisterous parties. When they appear, no fear is involved; no chandeliers crash to the floor, and no people have heart attacks or brain-deteriorating blackouts. Their visits are respectful and motivated by the best intentions. They come whether or not anyone is hoping to see them, almost always to help someone they know.

That being said, many dead people remain troubled by problems left unsolved. Some of them are frantic to reach the living, especially if their deaths were unexpected. When contact is made and their stories are heard, their inner exuberance is released. Others come back to confess the wrongs they committed in life. Even in the afterworld, strong guilt and regrets can persist, keeping the dead emotionally imprisoned. Until reconciliation is achieved between the two parties, ideally in conscious, heartfelt communication, neither the living nor the dead will be able to truly heal and move on. The desire of the dead can be so constant, they might wait for decades to be heard. Unfortunately, their attempts to get our attention are usually ignored or mistaken as a wish-fulfillment fantasy or an upsurge of grief.

When we do make contact, we don't have to be satisfied with a fleeting apparition or a one-line message. Instead, all of us, on this side and the other, are capable of sustained two-way communication, which can recur indefinitely. Although I have long been talking to the departed, I did not truly realize until after the death of my dear friend Michael that communication could be so direct and interactive. It can. That first contact with him lasted over an hour and stands today as one of the most ecstatic events of my life. He too was swept away, riding on the relief that someone could still see and hear him. That first stunning encounter is the real inspiration behind this book. We can have actual dialogue with our loved ones on the other side, with questions and answers, avowals, misunderstandings, and confirmations. We can discuss things, disagree, and even joke with each other. Communication can be passionate or calm, angry or loving, sad or joyful. But whatever it is, at the end of it, you are likely to feel pure elation.

It would be no exaggeration to say that the deceased are a dependable source of reassurance, encouragement, inspiration, wisdom, and sheer amazement. Just as important are their eyewitness accounts of the afterlife, each one unlike the next, which impart information about their reality that truly bends the mind. If we let them, the dead will charge our lives with greater meaning and redefine our concept of reality. All in all, exploring the afterlife through contact with those who are living it is an unparalleled adventure.

A REVOLUTION IN CONSCIOUSNESS

In the past few decades, we have witnessed an explosion of information about death and the afterlife, generated by an ever-growing number of psychologists and psychiatrists, physicians, hospice nurses and bereavement counselors, near-death experiencers, researchers in parapsychology, and, of course, mediums, who are working toward a better understanding of the world to come. This is one of many signs that the human race is poised to enter a new era, an era I would call a revolution in consciousness. Another sign is that belief in survival after death is on the rise, up to 89 percent according to some surveys.[7]

In Western countries, more and more people believe in a kinder hereafter. Instead of hell they expect joy, reunion with loved ones, and the complete absence of pain and worry. As concepts of the afterlife are inextricable from concepts of the Divine, when one changes, so does the other. Predictably, the fear-inspiring God of old is giving way to a more abstract Supreme Being whose laws are written in the spirit of love, compassion, and forgiveness rather than judgment.

The belief in communication with the dead is also on the rise and to such an extent that it has moved into the mainstream. We already see it dramatized in films and popular TV mystery shows, unrealistic as they may be. The near-death experience, which combines communication with the conviction of postmortem survival, has joined the pool of common knowledge since the groundbreaking work of Raymond Moody in the mid-1970s.[8]

According to all surveys, belief in after-death survival is extremely low among scientists, around 16 percent.[9] So it is ironic indeed that technology developed by science seems to be the launching pad of such a revolution. The connection between the medical technology of resuscitation and the proliferation of near-death returnees is self-evident. The fact is, the shift in consciousness started much earlier, back in the 1800s, with the invention first of the telegraph (1843) and later the telephone, which Alexander Graham Bell introduced to an astonished audience in 1876 at the Centennial Exhibition in Philadelphia. Bell's presentation publicly demonstrated that a disembodied human voice could be received and heard from an unseen distance (speaking, no less, Hamlet's soliloquy), a startling parallel to communication with the dead. Of all the devices invented in the past century and a half, the telephone is the most involved in afterlife phenomena and the most common symbol in dreams and visions for telepathic contact.

Since then the radio has broadcast sound, and television, sound and images, into almost every home.[10] With these old technologies alone we grew used to the idea of unheard sound and unseen images moving in waves through space. A transmission picked up by an open receiver is very similar to the projection and reception processes of telepathy, although telepathy is generally targeted to a specific recipient and is definitely faster. All these technologies also help make distinctions between the brain and the mind. As you will see in the following chapters, the brain neither generates nor contains thoughts, feelings, and memories any more than your television set has the starship *Enterprise* stuffed into it. Both are receiver-transmitter systems.

The Internet has been an even better training ground for expanding our conceptual frameworks, because it transmits information from multiple points that work like inner dimensions. The notion of cyberspace and virtual reality accustoms us to entire dimensions of activity where space is collapsed and distances do not exist — you are at most only one page away from where you want to be — which is analogous to the nonphysical, no-space nature of the afterlife. Like telepathy, information and communication are everywhere at once and respect no barriers.

Technology now allows us to peer into the atom. If you don't already know, you will learn in chapter 2 that the atoms that make up the world of matter almost entirely consist of energies, oscillations, and force fields. Matter is hardly solid at all and much less "real" than we realize, a fact known by physicists and naturally by the dead, but not one integrated into the day-to-day sense of reality. That means our bodies are not much different from the energy bodies of people in nonphysical domains. Those people are acutely aware that physical reality is moreover a projection or camouflage system, one from which they often borrow when they construct parts of their own environments. They know that the bodies they inhabit and the places they go are the products of thought projection. What you see, hear, smell, or feel when you make contact with them comes by way of telepathy. I will explain what telepathy is and how it works in chapter 15.

These new technologies together with the news and entertainment industries have further developed our perceptual abilities to take in ever greater amounts of information bytes at ever greater speeds. This helps train us for telepathic encounters, which are commonly transmitted in images arriving at high speeds. Precisely capturing these images is very important to the accuracy of after-death communication. You will learn how to do all this in chapter 16, so that the telepathy you already use every day will become more noticeable, more exact, and more reliable.

With the advent of airborne vehicles, our former ideas of distances and how to cross them have been erased. This and satellite shots of our little green-and-blue orb rotating in space have entirely changed our concept of the world we live in. Aware of the fantastic immensity of the universe around us, in which Earth is tucked away in one undistinguished corner, we can now think in terms of light-year distances that are so huge they bend time and space, and we can extrapolate the unbelievable diversity possible within it. No distance, no matter how great, is unthinkable to traverse, and envisioning reaching across the cosmos to hardly imaginable destinations in the centuries to come is no longer pure fantasy. When you really think how far technology has pushed us to open up our conceptual borders, propelled in turn by the media, the idea of exploring the last great frontier and communicating with its residents seems not just to be well within the bounds of realistic possibilities but actually unavoidable in the long run.

Lost in Translation

Again and again those who have dipped into the hereafter report extreme difficulties in describing what happened. As in the dream state, time, space, the sequence of events, emotions, perceptual capabilities, and sensory stimuli are altered in ways that cannot be satisfactorily expressed in languages developed for use in the physical world. Out-of-body experiences of nontime, simultaneous time, or compressed time (I'll explain more about this in chapter 8) and visits from the dead are nearly impossible to convey without resorting to media terminology, such as fast-forwarding, zooming, picture projections (in midair!), semitransparency, and backlighting.

At the most elementary level, those who have left their bodies in NDEs see without using their eyes. How can a person describe that kind of seeing with the languages we now have? How do you describe what it's like to have an energy body but at the same time to feel as though you are a point in space? If you have had an encounter with the dead, how do you describe hearing when no words were actually spoken? And then there are those impossibly gorgeous feeling states that encompass people within layers upon layers of otherworldly emotions and insights, leaving them awestruck and...well...speechless. Words like *love* and *beauty* are maddeningly pallid, maddeningly inadequate, for expressing what people perceive in dimensions outside the physical. One near-death experiencer exclaims that "the very best love you feel on earth is diluted to about one part per million" when measured against the "real" love she felt.[11] And this is just trying to convey the first minute or two out of the body!

Because of our present conceptual limitations, the dead generally stop trying to communicate anything of complexity and satisfy the need for contact with a few words of love and encouragement. Or they will enter into our dreams, where our conceptual paradigms are more fluid. If we want to know more, we will have to develop frames of perception that are as broad and as flexible as possible.

CONSCIOUSNESS

Perhaps the two concepts most pertinent to the afterlife are the surviving personality and the Divine. Both concepts continue to evolve and acquire new names as our awareness widens. Although the *soul* still stands as the most popular term for the surviving entity, with *spirit* second, the term *consciousness* is currently taking over. The older terminology of *soul* and *spirit* set up unnecessary disjunctures within the self and between this world and the next. A person is not called a spirit while alive, only after death. Similarly, a person can have a soul while alive, yet he or she becomes a soul after passing. Consciousness, by contrast, transcends these disjunctures and maintains the notion of the self as independent of physical identity. You do not have consciousness; you *are* consciousness, alive or dead.

What consciousness is has baffled scientists for decades. Once they identify it, hard proof of survival after death will quickly follow. I think of consciousness as sentient energy that tends to form constellations of identity, from simple cells to the most complex discarnates. When it focuses in material dimensions, it creates matter. The consciousness of each identity, no matter what the species, whether in the flesh or not, is unique. Yet all seek expansion and fulfillment. Discrete consciousnesses that make up individual selves form larger identities outside the physical, what mystics call oversouls. The oversoul is far more than the sum of its parts. It organizes individual consciousnesses, even giving birth to them. It is then our parent consciousness in a way. We are not lost in this massive superentity, nor are we diminished by it. I do not know enough about the oversoul, but one thing is clear to me: it is an inconceivably vast resource of knowledge, inspiration, and energy. If we were only more practiced in accessing it! Learning about the afterlife will help us do that.

ALL THAT IS

And then there is God, the ultimate ineffable. For me the word *God* is not enough, for it implies a distinct being who is located somewhere else, up far away in rarefied celestial spheres. My God is too immense to be a being and too indwelling to be somewhere else. For me, It is a consciousness of such massiveness that It dwarfs the cosmos. It is forever giving birth, spawning whole universes and reality systems, such as the physical one we are presently in. All thoughts, actions, and things, bodied and disembodied, human and nonhuman, alive and inanimate, visible and invisible, are made from Its tissue. As such, It permeates everything that ever is, ever was, and ever will be, while containing everything tenderly within Itself. Yet It also stands apart. Because It manifests all that is and is manifested in all that is, I use the name All That Is. But then I am trying to force All That Is into a nutshell.

How I experience the Divine is more important to me than what It is. For when I do, it is so engulfing that it soars above all experience known before or since. I hear my own experience echoed by those who have come back from near-death events. Struggling for words, they try to explain a light that is not light but something alive and aware and with which they merge. They try to convince us of the out-of-this-world depth of its love, its compassion, and even its humor. In my view, this knowing light is an aspect of All That Is that can best touch the hearts and souls of human beings.

The dead and some near-death experiencers speak of another manifestation of the Divine, not a being, but a radiant atmosphere that envelops them in the afterlife. I call it the Presence, and it has been palpable to me on and off since childhood. I remember it particularly when as a kid I had climbed to the top of a cherry tree in full bloom. As I gazed up at the glory of those vibrant pink flowers against a sparkling blue sky, the freshness around me intensified, gradually becoming independent of the physical environment. Somehow it came into its own, faintly at first, until it began to shimmer. I knew that it was aware of me and of everything around me, from the sky to each flake of bark. What strikes me most now is the intensity of its intimacy. It is intimately aware of the singular character of every atom and recognizes the importance of every stray thought, seeking always to nurture their potential as they move along their individual pathways through eternity. Through such divine manifestations we get a glimmer of the unfathomable magnitude and immeasurable love of All That Is. We sense the deeper meaning of existence, although we may not be able to make out its exact contours. And we know, finally, that death is not an end but rather a lifting out into that vast, knowing, luminous Presence, in which all things thrive and are made possible.

PART I

The Evidence for Survival

CHAPTER ONE

Can Survival after Death Be Proved?

The question of whether or not survival after death exists is an anomaly of modern times. To a large degree doubting survival or rejecting it altogether is the long-term result of the Enlightenment, when science began carving an identity for itself in opposition to religion. It took a few more centuries before scientists in the predominantly Christian West would dare to question an afterlife openly and even longer before they would adopt the stance of its being little more than religious drivel. Such a stance was tantamount to denying the existence of God and the central tenet of Christianity, the resurrected Christ. By the turn of the last century, the question of survival had become a legitimate and robust area of inquiry, preoccupying some of the most prominent scientists, scholars, and political figures of the time, from Nobel Prize–winning physicists to prime ministers.

By the dawn of the atomic age, the split between science and religion had become severe. Science's chief distinction from religion was its reliance on materialist explanations for how reality works, in which spiritual forces, primarily divine will, play no role. A second major distinction was its refusal to consider survival after death, the linchpin of all religions. In those heady days of atomic bombs and sending men to the moon, scientists believed that they alone could uncover the true nature of the universe, promising rational explanations based on objectivity and proof rather than on religion's subjectivity and faith. Human nature, which is too untidy for pure science to objectively observe and mathematically describe, was left to the softer sciences. Even there, the materialist view seeped in. Archaeologists, for example, founded "New Archaeology." Although they still studied man-made cultures, they gave archaeology a scientific gloss by reducing the human saga to dreary strings of statistics and plotted climatic shifts. The cultural monuments of myth and ritual were treated like poison.

The notion of objectivity itself suffered a crushing blow when physicists discovered that the observer influences the outcome of tests at the most fundamental level of existence, the quantum level. Heinz Pagels, former president of the New York Academy of Sciences, stated, "There is no meaning to the objective existence of an electron at some point in space...independent of actual observation. The electron seems to spring into existence as a real object only when we observe it.... Reality is in part created by the observer."[1] Until observation, then, it is not a "real object"; it has no objective existence or location in space or time. It seems, then, that we live in a subjective universe that sits on the razor's edge of matter and nonmatter.

I would not argue, as some do, that spirituality is the province of religion rather than science. To me, spirituality and materiality are not opposites; both are manifestations of the inner workings of reality, the study of which belongs to everyone. There is plenty of room for the desanctification of spirituality, just as there is for the dematerialization of hard-core positivist views of reality. On the other hand, the idea that hard science should have the last word is popular, and many today look to it for unequivocal answers about survival after death. This odd expectation supposes that the afterlife can be proved as an abstract law of nature, perhaps formulated mathematically and discovered at work inside an atom or at the core of a dying star or hidden somewhere in the massive, brooding stew of dark matter. Yet no one would expect science to provide proof for other invisible, unquantifiable aspects of reality, such as love. Although love cannot be proved, few scientists would deny its existence.

So far evidence for survival has come from the softer sciences, psychiatry and psychology, as well as medicine and biology, with specific, potentially revolutionary hints in neurobiology, quantum biology, and genetics. Survival evidence has been steadily mounting over the past century, largely because of medical advances that allow for more resuscitations. There is also much more awareness among physicians, more and more of whom are admitting to a belief in life after death, and especially among hospice personnel, so that more phenomena involving near-death experiences and nearing-death awareness are recorded and better documented than ever before. In addition, technology and engineering play a significant role in documenting the presence of the dead in sound and image.

In part I, we will look at the evidence from a number of standpoints. First, we'll explore the now-defunct materialist view of the universe. Materialists are people who believe that if you can perceive something with the physical senses or at least measure it, it's real. If you can't, it's imaginary. Hence, the brain is real, but the mind is not. A person in a body is real, but one without a body is not. We will then move on to the more conventional routes taken in search of proof: near-death experiences, after-death communication, and reincarnation. Given that the evidence is mostly composed of individual, somewhat isolated phenomena that do not submit to the scientific criteria required for proof, objective observation and replicability, later in this chapter I will briefly define the slippery line between proof and evidence as well as the especially tough problems parapsychologists face. In the interest of "objectivity," all of part I is based on the findings of other researchers, not my own. My job in this section is to present the evidence and evaluate whether or not it meets the standards of proof.

Typically, proof of survival is held to standards that are rarely met in other areas of research, the hard sciences included. Much of what the hard sciences present as proven is more extrapolation from a set of effects than fact. If this and that are observed to happen, why they happen is deduced. From these deductions, a workable hypothesis is formed and then tested. We don't know for sure, for instance, if there was ever a Big Bang, that stunning first moment in no-space, no-time, when something infinitely smaller than an atom exploded into what 13.7 billion years later would become the universe; nor do we know whether wormholes or even black holes actually exist. There has been no direct observation of these cosmic identities. The assumptions that they do exist derive from a set of discernible conditions that can best be explained — in the current state of our knowledge — by a bang or hole. The sorts of things astrophysicists and nuclear physicists now consider as probable conditions of reality also include equally fantastic notions such as the God particle (the Higgs boson), the many-worlds interpretation, string theory with its eleven dimensions — some of them "compactified" so we don't see them — the zero-point field theory, and the hidden-worlds theory, which all read like the wildest science fiction and make any theory of postmortem survival look as dull as dishwater.

These theories derive primarily from quantum mechanics, a branch of physics that describes what goes on at the subatomic level. Most support the supposition that our dimension is constantly interacting with other dimensions whose existences are so far not directly detectable. And we're close to proving it! If you think I'm kidding, consider the newest baby on the block, and she is a genuine showstopper — an actual physical object called the quantum computer. Because the quantum computer is based on the many-worlds interpretation, it helps to know what that theory is. The many-worlds interpretation claims that for every subatomic event, the universe in which that event takes place splits to create a second universe. This ceaseless bifurcation of universes, each one as complete and as real as the one you perceive now, results in so many worlds that their total approaches infinity. We humans do not notice when we and our universe split any more than we realize that versions of ourselves exist in an astronomical number of these different dimensions at the same time. Furthermore, you can be alive in one universe and dead in another.

The many-worlds interpretation of reality, also called the multiverse interpretation, is today the most widely accepted among leading cosmologists, quantum field theorists, and other scientists, including such geniuses as Stephen Hawking and the Nobel laureates Murray Gell-Mann, Richard Feynman, and Steven Weinberg. Although it seems logical that the concepts of multiverses, parallel worlds, and other spacetime dimensions would rapidly lead to discussion about afterlife dimensions, no one has as yet stepped on that bridge, as far as I know.

Formerly, physicists thought that these other universes could not affect our own. But David Deutsch, a leading proponent of the theory, says they do so all the time. And it was he who thought up the quantum computer. At least for now, the computer need not contend with all the nearly infinite number of universes out there but deals with only 256 of them. So when you submit something to it for calculation, it will compute that calculation in 256 dimensions, meaning 256 different universes, on 256 different computers, simultaneously. Consequently, what could take a conventional computer many millions of billions of years to find out would take a quantum computer about twenty minutes. Theoretically, in the future it should be able to compute in 10^{500} universes at once, that is, the number ten followed by five hundred zeros. Because the quantum computer is beginning to work, many scientists now believe that the multiverse interpretation is no longer just an interpretation of how reality works but a fact.[2]

Since there is no law in physics that prevents time travel, some of the greatest minds in science are beginning to consider interaction between different time dimensions of past and future with the here and now. Because the multiverse theory, string theory, and the hidden-worlds theory specifically propose invisible, interactive dimensions adjacent to our own, they may very well lay the foundations for future investigation of that other, all-important dimension called the afterlife.

The zero-point field theory is leading to a new way of looking at communication. The old view was mechanical or chemical: subatomic particles and atoms attract or repel by virtue of forces, mainly electromagnetic; molecules, cells, and genes, by virtue of something like chemical hooks. Now some scientists think that what is really going on has to do with frequencies of quantum waves. These waves are believed to be spread out through time and space into infinity and to connect every point of the universe to all other points. Such a conceptual breakthrough is a prerequisite for the investigation of consciousness as well as telepathy, the existence of which has been proved ad nauseam in clinical trials. The notable systems scientist and philosopher Ervin László has dared to propose that the zero-point field is actually consciousness permeating our four-dimensional universe. He is not the only one in the sciences arguing that consciousness, not materiality, is the primary reality.[3] All in all, these current theories seem to be preparing the way for scientific investigation of the afterlife.

Proof or Evidence?

Does the evidence we have now from near-death experiences, after-death communication, and reincarnation constitute proof of survival? If we consider it objectively, what has been garnered so far does satisfy most scientific standards:

- When considering a phenomenon, we can definitively state that something real is happening because of its effects.
- We can extrapolate a finite number of hypothetical causes from these effects, most of which can be easily discarded as untenable.
- Of the hypotheses that remain, the one that *best* and most elegantly explains all the observable effects of a given phenomenon turns out to be the existence of organized consciousness outside the realm of matter — in other words, life after death.

Unfortunately, deductions made by individual researchers from different fields have not been coordinated, nor are they individually or collectively considered sufficient reason to invest in a large-scale study of perhaps the most pressing issue we face in life. By contrast, we have invested some ten trillion dollars, the entire output of the nineteenth century, on developing the atomic bomb. We also have no problem sinking billions into the Large Hadron Collider, a particle accelerator sponsored by several governments. Compare this high-level coordination and mind-boggling expense with the small-scale, uncoordinated, usually private and unfunded investigation of life after death.

Can science prove life after death? Absolutely. If only 0.1 percent of the money and expertise that went into the atomic bomb were available we would have that proof within a few years. The problem is really science's ideology: there is no life after death. A scientist pursuing this line of investigation runs the risk of ridicule and loss of funding and even position.

Despite this, consciousness itself has become a big topic in many scientific circles, especially neurobiology. Symposia convene to discuss what it is and how it can be applied. In fact, the development of a conscious computer has already been thrown onto the table. One researcher has even combined living brain tissue with electronics in order to locate consciousness. Wouldn't it be better to study consciousness where it operates unhindered by matter — during manifestations of the dead? If my own body can register the presence of discarnates so dramatically, then surely science, especially the applied sciences, can come up with something sensitive enough to register nonrandom electromagnetic patterns in the atmosphere where an encounter is taking place.

Even if an instrument could reliably detect intelligence, we still have to find ways to distinguish the intelligence's identity from a personality, say, inhabiting one of the zillions of multiverses in which the dead still have no official existence. That means we have to communicate with it, get it to identify itself. This too has often been done, as you will find in the chapter on after-death communication (chapter 4).

Proof of identity presents a conundrum that we will look at fairly closely in the pages to come. If what a deceased person gives as proof of his or her identity can be verified by records or by testimony of the living, the fact that the sources of verification already exist in our world disqualifies the information. So, if I were to drop dead in the next few minutes and start communicating with you tomorrow, giving you my full name, the date and place of my birth, my professional publications, and my private particulars, such as while I was writing these very words I was sitting on a red velvet couch at a friend's house on the rue Daval in Paris with a dog named Lulu by my side, critics could throw it all out, because you, the receiver of this information, could have uncovered it by "normal" means, as unlikely as that might be. Others propose that you could come by the same information by less normal means, such as clairvoyance. You might have picked it up telepathically from the living, the dog perhaps or, better, her owner, and not from the dead. So whatever information already exists in our physical world is suspect, for it can be acquired either normally or psychically. Therefore it does not *prove* the existence of the dead. If, on the other hand, I were to tell you about my experiences in the afterlife, giving you information that does not exist in your physical present, there would be no way to verify it. Hence, it also is not proof. That's the conundrum. And critics love it.

Skeptics like to claim that because accounts of the afterlife as told by near-death survivors and the deceased differ from one another, they can't be true. The expectation of uniformity in the afterlife is naive, a by-product of the human need for reassurance. Fixed canonical versions of the afterworld are also necessary for religious leaders. How could leaders maintain authority if they waffled about what is to come? First of all, traditional conceptions of the afterlife are culturally constructed and change ceaselessly as society changes, even within the same religion, as chapter 6 explains. Secondly, what near-death survivors and the dead tell us about the afterlife varies according to the speaker's personal experience. Say you live on another planet with technology that enables you to communicate with various earthlings from different times and places. If one were to tell you about home in 70 BCE on the island that we now know as Manhattan and the other about home in 2084 CE Manhattan, it would be hard to believe they were talking about the same place. What if instead you were to speak with people in one time period but from different geographical areas, such as the Sahara, the Himalayas, the Amazon, and modern Manhattan? Which area would you designate as representative of Earth? The irreconcilable diversity might even lead you to believe that planet Earth is just a figment of the imagination.

Still, this is beside the point. If the afterlife does exist, it would not be in another quadrant of the material world. It would be in a non-material domain, one composed of projected thought forms and idea constructions, at least in the dimensions most immediately accessible to us. Thought forms do not take up space, but they can project the illusion of space, as dreams do. The afterlife would not be a place, although it could be made to seem like a place. It would be a nonlocal reality, and your place within it the result of your state of mind, a mental construction. An individual would be able to duplicate the physical laws of space, time, and matter if he or she so chooses, while never being bound by them.

Groups of individuals would reproduce portions of the world they left behind when wanted. Each society, each person would bring a bank of images and ideas from their own particular time and place for use as building blocks in their new reality in conformity to what was previously known. Replications can include idealized natural landscapes or gardens, architecture, clothing, and even bodies. They can also include situations. People's descriptions of the afterworld as they have been handed down to us by mystics, mediums, and near-death experiencers carry features plucked from their respective cultures. We would not expect an untraveled, illiterate Londoner in the Victorian era to reproduce a yurt in the afterlife. On the other hand, a Victorian gentleman who had traveled in the Gobi Desert might consider reproducing one. A Mongolian would almost certainly re-create a yurt.

The dead would of course not be confined to the real. Whatever could be imagined, such as crystal cities or heavenly realms composed of golden clouds, even fire and brimstone, could also be fashioned from thought. Because everything is a product of thought, anything can be changed in an instant simply by intention. This is all to say that uniformity in thought domains is not only the last thing we should expect; it is also the last thing we should hope for, as it would seriously constrict our creative abilities.

The dead's use of an already familiar imagistic vocabulary for creating camouflage systems similar to those they just left would of course change too. When that vocabulary expands with experience — a basic law of all consciousness — at a certain point, it would expand in directions that are beyond our range of comprehension. It may make some of you uncomfortable to posit an afterworld that offers no solid ground to stand on, so to speak. However, the freedoms would be unlimited, nurtured by a profound sense of safety.

So far I have talked only about what scientifically oriented communities can offer when it comes to the survival issue. Yet evidence is habitually used in other fields toward proving one thing or another, and I have in mind here the courtroom, where anything from forensic evidence to circumstantial evidence is used to establish guilt or innocence. The idea of following courtroom procedure instead of scientific procedure to prove survival after death is the brainchild of Victor Zammit, author of *A Lawyer Presents the Case for the Afterlife*. Many millions of people alive right now who have no links to science could be called upon to bear witness before a judge and jury. You might be one of them. If each one were to submit private testimony about his or her experiences with the world beyond and its inhabitants, the sum total would constitute evidence so overwhelming that we would not even need a lawyer to argue the case. Although there would be no one, no expert, no witness, to contradict such testimony, plenty of skeptics and cynics would jump at the chance to discredit the witnesses. What skeptics cannot do, what scientists cannot do, in fact, what no one can do, is *prove* that survival after death does *not* exist.

CHAPTER TWO

How Real Is Real?

The strongest opponents to survival after death generally make their stand on a single belief — that the material universe we are in is the only real universe. They consider this belief to be self-evident and take for granted that science is on their side. As we have seen in the introduction and chapter 1, while most scientists have a peculiarly low opinion of the afterlife theory, few who investigate reality from the tiny subatomic view or the gargantuan galactic view would claim that ours is the only real universe. Furthermore, the whole notion of what constitutes a real universe is in question. Some scientists have gone so far as to propose that our universe is merely a computer simulation made by the mental giants of some supercivilization. Would that still be a real universe?

Most of us take comfort in assuming we know what real is. Real is solid. Real is the book you are holding, the car you drive, the body you inhabit, the brain you think with. Real is what you can see, touch, taste, hear, or smell. Real may even extend to what can be perceived only through instruments, like a radio wave, for example. Still, it is eventually perceptible to the physical senses. The difference between people who are sympathetic to the possibility of an afterlife and those who are not is simple: the former allow for the existence of things beyond the horizon of what can be physically perceived, and the latter, the material realists, think there is nothing beyond that horizon.

What material realists don't take into consideration is that what we think of as real is not at all what we suppose. Scientists have concluded that 95.4 percent of the entire universe is not made up of something we can perceive. It is neither solid matter nor the sort of energy familiar to us. So what is that 95.4 percent made of? Twenty-eight percent of it is composed of dark matter, a mysterious something detected only by its gravitational pull. Dark matter affects how galaxies move and the universe expands, and there is six times more of it than ordinary baryonic matter. The huge remaining 72 percent is dark energy, which fills all space. It is not the same as our ordinary energy and can be detected only indirectly by its influence on the way the universe expands.

The rest, the 4.6 percent that materialists regard as real, is made up of the kind of matter and energy we are used to. A brick wall is of course part of that 4.6 percent. But how real is a brick wall? If you had super-vision, you would see that the brick wall is made up of atoms. You would notice that nearly all the volume of a single atom is created by forces and oscillations, not by matter, and by the pathways electrons take when they whiz around the atom's nucleus at velocities approaching the speed of light. Their movement produces the illusion of an electron cloud. The wall then is composed of atoms that look like infinitesimally tiny cloudlike dots. At this close an inspection, what looks solid from a distance looks more like patterns composed of these individual clouds.

Similarly, if you were to take a printed image and look at it under a magnifying glass, you would see that the image is made up of a pattern of dots or pixels. If you look too closely, you won't be able to see the overall image; you will just see the dots. The same is true of the images you watch on television and computer screens. If you had super-vision you would never see the whole picture; you would never see solid matter.

If your vision were again amplified to a point where you could look inside atoms, you would realize that these dots have hardly any substance. You would see that each atom contains smaller elements, the neutrons and protons, composed of the still-smaller quarks, and the gluons that hold them together, the electrons, and so on, up to some two hundred subatomic entities now recognized. What would be most puzzling is that the subatomic entities you find inside behave just as much like waves as they do like particles or objects. When entities are doing the wave thing, they can then be considered fields rather than objects. Conversely, we can talk about something we don't consider to be matter, such as light or electricity, as a stream of particles rather than waves.

If you were to take all the space out of the atoms in our brick wall, the amount of matter it contains would be the size of a pin prick. If you were to take all the space out of the atoms of the human body, you would be left with a microscopic dot. What makes us different from the dead is that dot.

To complicate "matters" more, you might remember from chapter 1, an electron will appear only when we observe it. In physics, this is called the observer effect. The simple fact is, without observation, the electron is only potentially there. That means that until we observe it, it is potentially anywhere in the universe. That's a pretty wide range of possibilities. The observer effect superbly demonstrates that attention calls matter into being. It gets more unreal by the nanosecond when you consider other components of "quantum weirdness," such as that quantum signals travel backward in time and that quantum entities communicate across great distances instantaneously.

All this is still not likely to be the end of the vanishing act of matter. Some scientists are considering the likelihood that quantum elements constantly appear and disappear at a rate too rapid to perceive. We perceive something only when it appears, when it's switched on in our universe, like a light. The author and physician Deepak Chopra refers to the place subatomic particles go when they disappear as virtual reality.

A photon moves from one point to another by disappearing, changing its location while in virtual reality and reemerging in another location. Theoretically, all quantum elements do this.[1]

When they reappear they are not exactly the same. Let's go back to the pixel analogy, only this time let's imagine that each pixel is like an atom made up of smaller elements, which we could call pixelettes, just for fun. In films, the pixel patterns differ from one frame to the next. What makes the pattern change frame by frame is the change in color and intensity of individual pixels. For every frame, individual pixels are replaced one by one. In our model, these changes would take place at the microlevel of pixelettes inside each pixel. These slight, smooth changes give the impression of movement, so that a sunset is really a series of slightly altered stationary patterns composed of pixels. When those frames run in rapid succession, they create a visual illusion of a mummy's face decaying into dust, for example. In the same way, minute changes at the atomic and subatomic levels give the impression of movement, but also of growth and aging. When you watch a plant grow from a sprout into a tree in your backyard, the same process is taking place. The plant is not really growing. Each time the plant's quantum entities flash back into our reality, they come back a little different, like our pixelettes. In the smallest possible units of time, one pattern is replaced by another, with more pixels added or removed frame by frame, making the plant appear to get bigger.[2]

What you consider a solid brick wall is not solid, save for an infinitesimal amount of matter, but rather forces and space, not stationary, but rather in movement and probably not always there but constantly blinking in and out of our reality. It is also capable of some sort of communication with consciousness because of the observer effect. I would say that the material realists are standing on rather unstable ground, figuratively and literally.

Maybe death is just a matter of blinking back in another direction, a change in focus or intention. After-death communication accounts agree that people in the hereafter change almost instantly. An aged and sick person can become youthful and healthy in the blink of an eye. The only difference between what we, the living, do and what they do is that we are confined to a pattern arranged in a tight sequence and they are not. In the physical world, we normally only blink from point A to point B and in such small increments that it looks seamless. There are many documented incidences, however, in which objects appear out of nowhere, usually somewhere just below the ceiling. These objects are called apports, things that disappear in one place and materialize in another, slightly hot to the touch. Most apports are achieved by human intention. The blinking-universe theory combined with the observer effect would explain how that happens: an object's atoms blink out and disappear into virtual reality to blink back in and, by intention, reappear in another location. Since distance is not a factor in virtual reality, the object does not have to go from point A to point B. Similarly, the dead don't have to blink in a series that is contiguous from our point of view, but can and do go from point A to point X or R or any other point they want. They control their next location simply by intention. And they can reverse directions, becoming younger or older, for instance. And like quantum entities, they can achieve instantaneous communication backward in time, as you will see in the next two chapters. Although they usually appear as light and energy, sometimes they appear so solid that people have touched them. In other words, the dead seem to follow laws much closer to quantum physics than the laws of classical physics.

If you think the universe at the atomic level is volatile, wait till you hear about the cellular universe. A person weighing 220 pounds (100 kg) is composed of roughly 10^{28} atoms.[3] These atoms combine to form molecules, and molecules, such as hydrogen and oxygen, combine to form substances, such as water, which makes up most of the body. Old molecules of the body are exchanged for new ones some sixty times between the ages of ten and seventy. That means that last year's body is not the one you are in today. Obviously, if atomic particles, atoms, and molecules are constantly coming and going, your cells must be on the move too. In fact, five hundred thousand of your body cells die and are replaced every single second. Every day, about fifty billion of them go through this process. Cells of the outer skin are shed and replaced every twenty-seven days on average, meaning that a person has some thousand new skins in a lifetime.[4] The microworld of atoms, molecules, and cells is busy indeed. Rather than being fixed and solid, existence at this minute level is in constant movement, in constant cycles of death and birth, appearances and disappearances. It's got to make you wonder, just how real are you anyway?

MIND OVER MATTER

Just as we assume a sharp divide between the real and the unreal, we assume that because intelligence is real, it must exist in a real thing — the physical brain. Whether this is true or not is under debate. Some neuroscientists, psychiatrists, and psychologists are asking if intelligence can exist outside the brain. Can what we call the mind, the seat of intelligence and generator of thought and identity, be separated from the physical brain and operate independently of the body? If it can be shown to operate outside the body, then there is some basis for believing that the mind, which holds your identity, your memories, your values, your hopes, and everything else that is you, can survive the body at death. To me, this is the central issue of the survival question.

Science cannot even explain memory, nor can it locate memories in the brain, despite all the brain mapping using CTs, MRIs, PETs, and EEGs. Small segments of the past can be stimulated by electrodes, but where the actual archives are stored is simply not known.[5] The neurosurgeon Dr. Wilder Penfield, who was among the first to stimulate the cortex during brain surgery, notes that a patient's mental activities went on uninterrupted and unaffected by the stimulation. Despite years of experiments, flashes of memory could be stimulated, but beliefs, problem solving, decision making, or any of the other activities of a thinking person could not.[6] Penfield and others have since demonstrated that neuroscience's current models of the brain cannot account for the subjective inner experience of the self.[7] All in all, they conclude that the mind is not in the brain at all.

Drawing a relationship between cranial capacity and mental ability is common. The bigger the brain, the greater a person's capacity for memory storage and, say, playing chess. If intelligence were just a matter of biology, then East Asians would rank highest in human intelligence, as their skulls are on average larger than those of other races. Furthermore, there would be no explanation for the amazing mental feats of some animals with brains the size of walnuts. I am thinking here in particular of parrots, which sometimes develop stupefying language abilities, whole grammatically correct sentences and a wide vocabulary, and the ability to count. Some are talented telepaths to boot.[8]

It is a fact that people who have had half of their brains surgically removed in an operation known as a hemispherectomy retain normal memory and identity.[9] Studies on children who went through this procedure show that they actually performed better in school with half a brain than they did when their brains were intact. And there are some science-defying instances in which normally functioning adults were found to have almost no brain at all. This was the case of a forty-four-year-old civil servant, married and the father of two children. Scans of his brain taken at the Université de la Mediterranée, in Marseille, showed a fluid buildup in his skull so great that it had compressed his brain into a thin sheet of tissue. Despite this, he led an entirely normal life.[10] If mental capacity does not always diminish when the size of the brain diminishes, the claim that intelligence resides in the brain is indeed dubious.

One mental skill that reaches far beyond the scope of the physical body is remote viewing. Certain people routinely perceive people, objects, and events at some other place on the planet; the distance between the viewer and the so-called target is of no consequence. Sometimes they see an event well before it occurs. The skill is reliable and accurate enough for the government to employ individuals to remote-view in order to locate such things as munitions stockpiles in enemy territories.[11] If the brain were running things alone, it could operate only in the same zone in which it physically exists, which is not the case in remote viewing. Furthermore, it could operate only in the time zones in which it exists, meaning the past and the present. Yet people individually and en masse repeatedly have knowledge of events to come, events taking place in a time zone in which materialists would agree the brain has no existence. The number of instances of this phenomenon could fill many hundreds of volumes. Impossibly dry tests conducted from 1935 to 1987 show that people with no known psychic abilities can successfully predict which "targets" or images will show up on a computer screen *before* the computer itself has even selected them.[12] The odds against chance are ten trillion trillion to one. How can this happen?

Equally mysterious are the accounts of children with savant syndrome. One boy, for instance, mastered Finnish, Arabic, and Mandarin at a young age. He not only learned these extraordinarily difficult languages on his own but also learned them from books he held upside down.[13] Another so-called idiot savant can take one glance at a parking lot and tell you the make, model, and year of every single car in it.[14] This child has not picked up such detailed information from sources such as automobile magazines, because he can't read. Furthermore, where does his precise knowledge of European cars come from when the cars themselves are nearly unknown in the United States?

Child prodigies present the same challenge. A famous modern-day Mozart named Jay Greenberg was already enrolled at one of America's most prestigious conservatories, the Juilliard School of Music, and had already written five full-length symphonies by the time he was twelve.[15] He began drawing musical instruments and notes at the age of three without any prior knowledge or training. Unlike Mozart, he did not come from a musical family. The boy tells us that the music just fills his head, and he has to write it down to get it out. An entire orchestral work comes in fully composed without need of revision. Furthermore, he seems to be able to keep two or three different channels going at once, hearing more than one composition at the same time, while keeping track of the channel of the daily reality most of us are tuned into.

Laboratory tests of the past few decades on perception continue to demonstrate that people react to stimulation before the brain has a chance to register it. This means that perception can occur before the brain's involvement. The literature on this is vast and constantly expanding, so only two examples are offered here. Benjamin Libet, a neurobiologist at the Medical Center of the University of California, has found that a person will react to a sensation such as being touched *before* the brain is aware of it.[16] Dean Radin, senior scientist at the Institute of Noetic Sciences, conducted studies using random selection by a computer of two categories of pictures, the one being calming pictures, such as pastoral scenes, and the other being emotionally upsetting pictures, such as sexual or violent scenes. Skin-conductance levels showed that people reacted to the computer's calm pictures neutrally and to the emotional pictures with stress. So far there is nothing extraordinary about this finding. What was not expected, however, is that the skin of some people consistently reacted appropriately to the picture some full six seconds before it appeared on the computer screen — that is, also *before* the computer had even made its random selection.[17] Clearly, if the computer didn't know what picture was coming up, the brains of the test subjects didn't, either. What part of a person's mental makeup did know?

Because matter itself is almost entirely energy and only lambently present in the physical realm and the mind is far more than just matter, it's not too great a step to reason that the difference between the mind of the living and that of the dead would be as infinitesimal as that itsy bit of matter in every atom. The central question remains whether the mind can operate fully disconnected from the material realm, that is, disconnected from the brain and body. The best evidence for this is yet to come. Just turn the page.

CHAPTER THREE

Near-Death Experiences

If it can be demonstrated that the mind can function independently of the physical body, then we can assume it can function
outside the laws of the material universe. If so, we have reason to argue
that physical death will not greatly affect it. Believe it or not, the mind's
independence of the body has been demonstrated. The two clearest
demonstrations each involve a rather lowly object when compared with
their lofty consequences — a shoe.[1]

THE BLUE SHOE

A migrant worker named Maria was brought to the Harborview Medical Center, in Seattle, in cardiac arrest. After three days of convalescing,
she went into cardiac arrest for a second time. Shortly after resuscitation, she told the following story to Kimberly Clark Sharp, a critical-
care worker in the coronary-care unit.[2]

Maria said that while the medical team was resuscitating her, she
found herself floating out of her body and toward the ceiling. From
there she was able to watch the team working on her body. She described
the people in the room, what they were doing, and the equipment

they used. She then found herself outside the hospital, where she took note of the design of the emergency entrance. Although all that she described was 100 percent accurate, Sharp admits that she thought Maria was "confabulating" and had learned the details of resuscitation and the hospital's architecture before admittance. This is all the harder to believe considering Maria had never been in Seattle before.

Then Maria told her that as she was rising outside the hospital building, she came close to a window on the third story of the north side, where something sitting on the window ledge caught her attention. It was "a man's dark blue tennis shoe, well-worn, scuffed on the left side where the little toe would go. The shoelace was caught under the heel." At Maria's bidding, Sharp went out to look for the shoe, a search Sharp was sure would be futile. Nothing could be seen from the outside, so she made the rounds of the rooms on the third floor from the inside. She came at last to the right room. When she pressed her face against the window pane and peered down at the ledge, she saw it. From her viewpoint inside the building she could not see what Maria had seen from outside, the worn spot at the little toe area, but all the other details were exactly as Maria had described them, even the shoelace tucked under the heel. She opened the window and picked up the shoe. There was indeed a scuff mark on the area of the little toe.

THE RED SHOE

A similar incident occurred in 1985, in a hospital in Hartford, Connecticut. A nurse, Cathy Milne, learned about it from a woman who had recently been resuscitated. The patient told Milne how she had floated up over her body and, like Maria, watched the resuscitation procedure. She then felt pulled up through several floors of the hospital until she found herself above the roof, where she marveled at Hartford's skyline. From her bird's-eye view she spied a red shoe lying on the roof. Milne related the story to another resident, who in a fit of skepticism got a janitor to let him out onto the roof. When Milne saw him later, he had a red shoe in his hand. Milne had not yet heard of Maria's experience.

❧

These two shoe-spying women were in the beginning stages of near-death experiences, when a person leaves the body but still remains in the world we acknowledge as real. There is no end to similar accounts of people who see and hear things while out of their bodies during this initial stage. They note the oddest things as well as the obvious — for instance, a nurse's plaid shoelaces, where their dentures were stored and by whom, pennies sitting atop cabinets high enough to be outside the field of vision even for a person standing.[3] Many attempt to get the attention of the medical personnel working on them. They shout at doctors and nurses, grab their arms, all to no avail because they are disconnected from the material realm.

They are able to recall point for point the medical procedures used to revive them, the equipment used, the monitor readings, the words spoken. From all accounts, their recollections of what went on while they were out of body have a level of accuracy and detail that sends shivers down the spine, especially in view of how few of these survivors have knowledge of medical technology. Dr. Michael Sabom, a cardiologist in Atlanta, Georgia, mentions one thought-provoking instance in which a near-death survivor made an apparent error in describing his defibrillation meter. What Sabom had not considered was that the man's NDE occurred in 1973, almost a decade before the interview. When Sabom researched the older model of this device, he found that the patient had described exactly the kind used in 1973.[4]

Survivors are taking all this in, and with uncanny clarity, while their bodies are undergoing surgery, being worked on in emergency rooms, or lying in streets after being hit by a car. They may also be in anaphylactic shock or a deep coma, having seizures, giving birth, grieving, in meditation or deep sleep, suffering from physical exhaustion or sleep

deprivation, or running a marathon. The instances that most defy medical possibility are those in which people are, by all classical definitions,
dead. There are no vital signs whatsoever. These patients have stopped
breathing, their hearts have stopped beating, EEGs have flatlined,
pupils no longer respond, and yet they see, hear, feel, think, reason, and
remember.

Occasionally, clinical death lasts for several hours or longer. This
is a medical impossibility, for the accepted time limit without oxygen
before the brain suffers permanent damage is ten minutes. Sabom describes a Vietnam veteran's account of his out-of-body state that lasted
for nearly a day. It began when he was badly wounded in battle. He
watched as the Vietcong came upon his body and stripped him of his
watch, gun, and shoes. He continued to watch as the Americans came
back later and put him into a body bag, which was then stacked on a
truck headed for the morgue. When the mortician made the first incision to inject embalming fluid into the left femoral vein, he noticed that
blood gushed from the incision. He called in the doctors, who determined that the man was still alive. The soldier was then taken to the
operating arena, where he watched calmly and peacefully from above
while they amputated his arm.[5]

When people are out of body, mental faculties and perception do
not just continue; they are enhanced practically beyond imagining.
One of these faculties is super-vision. People often take in supernormal amounts of information in 360-degree Panavision, observing the
ceiling, floor, every hair follicle on a nurse's head all at once.[6] When
venturing farther afield, they closely perceive the physical environment
around them, and not just rooftops and landscapes. Some, whose bodies have been hurt or flung from crashed cars and motorcycles, report
reading numbers high up on telephone poles or painted on the roofs
of buses. Others might visit friends during their time away from their
physical bodies.

Even more momentous is that the blind are suddenly able to see.
This sensational finding presents the most stunning evidence that the

mind and perception can and do operate independently of the body. Kenneth Ring and Sharon Cooper discuss numerous cases of the blind in out-of-body and near-death experiences.[7] Some of their research subjects were blind from birth with a lack of visual sense so total that prior to their NDEs they had no concept of color or light. Nor were they capable of dreaming in images but dreamed only in sound, touch, taste, and smell. Still while out of body they saw with the same super-vision of the sighted what color socks the people around them were wearing, the instruments and procedures used for their resuscitations, the names written on name tags of hospital personnel in other rooms. Their accounts have also been unfailingly verified as accurate.

The phenomena of seeing without eyes, thinking, reasoning, perceiving, and remembering in the absence of all brain activity and vital signs demonstrate that our minds — all that we hold as our thoughts, memories, awareness, and identity, as well as our sensory experiences — do not need a physical body or a brain in order to function. In fact, they seem to be hindered by matter. The evidence together shows conclusively that consciousness does exist outside the brain and is not subject to the laws of matter.

Yet skepticism abounds. Even physicians committed to the validity of NDEs still hedge the medically impossible by proposing that the brain is not "really dead" but carries on at a level too deep to be technologically tracked. But no one has so far argued in the case of the congenitally blind that their physical eyes were operating all along at an undetected low level.

The evidence still does not allow us to state that when consciousness is freed from matter by death, whether clinical or permanent, it moves into an afterlife reality. Some thirteen million near-death experiencers in the United States alone insist that it does,[8] and millions more in other places and times have too. Of course, sheer numbers do not make it true. After all, there was a time when nearly everybody believed the world is flat. However, if thirteen million believers had marched off the edge of the earth, they just might have had an argument for a flat world. There's a big difference between belief and direct experience.

Although no near-death experience is identical to any other, there seems to be some standardization among those types often referred to as "positive." "Less-than-positive" near-death experiences, which are not as common, seem to be more personalized.[9] They show much more variability in imagery and landscapes, in the types of events that occur, and in what beings are met. The degree of discomfort can range anywhere from confusion to extreme fear. Very rarely, a less-than-positive experience might involve some stereotypically hellish features or a feeling of void in which a person fears nonexistence.[10] Whether the experience was positive, not so positive, or even hellish, the subsequent effects on survivors have been more or less the same. As we will see below and in detail in chapter 9, all survivors report an astonishing number of lifelong benefits.

Despite the more homogenous nature of the positive types, few have all the elements of classical near-death experiences. The depth of the experience varies from illumination to true transcendence. Not all people go through Maria's initial stage of temporarily remaining in our reality after exiting their bodies. Many simply take off — down a tunnel or through a corridor or over a bridge or into a fog. The exact imagery can differ, but the purpose of the image (here moving from one "zone" to another) and its affect (the sensation of passage) are closely related. I'll discuss this phenomenon in chapter 11. Whooshing, ringing, or buzzing sounds may accompany this process.

Typically a person is greeted by deceased relatives. Occasionally what appear to be guides or angels come to assist. In several cases, a person was met by a family member or friend he or she did not know had died. The later verification of the death of the greeter in every instance presents strong support for the legitimacy of these events. Frequently, experiencers see a mysterious, beckoning light on the horizon or at the end of a tunnel that pulls them forward. As they draw closer, they become engulfed in transfiguring sensations of love and spiritual comprehension. Many come back with rapturous descriptions of this light, perceived as personalities of profound compassion and intimate understanding, of indescribable love *and* a surprising sense of humor. The being of light has been called Christ, Allah, God, the Big Guy, and the Big Kahuna, among other names. Interestingly, children also see female figures.[11]

At this point, many undergo a life review. Panoramic flashbacks of every single moment in their pasts (and sometimes in their futures) rush before them at impossible speeds or all at once in simultaneous time.[12] Despite the rate of information, survivors have no difficulty absorbing it. In this spacious moment they reexperience their every thought and deed, every emotion, and feel the effects their acts had on others. Although many episodes in life reviews provoke shame, there is no sense of being judged. The aim is rather the realization of where improvement is needed. By contrast, the life reviews in less-than-positive experiences are felt like judgments from an outside source.[13] Perhaps less-than-positive experiences stem from deep-seated feelings of guilt, feelings that are evidently purged in the process of the life review. In either case, the review seems to play an important role in the decision-making process of whether to stay dead or to return.

Near-death experiences of different cultures share many of the same general features, yet there are also substantial differences. In studies on survivors in India, for instance, people nearly always met deceased relatives and acquaintances and frequently beings of light. However, those in the Indian accounts had messengers escorting them to the other side and bringing them back, which is unknown in the West. The atmosphere is generally more bureaucratic, involving clerks with books in which names and schedules of deaths are written down. When the names of newcomers are checked against this list and it turns out that their arrival on the other side is a mistake, such as a mix-up in names, experiencers are not asked whether they want to stay or return but are simply told to go back to finish their lives. In the small sample studied so far, there were no instances of life reviews.[14]

It is one thing to accept that people in out-of-body states can spot shoes on a window ledge. It is quite another when what they report is happening in another reality. Unlike shoes and hair follicles, what is seen and felt cannot be verified from our standpoint. Accounts of meeting the being of light, for example, read more like fantasies. Some of the more cosmic experiences in which a person seems to shoot through intergalactic space are the stuff of science fiction. Hence, many physicians, neuroscientists, psychiatrists, psychologists, and cosmologists reject near-death experiences as real events.

In the 1970s and '80s, when NDEs were still largely unidentified, physicians regarded them as signs of mental disorders. Despite the current change in attitude, the skeptics' arguments have not altered much. Most still hold with various hallucination hypotheses. Chemical imbalances caused by mind-altering drugs and painkillers like Thorazine, Valium, Demerol, and morphine are believed to be the source of hallucinations. Or perhaps the brain's reaction to stress produces a flood of neurohormones, primarily the powerful endorphins. Then again, psychoses such as schizophrenia and bipolar disorders also involve chemical imbalances that may result in hallucinations.

Several things are wrong with hallucination hypotheses. Survivors' reports show that the events they experienced were not at all like hallucinations but lucid, coherent, orderly, and eminently not dreamlike in quality. In fact, unlike hallucinations, they are rather predictable. Experiences normally take place while a person is unconscious, whereas psychiatric and drug-induced hallucinations occur during conscious states. In cases in which the survivor's brainwave activity has ceased, hallucinations would be medically impossible.

Pursuing the mental aberration idea, critics of NDEs have considered them as episodes of disassociation, common to psychoses like paranoia and schizophrenia. Organic brain disorders like delirium and dementia are also thought to be causes. Temporal lobe epilepsy is also suspected, but such a violently electrical brain disorder is bound to show up on electroencephalograms.

Mental illnesses generally lead to despair, depression, and hopelessness, whereas near-death experiencers go on to lead more adjusted and fulfilling lives.[15] In general, sufferers from delirium and dementia are characteristically out of touch with their immediate environments, disoriented, and unable to concentrate. They tend to lapse into incoherence, sometimes followed by nightmarish hallucinations involving insects and animals. Nothing in the literature of NDEs approaches such symptoms.

A study involving psychiatric outpatients who came close to death shows that those who did *not* have an NDE had more psychological distress after their medical crisis than before it, whereas those who did have one had less distress in their lives after the crisis.[16] Similarly, several studies demonstrate that people who attempted suicide and had NDEs returned with healthier attitudes and never again attempted to take their own lives.[17] For those who were resuscitated from suicide attempts but did not have an NDE, depression continued, and suicide attempts were usually repeated.

Most often, NDEs are attributed to the brain "playing tricks" for various physiological reasons. Lack of oxygen to the brain (hypoxia), which has symptoms such as seeing bright lights and feelings of peace and of leaving the body, is a favorite argument. But other symptoms include jerking limbs, impaired memory, tingling in the extremities, fragmented thinking, and convulsions, none of which occurs during an NDE.

Near-death episodes are also thought to result from a psychological mechanism that kicks into gear when a person's life is on the point of termination. This reaction to threat is called "transient depersonalization." If an NDE is merely an automatic reaction to a life threat, then why doesn't it happen to everyone faced with potential death? Furthermore, many NDEs are not triggered by such a threat. More important, the mechanism hypothesis does not explain why people who survive cardiac arrest without having an NDE develop long-standing emotional problems, such as insomnia, irritability, anxiety, and fearful dreams, the opposite of what happens to cardiac arrest patients who do have them.[18]

We know that something real happens during near-death experiences, because the aftereffects on survivors are not only extreme and consistent but also measurable. This falls in line with standard scientific requirements. Measurable effects include lower mean body temperatures, lower blood pressure and metabolic rates, shorter sleep cycles, heightened sensory perceptions, increased intellectual capacities, enhanced cognitive abilities, and changes in the survivors' electromagnetic field. Occasionally people return cured of fatal illnesses.[19] In chapter 9, we will explore the psychological and spiritual transformations survivors go through. These beneficial changes are so thorough and long lasting that they cast a shadow over the more scientifically acceptable physiological changes. The dramatic aftereffects can leave no doubt that something momentous occurs. Since near-death experiences are sandwiched between verifiable initial stages and verifiable, measurable, and consistent aftereffects, when they are taken together it seems reasonable to assume that what happens in between is also likely to have some basis in reality.

In the end, NDEs present limited evidence for survival, not because we disbelieve something real happened, but because, for the first time in history, the old definition of dead — the absence of vital signs — no longer holds. Since even physicians can't be sure of the dividing line between alive and dead, they can't decide if experiencers were ever really dead. Most physicians would say they were not. If they were not, critics can claim they were never in the afterlife. Nevertheless, what stands glistening and clear for the survival issue from near-death research is that the mind can and does continue to function outside the body.

Chapter Four

After-Death Communication

*B**y now you might be asking,* if people survive death, why don't they just come back and tell us? They do — over and over and over again — and they have been since the beginning of time. The Afterlife Encounter Survey, the most extensive and broadest-based survey of its kind, found that 72 percent of the respondents believed they had either felt the presence of the dead or communicated with them.[1] In other research, this proportion went as low as 42 percent. If these surveys are representative of the general population, they suggest that on average some 57 percent of the present population has had some sort of encounter with the dead. That conservatively amounts to about a hundred million people in present-day North America alone, not including the dying, children, and pets. I'm not talking about ghost sightings, either, which, as explained in chapter 14, are not the same.

The problem is, we simply won't believe in communication with the dead. The resistance is peculiar considering the overwhelming amount of documentation and number of testimonials, the innumerable incidents in which provably accurate information was received, and the material remains, such as photographs in which the deceased appear or recordings that have their captured voices. It is especially peculiar considering that the dead hold the answers to the survival question.

Part of the problem is that after-death communication gets little support from scientific communities, largely because few scientists (about 5 percent) believe in it. It remains a fringe area of research, of concern to a handful of people specializing in bereavement or parapsychology. Science cannot monitor the content of thought or quantify feelings and intuition, the base elements of after-death communication. Since it has so far failed to explain thought, how could it explain telepathy, the process by which after-death communication is achieved? Lastly, scientific communities avoid after-death communication out of a justified fear of ridicule.

In this chapter, we will review a small portion of the accounts that best demonstrate survival after death, accounts that skeptics ignore or dismiss as delusions or fraud. What is offered here is not representative of the full range of how people communicate with the dead; for that see chapters 12 and 13.

SPONTANEOUS AFTER-DEATH COMMUNICATION

Most communication between the living and the dead occurs without conscious effort on our side. The data on spontaneous after-death communication were first systematically gathered in 1894 by the philosopher Henry Sidgwick, who pooled 1,684 accounts in England. Since those early years, many others have contributed, with one collection compiled by Bill Guggenheim and Judy Guggenheim, founders of the ADC (After-Death Communication) Project, which was topping 10,000 accounts at the time of this writing.[2] Spontaneous contact is typically short, and interaction either brief or nonexistent, primarily because recipients are too unprepared and overwhelmed to engage. The exception is the deathbed variety of communication, in which interaction is the norm. The messages conveyed are generally reassurances that the deceased have survived, are whole and happy, and that their love for us will never die.

Spontaneous encounters can occur anywhere from the split second a person expires to many decades after. In a few cases, they have occurred shortly *before* the visiting person dies, as we shall see. Spontaneous encounters are most frequent in the first year of mourning. They can be visual, auditory, or tactile or all three. They usually happen when a person is relaxed, often while dreaming or daydreaming, but also while active and alert, or when their attention is focused elsewhere, such as while driving. They especially occur during times of stress. In a survey of 596 respondents who had spontaneous encounters, 21 percent of them were with deceased relatives of the recipient, grandparents arriving more often than siblings, and siblings more often than parents.[3] Next in frequency were friends (13 percent), children of the recipient (11 percent), pets (10 percent), and spouses (6 percent). More than half of the pets showed up with a dead family member, even if that person had died long before the animal was adopted by the recipient. Figures unknown to the recipients at the time of the encounter made up 11 percent. Many were later found to be relatives whom the recipient had never met; their identities were eventually established by old photographs. Others in this category were the relatives of friends. Spiritual figures made up 5 percent of the encounters, and historical or famous ones, 2 percent.

Evidential accounts include encounters in which the departed reveals information not known by the living, which is later verified. A large proportion of these accounts involves the arrival of the deceased at the moment of death but before the recipient is aware of that death by other means. A fascinating group is composed of warnings to the living of impending disaster. Still others are about unsuspected, unthreatening future events. The dead directing their family members where to find things also belongs in this category, as does conveying the correct number sequence for winning the lottery! Transmitting exact information that is otherwise unknown to the living is a strong indication that after-death communication is real, involving real people, alive or dead, and is not hallucinations, fantasies, or projections. It also indicates that the deceased exist independently of the living, possessing minds that are not only intact but also broader in their scope of knowledge, including foreknowledge.

Perfect Timing

The sudden appearance of a loved one is all the more uncanny when it occurs at the moment of death. Lillian's story is not atypical. She returned home from visiting her husband, who was in the hospital because of a heart attack. While sitting alone on the couch, she heard his voice telling her he had to go on; his "job here on earth" was finished. It was 1:56 in the morning. Lillian understood what was happening and expected a call from the hospital. Fifteen minutes later, a nurse from intensive care did call. Time of death was recorded at 1:56 AM.[4]

A particularly poignant encounter involves a man who lay dying from heart disease while his sister was in a diabetic coma in the same hospital. He had a partial near-death experience. Now out of body, he met his sister, who had also left her body. When she began to move away from him and he tried to go with her, she told him firmly it was not his time. She then disappeared through a tunnel. When the brother regained consciousness, he told the doctors that his sister had died, which they at first denied. Finally a nurse checked and found out he was right.[5]

The timing in these instances is remarkable enough, but in each case death was expected. Other encounters present situations in which the living had no reason to expect a death and learned of it only from the deceased themselves. Dianne Arcangel tells us of a woman who saw her uncle glowing at the foot of her bed at exactly three o'clock on a Sunday morning.[6] This woman had been estranged from her uncle and his side of the family for thirty years. On the following Tuesday she and her husband read in the newspaper that her uncle had died at 3:00 AM that Sunday. A woman named Vicky perceived her maternal grandfather at 2:17 AM. Since she wasn't even aware he was ill, untroubled she went back to sleep. The following day her sister told her that their grandfather had died just before 2:30 that morning.[7] In several instances a person has died in one time zone and visited someone the same moment in another.[8]

There are equally plentiful accounts in which the visiting deceased was young and healthy at the time of passing. Melinda had lost touch with her childhood friend Tom for over ten years. One night she woke out of a sound sleep to see him standing by her bed in his navy uniform. He distinctly said, "Good-bye Melinda. I'm leaving now." What further confused her was that the last she had heard, Tom had become a priest, not a soldier. Three days later, she got a letter informing her that Tom had been killed in action. He had become a navy chaplain.[9]

Several people submitted reports to the Guggenheim project about appearances intended to ease the blow of bad news. One teenager named Heather appeared to her mother, Christine, just before the police came to the door. Christine was stunned to see her daughter, her only child, together with the daughter's grandfather standing in midair. They looked very happy and as solid as flesh and blood. The grandfather, who had passed six years before, told her, smiling, "She's okay, Baby. I have her. She's fine!" "Baby" was his nickname for Christine. She then went to answer the door, where the police informed her that Heather had just been in a fatal car accident.[10]

Similarly, Clare saw her friend Hugh while waking up. He was pinching her to get her attention. His message was puzzling: "I didn't make it…Good-bye." Just then her clock radio came on with the early morning news that Hugh's seaplane had gone down in the Columbia River the day before. Her friend didn't "make it" to the bank of the river and drowned.[11]

How can we explain these encounters? Could it be mere coincidence that a person is hallucinating about someone just at the moment of death? If so, what would prompt it? If they are hallucinations, fantasies, or wishful thinking, the chances that people would imagine the dead as cheerful and healthy are slim. Could it be wishful thinking that led a mother to see her daughter dead? Death-wish fantasies can be ruled out, because no account of this type suggests that a beholder harbored murderous thoughts for the visiting deceased. Precognition and subconscious knowledge can also be ruled out, because they almost never take the form of a direct encounter but, rather, surface as mental images of a person dying, say, in a bed, in a car accident, and so forth.

Warnings

Instances of the dead warning the living of a coming disaster or diverting them from harm offer some of the best evidence for survival. The Guggenheims have published accounts of warnings preventing car, truck, and plane accidents; crimes, such as break-ins and financial swindles; death by fire, lightning, and collapsing roofs; accidents in factories and constructions sites; and the deaths of young children. Warnings demonstrate the intimate knowledge the dead have of us, knowledge we seldom possess, and the expansion of awareness in time and space, well beyond the usual mortal borders.

Records abound of the dead averting motor vehicle accidents. While Glenda was driving her truck, she heard her dead father shout, "Stop the truck!" He had to say it twice before she did. Just as she came to a halt, a car sped out from a side street heading straight at where she would have been if she had ignored her father. Andy missed colliding with a semi because of his dead mother's warning. Jeff heard the scream of his friend Phil, "Wake up!" just as he was falling asleep behind the wheel. Phil had died at nineteen when he fell asleep while driving and hit a telephone pole. When Marsha was crossing train tracks and saw a train twenty to thirty feet away from her car, she absolutely froze. Then she heard her late friend Josh scream at her, "Drive this car!" She still sat there frozen. Suddenly she felt a foot press down over hers on the gas pedal. The pedal went straight to the floor, and the car shot forward. The next day her foot showed bruises. Josh had died five years earlier when his car was hit by a train. Other drivers are warned by their loved ones of mechanical problems, such as tires on the verge of blowing or wheels coming off. Sometimes the dead are not so direct but use diversionary tactics to steer the living out of harm's way.[12]

Saving young children seems to be another specialty of the dead. Debbie was visiting her friend Donna and Donna's six-month-old girl, Chelsea. Just as she was walking out the door to buy some groceries, she telepathically heard her mother's voice say, "You need to check the baby." Since her mother had died only the week before, Debbie assumed she was reacting to her own grief and started out the door again. Her mother firmly repeated her message, which sent Debbie to the room where little Chelsea was napping. To her horror, she found the baby suffocating, already turning blue from lack of oxygen. Another deceased mother woke her daughter in the night and brought her to the bedroom of the daughter's nine-month-old. The baby was choking to death on a piece of rubber nipple she had bitten off.[13] Both babies survived because of the dead's intervention. Several people in the Guggenheims' files had similar warnings but did not act on them. They came to bitterly regret it.

I'll leave it here with one that is simply too beautiful to omit. When a man lost his beloved wife, Ellie, it nearly destroyed him. After she died he made frequent visits to the cemetery. One such time he brought three pink roses and put them in the vase by her grave. Just as he settled onto a nearby bench, he noticed that one of the roses was rising out of the vase. He rushed over to grab it before it hit the ground. The second he reached it, a bolt of lightning struck the bench he had been sitting on as well as the tree shading it. It was so close that it burned the shoe off his right foot.[14]

Things the Dead Tell Us That We Didn't Know

Instances of the dead telling the living something they didn't know range from the dramatic to the trivial. Some have led to solving crimes.

Others, to correcting the placement of a tombstone or meeting a dead brother the recipient never knew existed.[15]

For Lucille, the encounter involved her biological grandfather, someone she never knew. He appeared one night at her bedside, calling her Mary, the name she was given at birth. When she was adopted, her new parents changed her name to Lucille. Although she saw him clearly, she had no idea who he was. The man said, "Mary, your mother loves you. Your mother is looking for you. Start looking for her. Find your mother! I love you." When Lucille asked him who he was, he simply replied, "You'll find out," and disappeared. She did find out when she found her biological mother. The mother had a photograph of him, conveniently wearing the same suit he wore when he had appeared to Lucille. Just before he died, he told his daughter to find her baby girl, a wish he made come true.[16]

Frequently, the deceased direct the living to find things of value, such as hidden cash, insurance policies, and heirlooms. Still others are directed to find things they never knew existed, buried in a trunk in the attic or stashed behind the drawers of a desk. If necessary the dead will alert a third party to initiate discovery. One such deceased was a man named Leland who showed up at the house of his friend Kitty the day after his fatal truck accident. He asked Kitty to tell his wife about an insurance policy he had kept secret and hidden in the bedroom. Kitty did and the policy was found.[17]

Communication Witnessed by More Than One Person

Postmortem encounters witnessed by two or more people go a long way in reassuring the recipients that what they experienced was fact rather than fiction. Oddly, the most common types of shared after-death contact are sensing a presence or smelling an odor associated with the deceased. Still, shared visual encounters are far from unusual. Frequently, several people watch the dead person enter a church at his or her own funeral service, for instance. What is interesting about shared sightings is that each witness usually sees the discarnate from his or her vantage point. Not everyone has an experience identical to the next. Sometimes one person may just feel a touch or hear a voice while the other may see an apparition.

Here's one example, reported by a woman named Lois. Two days after the death of her husband, Ray, Lois just happened to pass by her bedroom, where she saw her son Jesse sitting on the side of her bed. He was only eight at the time and was unable to deal with his father's death. Right next to him was Ray, who had his arm around his son and was talking to him in a calm voice. Ray looked up and smiled at his wife, then gestured for her to go away. She moved off to give them privacy, and after a fifteen-minute wait, Jesse came out to tell her what his father had said: "Daddy told me that he has gone and won't be coming back and not to worry about him. Everything will be all right."[18] This event marked the boy's turning point for healing.

Just as common are sequential after-death communications in which the deceased visits two or more people, one after the other. Leslie participated in one of these with her father four months after he had died. When she turned the light out in bed, she saw him standing in the doorway. He was glowing. He told her that he was fine and would always be with her. Then he announced he was going to look in on her mother and her three-year-old son, Curtis, who was in the next room. The next morning, Curtis told her that "Granddaddy" had come into his room the night before.[19] Corroborated encounters offer some evidence that a real event is taking place. Unless the integrity or soundness of mind of the witnesses is in question, double, multiple, and sequential after-death communications present the kind of testimony that would stand up as solid proof in any courtroom.

Physical Phenomena

The enormous number of spontaneous encounters associated with physical phenomena includes images and messages received on answering

machines, recording devices, pagers, televisions, room monitors, computer screens, and any reflective surface, primarily mirrors. The dead
have been captured in photographs and on film and their voices heard
on recordings or interrupting radio broadcasts. One woman was so
skeptical about a private message on her answering machine left by her
long-dead husband that she hired detectives. All they could establish
about the call was that it was not incoming.[20] Other phenomena affect
electrical and electronic devices, sometimes activating the object when
it is switched off, not plugged in, or even broken. Frequently objects
associated with the deceased move on their own.

Phenomena involving telephones are so common that a whole book
has been written on them.[21] People receive phone calls from the dead to
give thanks, to say good-bye, to warn them about danger, to tell them
where to find the will, and to wish them a happy birthday. Usually the
recipient is too startled to respond. If the "callee" does not at first recognize that the caller is deceased, the conversation may last quite awhile.
On a few occasions, a living person made a call and had an exceptional
exchange, only to find out later that the person he or she dialed had
already died.

The call phenomenon can involve more than one person. A couple
of hours after one woman had died, she phoned the nurses' station of
the hospice she was in. She repeatedly gave the nurse the same message:
"Tell my son I'm okay." Caller ID showed that the call was coming
from Room 256. When a quite-flustered nurse, along with the doctor,
rushed off to check on the patient in that room, they found that her life-
less body had already grown cold. No one else was in the room. The
son showed up a half hour later and told the doctor he had just gotten a
phone call from his mother, saying, "I am okay. I love you." In spite of
the static on the line, her voice was unmistakable, so he arrived at the
hospital fully expecting her to be alive.[22]

Hilda was with her daughter Greta at home two weeks after Hilda's
father had died. Because of work on the phone lines outside, her phone
service had been out for two days. Despite this, her phone rang, not

once, but several times. Greta answered it twice, and there was no one on the line. When Hilda answered it, she heard her father tell her in Polish that he loved her. Soon after, Hilda ran outside to ask the men working on the phone lines if service had been restored. The chief technician pointed to the wires, which were still lying disconnected on the ground.[23]

One last account of physical phenomena comes from Elisabeth Kübler-Ross, the psychiatrist who revolutionized the way we look at death. It took place after a long day of teaching at the Medical Center of the University of Chicago. On her way to her office, she met a vaguely familiar woman who asked her, "Do you mind if I walk along with you?" While they chatted along the way, Elisabeth kept wondering who this woman was. When they arrived at her office, she invited the woman in, studying her closely for a clue that would jog her memory. Finally, the woman leaned forward and said, "You don't remember me, do you? I'm Mrs. Schwartz."

"Oh, yes! Of course!" Kübler-Ross exclaimed. She now realized that the woman had been a patient of hers who died the year before. Inwardly she wondered if her long hours of work were causing her to hallucinate. If this was a genuine encounter with the dead, she wanted to get something tangible. So she gave the woman pen and paper and asked her to write a note for the chaplain, making sure that the woman signed her name. The hospital chaplain was thrilled.[24]

How can we explain away so many thousands of testimonies of spontaneous communication, especially when it has impacted our physical world?

Intentional After-Death Communication

Since the beginning of recorded history, people have invented means for communicating with the dead. They have sought to make contact through dream incubation, prayers, trances, rituals, letter writing, automatic writing, and table rapping, by burying themselves underground, gazing at reflective surfaces such as water and crystal, gazing at or inhaling smoke, swallowing specially prepared substances, reading cards and the patterns of stones, bones, sticks, leaves, and the flight of birds. More recent developments include the Ouija board and technological devices. Presently, those psychiatrists, psychologists, and bereavement counselors who realize the therapeutic value of after-death communication are working out new ways to conjure the dead.[25] Below, we will look at selected categories of intentional after-death communication that speak to the problem of proof.

Instrumental Transcommunication

A fascinating and promising field of research is instrumental transcommunication. This is a collective term for contact with discarnates through devices, historically tape recorders, TVs, radios, telephones, answering machines, computers, videos, and cameras. This fast-growing area of study developed from electronic voice phenomena, which began in the early twentieth century. It took shape in the 1950s with the discoveries of the Swedish researcher Friedrich Jürgenson and later with the book *Breakthrough* (1971), by Dr. Konstantin Raudive, which is based on an astounding seventy-two thousand recorded messages. Most investigators of instrumental transcommunication are dedicated amateurs, often with a background in electronics or engineering.

The voices are mostly unfamiliar, usually somewhat distorted, and display a full array of languages and dialects. Recordings typically pick up no more than a couple of words, few of which seem to be personal messages for the listener. Combined worldwide, they represent a massive amount of disembodied communication, yet their origins are still in question. Skeptics claim they emerge from random noise or stray radio and television transmissions. The softer skeptics believe they might arise from telepathic thoughts of living subjects.

The greatest achievements in the category of technologically assisted after-death communication were made by the late George Meek, an engineer and successful businessman who retired early to devote his life to survival research. He, along with his team, invented the Spiricom, a complex instrument that allows unambiguous two-way communication between the living and the dead. The participants besides Meek were William O'Neill, a high school dropout with a talent for electronics and communing with the dead, the physicist George Mueller, and "Doc Nick," a physician and ham-radio operator. What is exceptional here is that both Mueller and Doc Nick were already dead. Neither Meek nor any of his colleagues and acquaintances had ever met these men in the flesh or even heard of them before.

Through O'Neill and the Spiricom, the late Dr. Mueller furnished Meek with many specifics of his life for the verification of his identity. They are given here in full, because they represent one of the most extensive and accurate communications yet documented. The social security number Mueller gave was confirmed by the U.S. Social Security Administration; his BS degree in electrical engineering from the University of Wisconsin in 1928 was verified by the university's registry office; his MS, PhD in experimental physics, and a research fellowship from Cornell were all validated by a faculty member of that university; his memberships in the obscure Haresfoot Club and Triangle Fraternity were verified through thirty-year-old archived photographs; his Meritorious Civilian Award was confirmed by Tom Bearden, secretary for the U.S. Air Force Intelligence Service, who also confirmed Mueller's top-secret-clearance status and the nature of the design and development work Mueller performed for the U.S. Signal Corps and the NASA space program. Mueller's account of the place and circumstances of his death concurred with his death certificate.

Mueller also gave Meek two unlisted phone numbers of old colleagues, whom Meek then contacted. And Mueller gave the names of four family members who were confirmed by his wife, whom Meek found through the Social Security Administration. The widow Mueller also agreed with her husband's description of himself. After a two-year search, Meek located the training booklet Mueller said he had written for the U.S. Army, *Introduction to Electronics*, through the Wisconsin State Historical Society. Meek found the two pages Mueller wanted him to read for help in building the Spiricom. Mueller was indeed who he said he was.

Meek presented recordings of the Spiricom experiments to me personally at my home some decades back. The technical dialogue I heard going on between two worlds about how to improve their equipment was simply jaw-dropping. If the Spiricom and the precise dialogue it facilitated were a hoax on Meek's part, it certainly cost him many years of his life and a considerable portion of his personal fortune to pull it off. So far, his integrity has never been in doubt. Meek made his fortune from his patents, yet when it came to the Spiricom, he refused to apply for one. Instead, the plans are free to anyone through the Spiricom website. The Spiricom experiment stands as one of the most convincing pieces of evidence to date of postmortem survival. If just a fraction of what we spend on developing communication technology were invested in instrumental transcommunication, we would soon be connected to the most exciting, the most urgently meaningful domain in existence.

Book Tests

Book tests refer to when the dead direct the living to specific books and pages within them. On these pages, words or phrases are found that convey messages or answer questions. Although the dead usually set up book tests through a person with developed mediumistic abilities, sometimes they occur spontaneously, as one did with the psychoanalyst Carl Jung. One night while Jung lay in bed, a friend of his who had recently died appeared. He beckoned Jung to follow him. In a vision Jung followed him out of the house, into the garden, out to the road, and finally to his house. Jung was then conducted "to the second of five books with red bindings which stood on the second shelf from the top."[26] He had never been in this man's study before and was certainly unacquainted with his collection of books.

Curious, Jung went the next morning to his friend's widow, asking her for access to the library. "Sure enough," he writes, "there was a stool standing under the bookcase I had seen in my vision, and even before I came closer I could see the five books with red bindings. I stepped up on the stool so as to be able to read the titles.... The title of the second volume read: *The Legacy of the Dead.*" Jung's personal book test and his dreams and visions of the dead led him to believe that the spirit hypothesis was the best and most useful explanation for his experiences.

The Cross Relics

The cross relics represent a singular category of after-death communication.[27] In Redlands, California, in 1914, a poor, illiterate woman named Violet Parent began to fall into trances after recovering from a serious illness. The spirits of Spanish missionaries and Native Americans began to direct her to places where money had been buried. After six years, Violet and her husband, Gregory, had enough money to buy a house and a car. During the next ten years, the spirits guided her to some fifteen hundred sacred objects, mostly crosses, both Christian and Indian, in many different metals, including silver and gold. The Indian crosses are extremely rare. Before the Parents' discoveries, only ten crosses had ever been excavated, all from grave mounds. The Parents also discovered wads of bills as well as gold pieces and tablets dating from 1769 to 1800, and a score of miscellaneous objects. The finds were mostly uncovered in wild and remote places, buried in the sand, in streambeds, in rusted containers, and the like, over an area of some two hundred thousand square miles. Gregory's notes of their discoveries took up twenty-two volumes.

Mediumship

As far as we know there have always been people who specialize in communicating with spirits. Shamans and medicine men and women were indispensable and honored tribal members. Some mediumistic priestesses and philosopher-priests achieved such fame that they drew seekers from all over the ancient world. Today's equivalent, psychics and mediums, however, hold a dubious place in popular opinion. The difference between a psychic and a medium is a matter of emphasis. I consider mediumship as a subgroup in the panoply of psychic abilities, one that is turned to channeling the messages of discarnate entities. For professional psychics, mediumship is but one of the services offered should a dead loved one arrive. Until the past few decades, mediums typically went into trances so deep that they lost all awareness of their environments. The current trend is a lighter altered state, a kind of deep concentration, in which mediums remain conscious and interactive. Since serious investigation of the survival issue in the past two centuries has concentrated on testing mediums, the literature on phenomena occurring through them is overwhelming. Here I can only offer a few highlights.[28]

Although physical mediumship, which includes manifestations of objects, voices, human forms, and other physical phenomena such as levitation, does not bear directly on the question of life after death, it does allow discarnates to leave footprints in the world of matter.[29] These are largely traceable through technological devices that are sensitive to light, sound, magnetic forces, or electrical impulses. For example, infrared cameras and beams were used in one set of experiments with Rudi Schneider. When Schneider went into trance, something or someone arrived and moved objects. The equipment was set up to catch and record on film any instances of fraud, such as a mortal accomplice manipulating the objects. None was found.[30] This may not be more than telekinesis on Schneider's part, but in the following experiments, the paranormal occurrences are harder to explain. They involve the "direct-voice" phenomenon — audible voices manifesting out of thin air in the *vicinity* of a medium but not issuing *from* the medium.

Three such voices around the medium Shirley Bray were taperecorded. The tapes were sent to a voice-recognition device used by the British police in criminal investigations. These instruments analyze variables such as pace, rhythm, and accents and are as precise in distinguishing identities as fingerprinting. Analysis demonstrated unequivocally that the three voices around Shirley Bray had three distinctly different patterns that could not have been made by one person.[31] Similarly, an electroencephalograph (EEG) was used to measure the brainwave patterns of Elwood Babbitt while he channeled three different "intelligences." The EEGs changed dramatically with each intelligence, and none was similar to Babbitt's EEG when he was out of trance.[32] The voices around Etta Wriedt, a medium from Detroit, were so independent that she was able to converse with them, that is, if they were speaking English, Wriedt's only language. In addition, the voices spoke Dutch, German, Spanish, Norwegian, Serbo-Croatian, and Arabic.[33]

Testing After-Death Mediumship

Psychics participating in tests are often signing up for a true ordeal. They frequently have to wade through suspicion and even hostility on the part of investigators, which is keenly felt and causes faltering. Test-scoring methods are usually tough, with standards for "hits" that leave little room for nuance. The most successful tests in after-death research occur when the medium is faced with a human being, an anonymous sitter, since no matter how neutral the sitter attempts to be, need and hope are still present. In all cases, paranormal abilities reach their fullest capacities in response to genuine need.

Human error can arise from the way investigators set up the tests and interrogate the subjects. Sitters also make mistakes, usually because they are too overcome to think clearly. They have been known to give incorrect information, block information, and pronounce a medium's statement wrong only to find out later that it was actually right. And finally, mediums are not omniscient and have a lot to deal with internally while interpreting the images, sounds, and sensations coming to them. A wide margin of error is built into all fields that depend on interpretation; the astonishing 85 percent or higher accuracy rate of many psychics and mediums is as high as it gets in any professional sector.

Obviously investigators must eliminate any chance of fraud. In experiments of physical mediumship, subjects have been blindfolded, had their mouth and eyes taped shut, and been bound to chairs and tables, put in isolation compartments and Faraday chambers, buried, covered in drapes, spied upon by every conceivable surveillance device, and wired from head to toe. Some of them have been pricked or burned to test the validity of their trances. Researchers and certainly cynics have hired magicians who attempt to duplicate phenomena by "normal" trickery. In séances, the magician's role is to stay on the alert for any spurious signs, such as a cold reading. A person doing a cold reading gathers information not paranormally but by cues picked up through careful observation of the sitter-client's body language, facial expressions, breathing, voice patterns, and audible responses, in order to formulate a high-probability guess.

Gary Schwartz and his colleagues at the University of Arizona devised a test in which five mediums and one sitter with a history of six significant deaths participated.[34] The sitter, unknown to the mediums, was restricted to flat-spoken yes-or-no responses to statements mediums picked up from the dead. At the same time, Schwartz set up a control group who did readings on the same sitter based on pure guesswork. The average results for correct statements were 83 percent for the mediums and 36 percent for the controls, representing odds of ten million to one that the statements were chance. Further trials were conducted in which the sitters were put behind screens and not allowed to respond to statements. The mediums had no idea of the sitters' sex or age. Each read ten sitters in the first set of trials and five in the second. Test results ranged from 77 percent accuracy in the first set to as low as 40 percent in the second.

Some of the errors in the second series had to do with cross-communication when a deceased person who was *not* connected with the sitters arrived. In situations of cross-communication, accurate information from the dead intended for someone other than the sitter is still counted as a miss, which drops the overall score. If a medium comes up with nothing, it is also counted as a miss. Although the second set of silent readings had a poor rating in comparison to the first, the accuracy of the control group averaged about 50 percent lower than that of the mediums, making guesswork on their part improbable.

The most common deception in mediumship is attaining knowledge of someone or something before the séance, which the medium then passes off as coming from the dead. Hence, careful investigators go to great lengths to make sure that the medium has no prior knowledge of the sitters participating in experiments. Early researchers have gone to extremes. The great Bostonian medium Leonora Piper, one of those who was cut, pricked, burned, and exposed to ammonia while in trance, was perhaps subject to the harshest scrutiny so far recorded. She conducted several thousand sessions over three decades around the turn of the nineteenth to the twentieth century under the stringent control of five experienced researchers from the Society for Psychical Research. These were all scholars in their own fields, including William James, a professor of Harvard, and James Hyslop, a professor of Columbia University and a true skeptic. They brought hundreds of sitters to these sessions under false names. They hired detectives to follow Piper. While she was in England, she was kept in seclusion in the home of the physicist Sir Oliver Lodge and closely watched. She was not allowed to go out without a member of the Society for Psychical Research by her side. Her mail was read in order to be sure she was not receiving clandestine information. Lodge even went so far as to change his domestic staff during her stay to prevent her from learning anything about his private life. She was also forbidden to read newspapers around test days. In over three decades of this treatment and stressful examination, Piper never once came close to committing a fraud.

Like many others, I would rather not know the names of people coming to me for readings. Occasionally I do have some information on clients, especially when they're famous. So far prior knowledge has rarely worked to my advantage. Whether my approach involves a purist streak or an inbuilt trance ethic, I usually block whatever I have learned about that person beforehand. If I already know that a person has diverticulitis, for instance, or is an astrophysicist, I am likely to screen it out. On the other hand, when I do not know such facts beforehand, they normally surface through psychic channels during the course of the reading. This inner ethic makes doing readings for friends and relatives thorny business.

Distinguishing between what a medium knows or does not know before a test is not easy for anyone. An illustration of the problem occurred on October 7, 1930, at a séance held in the National Laboratory of Psychical Research, in London. The medium was the hugely talented Eileen Garrett. The session was held in the hope of contacting the recently deceased Sir Arthur Conan Doyle, who was in life the creator of Sherlock Holmes and an ardent supporter of after-death survival.

Garrett went immediately into trance. Instead of Doyle, a man who gave his name as Flight Lieutenant H. Carmichael Irwin came in. He told them he was the pilot of the *R101*, a dirigible built by the British Air Ministry and the largest airship then in existence. Little did anyone at the séance know that on its maiden voyage to India, it had crashed in a town north of Paris three days before, killing all but six of the fifty-four passengers and crew. Irwin was one of the dead. Clearly in extreme distress and desperate to explain what went wrong, he burst into an account of the crash. Like any eyewitness in shock, he spoke in excited, agitated spurts: "Starboard strakes started.... Impossible to rise. Cannot trim. Almost scraped the roofs of Achy. Kept to railway." The account was long, exceptionally detailed, and delivered in a technical jargon no one there understood, least of all Garrett herself. A transcript of the reading was given to the Air Ministry Intelligence for analysis. It was also published in newspapers throughout England, causing a national sensation and a giant headache for the Air Ministry. Subsequent séances produced much more information in equally technical detail. Others who died in the crash spoke too, including the minister of civil aviation. They all concurred with Irwin's take on the dirigible's problems.

Despite the torrent of accurate details given to Garrett by Irwin in the terminology of airborne vehicle engineers, controversy lingered. The problem was not that Garrett was suspect or that survival was denied but that the government wanted to cover up the disaster. Authorities therefore tried to discredit the accuracy of Garrett's account or suggested that she could have come by details of the ship's construction from press releases. How could Garrett have known details of the *R101* crash by normal means when the government had kept it secret at the time of the first séance? Furthermore, all involved, living and dead, confirmed that only Irwin was in possession of all the facts.[35]

During World War II, séances conducted through the Scottish medium Helen Duncan revealed the sinking of two ships: the HMS *Hood* on May 25, 1941, and the HMS *Barham* six months later. With the HMS *Hood*, the disaster happened more than an hour *after* the séance. This is a remarkable instance of the dead communicating backward in time. The second sinking was revealed by a young man who had died badly burned. In both cases, the British Admiralty kept the naval losses top secret for reasons of war strategy and to protect public morale. The admiralty authorities were so alarmed by the security risk Duncan's revelations presented that they had her arrested for witchcraft under a law dating from 1735. She was put on trial and convicted, thereby silenced for the duration of the war.[36]

The Garrett and Duncan séances expose the tough challenges to the survival explanation of mediumship. The super-psi (or super-ESP) theory claims that mediums are receiving information not from the dead but from something right here on this side of the veil. Therefore, supporters of this theory would charge Garrett with learning about the airship crash clairvoyantly from the environment rather than from Irwin. More simply, she may have picked it up telepathically from the officials who knew of the crash a few days before her séance, in which case parapsychologists would call it direct mental interaction between living systems, or DMILS. And Duncan might have precognitively plucked the HMS *Hood* disaster from the future rather than from the dead. In all cases I would add the possibility of retrieving information from mass consciousness.

DMILS between a sitter and a medium is a justifiable concern. Although I am risking voicing an unpopular view among survival advocates that DMILS can and does operate in readings and séances, normally it operates only to a certain degree. The better the medium and the stronger the contact, the less the medium will unwittingly fall back on information telepathically retrieved from the living sitter. Distinguishing between genuine contact, which is after all largely a telepathic process, and DMILS is not always easy for researchers and mediums alike.

There are many things the theories of super-psi and DMILS cannot explain, such as full dialogue between the living and the dead, including arguments. In addition, in a sufficient number of cases no living person possessed the information delivered in a séance. An interesting example is the case of the missing bone. It began in Iceland in 1937 with five sitters, each of whom signed an affidavit about the event, and the trance medium Hafsteinn Björnsson. The case was exhaustively investigated over the course of several decades, lastly by the esteemed scholar Ian Stevenson, of the University of Virginia.[37]

Björnsson was holding a séance with his regular circle of sitters when a dead man abruptly and rudely appeared, demanding snuff, coffee, and rum. When asked why he had arrived, the visitor announced gruffly that he was looking for his leg. Cantankerous and uncooperative, he refused to identify himself until his reappearance three months later, when he gave his name, Runolfur Runolfsson. He then related the circumstances of his death, which had occurred at the age of fifty-two, in October 1879, fifty-eight years before the séance. While drinking on the beach late at night, he fell into a stuporous sleep. A storm built up and carried him out to sea, where he drowned. When his body was recovered the following January, it was buried in the churchyard in Utskalar, Iceland. His thighbone, however, had been carried back out to sea. When it washed up onshore, Runolfsson explained, it was passed around and ended up in "Ludvik's" house. Ludvik was Ludvik Gudmundsson, who had recently joined the séance circle. Runolfsson also mentioned that he had been a tall man in life.

The church records confirmed the date of his death, his age at that time, and his place of burial. But no record of his missing bone was found despite years of investigation. Gudmundsson, unaware of a bone in his house, asked the oldest residents of his village if anyone remembered hearing anything about a missing bone. One of them recalled that a carpenter who had worked on the construction of the house for the original owner mentioned a bone he had buried between the inner and outer walls. It was put there because without an identity it could not be buried in consecrated ground. After Gudmundsson and others failed to find it, despite many attempts, the old carpenter was sent for. He showed them where to open the wall. In it, they found an unusually long thighbone, which was later buried in consecrated ground. Perhaps out of gratitude, Runolfsson became the medium's principal control for many years afterward.

This case is modest in comparison to the many spectacular ones involving murders, in which victims describe through mediums the exact circumstances of their deaths. As police forces know, the descriptive details given by mediums often lead to convictions. Yet Runolfsson's communication better satisfies the criteria for eliminating DMILS. While a murder is taking place, the murderer and the victim are alive and hence able to telepathically relay the event to anyone sensitive enough to pick it up. Furthermore, the sheer emotional force of most homicides could conceivably leave imprints on mass consciousness, putting the event in the public domain of telepathically available knowledge. Although I am personally convinced on the basis of my own experience that genuine contact is made with the slain victim, technically there is a possibility that DMILS or super-psi is at work. With Runolfsson, however, the man was already dead when his thighbone got lost. By definition then, knowledge about his missing bone, which he gained only *after* death, eliminates the possibility of a telepathic exchange between "living systems."

Unfortunately, the Runolfsson séances and others like them did not take place under controlled conditions with objective investigators documenting the events. Nor can they be repeated in the laboratory. In fact, most communication with the dead, whether private or through instruments or mediums, will not in the end prove survival according to the standards set by science. In order for the dead to establish their identity, they must necessarily give details that the living can verify, which brings us back to the conundrum mentioned in chapter 1. If the living can verify information given, then critics can argue that telepathy between the living is the source, such as between the mediums and their sitters in the University of Arizona trials. In the examples of warnings and the disasters seen by Garrett and Duncan, clairvoyance or precognition might be the source. If, on the other hand, the dead relate something not known to the living, who on earth can verify it as true?

CHAPTER FIVE

Reincarnation

The ancient belief in reincarnation is central to two world religions, Hinduism and Buddhism. Although it is still today predominantly an Asian philosophy, it was a tenet of certain Christian sects until the Council of Constantinople pronounced it heresy in 553. Despite church efforts, belief in reincarnation has been hard to kill and is generally on the rise in the West.[1] If reincarnation can be established as fact, then it provides clear evidence for the continuance of human consciousness.

Past-life recall can be spontaneous or evoked by hypnotism and therapeutic regression. The reason so few Westerners remember living before without facilitation — or, rather, why few adults remember spontaneous childhood memories of former lives — is addressed in chapter 8. In addition to considering memories, researchers also consider child prodigies, unusual skills, and atypical interests that spring out of nowhere at very early ages, phobias, behavioral idiosyncrasies, inexplicable strong likes and dislikes, sharp differences between identical twins, xenoglossy (speaking in a foreign language unknown to the speaker), birthmarks, and congenital deformities as possible signs of past lives coming to the surface.

Certain criteria must be met for a recollection to qualify as evidential. First, the investigator must be able to determine whether an account is a true past-life memory or a compensation fantasy. There are many ways to go about making this all-important distinction, as you will see. The absence of fraud and deception is also at the top of the list. Waking dreams, genetic memory, the collective unconscious or super-psi, and extrasensory perception, such as clairvoyance and telepathy, as well as possession have all been candidates for explaining away reincarnational recall. So has dissociation, as in people with multiple personalities. Channeling the memories of the dead is another possible explanation. Distinguishing a true memory from a story is especially difficult when the hypnotized subject has an imagination as fertile as a fiction writer's, capable of making up realistic tales elaborated with historical facts. The greatest threat to the theory of reincarnation is cryptomnesia. Cryptomnesia refers to when a person acquires information about an individual or historical period by normal means but afterward completely forgets it. The information might resurface under certain conditions, such as hypnosis, without the person consciously remembering its source. Fortunately, cryptomnesia is relatively easy to identify under hypnosis. All a practitioner needs to do is ask where the information came from, and the entranced subject will not hesitate to reveal the source.

PAST-LIFE THERAPY AND HYPNOSIS

Back in the 1890s in Paris, Albert de Rochas experimented with putting people in trance. He began by regressing them to early childhood, then to their births, and further back still until they found themselves in previous existences. His work marked the discovery of the most important source of past-life knowledge — regression. He and later pioneers of what would become known as past-life therapy, namely, Morey Bernstein (who made known the sensational Bridey Murphy case), Thorwald Dethlefsen, Edith Fiore, Bruce Goldberg, Denys Kelsey, Morris Netherton, Dick Sutphen, and Helen Wambach, have brought

about some of the biggest advances in the investigation of postmortem
survival beyond the advances made by near-death-experience researchers.[2] Neither the subject-patient nor the practitioner needs to believe in
reincarnation in order for recall to happen. Many hypnotherapists are
staunch nonbelievers. One was Dr. Alexander Cannon, a man awarded
degrees by nine European universities. In his groundbreaking book,
The Power Within (1950), he writes:

> For years the theory of reincarnation was a nightmare to me
> and I did my best to disprove it and even argued with my
> trance subjects to the effect that they were talking nonsense.
> Yet as the years went by one subject after another told me the
> same story in spite of different and varied conscious beliefs.
> Now well over a thousand cases have been so investigated and
> I have to admit that there is such a thing as reincarnation.[3]

Despite three decades of reincarnation research since publication
of *The Power Within*, psychiatrist Dr. Gerald Edelstein still could not
overcome a similar reluctance. Even though he had a strong bias against
reincarnation, many of his patients spontaneously fell into past-life
recall. The therapeutic results, he grudgingly admits, are phenomenal:
"These experiences, for reasons I cannot explain, almost always lead to
rapid improvements in the patients' lives."[4]

Dr. James Parejko conducted a study in 1980 at Chicago State University in which he hypnotized one hundred volunteers. Ninety-three
out of that hundred related previous lives, an enormous percentage. But
the point is, the subjects who gave the most thorough accounts of their
past lives were generally those who were known from earlier interviews
to outright deny the possibility of reincarnation.[5] Further studies show
that the subjects who do recall past lives under hypnosis are mentally
healthier than those who do not. Contrary to the popular belief that
people easy to hypnotize are weak-willed and easily led, successful subjects had a stronger sense of self-identity than unsuccessful ones. They

were also found to be more tolerant of stress and to have less guilt and fewer psychiatric disturbances.[6]

A past-life therapist typically collects many thousands of reports during the course of a career, providing us with a huge and extraordinarily important database from which the mechanisms of reincarnating can be gleaned. One of the most evidential studies is the work of Dr. Helen Wambach, author of two well-received books: *Reliving Past Lives* (1978) and *Life before Life* (1979). Wambach's ambitious research at the Monmouth Medical Center, in New Jersey, is based on a series of small workshops in which people were hypnotized in groups. Ninety percent of the volunteers had memories of previous lives, and an additional 5 percent were eventually able to recall past lives under personal supervision.

Wambach distributed questionnaires for the subjects to fill out in an attempt to organize an astounding 1,088 memories. Her analysis of the questionnaire responses is an eye-opener. First, nearly all previous existences were dull, with no significance to world events. According to descriptions of occupations, clothing, diet, habitation, décor, and objects used, 7 percent seemed to have had lives in the upper socioeconomic bracket, 23 percent in the middle bracket, and 70 percent in the lower one. Not one reported a life as a famous personality. Many past lives among the 70 percent group were characterized by violence, poverty, and early death. Such bleak recollections, from a group of workshop subjects primarily composed of white, middle-income Americans, are clearly not the stuff of compensation fantasies. In terms of sex, 50.3 percent remembered being male and 49.7 percent female, a ratio that is extremely close to the actual birth ratio. A hefty 90 percent had experienced their past deaths as pleasant, and only 26 percent looked forward to rebirth.

One aim of the analysis was to find discrepancies between what was reported by the subjects and what is known of a specific period: population density, climate, landscape, architecture, clothing, cultural customs, and moralities. Of the 1,088 accounts, serious discrepancies were found in a mere 11. More people regressed to periods and places where the population is known to have been high than to periods and places where it was low. Their memories also reflected known racial and economic distributions for any given period. Despite systematic agreement between the reports of Wambach's subjects and what is historically known, most researchers, and especially skeptics, reject her work as evidence of reincarnation on the allegation that the memories do not provide enough historical specificity.

Although her findings correspond to those of other past-life therapists, they also differ in some ways. Wambach's volunteers were not participating for therapeutic reasons, whereas people who go into regression therapy go in with a set of problems they want to solve. It is the therapist's job then to facilitate locating the past lives in which these problems are anchored. Therefore, the kind of past life that rises into conscious memory during therapy is nearly always traumatic or involves traumatic death. As with near-death experiences and afterdeath communications, something real must be happening, because the aftereffects are so strong. Thorough recall typically results in dramatic shifts in personal worldview and the rapid clearing up of an assortment of psychological problems and destructive life themes. From my own involvement with past-life therapy as a patient and as a therapist, I concur with many others that past-life therapy — which also addresses the problems of the present life — is the fastest, most effective all-around therapy currently known.

Past-life therapy has some surprising positive physical side effects too. I personally know of sudden remissions of cancer, the quick dissolution of a nine-year-long paralysis, the disappearance of many long-standing conditions, such as chronic urinary tract infections, gastrointestinal problems, ulcers, eczema, and other skin ailments, and the alleviation or elimination of arthritis, neurological pain, and epileptic seizures. Reports also include hair getting thicker, voice registers dropping, eyesight improving, and women's breast size increasing. Multiple sclerosis, obesity, stuttering, migraine headaches, depression, learning disabilities, addiction, allergies, and every conceivable form of phobia, irrational fears, and recurrent nightmares, as well as sexual inadequacies and nonbiological infertility, have also cleared up in a very short time. The claims that fantasy, deception, cryptomnesia, ancestral memory, possession, telepathy, split personalities, or channeling the memories of the dead can cure a person's deeply personal problems are to me unsustainable. Since when has someone else's memory cured another person? Deception and multiple personality disorders are also unlikely to lead a person to recovery. And ancestral memory is untenable when a Thai child remembers being an American soldier in the Civil War.

Single Memories

Dr. Morris Netherton, a pioneer in the field of past-life therapy (and my teacher),[7] relates the incident of a patient who returned to her previous life as Rita McCullum. Rita was born in 1903 and lived in rural Pennsylvania with her foster parents until they were killed in a car accident in 1916. In the early 1920s she married a man named McCullum and moved to New York, where they had a garment manufacturing company off Seventh Avenue in midtown Manhattan. Life was hard and money short. Her husband died in 1928. In 1929, her son died from polio, and the stock market crashed. Like many others during the Great Depression, Rita succumbed to bankruptcy and depression. On the sunny day of June 11, 1933, she hanged herself from the ceiling fan of her factory. Because this memory featured traceable facts, Netherton and his patient contacted New York City's Hall of Records. They received a photocopy of a notarized death certificate of a woman named Rita McCullum. Under manner of death, it stated that she died by hanging at an address in the West Thirties, still today the heart of the garment district. The date of death was June 11, 1933.[8]

Another validated single memory from Netherton occurred while he was giving workshops in Brazil. A local woman suffering from agoraphobia volunteered to be the subject. She fell into a memory of dying in a concentration camp. Just as she began reexperiencing the branding of a number on her arm, she started to scream. Red welts surfaced on her arm, which soon formed into numbers. They were quickly photographed before fading. The Brazilian woman gave many details of that life, including her former name, the names of her family members, and the name of the camp in which she was confined in Nazi Germany. Apparently, she had died from exposure after months of being left outdoors in harsh weather. The number, and only the number, was forwarded to the Holocaust center in Israel. The report the archivists sent back stated her name, birth date, parents' names, village of birth, date of death, and name of the concentration camp, all of which tallied exactly with what the Brazilian woman remembered.[9] There are many such stories in the files of past-life therapists.

Two or More People Remembering the Same Past-Life Events

Even more convincing are instances in which two or more people experience the same event from their respective standpoints. The hypnotherapist Dr. Bruce Goldberg, who has regressed some thousands of patients, provides us with a remarkable account of two patients who had never met and had no awareness of each other, yet individually remembered a past life in which they were together.[10] The first patient, a salesman named Arnold, had come to Goldberg complaining of feeling exploited and dominated by others. After some attempts, Arnold began to talk about himself as a young man named Thayer, who lived in Bavaria in the year 1132. Arnold found himself as Thayer eating under the table in the shop of a master goldsmith he specifically named as Gustave. Gustave had taken Thayer as his apprentice. He frequently beat him, sodomized him, and when he was away from the shop, chained him to the table, hence Thayer's dining under the table. Gustave also humiliated him in front of customers, especially Clothilde, the daughter of a local wealthy family. Eventually, Thayer got into a violent fight with Gustave, who stabbed his apprentice in the stomach with a work-shop tool. Thayer died.

Eighteen months later, an attorney named Brian showed up in Goldberg's office, troubled by an uncontrollable compulsion to manip-ulate and dominate others. He also had insomnia and eating disorders. When Brian was regressed, he began speaking of his life in twelfth-century Bavaria, when he was a master goldsmith named Gustave. He said his apprentice, a fellow named Thayer, was incompetent. He went on to relate how he had enjoyed beating him and sexually molesting him and that a girl named Clothilde was distracting the boy from his work. Many other facts corresponded perfectly with Arnold's version. Gustave/the attorney also told Goldberg that Thayer resisted being chained to the table, which one day led to a fight. He then killed the boy by stabbing him in the stomach. Although these accounts made Goldberg's skin crawl, the therapist was obligated to keep them confi-dential. His two patients never became aware of the other's existence con-sciously, yet the synchronicity of when and with whom they both sought help shows that they communicated with each other on a deep level.

Netherton reports that in a space of ten years he heard eighteen separate patients recount the same execution.[11] The late and highly respected Dr. Arthur Guirdham, once senior consultant psychiatrist in Bath, wrote a series of books detailing Cathar incarnations, of which he was one in a group of eight living together.[12] The Cathars formed a heretical sect that believed in reincarnation. It flourished in the twelfth and thirteenth centuries until the Albigensian Crusades exterminated it. Individual memories contained enough hard data for Guirdham to trace the identities of seven out of the eight people back to thirteenth-century France using records of the French Inquisition. Several gave details about the Cathars that at first seemed incorrect. Guirdham's subsequent investigation in obscure sources, sources that other group members were not likely to have come across, eventually confirmed the historical accuracy of their reports.

Dr. Marge Rieder, a hypnotherapist, took seventeen years to gather and document the last account I will give of multiple past lives. Among her patients, she uncovered more than fifty who remembered living in the little town of Millboro, Virginia, around the time of the Civil War. Only three of them had ever visited Virginia before, and none had ever heard of Millboro. All, however, pronounced the town's name as "Marlboro," exactly as residents of Millboro pronounce it today. Their stories and descriptions of life in old Millboro were consistent. They spoke of buried rooms and tunnels painted in unusual colors, used as an underground railroad for slaves and military escapees. No mention of an underground railroad was uncovered in historical documents or maps, nor did any Millboro resident know of one from oral tradition. It took excavations in the areas remembered by Rieder's patients to finally find this lifeline to the North.[13]

SPONTANEOUS RECALL

Only a small percentage of past-life memories are facilitated by thera-pists and hypnotists. Millions of people all over the world have sponta-neous recall all on their own. From childhood on, Jenny Cockell had dreams that were "swamped by memories." In her previous life her name was Mary O'Neil. At her death, Mary was in terror of what would become of her children, the oldest only thirteen. Jenny's memories of her former home, her village, and nearby towns were so clear she was able to draw maps. Eventually she identified her past-life hometown as Malahide, Ireland.

Jenny went to Ireland and made contact with all O'Neils in the Malahide area. She also obtained Mary O'Neil's death certificate and the names of her children. When her story was nationally televised, she met Mary's eldest son, Sonny, then seventy-one, for the first time. At the instigation of the show's producers, before Jenny and Sonny were allowed to meet, they independently wrote detailed descriptions of family events. On camera, the two of them compared notes. Sonny was able to validate Jenny's memories of the village two generations ago, the cottage, which had been demolished in 1959, the violent behavior of Mary's drunken husband, names, dates, family events, and a slew of private circumstances only a member of Mary's immediate family could confirm. What Jenny did not know was that when Mary died her children were split up and put into different orphanages. Through Jenny, they were once again united.[14]

Spontaneous Memory in Children

Young children offer especially evidential material for reincarnation, primarily because cryptomnesia, pseudomemories, and déjà vu can be ruled out. They also lack the experience to fantasize at the level of sophistication their memories exhibit. Children's past-life memories can emerge as early as the age of two and generally fade by the age of seven. Occasionally they will resurface at seventeen or eighteen. Parents might hear matter-of-fact statements from their toddlers, such as "When I died..." or "When I was big..." A three-year-old might talk about having a wife or husband and not always in the past tense either. Sad to say, parents usually think their children are making it up and either ignore them or scold them. Extremely clear and detailed memories often signal dramatic circumstances of a previous death, usually violent and sudden.

Such was the case for a little Louisiana boy, James Leininger, who by the time he was eighteen months old was already showing signs of obsession with military airplanes, particularly crashing toy planes. At two and a half he displayed a knowledge of aviation that far surpassed that of his parents, Andrea and Bruce. In that same year, the nightmares began. Several nights a week they heard his anguished screams, "Airplane crash! Plane on fire! Little man can't get out!" Over the course of the next few years, the boy gave his name as "James II" in that life, the names of other people in his squadron, specifically "Jack Larsen," and three more names of pilots who had died in the same air strike. He also told his parents that he had flown a Corsair, that his launch ship was the *Natoma*, and that his plane was shot down head-on, right into the engine, by Japanese antiaircraft fire in the battle of Iwo Jima.

Now it was the father's turn to become obsessed. Bruce's initial intention was to disprove his son's claims. But after investigating, he learned that there was indeed a USS *Natoma Bay* in the Pacific arena. Since a reunion of the men who had served on it was coming up, he decided to go. There he met a former rear-gunner named Ralph Clarbour, whose plane was right next to the one flown by Lt. James M. Huston Jr. (i.e., James II). Clarbour saw Huston's plane get hit head-on and right in the middle of the engine, just as the boy had said. He watched it go down at Chichi Jima during the raid on Iwo Jima, March 3, 1945. Military records testified that a Lt. James Huston Jr. had actually died in this mission at the early age of twenty-one. In fact, he was the only pilot from the *Natoma Bay* shot down at Chichi Jima. They also confirmed that Huston had been part of a special squad that test-piloted Corsairs. Bruce Leininger also found Jack Larsen in Arkansas, who turned out to have been Huston's wingman in the Pacific. Lt. James M. Huston Jr.: Died 1945. Reborn 1998.[15]

It is impossible to discuss children's incarnational memories without citing the life-long research of the late Ian Stevenson, founder of the Division of Perceptual Studies in the Department of Psychiatric Medicine at the University of Virginia. Stevenson collected more than two thousand cases "suggestive of reincarnation," as he cautiously put it, in India, Sri Lanka, Thailand, Burma, Brazil, Africa, Turkey, Lebanon, Syria, Great Britain, and the United States, particularly among the Tlingits of Alaska. He examined about two hundred of these extensively over years.[16] All together they present evidence for reincarnation that is by most standards impossible to refute.

In the most persuasive cases among thousands filed at the university, deaths were usually premature and almost half were violent. The time lapse between one life and the next was between one and four years, generally, and rarely more than twelve years. Because these intervals are short, past-life identities could be verified up to 75 percent

of the time, since family members from the child's previous life were
still alive. Memory is so vivid that children regard their previous lives as
continuous with the present, keeping largely the same habits, behavior,
and preferences of their former selves. Phobias, such as fear of water,
having to do with the manner of death, such as drowning, are quite
common, and birthmarks or congenital malformations frequently correspond to fatal wounds. Children speak of people and places they have
never seen in their present lives with an accuracy of up to 90 percent. I
offer here one of Stevenson's cases to illustrate the depth and sophistication of some past-life memories in children.

A boy called Bishen Chand was born in Bareilly, in Uttar Pradesh,
in 1921. When he was only ten months old he pronounced the name
Pilibhit, the village of his previous existence, also in Uttar Pradesh. At
three he gave his former name, Laxmi Narain, and details about his
father as a rich landowner of the Kayastha caste. At school, which he
mentioned was near a river, he had learned Urdu, Hindi, and English
and had a sixth-grade teacher who was fat and bearded. He spoke of his
former two-story house with one entrance for females and another for
males. His uncle's house was apparently green. He had kite races with
his neighbor, whose name he gave as Sunder Lal, who also had a green
house, but with a fence. He spoke of his servant, a short, dark-skinned
man named Maikua of the Kahar caste, whom he remembered as being
a good cook. In his former life, he went to court against some family
members and won. His favorite prostitute was a woman named Padma.
One night when he was drunk he saw a man leave her house and shot
him. With his mother's help, he stayed hidden after the murder until he
found work in Shahjahanpur, where he died at the age of twenty.

More than 90 percent of his recollections checked out. When his
family took him to Pilibhit, Bishen Chand recognized his house and
told them what changes had been made since he was last there. He
located the room in which he had hidden money, money that they then
found. He knew the house of his neighbor, Sunder Lal, as well as where
a trader had lived and where the office of a watchmaker once was. He

was quite attached to his previous mother, who accepted him as the reincarnation of her son. Contemptuous of the impoverished circumstances of his new life, he frequently tore off his clothing because it wasn't silk and refused food, ranting that it wasn't even fit for his servant Maikua. In his previous life he had played the *tabla*, a musical instrument, which as Bishen he mastered and gave up by the time he was five. Throughout his life, Bishen was also renowned for his skill in Urdu, a language he had never studied. At the tender age of five, he advised his father to get a mistress. His attachment to his own past-life mistress Padma was still so strong that when he was twenty-three and met her again (by then she was fifty-two), he fainted from emotion. Attempts to convince her to resume their relationship failed. He never repented for killing his rival, but remained proud of it.[17]

Other researchers have uncovered incidents no less remarkable for their detail and accuracy. One comes from Des Moines, Iowa, where little curly-headed Romy Crees began pouring out her memories as soon as she could talk. She remembered being a man named Joe Williams, married to Sheila, with three children. She vividly recalled dying in a motorcycle accident, which was consistent with her motorcycle phobia. As Joe, she lived in a red-brick house and went to school in Charles City. According to the three-year-old, her mother in that life was called Louise Williams and, she added, had a pain in her right knee. When Romy, her father, and two past-life researchers visited Charles City, 87 miles (140 km) away, she was able to lead them to the house of Louise Williams, who came to the door limping because of a bad right knee. Joe and Sheila Williams had died in a motorcycle accident in 1975, two years before Romy's birth.[18]

BIRTHMARKS

After decades of research Stevenson could not ignore the birthmarks and congenital defects of some children with past-life memories. Among 210 of these children, he found postmortem reports for 49 from their previous existences. In 88 percent of the cases, birthmarks were within 4 inches (10 cm) of the wound that had killed them.[19] Thiang San Kla believed he was his uncle Phoh reborn. Phoh had died from a stabbing. He was also known to have had a festering wound on his right big toe and tattoos on both hands and feet. Thiang was born with a large birthmark that corresponded exactly to the knife wound. His right big toe was deformed, and his hands and feet carried tattoolike markings.[20]

Fourteen children who remembered being shot to death had birthmarks of both entrance and exit wounds. A Turkish boy who told of a life as a notorious criminal vividly recalled shooting himself under the chin just before the police got hold of him. When Stevenson saw the round red mark under the boy's chin, he looked for the exit wound and found a round, red, bald spot on the top of the boy's head. Another child was born with a pattern of red dots on his chest consistent with the shotgun blast he claimed had killed him. Occasionally, the birthmarks appear after birth. When a Brazilian infant fell into a high fever a few days after birth, red stripes suddenly appeared all over her tiny body. The parents later learned from her that in her previous life she had died at the age of twelve, run over by a train.[21]

PHOBIAS

We have already seen a few examples of phobias directly related to past-life deaths. Phobias tend to be the first signs of reincarnation to show up. The list of phobias is long, with some of the most common involving water, found in 64 percent of the children who remembered drowning. Other children, like Romy above, are terrified of motor vehicles when their past-life deaths were caused by vehicular accidents. Claustrophobia is also frequently related to previous existences. Children might shake with fear when getting close to those places where their deaths occurred. One Indian boy had a strong aversion to yogurt, a diet staple in India, because he had died from poisonous yogurt in his previous life. Nevertheless, birthmarks and defects can be more objectively

measured than phobias and therefore better support the validity of reincarnational memory.

XENOGLOSSY

I have saved what is perhaps the most enthralling evidence of past lives
for last: xenoglossy, the spontaneous speaking of a language unknown
to the person speaking it. Most often, the person is totally incapable of
comprehending the language, let alone speaking it, outside of altered
states. Stevenson recorded many instances of this phenomenon in India.
Occasionally, however, the language stays in use, as it did with Bishen
Chand, who retained his uncanny command of Urdu. A thirty-seven-
year-old Philadelphia housewife, "T. E.," spoke Swedish while under
hypnosis. She had never been exposed to Swedish in her present life
and could not understand a word of it when she came out of hypnosis. Under hypnosis, her personality shifted from a woman to Jensen
Jacoby, a peasant farmer in the seventeenth century who spoke col-
loquial Swedish. Going from female to male, from America to Old
World Sweden, her voice also changed significantly, as did her worldview. After more than eight years of intense investigation, Stevenson,
together with linguists, psychologists, and other scientists, found no
alternative to the reincarnation explanation for this remarkably clear
case of xenoglossy.[22]

There are other instances of Americans speaking Swedish, oddly
enough,[23] but also Coptic from first-millennium Egypt. One English
sports instructor spoke a much earlier Egyptian, from the time of the
pharaohs.[24] A technician from England spoke elegant, upper-class
French while he was emerging from the fog of an operation.[25]

Netherton found one of the most amazing instances of xenoglossy
in a blond, blue-eyed, eleven-year-old California boy. Luckily, Netherton audio-taped the boy while he was speaking what sounded like Chinese! The taped example of xenoglossy was eleven minutes of unbroken
monologue. When it was given to a professor in the Department of

Oriental Studies at the University of California, the philologist identified it as a passage from an ancient forbidden religion in China.[26]

Since trance mediums speaking in tongues completely foreign to them is a matter of record, there is still the possibility that mediumship, not a past life, is behind xenoglossy. The California boy could have been channeling a long-dead Chinese monk, for instance. Another cause of xenoglossy might be possession, in which case the California boy could have been possessed by a long-dead Chinese monk. Yet, if either one was the root of xenoglossy, this would still demonstrate the survival of consciousness after death. The last case offered here eliminates mediumship and possession as explanations for xenoglossy.

Marshall McDuffie, a prominent physician in New York, and his wife, Wilhelmina, repeatedly found their twin baby boys talking to each other in a strange language. As it seemed to have a grammar and a consistent vocabulary, they took the twins to the foreign-language department of Columbia University in the hope of identifying it. None of the professors there recognized it until a specialist of ancient Semitic languages passed by. He was amazed to hear from the mouths of babes Aramaic, a language that flourished in ancient Syro-Palestine.[27] Unless we can accept that both of these babies were mediums, each one channeling a distinct dead person from, say, ancient Galilee, or that both were possessed, each by a different Aramaic-speaking spirit, the only explanation for this instance of xenoglossy is reincarnation. If there is reincarnation, there is life after death.

PART II

The Social Construction of the Afterlife

CHAPTER SIX

A Comparative History of the Afterlife

*M*ost of us were brought up to believe that where we go after death is a fixed place that is forever the same. We were also taught that the religions we belong to know the exact nature of that place. As we explore ancient beliefs about death and the afterlife in this chapter, one thing becomes clear: from the beginning of recorded history to the present, each society, each cult and sect, has remade the afterlife to fit its own needs, even when the official religion has remained the same. Here we will trace afterlife beliefs from the root cultures of ancient Mesopotamia, Egypt, Greece, and Israel to the Roman Mediterranean of early Christianity. Seeing our own beliefs as part of a wider, ongoing (but very uneven) sociohistorical process rather than divine decree is liberating and leads to examination of our own private thoughts about the hereafter. To this end, I have included a short section on traditional and personal beliefs that challenge mainstream religions and stir further reflection.

Almost all cultures have claimed that their visions of the afterlife are the only true ones, divinely revealed to their legendary founders, holy men and women, priests and prophets, of the remote past. In extreme antiquity, revelations were passed down orally through the culture's mythology. By the time they were written down, most societies had already evolved into urban civilizations composed of massive institutions and classes of clerics and ruling elites. The visions and oral wisdom of old were then heavily edited, rewritten in order to serve the people and institutions in power. The imposition of doctrinaire versions of the next world becomes an extremely effective political tool in the creation and maintenance of a centralized power. Although a nation or state can threaten bodily death, only religions can threaten everlasting doom or permanent extinction.

Christianity, Judaism, and Islam, the three Abrahamic religions, claim that the teachings on the afterlife can be found in holy scripture. As you read through this chapter, you might be surprised to discover that there is too little in the Bible on the subject to form a clear picture of the afterlife, and what is there is contradictory. From what we can glean from the writings and practices of early Christians and Jews, from which Islam later developed, the beliefs of these peoples have little in common with those a great majority in the West adhere to today. Beliefs about the afterworld are flexible and ever-changing. At the point when they fossilize as official religious dogma, they tend to serve sociopolitical ends.

There are no known cultures of the past or present that have *not* recognized an afterlife of some sort. It is, then, what anthropologists call a universal. Universals are beliefs or practices that can be attested for all cultures, places, and times. They are the chief organizers of group behavior. And they are extraordinarily rare. Another universal even the Neanderthals practiced is ritual for the transition after death, usually as burial rites. A third is the conviction in divinity, whether a single god or a pantheon of gods, nature spirits, or good and bad daemons. These are the basics hardwired in the human psyche: the belief in survival after death, the rites of transition, and the belief in supreme beings. One principle was constant among the ancients: death shapes life. Every culture seems to have hosted specialists who mediated between the two worlds mostly by communing with the dead, in the belief that the dead can intercede on behalf of the living.

For some regions in antiquity, survival after death was precarious, because it was not granted to everyone. In the earliest historical periods of Egypt, for instance, it was reserved for the highest elite, the rulers and their families. Eventually, who survived was based no longer on a person's social supremacy or won glory but rather on the virtue of the life lived. Even so, without proper burial rites and often regular ritual care for the dead on the part of descendants, continued survival was not certain. In ancient Mesopotamia and the Greco-Roman world, the underworld received everyone, the pious and the sinful, the rich and the poor, the lawful and the criminal. With the exception of deified figures in the Greek and Roman periods, the conditions of a person's afterlife were largely dictated by the burial goods and the ritual offerings given by surviving offspring.

Another chief difference among the belief systems of antiquity is where individual identity resides. If we look at the records, it seems that the location of identity was an ongoing debate. The ancient Egyptians and Mesopotamians were the most complex in their descriptions of incorporeal identity. Classical Greece developed the notion of an impersonal immortal soul, a kind of intellectual survival, quite unlike the earlier Homeric characters in Hades, who were colorful, impulsive, and decidedly acerebral. In the early phases of Judaism (certain sects), Christianity, and Islam, identity was understood as located in the physical body. Survival of individual identity then required physical resurrection. Today, the carrier of identity is commonly held to be the soul or spirit, assumed to be outside the body.

ANCIENT MESOPOTAMIA AND EGYPT

Beliefs from ancient Mesopotamia and Egypt are especially important, because they show the earliest indications of two basic and divergent tendencies in the way we think about the afterlife: as permissive and inclusive or as judgmental and exclusive. Although the two cultures were concurrent, and both left hoards of archaeological and textual remains, much more is known about Egypt's afterlife than Mesopotamia's. Because Egypt was unified politically under a single ruler and by a single geographical feature, the Nile, Egyptian after-death narratives tend to be more unified. The cults of the dead revolved around a single divine person, the pharaoh, further integrating their stories. Egyptians literally and figuratively put their hearts and souls into their burials, and what has come down to us from Egypt mostly comes from tombs. By contrast, Mesopotamia was a collection of differing ethnicities and a great number of individual city-states until the great warring powers of Babylonia and Assyria arose. The disunity resulted in wide variations in beliefs, which are harder to arrange into one comprehensible narrative.

Most of you are probably aware that mummification, spells, and rites were required in Egypt for postmortem survival. In Mesopotamia, everyone survived. Nevertheless, to ensure an untroubled passage into the underworld, a corpse needed to be buried. Burial rites were more varied, although far simpler, than Egyptian ones. Beyond the obvious differences, both cultures produced prominent written works concerning death and immortality. Egypt even had a literary tradition in which the author told his story from the grave, the best example being the postmortem autobiography of Sinuhe (c. 1960 BCE). In addition, both honored legendary figures who visited the afterworld while alive.

Mesopotamians and Egyptians held complex views about identity outside the body, all strange to us today. Mesopotamians saw humans as infused by several invisible forces. The *napištu* was the divine breath breathed into the first humans, whom the gods fashioned from clay mixed with divine blood. Another windlike force was the *zāqiqu*, which could operate independently of the body. It was often imagined as a winged creature, because it was seen flitting about. The *eṭemmu*, usually translated as "ghost," is the identity that resides in the Netherworld after death. It was a person's *eṭemmu* to whom the living appealed for help. There was also *kuẓbu*, an aura or light that emanated from charismatic people and ritually invested objects and buildings.

Similarly, the Egyptians recognized several invisible components of the human spirit. The *ba* corresponds roughly to the Mesopotamian *ẓāqiqu* in that it too functioned independently from the body and was commonly conceived as birdlike. Egyptians believed that the *ba* became active only after the body died, whereas the *ẓāqiqu* was also active any time a person was out of body, as in sleep. The Egyptian *ka* is harder to define. Highly mobile, it could dwell in a person's image or in the sky. The tomb was called the "house of the *ka*," perhaps because it contained afterlife images in which the *ka* dwelled. If the corpse should perish, the *ka* could step in for the body in an effort to continue life after death.

The oft-hailed Egyptian *akh*, a word connoting light and everlasting radiance, was the transcendent self. Originally, only a pharaoh could become an *akh*; later most people could if they passed a series of trials in the afterworld. As Mesopotamians did with *eṭemmu*, Egyptians petitioned the *akh* for aid. For transcendence, the *akh* depended on the elaborate technologies of mummification, in which funerary priests ritually prepared the corpse and laid magical objects in the wrappings. These rites, lasting anywhere from thirty to two hundred days, were acts meant to revivify the dead in the afterlife. If they were not performed or were performed improperly, the dead could not proceed to the afterworld. The spirit was either extinguished or turned into a much-feared earthbound ghost. By contrast, the Mesopotamian notion of an essential divine breath guaranteed some sort of immortality no matter what the circumstances of burial.

Both peoples closely commingled with their dead. Surviving family members provided them continual offerings of food and drink, usually beer. In Egypt, these rites were mostly performed where the corpses were laid to rest, in mausoleum parks, which Egyptians used for picnicking. In Mesopotamia, the dead were even less sequestered. Although there were public cemeteries, family members were also interred at home. Household burial ensured that the family stayed together and that those who inhabited the graves were undisturbed. Ancestral household shrines provided a place for daily honoring of the dead. Special offering rites took place at monthly communal meals, with more elaborate banquets at special calendrical events.

The rites also served the living. In a world where most human ills were attributed to unseen malevolent forces, people sought to keep the dead content. Neglect could turn a friendly spirit into a hostile menace. Even the transcendent *akh* could be malicious.

The living also cared for the dead in order to enlist their aid. Although both societies had necromancers and dream specialists, communication was generally private. Mesopotamians had instructions, for instance, on how to make spirits visible so that they could freely converse with them. Letter writing was popular in both lands. Some letters contain surprisingly specific requests, the cure of an illness, say, or placement in a certain office. Ancestral spirits were expected to fight for their relatives against ill-intended spirits or curses cast by witchcraft. The living brought offerings, said prayers, and wrote petitions to the dead in much the same way as they did for deities, treating ancestors as minor gods. A letter from Egypt illustrates the age-old practice of one hand washing the other.

> A communication by Merirtyfy to [his wife] Nebetiotef: How are you? Is the West [land of the dead] taking care of you according to your desire? Now since I am your beloved upon earth, fight on my behalf and intercede on behalf of my name. I did not garble a spell in your presence when I perpetuated your name upon earth. Remove the infirmity of my body! Please become a spirit for me before my eyes so that I may see you in a dream fighting on my behalf. I will then deposit offerings for you as soon as the sun has risen and outfit your offering slab for you.[1]

The writer clearly wants to make a deal, and he wants verification in a dream that the deal was accepted. Before we scoff at such practices, let's consider how many of us do approximately the same thing inwardly.

And who among us has not called on a deceased relative or friend for help in trying times?

In Egypt, mortuary cults determined the nature of the afterlife, much as religious institutions do today. Tomb images show an idyllic Nile setting. In gorgeous vignettes of daily life, the tomb owner and his family are portrayed in arrested, youthful perfection, with their servants and laborers flawlessly performing their allotted roles. The orderly, idealized picture of the afterlife, drawn or written, grew more complex over time without straying from Egypt's natural settings: orchards and gardens, fields of reeds, winding waterways, well-irrigated verdant plots, boats and ferrymen, and mansions, but not a jackal or scorpion around. By the Middle Kingdom (c. 2160–1580 BCE), tomb art began to depict star charts, imagery that might have influenced much later beliefs of a heavenly sphere. Becoming a celestial body, once the sole prerogative of pharaohs, could be achieved by anyone who had the proper burial rites and could pronounce the right spells.

There were less starry options too. One might choose to dwell in Osiris's lush Fields of Offerings or sail in an unending voyage in Ra's brilliant sun-bark. The cults seem to have operated a little like travel agencies. They issued the famed Book of the Dead, the Book of Gates, the Book of Caverns, and the Book of Amduat, early guidebooks on how to get to the afterworld and avoid perils along the way. Generally the books name and describe various daemon gatekeepers. If the deceased could not recognize and name the gatekeepers, they would not be allowed to pass.

The later New Kingdom Book of the Dead is almost entirely moral directives on how to behave in order to be "acquitted" of charges that would bar entrance into the afterlife. Thus the notion of a life of right behavior as an entrance ticket to the afterlife made its first appearance. The god Thoth weighed the heart, the seat of consciousness, against ma'at, the feather of truth. If someone failed the feather test, he or she was devoured by monsters straight out of a Nilotic nightmare, part hippopotamus, part lion, and part crocodile.

In Mesopotamia, the nature of the afterlife was not dictated by a centralized institution. In fact, the clearest single spokesman was not even a priest but the hero Enkidu, companion of the legendary king Gilgamesh. Enkidu made a trip to the Netherworld in a dream that presaged his own untimely death. He related a grim, lightless universe, where dust was the common fare and where — unthinkably — kings sat next to beggars. Other mythological sources give us more cheerful conditions. They describe the Netherworld as hardly different from the world of the living, a kind of shadow civilization modeled on the city-state, with entrance gates and palaces at the hub. Its residents even enjoyed drinking and sex. In this upside-down world, the sun god shone at night. All people, including the early deified kings, ended up there, with one exception, the prebiblical Mesopotamian Noah, who was granted immortality in the flesh. Unlike the Egyptian notion of postmortem judgment, Mesopotamia's was not based on morality. It was applied, rather, to maintain social order in the Netherworld. There are also vague references to souls being recycled back into life after a certain period passed.

In a very early Sumerian myth, "The Descent of Inanna to the Netherworld," the most beloved of all deities in Mesopotamia, Inanna (her Sumerian name is Ishtar in Akkadian), went down to the Netherworld and visited its queen, her sister Ereshkigal. The story is too complex for our purposes here. Suffice to say that Inanna, the lusty, daring patron deity of war and sex, virtually died but was saved and brought back to the world of the living. The work reads like a set of ritual movements, such as the removal of certain items of clothing or jewelry at each of the underworld's seven gates. The repetitive and numbered mental gestures resemble modern techniques for inducing hypnosis. "The Descent" may well be the remains of an extremely ancient liturgy, perhaps as old as the fourth millennium BCE, if not older. I am going to go out on a limb here and speak more as a psychic than as a historian. The Descent texts, together with my own private trance experience, suggest that in very early times certain priestesses were trained to visit the afterworld in deep trance. In ancient thinking, whenever Ereshkigal was enraged — usually because her pride was offended or her sanctuaries neglected — she sent "the dead up to devour the living." The priestesses, who stood in for her sister Inanna, would make the descent in times of mass death from natural disasters, famines, or war in order to placate the underworld queen and stop the killing.

The patterns that the Mesopotamian and Egyptian cultures present are foundational to later ideas of the afterlife. One is that the afterworld is primarily a social construction, built in accordance with what a culture values. Egyptians used imagery from the Nile, source of life and renewal, and, to a lesser extent, the starry heavens. In Mesopotamia, the afterworld was produced as a city-state, a social organization regarded as a gift from the gods. In later Akkadian texts, Ereshkigal was made to marry the god Nergal, who became king of the Netherworld, a political shift from female rule to male rule that reflects the androcentric values of the new rising military states. As you will see, politicization of the afterlife in later eras is more a rule than an exception. Since rivers dominated the lives of people in both regions (Mesopotamia means "the land between two rivers"), they both had traditions of crossing a river to get to the land of the dead.

A second pattern has to do with institutional monopolies on death and the afterlife. Egypt's mortuary cults, like later religions, decreed that unless a person adhered to the advice and rituals prescribed, he or she could not attain eternal life. Cults that enforced moral orthodoxy and compulsory rites performed by their own priests had immense control over the behavior of their members, not to mention their pockets. That they also inculcated fear is evident in the unparalleled preoccupation in Egypt with ensuring a place in the afterlife. For the comparatively decentralized religions of Mesopotamia and Canaan, as well as in later Greece and Rome, survival did not depend on specific cults. More important, people were not denied eternity or punished in the hereafter on moral grounds. That's a huge difference!

The third pattern involves how the journey to the afterworld was made. The journey in Mesopotamia was more familiar than frightening, like a long-distance trip taken from one city to another, though, admittedly, downward. The destination too was a comfortable re-creation of the known civilized world with recognizable values and social rules. Despite a few rare allusions of passing through unfamiliar territory, no texts explicitly warn people of threats and trials before the final arrival at death's literal gates. In Egypt, the way to the Land of the West was longer and fraught with a series of trials and exotic dangers against which people were equipped with an arsenal of apotropaic objects and spells they had to correctly pronounce. Although priests and family members could assist from their positions on the other side, for the grand finale at the destination point, the feather test, a person stood alone.

Most of today's religious institutions have taken paths parallel to Egypt's: obedience to cult creeds and participation in cult death rituals. The Egyptian notion of trials and judgment has been adopted by later world religions, although in later religions a person is subjected to them at different junctures after death: in the body lying in the grave, in the afterlife, or in the following reincarnation. As in Egyptian beliefs, most world religions teach that the spirit is upwardly or downwardly mobile. The Mesopotamian model, in which all humanity is granted a relatively effortless voyage to a familiar afterworld, is better attested in traditional societies. Interestingly, as organized religions become more decentralized in the modern West, the notion of death as an automatic passage into a comfortable afterworld of family and friends is returning in popular belief.

THE CLASSICAL WORLD

The conception of the afterworld in early ancient Greece and Rome was not much different from Mesopotamia's shadowy abode. In Greece, there were specially designated places, *psychomantea*, where necromancy was practiced, often through oracles. According to writings, heroes, mystics, and philosophers temporarily left their bodies to visit the realms beyond. One of the earliest known is the famous Homeric hero Odysseus, whose visit to Hades has left its impression on later Greek mystical literature. The prototypical journey to the afterlife is reminiscent of Egypt's. The dead were guided by Hermes and encountered Cerberus, the three-headed watchdog. On the final stretch, they paid their coins to the ferryman Charon to cross the river Styx. Although intellectuals held different views of the afterlife, this version of Hades was the popular view.

Ancient Greece offers many variations on the meaning of immortality. Great mythological heroes like Herakles, Perseus, and Orion were deified through fame and legend. Hence, they did not die and go to the underworld like other mortals but ascended to the heavenly realms to join the gods of Mount Olympus or to become astral constellations. Since Greeks regarded the dead as mere shades of their former selves, true immortality was possible only when the deceased was memorialized.

Others were no less celebrated for out-of-body trips, like Orpheus and Pythagoras of Samos. Schools were founded on the teachings of these mystics, which included reincarnation. At these centers of learning, the initiated were also taught how to make return trips to the afterlife. Such spiritual adventures were the hallmarks of wisdom in antiquity. Socrates was one of these adepts, according to Plato. In the *Symposium*, Plato relates a story about Socrates standing still for a day and a night in a trance journey (220c). In the last section of the *Apology*, Socrates analyzes death, positing transmigration into reborn bodies, human *and* animal, as the most plausible course. In *Phaedo*, he goes much further, suggesting that we undergo several incarnations in order to learn how to perfect our mental abilities. When separation of the soul from the body is fully grasped, then and only then is reincarnation no longer necessary. The supreme reward is total liberation from bodily existence.

Greek philosophers, including Aristotle, regarded the part that survives physical death as purely mental, an idealization drawn from what intellectual elites valued the most. The body was considered a lowly object that kept the soul in bondage, for Plato in particular. His dualisms of body versus mind (or soul) began infiltrating Christian thinking in late antiquity as Neoplatonism and continue to affect us today. Plato also envisioned a kind of judgment or trial after the first incarnation. Those who pass are borne upward to a celestial sphere, whereas those who don't are sent beneath the earth to prison houses. At the end of a thousand years, the worthy and the unworthy return to choose their next life.

Romans inherited a Hadean afterlife and a similar split in the concept of immortality. On the one hand, everyone had immortal life in the underworld; on the other, people of fame could be immortalized and gain divine or semidivine status, and so avoid Hades altogether. The split was further complicated by what became a chronic tendency among Roman emperors toward deification. Not only did emperors elect themselves and one another to godhood; they also included wives and lovers. In the *Aeneid*, by the Roman poet Virgil (c. 70–19 BCE), we see the incipient forms of heaven and hell, reward and punishment, that later transferred to Christianity.

ANCIENT JUDAISM

Without a doubt, the strongest influence on modern Western spiritual thinking is what has come down to us from Hebrew scripture. Yet it offers such a disturbingly vague and understated afterworld that some scholars have assumed there was no real conception of a hereafter in ancient Israel. There are a few references to Sheol, usually translated as Hades, and like Hades and Mesopotamia's Netherworld, it was not a place of reward or punishment but a final destination for all. The archaeological record, however, emphatically tells us of a strong belief in an afterlife. To understand the discrepancy between the written word and popular belief requires a little knowledge about the historical circumstances under which the books of the Old Testament were formed.

The writings as we know them today were shaped primarily during two definable waves of reform. The first occurred during the reign of King Josiah (640–609 BCE), toward the end of the First Temple period (960–587 BCE), when the military dominance of Assyria (northern Mesopotamia) over the Near East was weakening. In its wake, Josiah purged Judaism of Assyrian-influenced strains. In the interest of concentrating power and building a national identity, he instituted an official state cult centralized in Jerusalem, its temple, and its one god, Yahweh (Jehovah). All other cults, especially Canaanite cults and other local Jewish ones, as well as their gods, were proclaimed abominations.

In an unprecedented move, Josiah outlawed ancestral spirits, the *terafim*, whom the people had been accustomed to consult and for whom they built altars, as did all the peoples of the Middle East during this time. The ancestral spirits were sometimes referred to as *elohim*, meaning deities. As such they were "foreign gods," rivals of Yahweh's authority; hence, biblical editors eradicated them and their abode from scripture. Several laws went so far as to prevent priests from actively serving in funerals. Mourning and mourning rites were either curtailed or forbidden outright. Josiah further broke the connection by throwing out the mediums and necromancers (2 Kings 23:24). Eliminating ancestral spirits was tantamount to eliminating the dead and the realm in which they dwell.

The second wave occurred after the Jews, in particular Yahweh's clergy, returned to Israel from exile in Babylonia (southern Mesopotamia) after 539 BCE. This initiates the Second Temple period (539 BCE– 70 CE), and it was in this period that most of the Old Testament took on its present form. During the generations of exile, the Jews in Babylonia and those left behind in the homeland had reverted to the magical-religious practices common throughout the ancient Near East, remembered from before the time of Josiah. Creating a single cult devoted solely to the god of Israel required a renewed drive to stamp out external, "foreign" influences.

> When you come into the land that the Lord your God is giving you, you must not learn to imitate the abhorrent practices of

those nations. No one shall be found among you who makes a son or daughter pass through fire, or who practices divination, or is a soothsayer, or an augur, or a sorcerer, or one who casts spells, or who consults ghosts or spirits, or who seeks oracles from the dead. For whoever does these things is abhorrent to the Lord; it is because of such abhorrent practices that the Lord your God is driving them out before you. You must remain completely loyal to the Lord your God. (Deuteronomy 18:9–13)[2]

The central idea in this First Temple period passage is to rebuild the identity of a fractured and beaten people. A monotheistic state distinguished it from all the surrounding polytheistic ones, including Canaanite and Phoenician cultures, with which Israelites were deeply intertwined. Yahweh became the national figurehead. Monotheism at that time was not the same as it is today. An unbiased reading of scripture makes clear that for the ancient Jews monotheism did not mean there were no other gods; it meant rather that they should worship and obey only one particular god and no other. Special effort was made to separate Yahweh from the very powerful Canaanite god Baal. Baal's descent into hell and his resurrection linked him to the deceased and the afterlife. Yahweh, by contrast, was known as "the God of the Living." This deliberate differentiation removed Yahweh from Sheol.

The God of Israel was not present in the afterworld. Some texts refer to his abode as heaven. However, heaven in this period was not a place for the dead but a high place where gods dwelt, akin to Mount Olympus. In the absence of an underworld deity and with the eradication of the ancestral *elohim*, Sheol is emptied and nearly disappears as a viable concept. The God of the Living and his cult seem to have been hostile to the deceased and their realm.

The vehement prohibition against communication with the dead does not mean that ancient Jews disbelieved in their existence. The common burial, which ultimately ended with a person's dried bones added to the family bone pile, suggests a gathering to one's ancestors or fathers, as the biblical phraseology goes. It is probably not coincidence that this burial practice became widespread in the Second Temple period, when ancestor cults were forbidden. Before the reforms, Jews buried their dead as anybody else did in the ancient Near East: in the ground or under the household floor, with grave goods for use in the hereafter.

Nor did they disbelieve in communication with the dead. Mediums, seers, sorcerers, witches, diviners — anyone who crossed the divide between the living and the dead — were denounced as evildoers and punished by stoning (Leviticus 19:26, 31; 20:6, 27). The famous "Witch of Endor" episode is a fascinating account of an ancient séance. When King Saul fears God's disfavor he resorts to necromancy, which he himself has made punishable by death. The necromancer, afraid for her life, calls up "a divine being" from under the ground.

> When Saul inquired of the Lord, the Lord did not answer him, not by dreams, or by Urim, or by prophets. Then Saul said to his servants, "Seek out for me a woman who is a medium, so that I may go to her and inquire of her." His servants said to him, "There is a medium at Endor."
>
> So Saul disguised himself and put on other clothes and went there, he and two men with him. They came to the woman by night. And he said, "Consult a spirit for me, and bring up for me the one whom I name to you." The woman said to him, "Surely you know what Saul has done, how he has cut off the mediums and the wizards from the land. Why then are you laying a snare for my life to bring about my death?" But Saul swore to her by the Lord, "As the Lord lives, no punishment shall come upon you for this thing." Then the woman said, "Whom shall I bring up for you?" He answered, "Bring up Samuel for me." When the woman saw Samuel, she cried out with a loud voice; and the woman said to Saul, "Why have you deceived me? You are Saul?" The king said to her, "Have

no fear; what do you see?" The woman said to Saul, "I see a divine being coming up out of the ground." (1 Samuel 28:6–13)

After the Persian king Cyrus liberated the Jews from Babylonia, they lived under Persian rule until Alexander the Great's conquest in 333 BCE. During this time, a distinct afterlife belief began taking form — apocalypticism. There are many versions of apocalypticism, but all ultimately assume that the dead will resurrect at the End of Days. Many historians think it originated with Zoroastrianism, the state religion of Persia, despite problems with dating. More than any other contemporary religion, Zoroastrianism focused on dualisms of right and wrong, good and evil, light and dark, dualisms played out in apocalyptic visions as battles of an earth-shattering scale.

The book of Daniel is the first to unambiguously speak of physical resurrection. The trance visions are the product of the Maccabean period, a time of constant war and revolt. Daniel was primarily concerned with the Seleucid king Antiochus IV, ruler of Judea, who had sacked Jerusalem in 163 BCE. Antiochus enforced a policy of Hellenization on Jews. He placed an idolatrous statue in the Temple that conflated the God of Israel with Zeus, destroyed sacred texts, forbade circumcision, and forced Jews to eat pork. Noncompliance meant immediate martyrdom, as did dying in revolts. This is the beginning of martyrdom's glorification, which was to play a great role in Christianity and Islam. It was believed that Yahweh would resurrect all those who kept his covenant.

Another first in Daniel is the claim that only the righteous, those "written in the book," will be saved; the others will rise from the dust, condemned to everlasting shame and contempt. Zoroastrianism, by contrast, originally preached that time in the grave cleansed all people of their sins and primed them for resurrection.

Apocalyptic belief is set apart from other versions of postmortem experience, because it negates the reality of the body's death. Daniel refers to dying as "falling asleep," as did others in the apocalyptic tradition. A person eventually awakens in the same body, to the same reality.

Furthermore, for the postexilic Jews, together with the early Christians and Muslims, personal identity is bound to the body. Physical resurrection denies disembodied immortality and reduces the afterlife to an interim period of unconsciousness.

To those who lived under the crushing rule of foreign powers, the Seleucids and especially the later Romans, the end of the world must have felt imminent. Powerless to effectively fight back, they invested their hope of retribution in a supernatural mass destruction. Yahweh was expected to deliver them from intolerable subjugation and punish the oppressors. Apocalypticism was a corrective to earthly imbalances, a revenge mechanism more or less. Just as it avenged the people's unspeakable impotence, it also solved the wrenching tension of worshipping a deity who abandoned them at death.

Not everyone believed in resurrection. According to the first-century Jewish historian Josephus, the various sects hotly debated the whole issue of life after death, with the Sadducees rejecting an afterlife altogether. Resurrection was, however, central to extremist groups like the Essenes and Zealots.

The famous Dead Sea Scrolls contain scripture never accepted as canonical. From them we get glimpses of various spiritual systems and mystical beliefs circulating before Jerusalem fell to the Romans in 70 CE. One is the phenomenon of angelmorphism, reserved for those who reached the highest level of spiritual wisdom. More important are the fragments of the Book of Jubilees, composed during the late Second Temple period. That work gives us our best evidence of a perception of the universe completely missing in the texts of official Judaism, a perception that was later to make an enormous impact on the Western world. Written in a climate of real and constant warfare, the book presents a cosmos in perpetual battle. Yahweh and his angels are the forces of good, opposing a foe nearly equal in power, Mastema. It is here in a work of late date that the notion of a mighty satanic force makes its first known appearance in Judaism.

A central human figure in pseudepigraphical literature was Enoch, the father of Methuselah, in Genesis. The Book of Enoch, developed sometime after 300 BCE, picks up themes unfinished in Daniel. It contains a dozen distinct apocalypses and an enormous cast of good and evil angels. That Enoch did not physically die but was taken up to "walk with God" demonstrates the avoidance of mortality in ancient Hebrew thought. In the course of several visions, Enoch makes a journey to heaven, much like the two wise men from Mesopotamia, Enmeduranki and Adapa, who traveled to heaven and afterward founded divinatory priesthoods and ecstatic prophetic guilds. Enoch's heaven was a place where the divine dwelled, not the dead. He describes it as fire and wind and blazing angels. A flaming white marble palace features crystal floors and a throne room, whose splendor overcomes him. Traveling on to the far West, Enoch finds a great pit in which four categories of the dead await judgment. These holding pens make up the temporary afterworld of the dead and are emptied at the resurrection, after which angels hoist the select to heaven with ropes.

In rabbinic tradition, the Old Testament figure of Elijah is more important than Enoch. Like Enoch, he escapes death and is taken up, this time in a chariot of living fire driven by flaming horses (2 Kings 2:11). Unfortunately, he did not return to tell us what he saw, although his return was expected. Among certain Jews, including Jesus, Elijah's return was looked for as a signal for the beginning of the End Time. According to two gospels, Jesus proclaimed John the Baptist as Elijah reborn (Matthew 11:10 ff., 17:10 ff.; Mark 9:11 ff.). Whereas the early Jews regarded Elijah as a messiah in his own right, the later Christians took him as a precursor of Jesus. Both are hailed as having resurrected the dead, and both as having ascended alive (1 Kings 17:17 ff.).

EARLY CHRISTIANITY

The notion of an apocalypse and global resurrection might have been lost with the Diaspora after Jerusalem's destruction had it not transferred to Christianity and Islam. The teachings of Jesus and John the

Baptist, as they have come down to us, fit entirely within the apocalyptic discourse. The raising of Lazarus is nothing less than a demonstration of Jesus doing the work of the Father. It also prefigures his own death and resurrection. According to one Gospel, it even set his death in motion (John 11:38–53). Although the Gospel of St. John, in which the Lazarus miracle is related, was written more than seventy years after Jesus's time, the story stands out as a clear signal that the trumpet was soon to call.

In the Gospel of Mark, Jesus is quoted twice as predicting an end within his own generation: "Truly I tell you, some of you standing here will not taste death until you see the Kingdom of God having come in power" (9:1); and: "Truly I tell you, this generation will not pass away until all these things take place" (13:30). In the slightly later book of Matthew, it is more descriptive: "For the Son of Man is to come with his angels in the glory of his Father, and then he will repay everyone for what has been done. Truly I tell you, there are some standing here who will not taste death before they see the Son of Man coming in his kingdom" (16:27–28). The righteous are reincarnated in sexless angelic bodies: "When they rise from the dead, they neither marry nor are given in marriage but are like angels in heaven" (Mark 12:25).

The apostle Paul also expected the return of the Son of Man, a final judgment, and the end of the world as he knew it, during his own lifetime. Because his works are the earliest extant writings in the New Testament, they reflect the earliest Christian thought. Like his contemporaries, he preached to the poor, the oppressed, and the subjugated and attempted to palliate their suffering with the promise of a better life in the world to come. In 1 Corinthians (15), he relates to the newly converted that the risen Christ was witnessed by hundreds, some who are still alive. This truly astonishing statement worked to convince doubters of resurrection — if God the Father raised Jesus from the dead, then the followers of Jesus could also be resurrected.

As the New Testament describes it, at the End Time, God will destroy every ruler and authority in power. Obviously such a vision could only come from the oppressed. Not surprisingly, the last enemy to be destroyed is death itself, again reflecting the discomfort and denial inherent in ancient Hebrew thought. Instead of decaying, mortal bodies will be transformed into imperishable ones invested with angelic attributes.

Some of this is reiterated in 1 Thessalonians (4:14–17), in which Paul writes more directly about the dead. Grief is unnecessary:

> For since we believe that Jesus died and rose again, even so, through Jesus, God will bring with him those who have fallen asleep.[3] For this we declare to you by the word of the Lord, that we who are alive, who are left until the coming of the Lord, will by no means precede those who have fallen asleep. For the Lord himself, with a cry of command with the archangel's call and with the sound of God's trumpet, will descend from heaven, and the dead in Christ will rise first. Then we who are alive, who are left, will be caught up in the clouds together with them to meet the Lord in the air; and so we will be with the Lord forever.

In this passage, dead Christians are privileged over living ones, thus giving converts a motivation for accepting martyrdom. The missionizing in early periods provided some extraordinarily compelling incentives to convert, the most powerful being the promise of ultimately escaping death. The end of the world is at hand. If you convert, you are saved and will never die. If you do not convert, death and possibly eternal torment will be your lot.

But the end did not come. In the following generations, the Christian world sought reasons for the failure of scriptural fulfillment. One was to blame that failure on an evil force, a force that began to grow in the imagination as a mighty cloven-footed beast. For a solution, Christians began syncretizing the Greek immortal soul with a corporal hereafter. The most important adjustment was the relocation of the new Kingdom of God. It was removed from its original earthly setting of the New Jerusalem and cast into the heavens, a relocation suggested in the verse quoted above. More astonishing still, the God of the Living now shared his kingdom with the dead.

During the first few generations of Christianity, the threat of an immediate world end served to inspire Christians to faith and obedience. As time passed, the more the end was lost in sight and the further the reward for the good was pushed into the distant future, the more the conception of heaven and hell took hold. The longer sinners and oppressors thrived without penalization, the more vindictive the faithful became. Hell grew ever more horrifying and ever easier to get into. Over time, the softer intermediate zones of purgatory and limbo developed to reestablish the essential mercifulness of God.

The efforts to establish orthodoxy and centralize power in Rome led to a great deal of infighting and brutal silencing. Other versions of Christianity, the Gnostics, Ebionites, Marcionites, and so on, were suppressed along with their sacred books, many of which had pedigrees as legitimate as the canonical Gospels. Lay individuals who continued to practice divine revelation, healing gifts, or communication with the spirit in the apostolic practice of charisms were subject to persecution. The early Christian belief in reincarnation was also stamped out.[4] Obedience to the church and its clergy and participation in its sacraments, especially baptism, became compulsory for heavenly attainment. Christianity succeeded in colonizing the domain of the afterlife for itself.

❧❦❧

The tenet of the Last Judgment and global destruction still lingers in Roman Catholicism and in nearly every Protestant denomination. Among conservative groups, this tenet is alive and well. Most sects ignore the soul's descent back to earth. And few have made the attempt to reconcile the soul with the resurrected physical body, allowing old sanctions against cremation to be lifted. Similarly, the return of Christ is still expected, but not all groups believe it will be accompanied by an Armageddon. Some denominations believe that the prophecies of the

End Time have already taken place or, as Jehovah's Witnesses believe, are unfolding this very minute. In the various sects of Judaism and Islam, there is just as much apocalyptic diversity.

For most of us, the literal apocalypse as celestial warfare is no longer taken as a real possibility. Instead its enticingly obscure esoterica, the epic scale of Armageddon, the age-old appeal of a cosmic showdown between Good and Evil are a source of wonder and diversion, something we like to scare ourselves with, as the entertainment industry knows all too well. Nevertheless, at the approach of the year 2000, dormant expectations of the end reawakened in a fury wearing a secular face. Anxiety of world destruction was fueled by the entertainment media, flying rumor, and occasionally scientists. We anticipated the planet exploding in a nuclear blast or destroyed by a comet. More popular was the apprehension of a worldwide computer breakdown, caused by the date change, which would cripple modern civilization. In the end, all this stems from a fear of death embedded in the Judeo-Christian consciousness, projected onto a global landscape.

THE SOCIAL DIVERSITY OF AFTERLIFE CONSTRUCTIONS

No matter what an organized religion, sect, or spiritual philosophy teaches about the afterlife, descriptions of heaven and hell will generally follow the physical conditions of the time and place in which they were conceived. The Muslim notion of paradise, where fruit grows effortlessly on trees to feed Eden's inhabitants, mirrors the idyllic oases of the desert world of the Middle East. Just as the paradisaical garden is the operating image of a heaven world in Islam, the darker side of the desert is the model for hell. In the Sufi tradition, sinners boil inside and out and are tortured by bites from scorpions and snakes the size of camels. Hell in conventional Christian thinking is hot, a central feature borrowed from the searing heat of the eastern Mediterranean basin, the cradle of Christianity. The reverse was true in Anglo-Saxon England, where poets writing before the Norman invasion of 1066 saw hell as a cold and lonely place; condemnation meant being cast a-sea alone in a small boat, bare hands eternally paddling the frigid waters through the freezing gloom.

Cultural values are even more important building blocks, though they are not always so apparent. The notion that earth is a lowly plane, for instance, is fundamental to many world religions and philosophies, in contrast to traditional belief systems based on nature models, discussed below. Permanent release from the physical plane is the ultimate aim of Hinduism, Buddhism, and Platonism. These three systems also regard the ego, the by-product of physical existence, not as an aspect of the self that helps us grow but as something we must shed before we can reach the heady states of pristine awareness. As we will see in chapter 8, the modern West has inherited a great deal from such notions.

While constructions of life after death reflect what a society values, they also reinforce those values. Buddhist and Hindu notions of reincarnation uphold the hierarchies that pervade the political, economic, religious, and social fabric. The belief that a person's present status, high or low, is the just result of past lives legitimizes the pecking order. Reincarnation looks quite different in societies that take most of their cues from nature, where reincarnation is part of the cycle of birth, death, and rebirth. There is no ranking, no reward and punishment from lives before. Souls simply return to their families, assisted by shamans or midwives. Among the Yolngu, of Australia, the soul drifts up with the clouds at death and returns to the earth as rain. When women come in contact with water, drinking it, washing in it, the spirit in the water impregnates them. The cycle of leaving and returning, of death and rebirth, is carried forward by natural elements, thus reinforcing the trust in nature as reflecting the Mover of All Things.

For the early Teutonic peoples, like the Vikings, a single action could decide the incorporeal future. If a man were to die in battle, sword in hand, he expected to go to the most sought-after place in the afterlife, Valhalla, to join other brave hearts at the tables of kings for an endless round of high-spirited drinking. Early Teutonic expectations perpetuated a warrior society, exhorting acts of courage and aggression. Religions with strong missionizing precepts, like Christianity and Islam, promise instant paradise in exchange for martyrdom, thus encouraging crusades and jihads. A woman's place among the saints historically carried the prerequisite of virginity, maintaining chastity as the supreme spiritual ideal for females.

Modern American notions of the afterlife seem to be moving in the direction of a kinder, more permissive world to come. Yet more and more they reflect the cultural values of education and family. And in some recent works, the authors' visions of the afterlife suspiciously resemble group therapy. What seems to us to be common denominators of social good would have been regarded as insipid fare to our ancestors and severely limited to mystics who perceive the rapturous capabilities of life outside the body. To a Viking such an afterlife would be a hell of the most unspeakable dishonor. The celestial realms of biblical and early Christian descriptions with their palaces, thrones, and gates, their fixed ranks of angels, would spell insufferable imprisonment to the free-roaming, nature-loving peoples of precolonial America. When I read a matter-of-fact statement in one book about the afterlife, that there is a giant organ in heaven from which Liszt is played, my first thought was, how could that possibly interest a Watusi?

THE AFTERLIFE IN TRADITIONAL SOCIETIES

Like three of the oldest known philosophies of the afterlife, the Netherworld of Mesopotamia, the Sheol of the early Israelites, and the Greco-Roman Hades, the philosophies of traditional societies tended to be inclusive: everyone survives regardless of race, creed, or social rank. The home of the dead was constructed as a familiar place, and the passage there smooth. Knowledge of it was not controlled by a priest class but was thought to be present everywhere in the natural world. For many tribal societies, Nature — the winds and waters, the plants and

creatures, the skies and the earth — was the teacher and the manifestation of Divine Spirit. Exploitation, waste, and violence against Nature
were transgressions committed directly against Spirit, sadly a very different morality from our own. Harmony with nature, rather than dominance over it, was the chief spiritual goal. Not all traditional societies
held such ideal beliefs, but many did.

In most traditional belief systems (as opposed to institutionalized
ones), the dead and the living stayed connected. House burials and
ritual feeding of ancestors at the home altar illustrate the closeness of
one world to the next. For some tribes still today, the afterworld is not
someplace else, under the earth or in the sky, but coexists in a universe
parallel with the world of matter. Among the Yoruba of Nigeria, the
afterworld is much like earth but far more beautiful, filled with ever-
blooming flowers and perpetually green vegetation. It is a luminous
universe where friends and family enjoy uninterrupted peace and goodwill. People continue what they did while alive, farming, hunting, and
conducting business. Proximity is taken to an extreme in Nigerian vil-
lages of the Nembe. Because they believe that the dead want to stay
involved with village life, they are buried in their own houses or in new
houses nearby.[5]

For most traditional societies the journey is remarkably easy. The
Milky Way is regarded by many as the road to the afterworld, the millions upon millions of stars as brilliant souls moving along its path.
Nothing is hidden; there is no secret knowledge of the Way known to
only a very few. Instead this wondrous celestial roadway with its progression of souls is ever present, ever revealed to all peoples on earth,
night after night. Indigenous peoples of Australia and parts of the
Americas, such as the Guajiros, the Inuits, and several extinct Native
American Indian tribes whose beliefs are preserved in their mytholo-
gies, imagine the spirits of the dead simply flying up out of their bodies to join those resplendent souls moving across the heavens. What
a contrast to the Egyptian system, in which the starry firmament was

originally the sole province of the pharaoh, and reaching it involved the meticulous performance of rites and surviving appalling threats.

In traditional societies, it is the local shaman who usually assists the soul's transition, sometimes escorting the newly deceased on the first leg of the journey. Yet in Eskimo lore, a daughter eases her father's passage after death by singing a song with magic breath. This song conducts his spirit into the body of a wolf so that he can hunt the caribou for eternity. When the Fon people of West Africa turn ninety years old, they are acknowledged as intermediaries between the living and dead. They prepare other community members to die by telling them about the afterlife. Dead relatives and friends are expected to help the new soul from the other side.

Some in these societies choose a day to die, not because they have reached the bitter end, but because they have reached fulfillment. All things are in place, so it's a good day to leave this life. Instead of fear, there is trust that the Great Spirit will provide a good place for all things that die, as it does for all things that live. A person simply slips from this world into the next, with little or no struggle. As I write this, I can't help but remember one of my favorite messages from the dead in the Guggenheim archives, a father telling his daughter, "Honey, there's nothing to it. Dying is as easy as falling off a log."[6]

PERSONAL AFTERLIVES

Private beliefs can differ drastically from one person to the next, even if they belong to the same religious community, and beliefs change with age and experience. Where and when we live, what religion and which sect of that religion we were born into, all continue to shape our beliefs, even if we have rejected our religious education.

Most of us have witnessed radical change in our own beliefs as we grow older. Or without realizing it, we invest in alternative, sometimes conflicting renditions of the afterworld at the same time. I did this as a child. One part of my childhood picture was modeled on that masterpiece of dualism, Dante's *Divine Comedy*, because an illustrated copy of it was in our family library. The depictions of hell and its tortures were far more graphic and memorable than those of heaven, which even my young mind perceived as static. However, the damned did not speak to me. They were not people I would ever know. At that tender age I could no more imagine suffering down there with them than I could imagine having cancer or heart disease. It was purgatory that bothered me. Since no one in my family was a saint, I was sure that was where we were all headed. There was also little doubt that my recently dead grandmother was there, suffering and lonely, working off her minor sins, maybe for centuries. By the time I was ten I was paying indulgence money to get her out.

At the same time, my childhood intuition conjured up an entirely different afterlife, one filled with a golden, springtime energy. Trees dotted meadows blanketed with flowers, sparkling in sunlight. Chubby squirrels ran about, happily unafraid of people, so you could cuddle them like kittens. My guardian angel was there along with a fairy godmother right out of Cinderella and our long-dead dachshund Schatzie. Aside from the hodgepodge of equally idealized motifs that have moved in and out of this picture over time, the underlying spirit has stayed constant to this day. It never occurred to me as a child that having two incongruent sets of beliefs, one socially conditioned and the other based on intuition and a deeper trust, was a problem.

~≈❀≈~

Looking at the evolution of the afterworld from a five-thousand-year perspective makes clear that mainstream beliefs held in the modern West are surprisingly new. It also shows that they can conflict with what the founders of religions themselves preached. Contrary to our misplaced confidence in spiritual evolution, we have seen too that later versions of the afterlife were not necessarily more enlightened than earlier ones, but tended to be more judgmental and ever more exclusive. Instead of being a single, fixed truth, ideas of the afterworld are as flexible and ever-changing as the populations who invent them. On what basis, then, can any religious institution claim to know its real nature?

CHAPTER SEVEN

The Genesis of Sin

In chapter 6, we saw that there are loosely two models for what happens to us after we die. In one, all humanity goes to more or less the same place. In the other, individual judgment determines a person's postmortem circumstances. Despite enormous differences, the five principal world religions, Christianity, Judaism, Islam, Buddhism, and Hinduism, have taken the second option, in which judgment of some kind decides what happens after death. They also share another essential and equally damaging teaching, which is that humans are innately flawed. Each of us born to one of these religions necessarily internalizes judgment as part of the socializing process. Because judging others and self-judgment go hand in hand, internalized judgment impacts how we think about ourselves, others, and the world at large, as well as how we conduct ourselves each day. Whether we realize it or not, it plays a part in nearly every decision we make. It also shapes what we expect after we die. Internal judgment usually takes the form of tallying good thoughts and deeds against bad ones. It is so ingrained that most of us mentally adjust our personal debit and credit accounts unconsciously during the course of any given day.

The notion of sin also burdens us with guilt, one of the most counterproductive of all feelings. Shame that builds up around so-called sinful acts sets up an impenetrable wall between us and knowledge of our inner selves, a knowledge that leads to forgiveness and release. For example, many men and women who were sexually molested as children cannot get past the shame barrier to release the experience. I know one woman who was so caught up in her shame from repeated childhood rape that she became paralyzed in young adulthood. Life in bed with constant pain, especially during menstruation, was her way of punishing her sinful body. The extreme levels of shame, however, also kept the intolerable events of childhood at a distance. With just two sessions of light regression therapy, in which she relived a few of those devastating episodes in detail, she penetrated the shame barrier and rediscovered her innocence. She then got up and walked.

In the past century, the vocabulary of sin has been fitted to new philosophies. The essence of sin underlies the way psychology passes judgment in terms of mental health versus neuroses or the way spiritual communities judge in terms of positive versus negative or higher versus lower (see chapter 8). Walking on the side of right (good, healthy, positive) and avoiding the wrong (bad, unhealthy, negative) can result in a relentless mental balancing act that drains creative energy and silences our deeper interior voices.

Many organized religions have maintained tension between right and wrong by a system of watching. Religious vigilantism is well known from such dreadful epochs as the Inquisition and the New England witch trials. Any sect can call on its members to watch one another, thereby adding the very powerful weapon of social scorn to its arsenal of control.

The forms of watch engines are as numerous as they are ingenious. Some traditions invented a supernatural watch force in which good and bad deeds are seen, recorded, and measured. In Jewish folklore, angels stalk individuals throughout their lives, busily judging and recording their most minor deeds. Hindu tradition offers similar otherworldly watchdogs, which perch on a person's shoulders. Their accumulated records are given to an account keeper nightly. The notion that deeds and thoughts are somehow collected and then calculated is reminiscent of the Egyptian feather test, in which the worth of the soul is weighed on a scale. The greatest watchman of course has historically been God himself. How did this all start?

Since conventional thinking in the West considers sin as the main mediator between salvation and condemnation, it is worth taking a hard look at how and when the concept of sin developed. Sin is a newcomer on the world stage. Its earliest roots might be the Egyptian feather test, which first appeared in the late second millennium BCE. During the sweeping changes of the first millennium BCE, the tendency in the Near East to qualify survival in whatever form increased significantly. In general, survival was reserved for those who fulfilled certain conditions of a cult, such as the mortuary cults of Egypt or the apocalyptic cults of Israel. The criteria for survival changed too, developing more and more along the lines of compulsory compliance to given rules and moral codes. It was during this development that sin was born.

All these changes were accompanied by alterations in the way godhood was conceptualized. In earlier periods, the great gods were all somewhat well-intentioned, but none was entirely good, and they certainly were not omniscient. And none was completely evil. Selfish, perhaps, definitely grandiose, but not evil. What is more, all gods and goddesses were subject to criticism and occasionally active opposition from their peers. These checks and balances within a given pantheon prohibited any one deity from rising to absolute power. There were gods of judgment but not of morality. Shamash, the Mesopotamian sun god, was such a god on earth and in the Netherworld, yet he was moreover concerned with civic law, such as breaking a treaty oath. The temples of the great gods and their priests and priestesses generally left the curbing of moral behavior to local tribal traditions. Because the cult of Yahweh was itself a tribal development, the ancestral customs became codified as religious law when it became a state cult. Yahweh was at once the supreme tribal elder, lawmaker, and judge. As his cult grew, it continued to appropriate social conventions and regulations from sources outside itself, including myth and literature from other cultures, all of which it reshaped to assert its own system of morality, as all religions have done.

Important to establishing cultic law was the invention of sin defined as a violation against one deity and one deity alone. This unprecedented step was crucial for carving out a group identity that sought to distinguish itself from the overall polytheistic zeitgeist. According to scriptural accounts, the once nearly nonexistent notion of sin quickly came to the fore as the number one social directive, leading to the evaluation of quotidian actions in the light of what would please Yahweh and what he would condemn as an abomination. Obedience and disobedience to the rule formed the dividing line between right and wrong, good and evil, the saved and the damned. Born, too, was a unique kind of exclusivism: only adherents to this cult were divinely chosen.

The surprisingly late creation of sin stands as one of the most momentous shifts in worldview ever to have occurred. Nothing elucidates the shift better than comparing the story of Noah and the Flood with prebiblical Flood myths. Few realize that Noah's story is an adaptation of a Mesopotamian work that predates it by at least fifteen hundred years. The versions preserved in cuneiform tablets, based on even older oral tradition, refer to the ark builder variously as Atrahasis or Utnapishtim. The chief difference, and the most telling difference, was the reason given for sending this first-known weapon of mass destruction. In the Genesis story, Yahweh sends it as punishment for humanity's sins. In the Mesopotamian one, neither sin nor punishment plays a role. The people were destroyed because they overpopulated. Since there were too many of them, their collective noise disturbed the gods. Some of the gods, but not all, decided that the solution was eliminating them — or almost. The original Flood myth was not about morality; it is an archaic argument for ecological balance.

Since World War II, the way we conceptualize the God of the Bible has been changing with unparalleled speed. The wrathful, vengeful God of the Old Testament, a figure based on despotic rulers and severe patriarchal elders, has been transformed into a god of compassion and love. In antiquity, such a god would have been considered so distastefully feminine and lily-livered that no one would have followed him. As society becomes more permissive, the fearsome old man, whom our grandparents visualized with a white beard and sitting on a throne, is giving way to a more abstract Supreme Being. As this antique image of a god of judgment fades away, so does hell.

EVE AND THE SIN OF DISOBEDIENCE

Human sin is supposedly inevitable because of our right of free will. This assumption is unmistakably laid out in the greatest origin story ever told — the story of Adam and Eve. The Genesis account of the beginning, foundational to three major world religions, establishes the dichotomies of "light and dark" and "good and evil" as basic to the infrastructure of the universe.[1] The greatest transgression is emphatically disobedience. Disobedience drives the action, bringing about the Fall and the permanent loss of paradise. As a result of Adam and Eve's eating from the tree of knowledge of good and evil, all who issue from the seed of Adam are condemned to death. Mortality — dying, regarded as a *natural* act in most non-Abrahamic-based philosophies — is instead the *unnatural* outcome of sin. This is yet another demonstration of the Judeo-Christian discomfort with death. Eve and Adam's disobedience also brought down on us a host of lesser curses — shame, guilt, impurity, suffering, bodily pain, especially while giving birth, physical labor, desire, temptation, greed, crime, sex, and so forth. Why was this tree put there?

A little later in Genesis, the counterpoint to Eve appears, Abraham, the embodiment of perfect obedience. His story is a moral tale that reinforces unmitigated obedience as humanity's first obligation to God. At Yahweh's command, he is brought to the brink of slaying his only beloved son. The message seems to be that even murder is preferable to disobedience. Still worse, obedience triumphs over the instinctive forces of love and reverence for life. Yahweh rewards Abraham with offspring as numerous as the stars in heaven and the sands on the seashore (Genesis 22:17–19), appointing him father of his chosen people, the first patriarch. A covenant is initiated, inscribed only on males by circumcision. Placing Judaism's origins under Abraham is all about patriarchal rule.

Most scholars view the story of Adam and Eve as a later writing designed specifically to serve the state and its cult.[2] A chief aim was the elimination of the persistent and popular practice of goddess worship, including that of Yahweh's forsaken wife, Asherah. Goddess worship, traditionally an important channel for female devotion, is attested again and again from the archaeological record of ancient Palestine. The orthodox form of the story of Eve, the tree of life, and the wicked serpent was designed primarily to strike a severe blow against Asherah, whose symbol was the sacred tree, represented in the temple by a piece of wood or a pole,[3] and the cults of even more powerful goddesses in the East and eastern Mediterranean, some associated with snakes. Both the monarchy and the temple wanted to enforce an absolute obedience to male authority, from God to king to high priest. Female obedience was owed more immediately to fathers, husbands, and brothers than to God, which interrupted the connection between women and the Divine. In this way power was centralized and placed under masculine rule, and paradise itself was imagined primarily as a male province.

ORIGINAL SIN

In Christian theologies, humanity's inheritance from Eve is a two-ended punishment. Just as a person's life ends with the punishment of death, a person's life begins with another punishment, original sin. This doctrine, formulated four hundred years after Jesus,[4] claims that we come into this world with a stain on an otherwise spotless soul. The stain marks our direct descent from the disobedient Eve and her murdering son, Cain. It is the sign of our human legacy to do wrong.

The only way to rid oneself of original sin is by baptismal cleansing, a rite that also makes you a Christian. Without it, a person cannot enter the kingdom of heaven. Original sin and its ritual antidote demonstrate how institutional religions set up a dichotomy of a condemned "them" (here, unbaptized) versus a saved "us" (here, baptized), a dichotomy whose effectiveness hinges on the fear of death.

Because the doctrine of original sin tells us we are innately and inescapably flawed, it also serves to separate us from nature and the purer, simpler creatures of the earth. Worse, before the Fall, God was present with Adam and Eve in Eden. After their rebellion, humanity at large was sentenced to dwell apart from God. That is an immensely tragic verdict. Original sin serves as an additional wedge between us and the Divine. From the Fall on, the peoples of the three Abrahamic religions have had to earn the right to reunite with the Creator.

LORELLA AND JOE

The stories of Lorella and Joe illustrate how belief in sin can shape our expectations of the life to come and even affect our experiences after passing. Both of these people were brought up with the typical dualisms of their generation — heaven and hell, good and evil, right and wrong, reward and punishment, and so forth. In Lorella's case, she held the common conviction that the afterlife was bipolar and that getting into the upper hemisphere meant leading a life as righteous as possible. Joe was noncommittal, an "I dunno" kind of guy, who left it all up to religion. Both of them ended up being very surprised. We'll take Lorella first.

Lorella was a very intelligent person, curious, and capable of great warmth and humor. Her main fault, however, was her rigid obedience to church authorities, for which she expected reward. What it brought, rather, was the restriction of her innate abilities, significant damage to her children, and a very nasty shock after her death. She adopted all the virtues women were traditionally expected to have, including a self-sacrifice that leaned toward martyrdom. Although no prohibitionist, she was overly suspicious of drinking. Her moralistic control of family consumption resulted in her husband's sipping from bottles hidden in drawers and closets and a son who became a full-blown alcoholic. The tension Lorella set up between good and bad, obedience and rebellion, had the strongest effect on her daughter. The girl's strict upbringing was supposed to keep her pure in mind and body until her wedding day, a strategy that seriously backfired. She grew up instead to be a lying, cheating, drug-addicted nymphomaniac, often bedding more than one man a day.

Mother and daughter played opposite roles in the family drama, like Cain and Abel. I am certain the connection between them went beyond this life, for they seemed to have made an agreement to explore both sides of the obedience-and-rebellion/good-and-bad modality as it has long applied to the female sex. Both of them, in their extremism, missed the point. Lorella developed cancer of the uterus and suffered terrible physical pain in the months before she died. I read this as her attack on the "sinful" womb, that part of her that gave birth to such a daughter. Her daughter died a year later from a drug overdose.[5]

I was not present at Lorella's death. But within three days, while brushing my teeth, I was suddenly caught up in a whirlwind of rage. I felt under assault. Knowing instantly it was Lorella, I stood stock still and listened. This was one of those visitations that was so full of violent emotion, no organized sequence of thoughts was at first possible. In such circumstances, all you can do is memorize what the person is trying to convey and put it together later.

Once the storm had died down, the reasons for Lorella's rage began to emerge. She had just discovered that heaven and hell don't exist. Nor was there anyone "up there" to give her the Mother of the Year Award or, conversely, to chastise her for her failures. Instead, she faced an uncomfortable reckoning of what she had done with the gift of life. Because of her fear of sin, she had repressed her naturally exuberant love of life, closed down her intuitive nature as well as her sensuality, and limited the range of her intelligence and curiosity. Although the battle between good and bad, obedience and rebellion, was extreme between Lorella and her daughter, nearly all of us have seen it at work to some degree in families and within ourselves.

Joe's case is far more unusual. I didn't know him while he was alive. My involvement with him occurred some twenty years after his death and at the request of his son Michael, whom you met in the introduction. Michael, himself dead for three months, had found his father in an awful situation and wanted my help in getting him out. There was no direct contact between them, nor did Michael want any. His father was too immersed in his own hallucination anyway to notice him.

Joe was in a very bad state. He looked like an old man worn down by guilt and woes. I saw him in a dusty, yellowish wasteland, crouching as though doubled over in pain. There wasn't much else to see, except a vaguely reddish border of some kind that seemed to keep him in this solitary confinement. It was evident from his gestures, clasping his head and shaking it from side to side, and from his facial expressions that the man was in terrible anguish, which he appeared to experience as physical. It reminded me of the phantom pains some people feel in an amputated limb. This poor guy was trapped, isolated, in something akin to hell. Michael told me Joe was in a personal delusion of self-punishment. There is no way to tell how Joe perceived time in this state. From my standpoint, it had gone on for more than twenty years, yet he may have experienced it as hours or days or perhaps an eternity. Nor could I tell if he was seeing things or experiencing tortures or hearing voices. He definitely believed there was no way out. He was always a bad boy, a natural-born sinner. And God knew it.

Although I had no idea how to proceed, the solution spontaneously arose as soon as the problem was grasped. The solution was so unforeseen from my perspective that it could only have come from someone else. All at once a man from one of Joe's past lives appeared. He had been Joe's captain in some war during the nineteenth century. I had the impression it was the Crimean War (1853–56). What I did get rather clearly was that Joe had been a low-ranking foot soldier in that life. Because he idolized his captain, naively believing in the man's infallibility, he duteously marched on his superior's orders to his death. Joe's past-life hero, who had spiritually matured since his military days, took on his old appearance, complete with uniform and horse. Brandishing his scabbard and blowing a horn, he rode furiously into the psychic circle where Joe held himself captive. He gave Joe firm orders to follow him: "March!" Fortunately, the old soldier in Joe was reawakened, and without hesitation he marched, following the captain and his horse, straight out of hell. The illusion was finally broken.

I understood later that the captain felt he owed Joe something. Just as he marched Joe to his death in a past life, he marched Joe to a new life in the afterworld. The ruse he put on stimulated the side of Joe's character that lay dormant in this life, the side that obeyed authority.

Although I never actually made direct contact with Joe, nor did I hear about him after his release, it is hoped that once his delusion broke up he would see that the choices he made in both lives represented two sides of the same coin. The masterstroke came, of course, from the captain, who set up an opportunity for Joe to return to his "good" self — the obedient self. What else could have sprung Joe out of hell? A heart-to-heart talk about his hallucinations? Never.

I often wonder at the childlike simplicity of what goes on in non-material dimensions, including dreams. As in Joe's story, what happens and what is said can sometimes seem just plain corny, so corny it makes me hesitant to describe it. Nonetheless, corniness seems to do the job.

THE DUALISMS OF GOOD AND EVIL

The stories of Lorella and Joe show how strongly dualistic beliefs of good and bad, reward and punishment, can operate in both this life and the next. The whole concept of sin is based on such dualisms. They are man-made, and they dominate modern thought. They are also weighted, with one side of the binary considered better than the other, usually set in a "positive-versus-negative" formula, as in those above and in saved and damned, or in more neutral dualisms, like strong and weak, rich and poor, big and small, high and low. The examples are endless. The next time you have a conversation with someone, just try springing "death and life" on them instead of "life and death" and watch the reactions.

Dualisms are powerful. They extract parts from the whole, effectively obliterating the whole, and force distinctions that may or may not be there. They set up biases, create unnecessary opposites and false categories. Finally, they convey preset, superficial judgments that we assimilate thoughtlessly. "Light and dark," for instance, expresses an instilled cultural value that exalts light but fears darkness (i.e., Satan = the Prince of Darkness). This dualism therefore denies the generative powers of darkness — the great creativity of night, of dreams, of fetal gestation. It also denies all those shades in between that make light and dark not opposites but arbitrary points within a whole. Lastly, dualistic thinking fosters prejudices and bigotry, a them-versus-us mentality, in which the "them" side of the binary is different from, and inferior to, the "us" side. This alone promotes racism, as well as nationalistic, political, and sexual chauvinism. With dualistic thinking, there can be no unity, no global family.

In dualistic thinking, if there is good, there must also be evil. I have no reason to believe in evil, and from all the exorcisms I have conducted as a professional, I have yet to see anyone possessed by evil. I have seen only people who are possessed by a deep-down *belief* that they are evil. I guarantee you, a belief like that, if it is repressed enough, can explode into a host of unsuspected paranormal abilities that our meeker "good sides" would never allow.

The inner universe does not acknowledge sin or follow a dualistic logic. The inner universe operates more along the lines of intuitive thinking, only on an impossibly grand scale. In intuitive thinking — thinking with the heart — dualisms ring false, if they surface at all.

Intuitive thinking includes; it sees the whole, rather than excluding, which limits perception to only the parts. Because it issues from those deeper portions of the self, it knows without doubt that the universe, no matter what dimension, is benign, that all things are fundamentally created from the god-stuff of benignity. Evil as a real category in the good-versus-evil dichotomy is unimaginable. It is a false category, an artificial category. What analytic thinking labels as evil and sets opposite to good, intuitive thinking regards as no more than a distortion of good intention, a misdirected attempt to compensate for a weakness, an attempt to grow. Evil then dissolves in that great sea of good. When we can learn to trust our intuitive "brain," dualisms will seem silly and prejudicial and ridiculously, absurdly, preposterously too petty for the Divine Mind.

Even if we have rejected the orthodox views of the religions we were born to, most of us have still accepted the underlying precept that the matrix of reality is dualistically structured. In fact, we buy into that assumption every day. Telling your child or dog she's a "good girl" or a "bad girl," almost in the same breath, would be typical of the thoughtless, daily dualistic categorizing that does so much damage. It's enough to make your house pet schizophrenic! Take the reward-punishment paradigm. Common expressions such as "may he rot in hell" or "he'll pay in the end" are perhaps comforting but unrealistic. No one makes us pay after we die. This is not to say that people in the afterlife don't feel remorse. When we pass, we may regret many things: a lack of courage, not having loved enough, not having demonstrated the love that we did feel, not having used our creative gifts. We may feel remorse for hurting others, for attempting to crush the spirit, or for poisoning hope. The core of the Divine Heart is so filled to the brim with unfathomably limitless compassion, there is no room for punishment. The whole of the law is realization, not punishment. The only cure is true self-forgiveness. The only failsafe is the recognition that, despite everything, all of us at all times and forever and ever are part of All That Is.

IS IT FAITH OR FEAR?

We might ask, Was Abraham's willingness to slay his beloved son an act of faith or fear? Remembering how often Yahweh had favored him, protected him, and gifted him, sometimes even conversing with him face-to-face, we could easily conclude that Abraham acted with a great deal of assurance. Yet according to the account in Genesis 22, Yahweh sent the first patriarch this test in order to find out not whether Abraham loved him, not whether Abraham trusted his intentions or had faith in his goodness, but whether Abraham feared him. The ancients used the word *fear* to signify the way mortals were expected to respond to the terrible resplendence of gods and kings. Responding with the intimate feelings of love, trust, or faith was unthinkable.

The antiquated mandate of total obedience quashes creativity, spontaneity, curiosity, desire, and inspiration, the very same qualities that propel personal spiritual awareness. Pure obedience will never lead us to a real comprehension of the Divine. It will not even allow us to ask questions. Without at least some insight, our true natures and that of the afterlife we cocreate will remain impossible to grasp.

Historically, the notion of faith was all but interchangeable with the notion of obedience. Although this equation has significantly broken down in the past century, it is also returning with the current revival of fundamentalism taking place in the three Abrahamic religions. This revival of the old law-and-order faith does not flood up from a profound trust that our connection with All That Is can never be severed. It is instead a faith born from an inculcated fear of just such a severance. It divides humanity, setting one religious group or sect over another, the believers over the infidels.

Acceptance of a ready-made faith fills an emptiness that is otherwise difficult to fill. But acceptance also compels us to ignore the disturbing inconsistencies, contradictions, biases, and double standards we perceive in our own sects. It forces us to profess that our personal holy books, whether the Torah or the New Testament or the Koran, are the actual records, and the *only* legitimate records, of divine thought. All too often, faith in scripture is achieved with a hefty measure of fanciful reinterpretations that just bulldoze over glaring contradictions and crucial differences between our world and the antique worlds in which it was written. Of course scripture contains divinely inspired passages. We can feel them. And they can be so profound that they send shivers of revelation down our backs. Such passages are great gifts passed down to us and should be cherished. Yet they do not validate all the others.

Coerced faith is nothing more than a device for silencing our own inner voices. It distorts our private revelations and epiphanies, if not devaluing them altogether. It is especially devised, however, to protect at all costs the deep doubts and inconsistencies upon which that particular faith is built. In the most radical cases, such false faith can lead to a pathological denial of the self, fanaticism, war, and terrorism, as it has in the past.

Each person is born with a spiritual and biological faith that is personal, intimate, and optimistic. Real faith springs from innate awareness of our connectedness with all living beings, with nature and All That Is. It requires only that we retrieve that child part in each of us that *knows* the universe is good. Not good and evil, not even good and bad. Just good. It is knowing that every consciousness is uniquely meaningful and charged with purpose. That survival beyond the body is the only possible outcome. That the afterworld is not about judgment and condemnation. That All That Is is so all-encompassing, so unfathomably compassionate that even forgiveness is dwarfed into insignificance. This faith is what people who have returned from near-death states bring back with them. For the dead it is the ever-present state of grace in which they dwell.

CHAPTER EIGHT

"Spiritual Evolution," Nontime, and the Ego

S ince the New Age counterculture movement began in the 1960s, stock concepts like spiritual evolution, low and high planes (often called astral planes), low and high vibrations, new souls and old souls, as well as karma and karmic debt have infiltrated the popular imagination. We have also grown accustomed to the notion that the ego has no place in the realm of spirituality and will not survive death. These ideas are normally taken for granted in alternative spiritual communities, but how do they actually stand up under scrutiny? How, for instance, can spiritual evolution or karmic debt operate in the realities of nontime and simultaneous time, which rule the inner dimensions of consciousness and the afterlife?

New Agers include spiritual counselors, all-faith ministers, psychics, healers, writers, therapists, and workshop leaders. In the past decades many New Thought churches have arisen whose precepts are anchored more in New Age metaphysics than in the Abrahamic traditions. Liberal churchgoing Christians represent a large community who define themselves as spiritual rather than religious. The chief difference between the two is the rejection of an exclusionary, fixed set of religious principles in favor of a more tolerant, decentralized, and inclusive philosophy. The most significant influences on modern spiritual metaphysics, besides its Judeo-Christian heritage, come from Hinduism and Buddhism. Despite its broad-minded nature, New Age metaphysics has generally assimilated the stubborn notions of a morally dualistic universe and the inherently flawed self, notions we will examine in this chapter. But first I would like to introduce the Western esoteric movements for those unfamiliar with them.

The philosophy of Transcendentalism, launched by Ralph Waldo Emerson and Henry David Thoreau, flourished in the mid-nineteenth century. Influenced by the Quakers and North American Indian traditions, Transcendentalism called for an intuitive religion based on direct revelation, inspired by a godhood that was perceived as permeating the universe. Transcendentalists believed that directly received divine inspiration was possible, because at the core of every human being there is an indestructible, eternal self called the inner light or oversoul, which is itself divine. It is this light that guides us after death to return to the Source. Although unfortunately short-lived, Transcendentalism played a great role in elevating nature to a spiritual status. Through the voices of its prominent members, it also granted validity to personal interior experience and thus inadvertently opened the door to an upsurge of mediumship in the United States.

Theosophy, perhaps more than any other philosophy of its kind, impressed the Asian beliefs of reincarnation and karma onto Western spiritual thought. The controversial founder of what eventually became a worldwide movement was the Russian mystic Helen Blavatsky, founder of the Theosophical Society in New York in 1875. Blavatsky synthesized elements from Hinduism and Buddhism with her own personal understanding into a complex set of ideas. For Theosophists, the eternal spirit forever strives upward, climbing a ladder through a series of rebirths toward spiritual mastery and perfection. All individuals must undergo a long series of reincarnations before they can free themselves from matter and rise high enough to return to the Source from which they came. Although there are no outside judges, after each life a person must experience the painful effects that his or her personal thoughts, words, and actions had on others. When we return to life on earth, we return to the demanding ordeal of creating or settling karmic debts. Fortunately, "highly evolved" souls, the ascendant masters, help us through the grind of life after life.

Spiritualism emerged around the same time as Theosophy. It holds that the disembodied, particularly the dead, can reach us through the agency of mediums. Ignoring the injunction against necromancy in the Old Testament, Spiritualists draw their authority from the numerous accounts of speaking in tongues, of visions and revelations, of apparitions and voices, in the New Testament. Like Theosophy, Spiritualism teaches that the indestructible soul advances in wisdom and moral vigor until it, too, reaches the Source.

In contradiction to Theosophy, strict Spiritualists reject reincarnation. Instead of leapfrogging from body to body toward enlightenment, the spirit moves successively from a starting-point plane of low vibration (the earth) to higher and higher vibrational planes in nonphysical realms. According to some Spiritualists, there are also planes lower than the earth planes, where particularly delinquent spirits may go. Spiritualists do not believe in resurrection, a last judgment, heaven, or hell, despite their Christian base. By the end of the nineteenth century, a number of organizations had formed around the phenomenon of spirit communication. Henry Slade founded the National Spiritualist Association of Churches in 1893, which by 1930 had officially condemned a belief in reincarnation.

The Society for Psychical Research, one of the most important centers for investigation into the paranormal and survival after death, was founded in London in 1882. Among its august presidents were Arthur J. Balfour, prime minister of England in 1902, nineteen professors, ten fellows of the Royal Society, five fellows of the British Academy, four holders of the Order of Merit, and one Nobel Prize winner. On the American side, William James (1842–1910), professor of psychology at Harvard University, contributed significantly to the study of spirit communication and survival after death, even establishing a research institute at Harvard. Impressed by the London society, he helped found the American Society for Psychical Research. Obviously, investigation of the survival issue was once a highly respected endeavor.

MEDIUMSHIP

The credibility of mediumship and spirit communication declined seriously in the early twentieth century with the exposure of a few frauds. Since then, association with the paranormal has stigmatized those in the mainstream institutions of politics, the academy, and often religion. Yet no amount of law, religious injunction, scientific denial, or popular derision seems to be able to stop mediumship. In fact, the past two decades have seen a surge of séances, somewhat of a throwback to the nineteenth-century table rappers. However, the emphasis no longer lies on proving postmortem survival but rather lies on transmitting messages from the dead. Many of the messages I have heard from televised séances or read about are oddly concrete, if not trivial. The dead person might comment, for instance, on a dress the sitter wore the day before. No philosophy here. No captivating accounts of life after death. The simplistic nature of the messages and their materialistic orientation partly reflect the general conservatism of the late twentieth and early twenty-first centuries. Such messages also serve as obvious "hits" that boost a medium's believability — a crucial factor for commercial success. They also demonstrate the need of the dead to work as quickly as possible while that window of opportunity is open to validate their identities and to convey reassurance and love.

Admittedly, some mediums can pick up information telepathically from the living instead of the dead, and some are frauds. But most are solid and honest, know their sources, and can distinguish among different types or levels of information. Some exhibit spectacular abilities and relay messages with an undeniable authenticity and poignancy.

Because mediums work with humans, alive or dead, messages are bound to be socially influenced. For instance, séances conducted during the late nineteenth and early twentieth centuries in England and America were influenced by a straitlaced Victorian mentality with its taste for the gothic and therefore tended to produce dramatic, moralistic messages. Ancient accounts of mediumship often concerned the fates of kings. Up to the eighteenth century, the dead communicated in words. Since the twentieth, the tendency has been to send messages in images, no doubt because of our society's increasing emphasis on visuality since the advent of photography, television, and film.[1]

Mediums of a certain type do not deal with the usual human deceased. Although they also draw on discarnates for information, these discarnates are spiritual teachers or "entities" no longer focused in physical existence. The landscape of their consciousness is much vaster than that of the recently dead. Their teachings are channeled through deep-trance mediums. The bottom-line message is: each of us creates our own reality, with which I would fully agree. How we do that, as utterly fascinating as it is, is a topic of such immensity it could fill (and has filled) volumes. Information on the hereafter is usually incidental, slotted in only where it serves the greater aim of broadening understanding of the self and the fabric of reality. The quality of the teachings through deep-trance mediums is uneven. In a class of her own is Jane Roberts, who channeled Seth for two decades until her death in 1984. Unfortunately, many other deep-trance mediums, whether channeling an adept from the lost continent of Atlantis or a Taoist sage from China's misty past, teach that the soul evolves from a "lower" to a "higher" state through a series of reincarnations. Most also believe in a universal law, the law of cause and effect, which lies at the foundation of karmic debt.

The common view of karmic debt, as most readers probably know, is that one's bad thoughts and deeds from a past life must be compensated for in a future life. The good thoughts and deeds are a kind of down payment on the life to come. Ancient Vedic literature from the

dawn of Hinduism conveys a more mystical and complex understanding of reincarnation and karma. For the less mystically inclined, karmic
debt, like sin, is understood as a tally system, akin to banking, where a
person builds up credits and debits that drag from one life to another.
Again, this system is not all that different in principle from conventional
Christian ones of virtues and sins.

SPIRITUAL EVOLUTION
AND THE HIGHER-VERSUS-LOWER PARADIGM

The nineteenth-century notions of spiritual evolution and the law of
cause and effect, so crucial to the New Age after-death vision, permeate
Western spiritual tradition. Implied or articulated, they form the base of
moral aspirations — striving for the "highest" spiritual attainments and
mastery over the "lower" self. Fresh intuitive insight and personal inner
experience tend to vanish when forced into these canned paradigms,
which instead of furthering a real understanding of life after death, reincarnation included, more often sidetrack it.

The higher-lower paradigm is also not far from conventional Christian thinking. Sinners whose transgressions once cast them into hell are,
in the framework of reincarnation, reborn to a painful life of low vibration. For Spiritualists, sinners are transformed rather into "earthbound
spirits," inhabiting the cruel, shady world of "low" or "dense" planes
(see chapter 14). The mediocre souls of yesterday's purgatory or heav-
en's lower spheres, meaning the great majority of us, are those, according to reincarnationists, who are still too underdeveloped to be released
from the rebirth cycle. They are instead stuck in a purgatory on earth,
where they work off the mistakes of the past. Some Spiritualists, on the
other hand, claim that these souls are sent to school in the afterlife for
a perpetual round of lessons. Other Spiritualists actually believe that
learning occurs only on earth, so if you blow it in this life, there is no
second chance and no redemption.

Moving on to the upper realms of higher vibrations, the pure soul who goes directly to heaven in the more orthodox view is now in the vocabulary of reincarnation an "old soul" who has accumulated enough wisdom to leave the earth planes altogether. In the Spiritualist's view, this purified soul is considered "advanced." When it is released from the body after death, it soars to join the ranks of superior beings. The celestial realms of many spiritual philosophies seem to have more hierarchies than the realms of "lower vibrations," for here we find "highly evolved" discarnates of all levels, from guides and teachers to ascendant masters. In Theosophy and Spiritualism, these hierarchies largely replaced the former pecking order of angels. The Aquarian Foundation, founded by a Spiritualist minister in 1955, has emphasized contacting these masters, a practice still attempted today. According to the Aquarian movement, the masters belong to the Great White Brotherhood of Cosmic Light.

Hold on now! Men's clubs in the afterworld? I thought the spiritual movement wanted to discover something real about life after death. Instead of case-by-case studies from which we can compile *tentative* interpretations, we have time-worn categorizations that steamroll over personal experiences as well as differences of race, sex, time, and place. Instead of exploring the ever-restless, ever-unfolding individual soul on its journey, the rank-and-file conceptual structure seeks to pin it like a dead butterfly onto a classification board.

Are There High Souls and Low Souls, Old Souls and New Souls?

The common conception of a new soul refers to a personality who has emerged into flesh for the first time with no past lives and little to no spiritual experience. But the records from the thousands upon thousands of people on the couches of hypnotists and regression therapists tell another story. No one so far has ever been found *without* past lives.[2] So from the data we have so far, the idea of a new soul is unattested. Furthermore, categories of old and new are based on linear time. Since the soul outside the body does not exist in a time-bound universe, as I'll soon explain, such categories are meaningless.

From what I have seen so far clairvoyantly, all souls possess a spectacular grandeur, a kind of cosmic immensity. Looking into the human core — the eternal self — is like looking deep into a vast and clear starry night. It simply never ends. The part of human consciousness that is bustling away just outside its narrow focus on physical reality is so enormous it *contains* the full spectrum of human experience. We could look at it as containing the sum total memory of humankind, past, present, and future, good and bad, exalted and tragic. This memory is the spiritual equivalent of our genetic heritage. The innate urge for self-fulfillment and growth continually pushes us to assimilate more and more of that sum total. It then comes into conscious awareness and is actualized. In the long run, we cannot really avoid this process any more than a baby can deny the biological urge to actualize its potential to walk. Of course there are teachers, guides, advisers of all sorts in dimensions adjacent to our own. But they too usually share the same jumbled heritage.

The eternal, individual personality dwells within an even greater self, the oversoul, the entity that gives birth to the personality. The oversoul also works as command headquarters, generating and orchestrating the past, present, and future lives of all it spawns. In comparison to the individual personality or self, it is "way out there," encompassing immeasurable regions of knowledge and potentials from which the individual self constantly draws. Enhanced by the profound and constant connectedness to the oversoul, our individual eternal selves are our own greatest personal teachers, ever present and alive within. That part of us that knows eternity also serves as a guide to others, helping people pass over, make crucial decisions, and deal with crises, whether we are aware of it or not. The human soul cannot be bound, not even by itself, but surpasses all limits while containing all limits. You are now and always will be transcendent.

The Foundations
of the Spiritual Evolution Model

The grafting of "high" and "low" onto spirit relies heavily on the authority of Darwin's theory of evolution. Before launching into discussion, I want to state here clearly that although I see significant faults in the theory, I am by no means subscribing to creationism. The theory of evolution is one of a group of contemporary "conflict theories" that rose out of the massively troubled climate of the late nineteenth century. All of them, including Freudianism and Marxism, propose an innate nature for humans and animals that is hierarchical and violent. Their central claims are fundamentally the same, that one part or sector of the whole will always struggle for dominance over the others. For Darwin, the conflict was between the so-called superior and the inferior, the powerful and the weak. Blinded to signs of cooperation within the animal kingdom, he saw ruthless competition. All creatures struggle upward along the perilous ladder of evolution to a higher life-form. The weak, the unfit, the ill adapted fall off, vanishing into oblivion, tripped up by genetic failures. In this model there is no room for consciousness and choice or for altruism and grace. If it were true, the creatures of this earth, humans included, would have annihilated one another long ago. In essence, the Darwinian premise of "survival of the fittest" takes the human fear of death and projects it onto the natural world. Fortunately, important recent research has now put the basic precepts of Darwinian genetics in doubt.[3]

The same environment of hierarchical struggle spawned Theosophy and Spiritualism, which bent the amazingly widespread theories of social Darwinism to their own use. In both spiritual philosophies, the human soul begins its climb via a series of unending lessons and, rung by rung, is purified by suffering. Its supreme aim is complete mastery over the lower (i.e., animal) self, so that it can merge with the Divine Source. This is too close to Darwinism for comfort.

THE CAUSE-AND-EFFECT VIEW OF THE UNIVERSE

The theory of spiritual evolution could not have been conceived without a regrettable bottomless trust in what is often called the universal law of cause and effect. Spiritual evolution is imagined as a chain reaction of cause producing effect, effect producing cause, and so on, ad infinitum. Although causes are moreover self-generated as choices made by virtue of free will, effects — for good or ill — seem to lie outside our control. They descend on us with a mechanical force, the inevitable consequences of a natural law, like the fall of an apple from a tree. Some esoteric thinkers have sought to mitigate this impersonal harshness by introducing spiritual agents, sometimes known as the lords of karma, who step in and manipulate the law toward kinder ends.

Even though higher evolvement is regarded as never smooth but constantly sidetracked by wrong turns and dead ends, it is thought to follow a definite trajectory. The trajectory is imagined as laid out on a time line. Past, present, and future are arranged in an unbroken sequence. Since effect is perceived as the result of cause, it always occurs later than cause. Even in the domain of eternity such a time line is assumed.

Karma

For nearly all believers in reincarnation, sequential time and the law of cause and effect are especially germane. According to the principle of karma, our present lives are largely the accumulative effects of causes — the good and bad thoughts and deeds — set in motion in the previous life. So, say, if you were a feudal lord in a medieval life who exploited your serfs by forcing them into slavelike labor, refusing aid in times of famine, sexually abusing them, and the like, the laws of karma dictate that in some future life you too will undergo terrible suffering, probably exploited and abused by others. Although this example is unforgivably simple, I offer it here merely to illustrate the moral balancing karma is supposed to achieve. As with the revenge mechanism of hell in traditional Western religions, the bad guy will pay in the end. The karma system, also like Western religions, employs the notion of rewards as well. A life spent in good thoughts and deeds will be followed by one of happiness. The differences between the two systems are who judges (God or the self) and where judgments are lived out (in the afterlife or in a reincarnation).

Is there a law of karma, as many esoteric systems claim? The people who have worked most directly with reincarnational memory, Ian Stevenson and Helen Wambach, introduced in chapter 5, were themselves surprised to discover that the answer is no. Stevenson found only weak indications of karma in fewer than 4 percent of the children he studied.[4] Wambach, working with adults, found that 30 percent of more than a thousand participants seemed to have some sense of karmic obligations, whereas another 30 percent felt they were free to design their present lives any way they wished. The remaining 40 percent were unclear or somewhere in between.[5] Of the 30 percent who felt a karmic pull, *none* came back to work off past misdeeds or reap their just rewards. Instead, they came back to work on relationships with people they had known before. If karma is not evident in 100 percent of the cases, it simply cannot be regarded as a natural or universal law. Even in those instances in which people came back to work on something we might regard as karmic, they did so by choice. Choice and law are two very different things.

SEQUENTIAL TIME, SIMULTANEOUS TIME, AND NONTIME

The Western concepts of a cause-and-effect universe and the upward progression of spiritual evolution are based on two assumptions. One is the concept of a Supreme Being or Divine Source that is outside us rather than indwelling. The Being or Source is envisioned as awaiting us up there, at the last moment of eternity, at the end point of the evolutionary trajectory, until we are advanced enough to merge with it. In some thinking, it is a place or state rather than a being, an ultimate cosmic summit, which looms above us, beckoning us, challenging us, but is not part of us.

The more influential assumption is the notion of sequential time, which carves definable pathways through eternity. Without sequential time the law of cause and effect and spiritual evolution are nonsensical. Time is far more complex than before, during, and after, or past, present, and future. Just below the surface, different kinds of time are simultaneous and interactive. At the deepest levels of consciousness there is no such thing as time at all. To make matters more complicated, many different versions of the past, present, and future coexist with, or parallel, those we choose to bring into our awareness, whether we are alive or dead. Yet they are equally real, equally concrete and valid, somewhat like science's multiverses. Although each of us experiences the deeper reality of nontime and simultaneous time in dreams, the way time and nontime work is a particularly difficult topic to explain and nearly impossible to grasp without leaning hard on intuition. Nevertheless, some discussion is needed for at least a rudimentary comprehension of how the folks in the afterworld function.

Throughout this section I will also introduce several time anomalies that crop up in our own everyday lives. Recognizing how time experiences of the afterlife are likewise present in the here and now — if we pay attention — helps bridge the gap between these two states of reality. Time as we *think* we know it is little more than a side effect of physical life. It reflects the way human nervous systems sequentially order incoming data. Obviously, the nervous system of one creature will construct a sense of time different from another's. An insect with a life span of a day or two cannot possibly experience time in the same way a house cat or a human does. The human experience of time is largely the result of cultural conditioning. An infant does not perceive time in the same way adults do. Nor does one culture or one era perceive and use time in the same way as another. Which sense of time is real?

If we are honest about it, each of us experiences different kinds of time on any given day. Expressions like "Time flies when you're having fun" and "Time stood still" have more profound meaning than we are willing to admit. Our current obsession with clock time, an extremely new invention, tricks us into believing that clock time is based on some absolute law. Because clock time is supposed to be more real than personal perceptions of time, we have lost our trust in those perceptions. Clock time is still based on human perception, primarily on how the human nervous system *orders* solar data. It is meaningless to a gadfly.

The time anomalies in the afterlife and in out-of-body states arise because the nervous system no longer orders action and events. In one study of near-death experiences, 71 percent of the respondents said that they experienced timelessness.[6] In other research, subjects were asked to estimate the length of time they spent out of body. Rather than the one to five minutes typically recorded by clocks, 8 percent reported hours or days, and in one case, believe it or not, the perception of how much time had passed during a near-death episode amounted to months.[7]

It is natural for children to have encounters with infinity and nontime, as I did as a child, when a few seconds expand into an eternal present so spacious that all time utterly vanishes within it. The momentous events of birth and death frequently inspire similar experiences. Whether you are a near-death experiencer, a child, a new mother or father, or recently bereaved, the experience is nearly impossible to describe.

The life review, a regular occurrence of NDEs, offers many novel perceptions of time. Experiencers often see events from birth to death or from death to birth as a series of sequences. But those sequences usually take place all at once, in one single instantaneous revelation. This is not just time speeding up; this is simultaneous time in which the *impression* of sequential time is still preserved, a striking example of how sequential time is actually *contained* in nontime.

Some survivors have reported past lives in their flashbacks. Even more remarkable, others also saw future lives in what you might call a flashforward. For example, in a 1941 NDE, a ten-year-old boy learned that he would marry at the age of twenty-eight. He also *fully experienced* a specific moment in the future in which his wife stood by while his two children played on the floor. That future memory was eventually reenacted in physical terms in 1968.[8] Usually, a survivor feels the psychological environment of each instance, past or future, in its entirety, including the emotional responses of the people involved.[9] It takes my breath away to ponder what unimaginable feats of genius human consciousness is really capable of.

Another common anomaly in the afterlife is the time lapse. Instances of time lapse are most noticeable during communication with people who have died but have not yet accepted or realized the fact. They seem to make time literally stand still. One enthralling example occurred during a séance in the late 1970s.[10] A man who had died during a battle in World War II came forward through a medium and announced himself to his old combat buddy, an attendee of the séance. Despite his panic and confusion, the deceased soldier was able to give his name and rank, Lt. Gazelle, and easily recognized his old friend. They had fought side by side in the battle that cost the lieutenant his life. Astonishingly, this long-dead soldier still experienced himself alive and fighting on the battlefield. He was so convinced of this that he demanded to know why his friend was not out there fighting with him. Where had this guy, this dead soldier, been for the past thirty-five years? Obviously he was hallucinating. But what kind of time was he hallucinating? It is doubtful that he perceived himself fighting in the same battle for thirty-five hard years, the length of time reckoned by the living. What to us were decades must have been days or even hours to him.

Remembering that consciousness transcends time zones allows us to know more accurately how the afterlife is actually lived. For the dead, time is psychological, an elastic expression of consciousness, and can be manipulated to meet specific ends. It can be mixed, jumped, reversed, looped, condensed, and expanded, or it can cease altogether. Time as we think of it is largely meaningless in the after-death state.

Reincarnation in Simultaneous Time

Within the nontime of the afterworld, a person can experience simultaneous existences. A few months after Michael died, he experimented with different versions of himself from other reincarnations. Before his death, he had only a nodding acquaintance with reincarnation. After his death, he reveled in it. He had called together a number of personalities from other lives, and with them came the time zones in which they had lived and died. It was a joyful meeting, in which past, present, and future versions of himself interacted, filling in gaps of self-knowledge and just playing together for sheer fun. At the same time, Michael transformed himself into one personality after another, like trying on period costumes.

These distinct personalities, of which only seven participated, were, like Michael, in the after-death state. Because the standard notion of reincarnation is built on sequential time, it dictates that once a person reincarnates, his or her past-life personality somehow dissipates to make way for the new, incoming personality. This is not true. Each identity, past, present, and future, remains inviolate. Each endures. Each continues to find ways to fulfill itself.

Years ago, I had communication with Peter, my first great love, in two separate afterlife states. They happened back-to-back, twenty-three years after his death. In one, it was the Peter I knew in this life, but in the other, it was the man I knew when we were together in Victorian England.[11] His double visit blindsided me. As a Victorian, he used the elaborate speech he had adopted in that life. His expressions were colorful and laden with period metaphors that still leave me baffled. He seemed desperate, pushed to the edge by an exaggerated dread of the wrong he had done. He was clearly seeking resolution. All these characteristics dated explicitly to the personality of some 150 years ago. The force of feeling succeeded in prying open a door that had been shut for well over a century in our terms.

Happily, the later incarnation carried no trace of the Victorian penchant for high-flown remorse. In the earlier life, emotional intensity was the driving force. In the later life, what drove him was intellectual achievement. In Peter's present after-death state, he is engaged in highly charged, ever-cheerful, mentally creative research.

These two sets of after-death encounters, as I understand them, demonstrate that individual personalities from different reincarnations can and do coexist in the after-death state and with a considerable degree of independence. There is no dismantling of the old identity to make way for the new. There is no privileging of the new identity over the old, no ranking of lives. In fact, as they all exist simultaneously, there is no acknowledgment of old and new souls, high and low souls, or of past, present, and future. Simultaneous time and simultaneous past lives answer a very common question about reincarnation: How did so few people in the Stone Age turn into billions in the twenty-first century without the creation of new souls? Well, they do that by ignoring sequential time!

A different perspective on the simultaneous existence of past lives shows up regularly in the offices of hypnotists and past-life therapists. Past-life personalities frequently interact with present personalities, exchanging information and insights. They are alive and kicking in our greater consciousness, with their individual characteristics intact. The British hypnotherapist H. W. Hurst conducted a battery of psychological tests on patients in their normal waking state and again while regressed in a past life. When he later had the results analyzed by two independent psychologists, they found that the average similarity in psychological traits between a person and any one of his or her past-life personalities was only 23 percent.[12]

The differences can be extreme. Prominent white men remember being female African slaves; Chicanos recall fighting as British soldiers in World War II; and don't forget the blond, blue-eyed, eleven-year-old California boy from chapter 5 who spoke ancient Chinese. From the point of view of the young Californian, he was in contact with a part of his greater self that is *still alive* in a *still-existent* ancient China, a person we would consider dead. But from the point of view of the ancient

Chinese man, he was talking to someone who is alive in a futuristic place called the United States.

Once in a blue moon, people do meet their future incarnations. It happened to me some thirty years ago in a trance. I was a man living two centuries from now. I saw him sitting at a desk in front of unfamiliar instruments. He was (will be?) an expert in communications. He easily recognized my presence and was fully aware of me as his own past-life incarnation. With utter clarity, he announced his name as Bernerd. His only remark was: "So, you finally figured it out, huh?" Bernerd obviously considers me a dimwit when it comes to interdimensional communication.

Although we reviewed some of the more convincing cases for reincarnation in chapter 5, chances are you still don't believe in past lives because you don't remember them. Well, actually, you do. You have just learned to blank the memories out. Not having conscious memory of something is not the same as having no memory at all. What do you consciously remember about your first few years of this life? For that matter, what do you remember from the dreams you had this morning? Memories from past lives as well as from the prenatal and infancy periods in this life are right there under the surface and can usually be retrieved with little difficulty if aided by a few relaxation techniques or a light altered state.

As you know, children between two and seven, before they conform to social censuring, frequently have past-life memories, which they seamlessly integrate into their play. Later, blockages arise because our society dismisses them as fiction, and some children are even punished for lying when they bring them up. Research conducted in Asian countries where reincarnation is accepted as fact shows that 77 percent of the children interviewed had had past-life memories. And those memories were evoked with little or no prodding. Nevertheless, Asian parents still try to suppress them, partly because of the superstition that those who do remember die young.[13]

Spiritual evolution dictates that we progress from "new souls" to "old souls." But looking at the records of past-life memories in sequence shows that many of us have been better people, more spiritually aware, in a past life than we are now. I certainly have had incarnations I am prouder of than the one I am embodied in now. In the deep regions of the psyche, our various personalities participate in a cooperative venture, with the tensions and resistances typical of any relationship. If we were to embrace reincarnation more consciously, we would have access to vast areas of information. We could draw strength and wisdom from those portions of the self in past and future dimensions, portions that have plenty to offer in helping less fortunate portions of the self in their current struggles. And because nearly all of us have lived lives as a different sex, as a different race, and with a different social standing in the world, active experiential memory of those lives would lead to a breakdown of prejudices and open up the way to empathetic compassion.

But since this is not a book about reincarnation, let me just summarize here. Our past lives and our future lives do indeed influence us. (In fact, I would not be writing about interdimensional communication were it not for my future incarnation, Bernerd.) They often set the overall directions of our lives, along with the parameters of strengths and limitations within which we have chosen to operate. Furthermore, they constantly affect our choices. Say, for instance, that in another life — and remember, it could be one from the future — you are a man in a society in which wholesale slaughtering is the highest measure of your manhood. In such a life, slaying would carry positive social values, counted among the prerogatives of heroes. The intensity of such a life could affect you in a variety of ways, depending on other variables. It could also spawn a number of life choices spread out over several lives that revolve around the same theme. Perhaps you might choose to be an unusually feminine woman or a male weakling in one or more lives either to avoid the whole issue or to develop other aspects of yourself. Or you might grow up to be a passionate pacifist instead or perhaps a war historian in order to examine the theme from a comfortable distance. Conversely, that life of slaughter might seduce you into situations that involve mass death from war or natural catastrophes. In yet another life, you might even murder in order to recapture a lost sense of power. Or you might take the role of the murdered victim, engaging in the same theme from the opposite view. Finally, it is also more than possible to have a whole range of lives in which the slaughtering life plays virtually no role. The choice is yours.

Although we plan out the general directions before we land in the womb, the plans themselves are usually triggered in childhood. Often extreme emotional intensity in one life serves as a departure point from which highly charged strands of influence radiate in all directions to affect other lives in other dimensions. It is also true that themes that are only brushed against lightly in one life may be the chief thrust in another. Some people, like Lorella in chapter 7, might experiment with a dualistic set of ideas, such as the rich and the poor, the powerful and the meek, the murderer and the victim, the intellectual and the emotional, and so on. People who want to explore a set of past lives following binary themes often discover surprising similarities rather than differences between opposites or reach unexpected outcomes, for example, that the impoverished life yields more rewards than the rich one. When the cycle of exploration is complete, the end result is ironically a holistic view in which dualisms cease to exist.

Time Anomalies in the Present

The disparity in time perceptions between you and your departed loved ones might cause discomfort. From our restricted point of view, such substantial differences seem to separate us psychologically and temporally from the departed, adding to our grief. We want them to stay as they were, in the reality we know, using the same familiar reference points we use. They can and do use our reference points when they want. But unlike us, they are not limited to them. Usually a sense of sequential time lingers with the newly dead. They re-create a version of our time in the same way they re-create their bodies or places that were dear to them on earth. In the long run, however, chronological time is an imprisonment from which the deceased quickly free themselves.

Discomfort can also be assuaged by recognizing similar time anomalies in our own lives. One I call time looping, the intrusion of one time zone on another. From our positions in the "now" zone, time looping can be experienced as the past bleeding into the present or, if we are extremely alert, the future bleeding into the present. Many of us experience time looping as that peculiar feeling of déjà vu, in which we recognize that a present event has already happened before. People in old age often accomplish time looping in very real ways when they relive the past, a subject we will return to in chapter 10.

We can logically explain away the past intruding on the present by calling it a memory. But it is often more than this. The past is fluid and present in a dimension adjacent to now. In fact, we are busy reshaping it. I don't mean fiddling with our memories; we are *changing it* — our childhoods, our early adulthoods, our past lives — and we do it ceaselessly below the surface. This is one reason why two people who clearly remember the same event in the past remember it differently. The dead do this too.

The future intruding on the present is more difficult to accept. Whether we know it or not — and whether we like it or not — it happens constantly. Most of us realize that we influence the future, intentionally manipulating the present toward certain desired ends. We are comfortable with this, since we believe that the future has not yet happened. Visions of the future are taken as daydreams. Although some visions and dreams are not more than experiments with potential futures (and parallel futures), others are *forward memories* from the future or actual apparitions from the future emerging into the present. We have seen many examples of the future intruding on the present in after-death communication, when the dead appear to tell us about something that has not yet happened.

When I was about seven, I was walking toward a highway with the intention of crossing it. Just as I reached the curb, I felt a tapping from behind on my shoulder. I knew there was no one there, so I ignored it and put my foot down over the curb. I felt the tapping again, this time so persistently that it made me turn around. Standing a few feet behind me was a woman wavering vaporously on the sidewalk. I immediately recognized her as my adult self. Mesmerized, I walked toward her, away from the highway. As I stood there gawking, a car sped along out of control and ran over the curb, exactly where I had just stood. It makes me wonder how often the doings of guardian angels are really the doings of our own future selves.

Professionally, I regularly see future events, that is, future versions of the self, affecting the present. One man in particular stands out. He was a very beautiful blond, a professional model and would-be actor. At the time he consulted me, his life was in turmoil. Because he was flamboyantly gay, I was hesitant to explain that it was caused by an as-yet-unforeseen event to take place in two years, the birth of his baby girl. As the child was vibrantly present in his auric field, he must have been aware of her on some level. Mustering courage, I got the news out. He was furious and refused to believe me. He would never touch a woman, let alone impregnate one. I never saw that man again. But a few years after our session, a friend of his came to me for a reading. It was then that I learned that he indeed had had a daughter and was wonderfully happy. Children waiting to be born frequently hover over their chosen parents. I usually see them around the ages of three to five, as do near-death experiencers.[14]

Many scientists consider past and future time as simultaneous with the present. Among many fascinating theories is the "block universe" model of reality, which says that the worlds of the year 1452 and the year 8346 are just as real and present today in spacetime as New York and New Delhi are. In addition, wormholes are thought to be the portals between different time zones, and in some universes time probably runs backward.[15] So some would agree that the past, present, and future zones we think of as sequential, or other kinds of time, which I would call psychological time and enfolded time, are dimensions that all occur at once. Each zone is far from fixed but, rather, ever-changing, with one influencing the others.

In those rare moments when we can grasp the simultaneity of time, when eternity becomes real rather than theoretical, the revelation that all things happen at once comes easily and makes "infinite" sense. When you experience eternity in what I call an infinity moment, you understand perhaps the most profound fundamental of life after death and of your own greater self.

THE EGO, THE PERSONALITY, AND THE BODY IN THE AFTERLIFE

The issue of survival after death has a lot to do with the ego. On the one hand, people who don't believe in survival do believe in the ego, that part of the human psyche anchored in the material world. On the other hand, people who do believe in survival generally agree that the ego is anti-spiritual and will not survive after death. There is also a popular idea among spiritual groups that the ego pulls us "down"; we cannot, then, reach the "higher planes" until it is either tamed or crushed. What complicates any discussion about the ego is that the word itself can also signify conceit and self-centeredness, characteristics antithetical to common spiritual ideologies. All in all, the ego and spirituality seem to mix about as well as oil and water.

In the most general sense, the ego is recognition of the self, the "I," as distinct from all other things, animate and inanimate. Humans and many animals have developed an ego in order to better meet the demands of their environments. Its job is to interpret the constant stream of data provided by the senses and make adjustments in order to preserve physical life. The ego works like a lens that faces outward, mediating between us and our surroundings, just as another lens faces the inner self and the nonphysical dimensions. The ego was the wedge that allowed humans to distance themselves from nature in order to maintain better control over it. This separation has gone to such extremes that we are now on the verge of irreversibly damaging the planet.

Along with its growing estrangement from nature, the ego's ever-increasing vigilance in the world of matter has eventually led to blocking out a great deal of the nonphysical inner self as well. Since its ultimate function is to protect the body, it strongly identifies with the physical self and trusts only information that the body's senses give it. During the course of the "civilizing" process, the ego has succeeded in dominating the human personality to a point at which it focuses more and more on the material domain to the exclusion of others. Most of us have been taught that the physical world is the only one that counts, and manipulating matter, which I call ego function, is our only legitimate activity. Creativity is not valid unless it manifests as something concrete or usable, like an artwork or a software program for bankers. Clearly, these are not conditions that foster mysticism. By now, ego thinking has taken over in the West, setting us against nature as well as against the inner eternal self — the two arenas in which death takes place.

What we customarily think of as our personal identities is today so prescribed by ego function that it's easy to mistake the ego for the whole self. People who are comfortable with that mistake are the material realists we first met in chapter 1. The most hard-core frequently belong to scientific and intellectual communities, who take the view that consciousness is a by-product of electrochemical activity of the physical brain. When your body dies, you die. This is the ego talking, not the whole self. Because the ego was developed solely for maneuvering in physical reality and keeping the body out of danger, it has difficulty seeing beyond physical life. It therefore fears annihilation when the personality sloughs the body off. The materialistic attitude of the "objective realist," which is supposed to reflect a tough ability to face the facts, boils down to the ego's fear of extinction.

The view that the ego has no place in the world of spirit has a long history, beginning perhaps with Plato and his theory of the soul as pure mind. He regarded the body as a foul ensnarement of the soul, which during the revival of Platonism in the Middle Ages resulted in the idea that punishment of the body — self-flagellation, fasting, the wearing of hair shirts, and so forth — made way for redemption and enlightenment. Purity was described by an ethereal look cultivated by the elite; and stone figures of apostles, angels, and saints on the facades of Gothic cathedrals were often sculpted to look as though they were dissolving into spirit. The body's postmortem putrefaction was of intense interest too and seemed to expose the corruption and rot at the mortal core. It was unfortunately during that same period that the classical visions of heaven and hell took shape.

Souls in the medieval hell were depicted as still burdened with bodies. Nude or clothed, they also wore the lowly colors of the earth, blood reds, night blacks, and dung browns. The condemned dead also had bodies, because bodies could be graphically tortured and feel pain. By contrast, the souls in heaven were nearly bodiless, represented in light-filled whites like the clouds, transparent blues like the sky, and golds like the rising and setting sun. They felt neither pain nor the immoral indulgence of physical pleasure. They could hear, in order to listen to celestial music, and see, to behold the glory of God. But touch was too immediate, too intimate.

Heaven itself was envisioned as a perfect state, in which the body, the ego, and personal uniqueness had no place. Since individuality cannot survive perfection, the model of heaven up until recently banished it, thus adding to the ego's fear of death. Perfection is, after all, total conformity to a perpetual state of nongrowth, a state that can exist only theoretically.

Current spiritual philosophies have incorporated many of these poorly articulated ideas about the ego, the personality, and bodily functions in the heavenly afterlife. Bodily wants are assumed to be absent, contrary to almost all other models of the afterlife from early antiquity and nature religions, in which eating, drinking, and making love continue after death. Spiritualism usually conceives of the surviving soul as extremely passive, without ego drive, much like the perfect souls in a medieval heaven.

The demise of the ego in a heavenly abode is in part modern spirituality's inheritance from medieval Neoplatonism, yet it is also influenced by Buddhist and Hindu beliefs. They, like Neoplatonism, hold the material world and its body as imprisonment and specifically blame the ego, with all its desires and attachments, for setting the traps that ensnare them. It is the ego that seduces us into believing in the illusion of physical reality. For Buddhists, desire is the cause of all suffering, whereas I would argue that desire is the cause of all growth. In the Eastern belief system, the soul eventually reaches a state in which individual identity dissolves into ecstatic nothingness. This model is very close to the Western notion of merging with the Source.

The fear of the ego, that part of us that desires, that goes its own individual way, that recognizes and evaluates the self, looms darkly in nearly all modern conceptions of the afterlife. The ego, along with its individuality and drives, is eradicated from the exalted state of nothingness and its close cousin, diffusion into mass consciousness, as well as from the more orthodox versions of heaven, where the highest choirs of angels, the seraphim and cherubim, have only one reason for existence, to gaze eternally at the face of God.

Does all that we typically experience as our individuality disappear when we're pushing up the daisies? The answer is quite simple. No portion of our identity ever dies, not even the ego. This is not to say that the ego runs things in the world to come, as it does here. Nor will it produce the kind of fears it produces in this life. Instead, it relaxes and integrates more with other portions of the self, while continuing to expand.

There are deeper regions in the nonlocal realities of the afterlife where the ego has very little significance. In the grandeur of becoming, in the expansion of the soul, the ego is preserved in much the same way as a momentary memory from childhood is. The memory, say, of your fourth birthday when you blew out the candles on your birthday cake, can be used to stand for a you that you recognize as yourself but no longer are. You may nostalgically indulge in it, even reenter the magic of that moment and reexperience being the child you once were, and you may know that somewhere this child is a living part of you, but you are not that child. Instead you contain the child as a small portion of your greater identity. In the same way, the ever-expanding self lovingly holds the ego.

With all that said, there are many accounts from the deceased of full-blown ego activity. People quite frequently re-create favorite rooms or environments, such as a library or garden, in which they function much as they did while still corporal. Some even smoke cigars and drink alcohol, at least in the early stages of death.

Just as personalities from past and future lives exist simultaneously in the afterlife, re-creations and activities also take place side by side with others, many of which are so expanded that we cannot at present access them. It is in these activities and states of being that the ego most loses its significance. Nevertheless, the ego is not automatically discarded after death like an old coat. Nothing is innately wrong with the ego, although we have let it run away with itself. We merely need to reintegrate it with the natural and spiritual worlds to which it also belongs.

The Self-Serving Ego

The ego also goes against the spiritual grain because of its secondary connotations, namely, self-aggrandizement and a selfish preoccupation with gratifying personal desires. In my view, Satan is a personification of the self-serving ego, seducing the vulnerable to sell their souls in exchange for fulfillments of the flesh. Another personification of the ego is the biblical "rich man," whose chances for entering the kingdom of heaven are worse than a camel's for entering the eye of a needle. Yet not so long ago, self-glorification achieved by doing great works or accumulating enormous wealth was considered an entirely valid spiritual maneuver. The people of yesteryear assumed that God privileged those who attained fame and wealth, at least if you were a man.

Another big part of the modern anti-ego/goodness package is maintaining a steady flow of love, and the more unconditional, the better. Unconditional love does not judge. The very definition is a usable antonym for an unbridled, self-centered ego, which would be perfectly willing to judge others, even harm them, for the purpose of elevating itself. The paragon of modern spirituality presents quite a contrast to the ranting, raving, finger-pointing prophets in scripture. No one expected them to be understanding. The people of the past who dedicated their lives to God, monks, nuns, hermits, church fathers, were often unabashedly nasty and aggressively competitive. All in all, until recently, lovingness was not looked upon as the fast track to heaven. I am of course not advocating a return to these old mores of saintly conduct. My purpose here is to point out that in earlier times the route to divine favor was wider, more bendable, more ego driven than it is now.

Members of spiritual sects characteristically strive to keep their egos under wraps and their hearts pure. From what I've seen as a therapist, healer, and psychic serving such communities, the attempts to repress or hide anything incompatible with their notions of spirituality — and that's a lot, including roast-beef sandwiches! — are the main reason these cults ultimately fail. Just behind the outward show of joy and love is often an atmosphere of vigilance against ego displays and "negativity." The common result of too much blocked energy and spiritual paranoia is an anxiety-ridden passivity.

I remember one woman who desperately wanted to get pregnant. Yet, no matter how many times I provoked her, she would not dare utter the words "I *want* a baby." All she could get out was, if the universe willed an entity to come through her, she would be grateful. Now that's passive. She never did get pregnant. Her marriage failed and she became permanently ill.

Egoless passivity also manifests in specifically American schoolroom or group-therapy versions of the afterlife. As student/patient souls, we submissively absorb lessons and wait for directions from higher teachers/therapists, who determine when we are ready for advancement. The truth is, learning is a weakling compared with what really goes on in the afterlife, the adventurous, creative exploration of the whole self — past, present, future, and probable selves.

❧❧❧

The innate urge to expand eventually leads to the breakdown of a division between the self we currently identify with and those outside it, not all of whom are strictly human in our terms. We are all in this process, whether alive or dead. It is not something that we have to wait for until we come to the top of the evolutionary ladder. It is happening right now in other levels of awareness and may intrude on us at the most ordinary moment, while we're taking a shower or frying a piece of fish. When it does, we spontaneously step into the spacious present where all things exist at once. In these precious, eternal seconds, the fundamental unity that underlies *all* creation becomes apparent. Ranking and judgment perish in the face of that realization, as do fear and anger. There is only empathy and compassion for others and, where it is most needed, for ourselves. For most people, such revelatory episodes do not last very long while they are in the body; nevertheless they are still powerfully representative of a greater self, already fully formed, who knows the spacious present and dwells in it. As this expansion pushes forward, felling the barriers that separate us from our natural oneness along the way, unconditional love is unleashed.

PART III

Dying, Death, and Beyond

CHAPTER NINE

The Fear of Death: Causes and Cures

In part II, we looked at how Western religions and alternative belief systems developed views about the afterlife that breed fear and undermine trust in humanity's natural goodness and a benign universe. We have also seen how the ego is afraid of annihilation when the body dies, in terror of losing its identity. Religio-spiritual philosophies and the ego are not the only ones that gang up on the side of ignorance. Society plays just as great a role in maintaining ignorance and inculcating fear. Because few of us are willing to engage in a personal exploration of death, what we intuit independently, what we have experienced at the death of another, we remain captive to untested social conventions. Most of the secular institutions of today's world — government, education, economics, science, medicine, pharmaceuticals, and insurance companies, as well as the news and entertainment industries — don't just produce the fear of death; they also exploit it. More than religio-spiritual institutions, they foster the assumption that being alive is in all cases superior to being dead. We live in a culture that thrives on this fear. It dominates daily life and diminishes our inborn capacities. It turns dying into a frightening process of failure and darkens our experiences after we die. It also prohibits the very idea of contact with the dead.

This fear has made our society schizophrenic. On the one hand, the topic of death is scrupulously avoided; on the other hand, it is a cultural obsession. When I ask people what they believe happens to them after they die, I am shocked by how often I hear answers like: "I don't know. I try not to think about it." But that same person probably spent last evening watching people getting shot, stabbed, garroted, drowned... over and over again on television. Avoidance of death in the real world will get us nowhere in understanding the fate of each and every one of us. Obviously, we will die whether we've avoided thinking about it or not. But how we die and what happens to us directly afterward are another thing altogether.

Discussing death with the dying is practically taboo. We collude in the belief that it is too stressful for them. What is disguised as good bedside manners is really rather a ploy for dodging awkwardness, confusion, and powerful emotions on everyone's part. We are too uncomfortable to tread on religious beliefs or to encourage the ill to confront their ambivalence. If you have private ideas of the afterlife that contradict the status quo, discussing them can expose another anxiety: What if my version is wrong and my religion was right? What if both are wrong and the material realists and scientists are right and there is nothing afterward?

Challenging old ideas, broadening new ones, and working through doubts greatly benefit the dying and the deceased. For those who hardly dared to question religious doctrine before death, the clash between what they actually experience after death and what they were taught to expect can leave them perplexed and sometimes very, very angry, like Lorella in chapter 7. And like Joe in the same chapter, the guy who needed to be sprung from his own hell, some will go so far as to hallucinate what they were taught to expect.

Hard-core denial or habitual avoidance of death and the survival question can lead to the newly dead remaining stuck in an in-between zone until someone or something sets them straight. Avoidance can lead to being so poorly prepared that people may never have considered how the lives of their families and friends will unfold without them. It is surprising how many feel desperation or rage when they realize that a spouse left behind is planning to remarry. Unsettled inheritance issues have been known to trouble the newly departed, as has neglecting to resolve problematic relationships. Such distressing issues could have been adequately put to rest with honest, courageous discussion.

A young woman I knew spent more than two years dying from a brain tumor, and in all that time not one person mentioned a single word about death. They pretended to be protecting her. Although she endured repeated failures of brain surgery and over a year of wasting in bed, in and out of consciousness, the fact that medical treatment was not going to cure her was never brought up. The family also chose to believe that her traditional Christian upbringing would be enough to see her through. Well, it wasn't. Eight months after she died, she was still fuming mad with her family for not telling her what was going on. She felt lost, betrayed, and abandoned. Telepathically she knew that her young and, I must say, vigorous husband was already thinking about other women, which made her crazy with jealousy. She also accused her parents of deliberately stealing her only child out from under her. It took me two days to convince her that she, too, was responsible for this out-and-out denial and to persuade her to accept her disembodied state and move on. Obviously, it would have been much better for everyone if they had all talked openly with her about dying. Then she could have used the time before becoming comatose to work through these difficult issues. Doing so would also have freed her parents and husband from their own burdens of guilt, which, from what they have told me, are still very heavy.

We especially avoid talking straight about death to children. Young children are still strongly connected to creature consciousness. Rather than fearing death, they try it out in play, routinely falling over dead in fantasies. Few parents I know stroll over to their child lying heroically dying in the backyard from an imaginary bullet and ask casually, "So, Billy, what's it like to die?" Although dying is a natural part of the young child's imaginative repertoire, we think that talking to them about it will pollute their purity and rob them of their innocence. They learn from our silence that death is a very bad thing.

Death is the most ordinary of life's occurrences. It happens all the time, in every household and hospital, in the streets, in cars, on planes, trains, and boats, every fraction of a second all across the globe. And I guarantee you, it will happen to each and every one of you. So why on earth are we so frightened to talk about it, especially to the dying and the young? We like to think that we are afraid of death because it is the great unknown. But what face have we put on the unknown? Think for a moment of some of the associations we have with the words *death*, *dead*, and the already-mentioned *the dead*. Then there are related words like *fatal*, *terminal*, and *deadly*. How about *corpse*, *grave*, *coffin*, *casket*, and *tomb*? Do some of these words send a shiver down your spine? When you think of death in the abstract, what feelings do you associate with it? Panic? Anger? Powerlessness? Regret? Repulsion? What occurs to you as soon as you find out that someone has passed? Do you visualize a corpse already cold, hardened, and discolored? Do you wonder where that person has gone? Do you imagine being dead as a suspension in a still place, without the slightest spark of personality, as the terms *eternal peace* and *eternal rest* suggest?

What other images arise when you pronounce related terms such as *death rattle*, *death throes*, *death knell*, and *deathbed*? Think for a moment how common symbols for death affect you: the Grim Reaper; a skull and crossbones; a black cross, sometimes impressed on a schematic image of a coffin. If you associate death with hospitals, funeral parlors, or graveyards, what sorts of feelings does each place convey? Project yourself into them and notice what you think and feel. It's probably all pretty creepy, no?

Most of the responses you might have to these questions are no more than enculturated knee-jerk reactions. A great deal of what we associate with death stems from how our cultures produce death, how they package it. Just one quick example: in Japan the color for mourning is white, not black. In some cultures, contrary to circumventing the subject of death, people spend a considerable part of their lives preparing for it. Although we think of the passing of a loved one as a bleak occasion of mourning, other mind-sets consider it a liberation to be celebrated. In Madagascar, people dance about during special festivities carrying the perfumed bones of their late relatives in the spirit of gratitude and joy.

I can't help but think of a joke here that nicely illustrates contrasting views. A Tibetan monk is called in by a family during the final moments of the aged paterfamilias. The terrified, grieving family hopes that the monk will do something to save the old man's life. The monk stands over him calmly, watching him intently, but without making a move. Suddenly the old patriarch draws his last breath. After a brief pause, the monk looks up into the anxious faces of the surviving family members and pronounces, "Oh, he's fine now." Although the story is intended to be funny, it is truthfully grounded in the Tibetan Buddhist philosophy of conscious dying.

Death is not the problem; fear is. And fear is something we create. It is why there have been so many attempts to systematize the afterlife, as though we can trap and control something as vast as eternity. As far as I can see, no systematized set of convictions in Western cultures has been able to dislodge one jot of our fear. Later in this chapter, we'll look at a significant group of people who have conquered it. Consequently, they have less fear of life and live life more robustly with enhanced physiological, intellectual, and spiritual abilities. They know that death is where we most powerfully reconnect with our greater selves and the magnanimous nature of reality.

Fortunately, ready-made, set explanations can no longer hold back the tidal force of intuitive knowledge. More and more people are speaking up about what the dead tell them about the other side; others are talking about the real inner experience of dying; and still others, about

their experiences while clinically dead. What they say typically contra-
dicts standard teachings and social attitudes.

THE SOCIAL PRODUCTION OF FEAR

Because the fear of death is a big chunk of our social conditioning, it
lies at the base of many of our institutions and cultural ideals. It is a
main driving force behind our economy and aspirations for wealth and
beauty. Think about it. An economy based on constant growth is at
bottom based on the fear of survival. Just as material growth is seen as
the antidote to stagnancy and decay, the accumulation of wealth is supposed to give us a sense of security and power. As possessions mount
up, the houses get larger, and the cars more expensive, we expect our
identities to get sharper, bigger, more solid. Material increase supposedly removes us from the side of the weak and puts us on the side of the
invincible. Some of the superwealthy even believe they have attained
a kind of immortality on earth. This is the fearful language of aging
and dying; as long as we continue to grow, we have not yet started the
downward turn toward death. Ironically, a constant-growth economic
policy will eventually lead to a planet so choked with waste and depleted
of resources it will no longer be able to sustain us.

A huge proportion of the elderly's savings frequently goes to prolonging life, even when the quality of life has eroded past salvage.
Witness too the outrageous amount of money spent on maintaining a
youthful appearance, no matter what age you are. Our natural bodies
with all their unique characteristics and irregularities are not what get
the limelight; rather, the idealized body, the overdisciplined and surgically corrected body, does. Men with pumped-up muscles and women
with Hershey's Kiss breasts are the icons for the pinnacle of youthful
adulthood just before the long, painful slide to aging and death. We fear
what will happen to us if we don't exercise the way we are told to, and
we fear what we eat and what we breathe. Few of us can enjoy the Sunday roast anymore without genuine unease for willfully ingesting fatal

amounts of cholesterol. The anxiety around it all produces toxicity in our bodies and pollutes the psychological atmosphere.

Equally close to the point are national ideologies, in particular that of a nation's war industry, which rationalizes its exorbitance with the cliché "kill or be killed." It is truly shocking that world powers are still measured by their capacity for meting out death. Wars would not occur, of course, if death were not the ultimate threat. The war industry thrives by propagating a vision of an unsafe world.

Religions that preach of a supernatural evil roaming the planet also spread an unsafe-world outlook. Less obvious are insurance companies, which coerce us into paying for "protection" against a host of perils that rarely happen. Just as pernicious is the way we mark history by wars, plagues, famines, massacres, murderous dynastic takeovers, and the occasional natural disaster, such as the caldera explosion that snuffed out the Minoan world. Without realizing it, we assimilate messages about an unsafe world and, worse, an unsafe universe from nearly all the sciences, including biology and medicine, climatology, geology, oceanography, physical and cultural anthropology, sociology, primatology, even astronomy, and to an alarming extent the news and entertainment industries.

The lethal scenarios generated by defense ministries, the academy, the sciences, health industries, the media, and religious institutions work in two directions. Either we are victims of something coming from outside — epidemics, global warming, atomic warfare, mega-asteroids, and entropy — or we are victims of some uncontrollable inner force that leads to disease, violence, and insanity. In biology, the inside force might be a genetic flaw. In psychology, it is the uncivilized subconscious. Either one reflects religious beliefs of an inherited wrongness. Between what we learn in church and school, we can't escape feeling that something will get us and, worse, that we deserve it.

As an academic who deals with the making of history, I am often enraged by how scholars distort their findings to fit the model of an unsafe world. Archaeology is no less prone to manufacturing interpretations of war and conflict out of nothing. The slightest hint of a town wall, for instance, becomes a defense wall against invasions. I remember one instance in which archaeologists took a single image on a gemstone carved in ancient Crete of a young male, mostly nude, with a dagger tucked into his belt as the depiction of a warrior. From this solitary picture, they extrapolated a warrior society. Why? From the same region today men carry such small knives in their belts to slice up their cucumbers when out lunching in the fields.

The supposed cutthroat instinct for survival that anthropologists and primatologists claim as forming the very foundation of human nature bends to a "kill or be killed" imperative, like the war industry. Science, together with history, supports the war industry's argument that man has always been and always will be aggressive, hierarchical, and prone to killing. The survival instinct goes hand in hand with the "preservation of the species" instinct. Although both impulses do indeed exist, the sciences have awarded them an unfounded primacy. As these so-called instincts are now conceived, they are the ever-vigilant, front-line agents that fight tirelessly against personal and social annihilation. We and all the creatures of Earth have supposedly taken a genetic oath to spend our lives crusading against death. Because we imagine that life operates from a stronger-versus-weaker blueprint, those occasions when individual and even mass death are *chosen* over continued physical existence are misinterpreted as proof of inferiority. Given our attitudes, we will never be able to perceive a species' disappearance from earth as the result of a collective decision any more than we can accept a person's decision to die. We prefer to believe that a species will always strive toward dominance to avert extinction. Paradoxically, these strongly invested assumptions about self-preservation have caused more death than they will ever forestall.

Rather than incorporating into our models the creature characteristics of altruism and cooperation, we inflate instances of conflict, especially among males. We claim that we are objectively studying the great apes, whereas the way we study them influences not only what we see but also how they behave. Furthermore, we have refused to reconcile the contradictions presented by a very humanlike group of primates, the bonobo, who, like chimpanzees, share all but 1 percent of our genetic makeup, according to some studies.[1] The gentle, matriarchal, and highly sexual great apes are noncompetitive, with a social structure organized along inclusive rather than exclusive principles. They are therefore simply left out of the narrative, ignored, or dismissed as anomalies.

Our ideas about "Early Man" are moreover mere hypothesis. The endless portrayals of the first humans as suspicious and brutal, forever on the alert against long-toothed predators and crafty enemies from competing clans, have led to the view that this young pristine earth was full of extraordinary threats in which the only defense was, again, kill or be killed. They have also led us to believe that the people of the remotest past fought ferociously against death itself, just as moderns do. This anachronistic insertion of our own attitudes into the Dawn of Man story has naturalized the fear of death. The inexcusable fabrications arising from anthropology and Darwinian theory pretend to present a real portrait of man in the raw, the genetic nuts and bolts of humanness. Because we have accepted them as true, we have seriously diminished our prospects of a better world.

Perhaps worse is the central tenet of the survival-of-the-species theory: that we are genetically driven to constantly procreate. What has this truly alarming rise in population really done for us? It has reduced the quality of human life and caused famine, ever more disease, competition, and waste, and an incomparably rapid devastation of the planet. We are led to this by skewed, fear-based scientific conjectures and by gross ignorance about the true nature of immortality.

The death process moves from the deepest regions of the self and is a spontaneous operation of nature. If neither the self nor nature can be trusted, then how can we place any trust in the death process? Perhaps when we begin to see death for what it really is, it will lead us back to a conception of ourselves as part of nature rather than against it. Within our current social framework, fear is logical. But it is more than that. It is also a habit. It takes a great deal of faith indeed to leap over it to some measure of freedom.

THE MEDICAL INDUSTRY AND ITS DEATH THREATS

No area of modern life is more effective in spreading the fear of death than the medical industry, and here I am including the makers of pharmaceuticals and medical technology. The industry's fanatical focus on disease rather than health has produced a national paranoia. Medical experts sponsor the idea that the body is constantly vulnerable to diseases that will lead to decline and death. Silent and unseen, viruses, environmental contaminants (ultraviolet rays, secondhand smoke, free radicals, parasites), bacteria, and a multitude of other evils can arbitrarily strike at any time. This picture of an unsafe world is loudly promoted by a science that has the most intimate influence on us and on which we are forced to depend to save our bodies from invasion.

Physicians often use extremely harmful fear tactics when something is found and a patient will not cooperate with their prescribed course of treatment. Alarmingly, fear tactics also work as hypnotic suggestions that actually promote disease. Because I am an uncooperative patient, my own general practitioner, a woman I simply adore, has used these tactics on me. When I refused to submit to a mammogram, she suddenly produced two patients who "just last week" were diagnosed with breast cancer. I have a thyroid that is four times larger than it should be, overactive, and packed with nodules. When I refused to rush into surgery to get the poor little thing ripped out, this same doctor suddenly manufactured a patient who "just this month" was diagnosed with thyroid cancer. She then described the horrendous procedures for treating it and the chronic life-threat her patient has to live with. Steeling myself against her graphic hypnotic suggestions, I understood that she means well. I believe she has such patients, maybe not all within the same month, and I know she feels responsible for me. Nevertheless, I will not get a mammogram, and I will not get my thyroid removed. At the moment of this writing, I have decided to trust my body's natural inclinations toward health — or at least try. After all, I'm the one who is creating the problem. Finding out why I'm doing that will heal the condition while evoking invaluable insights about myself. If I simply get the thyroid torn out, there is no possibility of healing. So far, it has improved without medical assistance and a year after diagnosis is again within the normal-function range. The route I am taking is not for everyone. Each of you must make your own decisions.

The medical sciences promote a model of the body that is fickle and unreliable, a body that must be kept under watch. We have been handed the tricky task of balancing mistrust of ourselves with self-control. How can we expect to have control if we also believe we can't be trusted? If we fail to eat healthfully and get regular exercise, if we drink too much or smoke, we are surely dooming ourselves to an early death, or at least social shame.

There is a famous case of a woman in southern France (Arles) who lived to 122, the oldest documented supercentenarian known. Jeanne Calment's remarkable longevity was largely attributed to genes and the pure quality of her food. Before we completely buy the idea that genes determine the body's destiny, for better or for worse, we should look hard at cases like Jeanne's and at why siblings, especially identical twins, differ in health or come down with unlike afflictions. Despite having a similar genetic makeup and eating the same food, no one else in Jeanne's family lived to see 100. She ate two pounds of chocolate a week until the age of 119 and loved her wine. She was physically very alive, taking up fencing at 85 and still riding a bike at 100, not for exercise, but for fun, doing what was right for herself spontaneously. Lastly, it was not until she was already 119 that she quit smoking! Clearly the factors that led to her long life lie outside currently accepted medical knowledge.[2] She claimed the reason was gobs of olive oil lavished on her food and skin. She was also prone to fits of laughter, a documented health benefit. Jeanne's philosophy — don't worry about what you can't change — set up a high immunity to stress. Unfortunately, modern medicine is still not ready to fully come to terms with the huge role the psyche plays in health and disease.

This is not to give license to eating, drinking, and smoking with abandon while watching TV in bed all day. Rather, if we were to trust our bodies, we would pick up their cues and automatically do what is good for us, like other animals. And we would do what is good for us, *not because we are afraid* not *to do it*. Instead of forced regimes — or guilt for the lack of them — we would spontaneously choose the foods we need, spontaneously get up and go for a walk or take a nap. We would instinctively gravitate toward pets to lower our blood pressure or to situations that bring tears of laughter to break up physical tension, release needed hormones, and eliminate toxicity.[3] In fact, most of the body's repair work takes place while we have the least control, when asleep, especially in the early-morning hours. The body knows how to heal itself, if we just let it. Unfortunately, the mistrust physicians have in the body's own ability to heal and their disbelief in healing agents outside medicine leave them in ignorance about how spontaneous cures happen. Instead, they regard the body as a time bomb. There is so much fear around illness and death that it's literally killing us.

Medicine takes the stance that death is the ultimate enemy and must be conquered or at least delayed as long as possible. A person who overcomes a death-threatening disease is admired as a "fighter." The war imagery extends to the common metaphor for death as "losing a battle" against, say, liver cancer. Because dying is considered a failure of the body alone, the mind and the will are disconnected from it in our thinking. We then read dying as a conflict between the body and the will rather than as a cooperative effort between the two. Doctors team up on the side of the will and take control over the body, severing it from the personality. It is no longer yours. Eventually even your will is subsumed in the medical agenda. Your body becomes an object, something for others to commandeer, probe, measure, observe, manipulate — a thing. Although it is your most intimate creation, it is now foreign to you, and only experts are qualified to understand it. It becomes in the end your enemy. When that Good Night finally arrives, we are expected to go kicking and screaming.

Medicine is not entirely to blame for its production of fear. Part of the Hippocratic oath is, after all, to save lives, but this should not compel us to go overboard. Medicine is partly a victim of the post-Enlightenment scientific mandate of material objectivity. Since the nonmaterial — the soul, the spirit, the psyche, the mind, the heart, and consciousness — cannot be tested or measured, it must be denied or at least skirted. Although we entrust the dying to physicians, most of them don't have a clue what's really going on. Courses on dying and what happens after death should be requirements for any medical degree so that doctors, nurses, and paramedics approach the dying with knowledge and trust in the process. And they are more than capable of perceiving deathbed phenomena for themselves. I have never met a doctor who wasn't also psychically talented. Nearly all of them have the ability to see into the body without the help of instruments, what I call x-ray vision. My own father, following my grandfather and great-grandfather, all of whom were doctors, never missed a diagnosis in forty-eight years of practice because of this ability, and this was in the days before diagnostic devices. It takes me a matter of minutes to get physicians to become aware of it and to use it more consciously. Still they are unwilling to apply their psychic abilities, partly for insurance and legal reasons, let alone to turn them toward perceiving what happens beyond the body during and after dying.

Medical personnel can and do understand a patient who wants to die because of pain or because there is no other possible outcome. But if a person wants to die before a given condition reaches the fatal stages, he or she will rarely admit it. We consider a desire to die as alarming, aberrant, a transgression against human nature, and a slap in the face to the living's superior position over the dead. The fundamental truth is, we all choose to die. As you will see in the next chapter, young or old, in sickness or in health, we choose when and how we meet death. If we were even slightly more aware of this choice and if we were more trusting of ourselves and our bodies, many more of us would elect to skip the debilitating breakdown of the body (and too often our finances) and just leave in our sleep.

We are all caught up in this devastating spiral of fear and confusion generated by the big and very competitive businesses of the body. In the end, it's all about money, not about the welfare of human beings. Physicians, squeezed between the threat of lawsuits and the payments of huge insurance premiums, are just as hamstrung and dismayed as their patients. They no longer have the right to act on their instincts or the leisure to consider the needs of the whole personality of a patient. They are also helpless when faced with someone in the end stage of disease who is ready and willing to die. Lacking the training and the spiritual and emotional resources to escort death, physicians are left with one option: suppressing its symptoms with drugs.

When my mother had her first major stroke she made it clear she did not want to recover. A series of catastrophic strokes within two days put her in a permanent vegetative state with no possibility of improvement. She stayed in the hospital under twenty-four-hour nurse supervision for a few months, fed through a feeding tube directly into her stomach. To complete the dying process, we had to get her out of the hospital. Although no words were spoken, her doctor understood that we were going to let her body starve and dehydrate until it let go. Had we told him, he would have felt officially obligated to regard our intentions as unethical, if not legally dubious.

The medical industry has taken dying away from us. It is no longer our province and our right as creatures but a disease requiring medical attention. It is furthermore hidden in hospitals, as though it were something too odious to be seen. In short, the medical industry has *denaturalized* death. The truth is, dying is without a doubt one of the strongest of all inborn instincts. Just as all infant creatures know instinctively how to be born, to take that first step or swim or fly, or a wound knows how to heal and a lung to breathe, we know how to die.

Many have remarked how courageous and graceful children are

when they are approaching death. And I must add, it forever astonishes me how my pets die, *actively* setting about it, preparing a place for themselves where they will not be disturbed, refusing to eat. All along they seem so serene, basking in trust that the road ahead will lead to something good. With just a measure of that creature faith restored, we can begin to trust our own dying processes.

THE MEDIA AND THE MAKING
OF REPETITIVE NIGHTMARES

The overall denial of death has led to mass repression. And as with any repression, what is repressed must surface eventually. The more fear there is around a given repression, the more frightening the repressed material is likely to appear. When it is stored in the body, it will manifest as an illness. A healthier way to release it would be in dreams, where pent-up fears often take terrifying forms that chase you or lurk menacingly in shadows or behind doors. They do all this hiding because your subconscious is trying to tell you that you are hiding something from yourself. Nightmares depressurize repression while containing information about what we refuse to face. Since we seldom have the courage to directly confront what we repress, it appears indirectly, couched in codes and symbols. If we don't get what a dream is trying to show us and acknowledge the source of the fear, it will repeat itself over and over again.

To a great extent, the news and entertainment industries are producing the nightmares needed to depressurize our collective dread of death. Instead of a dream, we have stories. Rather than confronting our real-life fear head on, we confront death vicariously through books, newspapers, films, TV shows, and computer games with their endless feed of wars, terrorist attacks, famines, earthquakes, tsunamis, hurricanes, epidemics, crimes, fires, and so on. Just take a look at what's on television tonight. How many shows revolve around death, for example, hospital dramas and murder mysteries, especially those featuring

forensic medicine? Through probing and scientific analysis, patholo-
gists make the dead speak. Although such series purport to show a sac-
ramental respect for the dead, special-effects experts shock and turn
the stomach with sheer dripping gore concocted through lurid colors,
camera angles, and zoom-ins on sickening wounds and mutilations,
exposed organs, the body's bloody interior, gunshot holes, amputated
body parts, missing jaws, eyes, and fingers, corpses blue and bloated
from poisoning or drowning or blackened and shriveled from burning,
blood pooling underfoot or splattered in readable patterns, and maggots
wriggling out of orifices.

This absorption with death, decay, and the macabre is intensifying.
Think of the old show *Quincy*, in which Jack Klugman played the role
of a forensic pathologist. Either the means by which a corpse became a
corpse was visually understated or it was never shown. In those days
of only a few decades ago, the dead were rarely featured lying on the
laboratory table, let alone having their livers ripped out and their skulls
sawed off. The macabre presented in a "realistic," "scientific" package
allows film and television-show makers to exploit our deep-set fears on
several levels at once.

Added to the pickings from your major television networks are of
course action films, thrillers, and horror films in which killing, often
by the hundreds, or environmental tragedies, sometimes of such scope
they threaten to wipe out all life on the planet, form the plots. There is
also the reworking of scary legends about vampires and other undeads
— mummies, zombies — who prey on the living. They, like bodies
inhabited by hostile aliens, viruses developed in secret government
projects, or satanic entities, actualize the widespread fear of losing our
individual identities after death.

The messages are characteristically all the grimmer in productions
about discarnates, ghosts, poltergeists, and the realms they inhabit. I
include stories about devils and possession here too, since evil spirits
are supposed to issue from that region of the afterworld we call hell.
All of these beings are usually portrayed as malevolent. They not only

have the power — and the intent — to drive us mad with fear or kill us; they can also suck our souls into hellish dimensions from which we are never released.

The way the dead have been represented in the media is for the most part appalling. We almost never see them as mundane and friendly. With few exceptions, they are in trouble, caught between worlds, usually in such psychological pain, they are demented. Just as damaging are the portrayals of those who can see them. People who communicate with the dead are usually depicted as abnormal, possessing what is presented as an extraordinarily rare ability akin to a bizarre gene or disease. In earlier years, films featured mediums as physically or mentally defective. Psychic visions often resulted in loss of life or blindingly severe headaches from massive brain-cell death. The more recent portrayals are of reasonably normal, good-looking people. Nevertheless, their gifts are unwanted burdens, separating them from the rest of humanity, and inevitably lead them into danger. Lastly, the way media present psychic perception of the dead is misleading. Even for real-life mediums, the dead do not appear as solid flesh and blood. Such an appearance does sometimes occur — about as often as a blue moon on February 29.

Our nonstop engagement with such prefabricated nightmares is a sure symptom of a big dilemma at the root of our society. If individuals were to have private fantasies or dreams as horrid and twisted as what the entertainment industry offers up, they would be diagnosed as psychotic and pathologically antisocial.

Transforming the Fear of Death

What can we do about all this fear? We can get rid of it by finding out what death is really like. There are many ways of going about this. You can die yourself, temporarily, that is, in a near-death experience. Less dramatic but almost as life-changing is talking with the dead themselves, a route so important that I have devoted all of part IV to it. The dying can also tell us a great deal, if we learn how to pay attention. You'll get many pointers on that in chapter 10. One facilitated technique for experiencing death is given below, although many others are available. Right now I only want to show that, contrary to its bad reputation, death is good for us.

Death, the Miracle Cure

If you talk to the people who have been through it, and here I am referring to the many millions of near-death experiencers, they will all tell you that death is the best thing that could ever happen to anyone. It's a miracle cure for the body and the soul. Even better, near-death experiencers are living demonstrations of what people are like when they lose the fear of death. The story is pretty remarkable, so hold on.

You will remember from chapter 3 that some near-death survivors were definitely pronounced dead — no vital signs, no heart or brain activity — yet revived with vivid accounts of life outside the body. Because "near" deaths usually take place within a hospital setting, the readouts that track a person's demise and resuscitation are available in plain black-and-white. What happens to them while they are dead varies.[4] As you know, the great majority have reported experiences so sublime, so sacred, they cannot find the words to describe them, while a very few have experiences that are frightening. Whether the event lasts moments or hours, whether it is transcendent or hellish, people come back with little or no fear of death. Then life really begins.

For those who have met death, the recurrent nightmare is finally over. When they return, there is no sense of having triumphed over death or having conquered it. How can you triumph over what feels like a homecoming, an escape from jail, or an awakening? The magnitude of love and compassion is overwhelming. Survival after death becomes an unshakable truth; and the cosmic infrastructure of benevolence, a palpable reality. The aftereffect across the board is a sea change in worldview. Ironically, death stands as the single most inspiring event of their lives.

Deeper investigation could tell us much about the true nature of health and disease, about perception and the relation of consciousness to matter, and about reality in general. Scientists have not even begun to assimilate the material these revivified dead have brought back to us. Their very terminology of *clinically dead* or *near death* underscores their ambivalence. By all medical standards, the complete absence of heart and brain-wave activity defines a person as dead. The body is dead; therefore the person is dead. Sometimes they have even begun to stiffen. Since science holds that life without a body is impossible, these people could not have been *really* dead. Tell that to someone who comes out of it with a toe tag in a steel drawer! At the very least, near-death experiences force us to admit that the line between alive and dead is neither as solid nor as stable as we pretend it to be.

As we've seen in chapter 3, equally troublesome to science are the people who are blind from birth but upon leaving their bodies can suddenly see in brilliant detail what is going on in their hospital rooms. Some travel during their NDE to view for the first time the landscapes and buildings of their home turf and to visit people they know but have never actually seen before. In all accounts, their observations are accurate. A few return with sight restored. Just as remarkable, other experiencers come back healed of the incurable diseases that were killing them, such as kidney failure, aplastic anemia (bone-marrow shutdown), cancer, and end-stage liver failure.[5] These fact-defying incidents of seeing without using eyes, perceiving without using the brain, and cures without medical intervention remain unexplained and uninvestigated scientifically.

Mellen-Thomas Benedict presents one of the most famous examples.[6] In 1982, he died from a malignant brain tumor and stayed dead for a full hour and a half, a length of time not credible by medical standards. His body had already started to grow cold and stiff. According to medical science he should not have revived at all, and if by some miracle he were to, he should have returned with permanent brain damage from oxygen deprivation. But he did return. It took him three months to get up the nerve for a brain scan. The results were spectacular. Instead of brain damage, his brain was clear of any malignancy, even though the type of cancer he had is known as the least likely to go into remission. Others who survive come back with lesser ills gone, like chronic migraines, cramps, stomach problems, susceptibility to accidents, and poor coordination. There is also a general diminishment of pain.

Researchers note additional, subtler physiological changes in the reduction of body temperature, blood pressure, and metabolic rate. Survivors need less sleep and have more energy. They also show heightened sensory awareness of smell, taste, and touch and a lowered tolerance to pharmaceuticals and alcohol. Their sensitivity to light, sound, and atmospheric conditions intensifies significantly. There is little doubt that near-death experiencers undergo some sort of electromagnetic transformation, since a surprising number of them short out their cars, computers, and appliances, or their digital watches and recorders stop working. In one study called the Omega Project, 50 percent claimed that their nervous systems were functioning differently. More than one-third felt that their brains had been physically altered, and indeed, several studies show that their mental and intellectual capacities did measurably increase.[7]

All these benefits are great in themselves, yet they pale in comparison to the dramatic cognitive shifts reported. Even near-death experiencers who were upset by the event speak of deep changes in their psychological orientations, with substantially altered values and life goals. The changes are lifelong, with the effects growing stronger over time.[8] Survivors become immediately awake to the greater human potential. They discover in themselves a reverence for all life, feel connected with all things, and live with the feeling of a surrounding divine energy. Spurred on by a sense of personal destiny, they become determined to fulfill it and live life more intensely, more purposefully, up to the last. Even though they gain a greater sense of self-worth, their brush with death instills humbleness, a sober, nonjudgmental self-awareness that allows a person to admit accountability and truthfully evaluate where changes are needed. Because they recognize that their lives are the products of their daily choices and free will, they feel more in control and take more risks.

Tolerance, concern, and compassion for others vastly increase, dismantling old prejudices and blame and dispelling the need to compete. Experiencers also lose interest in material gain, in living up to social expectations, or in winning approval. Newfound emotional expressiveness and open-mindedness, as well as enhanced creative abilities, are also typical. Near-death survivors become more reflective, more philosophical, and develop a hunger for knowledge, which frequently leads to higher education.

Wonderfully for them, they also become immune to society's fearmongering about death. Consequently, they have a broader, longer view of the planet's future and the role each individual has in shaping it, a view that frequently triggers a desire to serve humanity and a greater sensitivity to nature. Love becomes uppermost. Orthodox religious orientations give way to a more universalist spirituality, involving personal intuition, prayer, and meditation. What were formerly only abstract notions of a Supreme Being now become profound certainty, even for atheists. All that in a few minutes — phew!

But wait, there's more. Most have noticed a dramatic increase in psychic abilities — telepathy, clairvoyance, precognition, reincarnation recall. They have more mystical experiences and out-of-body episodes and are able to see auras as well as the dead. Lastly, from 42 percent to 65 percent, depending on the study, feel they have developed the gift of healing.[9] The awakening of such latent aptitudes has caused some to establish radically new careers in the healing arts and spiritual counseling.

Although the modern West has so far not acknowledged near-death experiencers as a distinct group, traditional societies the world over have customarily honored them, valuing the wisdom and paranormal abilities that were sparked to life during their walk on the other side. Many shamans, for instance, are known to have survived a fatal illness

or accident in their youth. The newly awakened psychic-spiritual connectedness is the force that powers and sustains the shift in worldview.

Pushing the Reset Button

Fortunately, we don't have to wait to wake up in the morgue to share
in these transformative experiences. Years ago, I led a special group of
students through their future deathbed scenes. The idea was to look at
their lives in hindsight, which people often do spontaneously shortly
before or after passing. The results were astounding. The students, like
near-death experiencers, fell into a hyperawareness of an exhilarat-
ing miraculous essence. From the position of the deathbed, they were
able to look back on their lives to evaluate the roles they had played,
their strengths and weaknesses, and above all, the fears and beliefs that
blocked the flow of love and creativity. Some had life reviews.

Just as they "got" what their life purposes were, they also saw where
they were steering off the track. They recognized where they were
withholding love, where they were hurting others, and where self-pity
or cowardice was holding them back. When we are poised in that final
moment, the inhibitions that rule so much of our lives seem ludicrous.

Most of the students caught glimpses of passing over into death,
though it was not part of the experiment, and came away with a comprehension of life, death, and the afterlife as one glorious sweeping
cycle. And how deeply safe they felt in death, immersed in a love-
drenched safety that allowed unimagined freedom. Sadly, it's often not
until we're on the verge of death that we realize how secure we really
are — and have always been.

The experiment shows how much we actually know about ourselves when we suspend the fear of death. It also shows how much that
fear inhibits life. For the students, just envisioning the end of physical
life was like pushing the reset button. Buried personal truths rose to
the surface: the importance of love, courage, emotional honesty, creativity, and helping others, of paying attention to sunsets, animals, and

children, and above all, of holding all life as sacred. The students felt a firm resolve to conscientiously honor these deeper values rather than just paying them lip service. They also emerged determined to conquer whatever stopped them from fulfilling their individual potentials.

One of the best things about fast-forwarding is that you can change anything you don't like. You can, for example, take steps to prevent the disease you see yourself dying from or, if it has already started, work on healing it. Even in the lightest of altered states, problems and solutions have a way of appearing together, so that an illness can show up along with the reasons for developing it, which is essential to a complete cure. You can mend relationships, seek forgiveness where needed, start loving wherever you withheld, and call a halt to judging others. Where you have allowed yourself to hide behind fear or have eroded your self-esteem by not living up to your own principles becomes so glaringly apparent that change is unavoidable. The emotional honesty is simply liberating. Why waste life stuck in our own traps?

Fast-forwarding to the last moments in the body is not all that difficult. It is best accomplished with the assistance of a responsible and trusted friend. Just lie down, relax, and imagine yourself on your death-bed. If you are too uncomfortable with a deathbed scenario, simply imagining the whole of your life as though you have already lived it can result in many of the same insights and reduce the fear of death.

Meeting the Eternal Self

Nearly any direct meeting with that part of you that is independent of space, time, and matter will bring some form of revelation. Meeting the inner self also has an uncanny way of unleashing natural psychic abilities. Such a meeting can come about in many ways. With children it normally occurs spontaneously, most often through contact with nature. Altered states brought on by sickness, accidents, childbirth, and the like frequently lead to encounters. We can set up intentional appointments with the inner self, ideally through meditations or deep relaxation; in either case the positive effects grow stronger with practice. Or we can simply go to a hypnotist or a regression therapist. In fact, almost any situation that lets us disconnect from our physical bodies has a tendency to put people in touch with their immortal natures. The inner crossroads, where immortality meets mortality, is a place of unending potential for transformation. Encountering your eternal self also means encountering that part of you that knows eternity, that part we would call dead. The immortal self has been through death over and over again. From its *Sputnik* perspective it sees death as a crucial part of the psyche's continued growth.

I was in my early twenties the first and only time I went to a hypnotist, and I had no idea what to expect. The hypnotist gave the suggestion that I go into the after-death state of my present life. I plunged ebulliently into the experience, shooting out of my body and exploding into a dazzling universe. I was transformed into George Bush the Elder's "million points of light," bursting forth in all directions, traveling at rocket speed through the stars. For me, the experience was ecstatic and revelatory, but it scared the hell out of the hypnotist. He abruptly ordered me to return. As a therapist who has helped many over the threshold of past-life deaths, I guarantee you that no one leaves the body permanently on a lark. The decision to die issues from a far deeper place and involves agreement on many inner levels. My experience of decades ago is still vibrant today. Because of it, I have a good idea of what my first moments after death are likely to be. If I ever feel the least twinge of fear, just recalling that ride out of the body is enough to abolish it.

❧

A moment on the other side of death's door is the most powerful transformative event there is in life outside of birth. It is the ultimate conversion, utterly without hype. It is here where we watch our greatest fears collapse into nothing. Where survival outside the body, outside time and space, becomes an absolute truth. It is here where we meet the eternal self — the real self — face-to-face. Where we are stunned by the realization that in or out of the world of matter, we are immeasurably safe, immeasurably free. It is here where the fundamental goodness of the universe is directly felt. It is here too where death's real nature is revealed. We also experience all this when we are in contact with those already on the other side. Since they perceive our immortality so clearly and speak directly to it, we can't help but experience it ourselves. They too reveal death's real nature. Death is a beginning.

CHAPTER TEN

Preparing to Die

The cycle of passing over — preparing to die, leaving the body, and the first experiences on the other side — is unique for each person. It also varies according to beliefs. Yet to a great degree, the inner experience of this cycle floods up from a deeper source, like a single subterranean river that rises to the surface in different places and times. Hence, no matter whether a person dies quickly from an accident or violence or gradually from illness, when old or young, in China or Brazil, there is an awareness of something of enormous magnitude happening underneath, an awe-inspiring recognition of being in a partnership with greater powers.

In this chapter, we are going to look at the preparation for death, step-by-step, from several points of view. Chapter 11 will take us through the moment of death and into the first days or weeks in the afterlife. It must be mentioned that the material I draw from, whether from my own observations or from the experiences of others, is situated in a modern Western tradition with few exceptions. If I had been brought up in a cave fifteen thousand years ago or in a Tibetan monastery and were writing about death, these chapters would not be the same.

Our own society's approach to dying is forever changing. Before World War II, death usually took place at home amid family. After the war, the dying were removed to hospitals, where all too frequently as little energy as possible was spent on so-called hopeless cases. The nourishing continuity of family, local pastors, priests or rabbis, neighbors and friends was then ruptured. Everyone involved was left to struggle with feelings of alienation and helplessness. Patients were plunged into isolation. Regarded as no more than bodies in an unstoppable breakdown, they lost their personhood as well as their agency. Relatives and friends, the custodians of old, were warned not to interfere. Confusion and anxiety rose as loved ones passively watched the spectacle unfold in the foreign setting of medical props and inhuman schedules. Patients were too numbed by drugs to respond to their environments, further driving a wedge between the dying and those who loved them most. Severed from their own inner experiences, the dying lay suspended in nowhere, waiting for their bodies to make that final step.

Although many still die in such an ambience, the picture is changing. In the late 1950s, a movement began that sought to rehumanize dying, propelled by the physician Dame Cicely Saunders, who resurrected the hospice in London, and by a psychiatrist, Elisabeth Kübler-Ross, with her 1961 publication, *On Death and Dying*. Kübler-Ross's psychological stages of dying — denial, anger, bargaining, depression, and acceptance — reestablished the importance of the mind. With the advent of near-death-experience studies in the 1970s, the psyche made a splashing entrance, to the discomfort of many medical professionals. Since then, the steadily growing hospice movement has more and more approached dying as a holistic event in which the body, the mind, the heart, and the soul play equally significant roles.

The best hospice workers follow a patient-centered principle, meaning they assume patients are right, even if at first they don't make sense. Rather than ignoring the efforts of the dying to communicate, hospice caregivers encourage them to speak while listening and observing very closely. When the dying say they have a visitor from the other side, instead of dismissing it, hospice nurses recognize it as a signal that death is approaching and call in the family. Likewise, when the dying pronounce the time of their own deaths, the nurses call in the family. Patient-centeredness represents a big step in the restoration of dignity to the dying and respect for their wisdom.

In 1992, two hospice nurses, Maggie Callanan and Patricia Kelley, called the expanded consciousness of the dying "nearing-death awareness" in their book, *Final Gifts*. They have observed that when the needs of the dying are understood and met, death comes peacefully with little or no pain. In the stories to come, we will see nearing-death awareness at work, as well as many other phenomena from my own observation.

There is one point I need to mention right away. Family and friends typically dread the final moment. Time dilates. Every detail of the event, every gesture and facial expression of the dying, every word becomes intensely meaningful. While most seem to gently slip away, others may go with such difficulty that it horrifies those around them. Whatever the case, the moment of death usually impresses an indelible memory on those who witness it. The memories are seldom pleasant. In some instances, as with war veterans, the images can haunt them for the rest of their lives. For the dead themselves, the last moment is rarely that important, which they will tell you if they get the chance.

My earliest death memory is of my grandmother's passing. At the age of seven, I watched with morbid fascination blood gurgling out of her mouth. This was the last and the strongest recollection I had of her until I met her in spirit as an adult. What stood for me and my family as her last tortured moments was for my grandmother almost too trivial to remember. From her perspective, she went on to a swift recovery. Usually the deceased recall their deaths in the way we remember getting over an illness. Most who died suddenly in car accidents or natural disasters reassure us that they left their bodies very quickly and felt little or no pain. Evidently, some leave their bodies *before* impact,[1] a phenomenon that may well be quite common. If you have a disturbing memory, when it returns, shift to the dead's healthy perspective for immediate relief.

LEADING UP TO DEATH: AN OVERVIEW

Ideally, a person dies when the body simply "wears out" from old age, as my dead mother once told me. Despite what it seems, the period from old age to death is actually one of accelerated growth, similar to puberty in the sweep of its psychophysiological changes. Qualities that have been suppressed often come to the surface. A man who in his prime exercised aggressive power might grow more passive or childlike as he ages. Similarly, a woman who was once passive might become more masculine and aggressive. The sweet ones might become nasty, and the cantankerous sympathetic. Of course, many retain their lifelong characteristics, but the general tendency is to balance out inner experience.

As you know, people in advanced years frequently visit the dimensions of the past. Because cellular consciousness largely organizes our perceptions of time, it loses focus with aging or illness, causing perception to loosen, so more than one time line becomes apparent. Short-term memory might fade while long-term memory becomes more real. Events, relationships, beliefs are reworked toward an overall healing. Although some portion of a mixed-time reality may be delusional, it is still a way of assimilating the formative belief structures of one's life normally set in early childhood. This kind of time looping also allows people to reacquaint themselves with loved ones they are soon to meet again.

If we were to understand better how the psyche prepares to make that great jump in focus from the physical to the nonphysical, we would not need to cast symptoms of rapid growth and mixed-time experiences in the form of senility and disease. Nor would we feel compelled to blunt them with drugs. If we begin to acknowledge these rarely recognized transformations as legitimate processes, the dying might enjoy having their feet in more than one reality at once, rather than fearing it.

As far as the physiological changes of people with long-term illnesses go, Callanan and Kelley will tell you that nearly anything goes.[2] For some, the last months might bring complications and discomforts, whereas occasionally, a person might feel and look very much the way he or she did when well until the last few days. Some may go through waves of feeling extremely sick and then well again, while others "decline" steadily. People once in a while die in their sleep without any forewarning of disease. Others may lie in a coma. It is not unusual for a person to temporarily come out of a coma shortly before death to reconnect. When my cousin Albert saw his wife's eyes opening and realized she was conscious, he made a joke. She looked up at him, chuckled, and then sank back into oblivion to die shortly thereafter.

The most commonplace symptoms are weakness and extreme fatigue to the point that the dying can neither move nor react to their surroundings. Sleep takes over at any opportunity, often deepening into unconsciousness. At this point, the dying are more on the other side than here, using the metaphors and symbols of their inner world to communicate. There is no more desire to eat or drink. The eyes characteristically take on an unfocused, glassy look as though they are no longer able to look outwardly. The physical senses withdraw, with hearing the last to go. Within days or hours of death, breathing normally begins to change, becoming more irregular, perhaps stopping and then starting again, slowing down and speeding up, getting louder and then softer, until it ceases altogether.

Once a person accepts that death is on the near horizon, an orchestration of body and psyche takes over, automatically enacting those changes that best accomplish the goal. The psyche's drive toward death can be so strong that it can be felt like the thrum of a high-energy engine. The destination can be so uppermost that the suffering it takes to get there is incidental by comparison, much like reaching the summit of a mountain or giving birth — hard, yes, but more than worth it.

Resistance and Politics around the Deathbed

People resist the corporal departure of their loved ones in all kinds of ways. It may show in the form of manic behavior, for instance, or draining distractions. In the face of helplessness, often overwhelmed and confused, we may irrationally scream at the doctor or the dog, compulsively plump pillows, wash the car, paint the attic, stay late at the office, or just run away.

Resistance may also mean trying to save the dying from death. I have seen a woman in the hope of prolonging life spoon hot soup into the mouth of a man already in a death coma. One of my own reactions has been abruptly going on a health kick, the more violent, the better, with the hope that the life force I pump up can be transferred to the dying to restore health. The case of a five-year-old boy dying from a brain tumor should give us pause. The three weeks he was in a coma, the family never left his bedside but prayed day and night for his return to health. Finally, the family's pastor came to the hospital with a message from the boy, who had visited him in a dream. In the dream, the boy told him, "It's my time to die. You must tell my parents to quit praying." When the parents heard this, they said one last prayer and told their son they would miss him but understood his need to go. The boy suddenly regained consciousness to say he would die soon and did the following day.[3]

Family politics also come into play. One family member may go so far as to limit contact with the dying or forbid it altogether. Most problems stem from a need to get approval from the dying before it's too late. Although detachment is part of the natural process, it is frequently read as rejection, causing people to compete for attention. With all this going on, what the dying need is often overlooked. If we were to realize that relationships not only continue after death but improve, the dying process would be easier on everyone. We would be emotionally freer to participate more fully and sincerely in the final preparations for the voyage ahead.

To Be or Not to Be

As I have mentioned, we choose when and how we die, a fact that may be difficult to accept for now, especially since these deep, personal choices are very seldom conscious ones. The decisions we make around death are generally formulated in inner awareness, where simultaneous time and nontime operate. In that inner place, the future is known. Just below waking consciousness, we try out probable futures and pick which ones we want manifested. We cannot exist without this future-probing mechanism, nor can we die without it. Social influence is another factor. As life spans continue to lengthen, mass consciousness adjusts to a longer life expectancy. Nevertheless, the decision of when to die is always open.

Since near-death experiencers are constantly faced with the choice of "to be or not to be," they expose the decision-making process with stunning clarity. The literature is full of stories about them *not* wanting to come back. More than once, a person has returned and felt angry at the doctor who did the resuscitation procedure. Most return for someone else's sake.

The reasons for dying are as numerous as the stars. In general, a person reaches a point when dying is the healthiest choice he or she can make from the psyche's point of view. This usually takes place in old age as a gradual process. Still, there are souls who want only a tentative exploration of physical life, abandoning the experiment as young children or even in the womb. When prenatal and infant death occurs for physical reasons alone, those little ones who are planning to stick around tend to come right back in another body. According to information that comes to light during rebirth therapy sessions, returning shortly after death with a fresh start in a stronger body is common, and the fetus or baby usually reincarnates to the same parents when possible. Dying young occurs for any number of reasons. Actors may want to be remembered at their peak, for instance. Others might die young to avoid a future calamity or disease.

Choice operates for all causes of fatality, whether sickness, violence, or accidents. If more than one person is involved, individual decisions combine to form agreements. Even in mass events like war, natural disasters, or epidemics, the degree to which we participate is still a matter of agreement. For those who elect to die in group or mass events, altruism is often the reason, whereby forfeiting the body is believed to serve a greater good. Past lives also play a role, as do general life decisions made prior to conception.

The prevailing notion that death is an accident of fate, a genetic misfortune, or the result of cells going berserk is to me more offensive than the fact of personal choice. I know many people will feel outraged at the idea of choosing death. Outrage is also a perfectly understandable reaction for people in extreme grief over a loss. However, the more we truly understand death and its profound purpose in maintaining the psyche's well-being, the more we will welcome this idea as fact. Similarly, if we were to know more about the afterlife and how our loved ones are living it, we might wonder instead why so many wait as long as they do to get there.

Foreknowledge

When a choice is made to die, it sometimes surfaces into consciousness, often through dreams. It is then called foreknowledge. Whether conscious or not, inner awareness still sets things in motion. Without knowing why, a person might make a change in life course that prepares him or her for death. Another might have presentiments or precognitive dreams even before there is any indication of an illness. One woman, for example, announced to her daughter while they were out shopping that she (the mother) would pass on in exactly six months. The daughter was puzzled, because her mother was in excellent health. Six months to the day later, the mother did indeed die.[4]

Precognitive dreams are occasions when information from the inner self is allowed to filter through. There is no way of telling how many of them are remembered and how many are suppressed. Abraham Lincoln was one who did remember. His precognitive dream occurred a few days before he was shot. He saw a corpse resting on a catafalque in the East Room of the White House. All around people were weeping. When he demanded to know who was dead, he was told it was the president, killed by an assassin.[5]

Family and friends may dream of the imminent death of their loved ones. There is nothing morbid about precognitive dreams for others; they are simply cases of shared information at the inner level. Very rarely, the dead will tell you outright that your time has come in order to prepare you. One afternoon while washing his car, Gary's late wife appeared to tell him that he would be with her soon. This troubled him, since he was young and healthy and finally over the grief of her death. He died shortly thereafter in a freak car accident.[6] Although Gary's story may seem macabre, his wife was doing him a favor. At her suggestion, he was able to enjoy his family and friends in the time he had left. He also had a firmer belief in survival. By the time the accident occurred, he was much better prepared.

If the dead can know when a person is likely to die and close relatives and friends sometimes know, chances are that the person involved is sending that information at some level. One way this is done is through auras, which diminish in terminal illnesses and prior to fatal mishaps. Edgar Cayce, the famous "Sleeping Prophet," told of one such incident in which he was about to enter a packed elevator. Suddenly he noticed that the auras of the riders were reduced to nearly nothing. He quickly stepped away. The door closed, and the elevator plunged to the basement, killing everyone inside. Nevertheless, no precognitive dream, no announcement from the other side, no psychic peeping writes the time of death in stone. Instead, individual personal decisions about when and how death will occur are usually under constant revision.

Foreknowledge also occurs on a mass scale. Since 1998, research laboratories have been analyzing the relationship between random noise, meaning white noise, and mass consciousness. Fifty computers around the world have been set up to uninterruptedly record and analyze white noise. When it shows signs of organization or nonrandomness, this is a signal for scientists that something has affected it. Among many remarkable findings was one that occurred in the early hours of September 11, 2001. The changes in white noise recorded from this worldwide network of computers showed that something dramatic had happened in global consciousness. The alert occurred at 4 AM (EDT), five hours before the first plane hit the World Trade Center, which was about the same time the terrorists began putting their plan into action. Similar white-noise changes have been logged for floods, bombings, tsunamis, earthquakes, other plane crashes, and more, with the chance of coincidence of less than a million to one.[7]

Humans, even better than machines, are aware of such future events. Larry Dossey relates many riveting accounts of premonitions of 9/11, many of which saved lives. As he notes, this event generated the largest outpouring of individual precognition ever recorded.[8] The same students whom I took through their deathbed scenes in chapter 9 saw the Chernobyl disaster more than a week before it happened and in such detail that one of them described helicopters dropping sandbags to quell fire. In those days, nobody in the West had ever heard of Chernobyl. For such mass events, we try out future probabilities in sleep states, typically dreaming along with others of a possible catastrophe in the near future. We then either agree to participate or not.

Sidestepping Fatality

Foreknowledge is also evident in the countless number of stories of people who sidestep fatal accidents, supposedly by sheer luck, or survive natural disasters and epidemics because of a series of uncanny happenstances.[9] Usually this is instinctive rather than conscious. An inexplicable feeling of dread may lead to canceling a trip on a train that later crashes. A person might be running late and just miss that train or fall sick and stay at home. Others step in too. The train might be missed because of an important phone call, for instance, or because the dog got injured and had to go to the vet.

In chapter 4 we saw examples of the dead warning people of a potential accident or death. Others may become aware of a personal fatal event from dreams. Still others may learn of it through psychic readings and are then able to avert it. Although such events are sometimes foretold to psychics by a dead relative of the client, the knowledge usually comes from those unlooked-at edges of the clients' own energy fields. If a psychic or the dead don't warn them, people not ready to die just find another reason for sidestepping fatality.

Research on near-death experiences in combat has turned up some incidents in which the sensory perception of a soldier in the midst of battle has abruptly kicked into supernormal gear. There are reports, for instance, of men who were suddenly able to see in 360-degree vision and were thus able to escape harm coming from behind. Even more astonishing, soldiers occasionally exhibit an ability that seems to slow down time and magnify objects. Two veterans out of the forty interviewed by Robert Sullivan said they saw the bullets coming at them while in combat. In this heightened sensory state, the bullets looked so large they were likened to baseballs and so slow that the soldiers were able to get out of their way.[10] These guys were simply not going to die. Of course, civilians can develop superhuman powers too to prevent disasters.

Some people will agree to participate up to, but not including, the point of expiration. Nonfatal accidents and natural disasters generally serve as a catharsis for those involved, a kind of wake-up call that brings about much-needed emotional and psychic clearing. Agreements are usually made on the inner radio waves. A one-time client of mine presents an interesting example. She came to me for information about a lawsuit she had filed against a man who ran her over in his car while she was crossing a street. The hit had resulted in multiple fractures. She arrived at my office in a body cast and full of rage at the driver. I saw at once that she and this man had strong past-life connections, although they were strangers in this life. Much to my own surprise, he had agreed to hit her in order to save her from a worse fate. This woman had been psychologically and spiritually poisoning herself for years. Had she continued on this route, she would have ended up friendless and riddled with disease. The "accident" was designed to get her fight up again and her healing juices flowing. It also gave her a badly needed focus, physical recovery, an objective that was concrete and doable.

Spontaneous Cures

Diseases, like accidents, do not come out of nowhere. Whether terminal or short-term, they too represent choices and are largely tailor-made from a person's inner patterns. Nearly anything outside of birth defects can be cured if the beliefs and repressed material that settle into an illness are uncovered and changed. I am a big believer in the treacherous power of repression. Releasing it almost always involves penetrating the shame barrier touched on in chapter 7. In general, healing is normally a slow process of altering inner decisions and beliefs as a person searches out alternatives to death. Cure can also come about suddenly from a conversion experience if it is powerful enough to restructure those undesirable beliefs and dislodge repression, as NDEs often do. The wide-spectrum effectiveness of these deeply private experiences is thorough and lasting. Public conversions and charismatic healings in religio-spiritual venues occasionally produce cures. However, they often don't last, or new ailments crop up, because the underlying problems remain unresolved.

If someone is not ready to die, almost anything can serve as an agent of recovery. I remember a little house near Bakersfield, California, where people gathered to pray in front of a shadow on the wall that resembled the classic image of the Virgin Mary. It was painfully easy to see that the shadow was caused by trees blocking the glow of outdoor Christmas lights. But those who gathered there empowered one another and so infused the air with hope and faith that some did have inexplicable improvements.

The dilemma of whether to maintain hope for a spontaneous cure or to capitulate to a terminal prognosis must be met case by case. On the one hand, waiting for a miracle may be playing into denial. On the other, a fixed belief in the inevitable fatality of a given condition works to preclude spontaneous reversals.

INNER PREPARATION FOR DYING

Dreams

From what I can see, once the choice to die is in place, the psyche initiates a process of inner preparation, sometimes well before a medical basis is identified. Again, a person may not be consciously aware of this activity or may notice it but not link it to mortality. Dreams are typically the strongest vehicles for carrying the process forward. My mother had preparatory dreams before any indication of illness. Many months before a series of strokes put her in a vegetative state, she was telling people about dreams of dying in her sleep, a subconscious euphemism for coma. I participated in some of them. The last one I had with her, we had gone together on a test run in the afterlife. We rose through layers of light grayish-blue clouds, staying there for what seemed like hours but was probably only minutes by clock time, and then descended slowly back through the same layers into a waking state. The next morning while she was telling me about the same dream on the phone, her speech seemed to short-circuit. It was the first sign of the big strokes soon to come.

Dreams help people already aware that they are dying and are an important part of nearing-death awareness. They help release fears about the process of physical death and about what happens afterward. They also point out what is worrying a person and what needs resolution.[11] Since the dreams of the dying are rarely insignificant, unraveling their meaning deserves full attention. Encouraging the dying to talk about them, especially about the feelings a given dream provokes, often brings insight and relief.

Early Preparatory Visits from the Dead

Inner preparation can also summon visits from deceased relatives and friends long before a person dies. The visits might be regarded as a very early sign of nearing-death awareness. Sometimes the encounters occur before a person is aware of being ill or even earlier, before the illness has set in. Visits are also known to occur shortly before a fatal event, as Gary's story above illustrates. Don't be alarmed about this. It doesn't mean that an appearance of the deceased is a precursor of your own death. If that were true, statistically most of the world's population would already be six feet under.

My late friend Al visited his mother long before she died. Even though his visit was definitely preparatory, no words of demise were mentioned. It was designed, rather, to recharge Mary's will to live and to set growth and acceleration into motion. When Al died from AIDS, Mary languished in despair. She went into seclusion, sitting in the house without even bothering to turn on the lights at nightfall. Eric, who was Al's partner, tried to step in, calling her frequently and stopping by. Normal measures were not working, and her condition worsened. Then one day she called Eric to tell him that Al had come. She found herself driven back into a closet, crouching on her knees. Al was taking control. He screamed at his mother to stop brooding. He was perfectly all right. Not really dead. No one is really dead. And then in words typical of him he roared, "Mother, get a grip!" She did. From then on, she grabbed at life, started to travel, including taking trips to Atlantic City for some high-spirited gambling. She did everything she had never before allowed herself to do. Mary joined her son within the year.

Acceleration and Orchestration of the Psyche

A man I will call Edward serves as an excellent example of orchestration and acceleration. Edward had come to me for a reading. His doctor suspected he had cancer, and Edward didn't want to wait a month for the tests. The reading uncovered his cancer and why he had it, at least in broad terms. He was trapped in a horrendous marriage. Although his children had grown up, he felt a responsibility toward his wife, who had a long history of mental illness. I rarely talk directly about a person's illness when I find it in a reading. Announcing to someone that he or she has a specific disease goes a long way in establishing it as ineradicable fact, which in turn reduces the possibility of a spontaneous cure. So rather than talking to Edward openly about the cancer festering in his stomach, I talked about what it represented. As gently as possible, I laid out two choices: to get out of his marriage or else. He wept. A week later while out shoveling snow, he dropped dead from a heart attack despite having no history of heart disease. He got out all right, out of the marriage and out of the misery of a dreaded disease.

While attending his funeral, his children spoke to me about his last week. For the first time in many years, all four of them and his grandchildren came home for a family reunion more than a week before his death. One of them even came in from the Middle East. And they were all still there to arrange his funeral. Edward was an active presence at his funeral and positively thrilled to be dead!

Edward's highly orchestrated race toward death and Mary's yearlong acceleration are atypical. In most cases, discernible acceleration occurs during the dying process, usually somewhere in the month before expiring. A person who has lingered for a long time might enter a period of feeling better. Energy is renewed. Alertness is restored, sometimes to a point of hyperalertness. Frequently, the dying suddenly fall in love with life, savoring its bittersweet transience. This quickening is familiar under much less dramatic conditions to anyone who works under deadlines, the big deadline being death itself.

Because we can see how preparation occurs on many levels at once, we can safely say that the province of death and dying ultimately belongs to the psyche, not to the body. Once the decision is made, the psyche goes about arranging the necessary future circumstances that will facilitate the body's demise. The energy of the psyche for preparing the change of focus is enormous and capable of fabulous orchestration. Much of it goes toward bringing about closure, resolution, reconciliation, or the conclusion of unfinished business. My first husband, Jacques, who died rapidly at the age of twenty-eight, is a case in point. An Armenian born and raised in the Old City of Jerusalem, he spoke six languages, had a strong penchant for French philosophy, and possessed an ironical charm. Before he consciously knew he was sick, his greater awareness was at work setting up some hefty milestones. Within twelve days of his death, his long-fought-for green card came through, and he got married. His status in America changed from foreign student to married legal resident, in short, from boy to man.

Jacques went to the hospital the day after our wedding. As news spread that he was a newlywed, he quickly became the nurses' darling. More important, he now had me, a relative with U.S. citizenship, who could officially interface with his doctors, make decisions, and take care of the many legal and financial concerns that arise at the close of a life, including arrangements for his bodily remains.

In addition were the small wonders that swept in on the tide of his acceleration. People often call them coincidences, when in fact they are evidence of the psyche's precise coordination to fulfill certain conditions. A minor piece of Jacques's unfinished business was getting me a television set. Somehow strangers I met at the hospital spontaneously gave me one of theirs. Another "coincidence" occurred when he was in delirium and spoke the street Arabic of his childhood. An American patient a few beds away had learned enough Arabic while stationed in the Middle East to translate Jacques's needs to the nurses.

On the ninth day of his hospitalization, he was transferred to a solitary cell of the intensive-care unit, where he was hooked up to an iron lung and closely watched from the other side of a large glass window. The cause of his illness was still unknown. At this point, I was staying the night with him. Two nights later, when I stepped out for a smoke, he seized the moment alone and ripped the respirator tube out of his throat. His shocked body sprang tiny leaks of spurting blood. Nurses panicked; one even cried. A tourniquet was applied, dividing him at the waist, concentrating the blood in his upper body to keep his brain and heart alive. He died only twenty minutes afterward. When I got home at four in the morning after that grueling night, there was a single message on my answering machine, spoken in Jacques's unmistakable voice: "Thank you, Julia."

On a lighter note, for my great-aunt, an Italian immigrant, acceleration occurred just a few days before her death. To everyone's surprise, she suddenly started speaking English at the age of ninety-three. We had not even realized she knew English, for in the nunlike seclusion that characterized her life in America, her circle of communication was confined to Italian-speaking relatives. It was as though she finally awoke from a lifetime of dreary denial to discover herself living in America amid English-speaking people.

Reconciliation

Reconciliation is perhaps the dying's strongest drive and seems to be the leading requirement for a peaceful death. Reconciliation is mostly about other people, healing old wounds, asking for forgiveness or offering it, expressing love and gratitude. But it can also involve reconciliation with oneself, spurring the dying on to rectify old sources of sadness, guilt, anger, and disappointment as well as to clear up unfinished business. As Callanan and Kelley note, the drive may lead them to reconcile with God and religion, as well as with local clergy and members of the congregation. The need for rituals, prayer, and confession, formal or informal, might arise. Or there may be a sudden upsurge of spirituality independent of organized religion. In general, nearing-death awareness seeks closure by embracing whatever was formerly divisive, smoothing whatever was contentious, and finishing whatever was left undone.

As the process progresses, the dying have to rely more and more on the assistance of others to bring reconciliation about. Verbal requests and signs can be unclear or go unnoticed. Some of the issues needing attention may seem insignificant or irrational to those on the outside and be ignored. If the need for reconciliation is not met, it can result in such emotional unrest that a person appears agitated, physically distressed, and perhaps confused. The dying may compulsively pick at their clothing or bedding, for instance, or have troubling dreams. One of the most important signs is the delay of death itself. When the need for reconciliation is satisfied, people usually pass away quickly and peacefully.

There is no end of stories about how the dying achieve reconciliation, one more remarkable than the next. It can come in many forms, symbolically, say, like expiring on the birthday of someone the dying person had hurt. And it can begin at any time, though it is most strikingly evident at the deathbed. Even the most ordinary cases show that the psyche *routinely* reaches closure in such complex ways that it borders on the unbelievable.

My father presents such an ordinary example. He had been divorced from my mother some thirteen years before he died. During that time, what little contact they had was unpleasant, and many things were left unsaid. To make matters worse, his two sisters, with whom he lived, "protected" him from my mother primarily by screening his phone calls. After a few days of lying in bed, he slipped into unconsciousness. The so-called death rattle began, coming in fits and starts. On the basis of his outward symptoms, we were told that he only had a few more hours left. Instead, he hung on for three more days. The ragged breathing seemed to grow louder and more desperate, as if his throat alone were trying to form words without the help of his brain.

Finally, it occurred to my niece that he would not die until he heard my mother's voice. Those miraculous coordinating powers of the psyche got busy setting up the circumstances that would allow this to happen. His sisters left the house for the first time in days. In a pause of those few minutes, we found a way to set up an incoming phone call from my mother. Holding the phone receiver to his ear, we were able to hear her speaking to him slowly, softly, but with courage and purpose. She reviewed for him the love they shared, prayed for him, asked his forgiveness, and forgave him as well. At the last, she said perhaps the hardest words anyone can ever say, words of release. My father was unconscious, yet he heard her. The death rattle stopped immediately.

At that point I was startled by something appearing around his bed — angels. They were so tall their heads seemed to penetrate the ceiling. They were standing at each corner of the bed, like gentle human-shaped lights, keeping the space around his body sacred and free to make way for the last of his consciousness to depart. By then, his sisters had returned. Meanwhile, my own sister took her two-year-old daughter out for a short walk. From what I know now about how the dying time their deaths, I can say with some confidence that my father did a great job. He knew that if his sisters missed his last breath, they would never forgive themselves. On the other hand, there was no need to expose his baby granddaughter to the grief that would ensue. With the right conditions in place, he died. This was about twenty minutes after my mother's words of release.

DEATHBED VISIONS

Deathbed visions are extremely important to the process of dying. Although a great majority of them happen within the last three days of life, others occur a month or even a year before death, as Mary's story has shown. If you remember, the phenomenon falls into two subcategories of visions: incorporeal visitors and otherworldly environments. In general, deathbed visions are often followed by "mood elevations"; some patients may temporarily revive, exhibiting renewed strength and mental clarity. Others may become quiet and peaceful. Many witnesses over the centuries have remarked that the faces of the dying during these experiences have a look of wonder and elation, but now and again also puzzlement.[12] Sometimes bystanders see or sense things around the body of the dying, such as a glow or an invisible presence. The more familiar caregivers become with deathbed visions, the more they are likely to perceive them themselves. Sadly, many of the ill are too sunk in a chemical haze to have these experiences or at least too drugged or weak to report them.

In 1926, Sir William Barrett published his book *Death-Bed Visions*, the first known study of its kind. In 1961, Dr. Karlis Osis presented more comprehensive research that when combined with later studies became a popular book.[13] Data were collected from more than a thousand attending physicians and care workers in the United States and India, totaling some 35,540 observations of dying patients. Although the visions differed culturally, they occurred irrespective of age, sex, religious beliefs, and whether or not people expected to die or even believed in an afterlife. The one factor that inhibited visions was mental impairment from either drugs or brain damage, a factor that also blocks near-death experiences.

Visitors from Beyond

According to Osis, apparitions of the departed occur with a substantially higher frequency than afterworld visions. In his research, the average interval between the first apparition and death was about four weeks. Eighty-three percent saw deceased relatives, 90 percent of whom were from the immediate family, which loosely accords with most other research. Appearances of religious figures were higher among Indians than Americans and corresponded to the beliefs of the recipients. Christians saw Jesus or angels; and Hindus, their god of death or his messengers.

It may be no surprise that differences are reflected at a microculture level as well. Recently, John Lerma, a deeply Christian physician in the heart of the Bible Belt, wrote about his hospice work. A full 90 percent of the five hundred patients he personally surveyed saw angels, a dramatic incongruity with Osis's findings of 24 percent from the American survey and none from the Indian one. Some of the patients Lerma attended described angels of different colors, gold, blue, and even black, complete with feathered wings. He was also told that up to forty angels could be in the room as the hour of death approached.[14]

Crowd scenes are not unusual. Unlike Lerma's patients, however, the dying are usually familiar with those who show up. Still, some are not. A man close to the end from kidney cancer saw many people just standing overhead, people he was unable to identify. He did not rationalize their presence or assume they were angels; he just accepted them as friendly people who brought him peace and comfort.[15] In another instance, a man repeatedly saw a little boy days before he passed. His family as well as the hospice agency decided the boy was an angel, although the man himself had no such assumptions.[16] Were Lerma's patients seeing angels, or were they projecting what they wanted to see onto the human dead?

Angels

Over the years, I have come to recognize a discrete group of entities that I can only regard as angels.[17] In my experience they have mostly appeared around the dying, yet they have also appeared while I was alone. Let me say right up front that, like children, I have never seen angels with wings. They did not fly around or descend from the heavens. They simply arrived. To my vision, they appear in the form of tall, slender humans, all possessing an almost identical beauty, which is delicate of feature, youthful, and androgynous. But here the resemblance to humans stops. They seem to have neither substance nor real color. They appear instead to be composed of a fluid luminosity, their features traced out in a living ink of shimmering, deep, liquid gold. Their brilliance and the streaming, pulsating mobility of their lines somewhat confuse visibility. The many trajectories of light radiating in different directions from their heads, for instance, form configurations that look something like crowns. Similarly, they appear to be wearing the conventional long flowing robes, an observation that leads me to suspect that my own projections play a part in their outward appearance.

Despite their unceasing vibration and flow, they give the impression of intense stillness. In my experience, they exhibit neither the joyousness we associate with angels today nor the fiery anger of biblical accounts, but rather a steady, composed solemnity that could be read as emotionless compassion. Although angels have been traditionally regarded as messengers between God and mortals, I have never once picked up a pronouncement or message from them, let alone a thought. To me at least, they are silent.

I have seen them most often arriving in pairs. Two might take their place at either side of the head of the dying person and the other pair at either side of the feet. Once, I watched amazed as one of them leaned down and lifted the etheric body of a person out of the dying physical body. And as unlikely as it may seem, three tiny ones, no more than nine inches high, appeared around my cat Twyla a few hours before she died, identical to the others but for size.

When these glorious beings arrive, death is not necessarily immediate. Just recently, my friend Timothy called me in a high state of excitement two days before his sister's death to tell me he saw four angels around her. It was quite gratifying that his descriptions of these beings exactly matched my own. He did not see them stay for the actual moment of her crossing over. The presence of angels seems to be preparatory to the transition. I have the strong impression that they create and hold a sacred space, a kind of safety zone through which the dying make their final passage. From my perspective, they work with grave concentration, as though the individual, animal or human, is the most important on the planet.

Discarnate Friends and Relatives

For the most part, deathbed visions involve deceased friends and relatives (not always from this life). They come to assist the transition, bring comfort, and help resolve life issues. Many come to take the dying away, as some close to death have stated outright, which is further evidenced by the frequency with which death ensues shortly after.[18] It is not unusual to hear the dying say things like "Yes, dear, I'm coming" or "I'm coming, just give me a few seconds" and die right afterward. Occasionally, however, visitors arrive to tell them that the time has not yet come, in which case the physical condition inexplicably improves.

Most hospice personnel are by now aware of unseen visitors. Dianne Arcangel, a seasoned hospice worker and researcher, states that she has never sat with a dying patient who was not in the presence of an apparition.[19] How does she know? Sometimes, of course, the patient simply tells us, if they can. Others may call out the name of the person appearing or speak directly to the unseen visitor. When there are no verbal cues, behavior and body language, such as a radiant face or staring at a fixed point near the ceiling, often indicate that the phenomenon is taking place. Callanan and Kelley describe patients smiling at something in space, waving, reaching their hands out, or opening their arms, nodding as if in answer to something heard, trying to speak with someone, even attempting to get out of bed.[20]

And finally, some people know when the dying see the departed because they see them themselves, as I do. In fact, nurses are particularly adept at this.[21] If you're not, the worst response is to try to invalidate the experience of the dying. For them, their visitors are ultrareal and accepted without question. And they are real, after all.

In one case, Ralph began having visions of his childhood friend Steve a few weeks before he passed.[22] As children they had spent many happy summers swimming together, but as adults, one living in Boston and the other in Ohio, contact had dwindled to Christmas cards. Both men were young. Ralph's wife considered the visions as a symptom of confusion, as most people do. Moments before he died, he sat up and cried out, "Oh look, it's Steve! He's come to take me swimming." Soon after, the young widow wrote to Steve to inform him about her husband's death from cancer. But Steve had already died a few weeks previously from complications arising from a car accident. He was not yet thirty. I have picked this case from the host of others because of the youth of the people involved. Ralph had indeed seen someone from the other side, even though he had no reason to think that Steve had already died.

What fascinates me is how the dead know the exact circumstances of the dying. They also seem to know just what to do to open minds and hearts for what is to come. Steve's promise to take Ralph swimming, for example, was just what Ralph needed to hear to go happily forward and make that plunge into another realm. In some instances the dying are in unbearable pain and cry out to the deceased for help. When that person comes, the pain seems to vanish, and the dying person sinks into a peaceful death.

What a service the dead perform! The literature is full of them arriving with secondary agendas of healing and reconciliation. The return of a dead child, for instance, is invariably an enormous healing for a dying parent. There is even an account of four murdered boys coming to their killer as he lay on his deathbed, expressly to forgive him and lead him to self-forgiveness before his demise.[23]

Previews of the Afterworld

Although visions of the afterworld are statistically second in frequency to apparitions of the dead, they are probably more common than we realize. The outward signs of seeing the dead are often clear, because we can watch interaction taking place. Since the dying don't interact with otherworldly environments, visual and verbal cues are normally missing. When descriptions are spoken, they are usually brief.[24] A person might mention seeing a light or utter something like "It's so beautiful," not to forget Steve Jobs's "Oh, wow! Oh, wow! Oh, wow!" Such exclamations are often the final words. It's as though the vista of the world to come suddenly opens before their eyes, inviting them to enter.

Some people have visions while they are still responsive enough to fully describe them. Near-death experiencers have them too. You may recall, however, that a small percentage of near-death experiencers find themselves in unpleasant if not hellish environments. If the dying have frightening or hellish visions I have not yet heard of them. A third source for descriptions of the afterlife is the dead themselves.

People struggle to articulate what they see — the staggering beauty, the extraterrestrial light, brilliant foliage of preternatural vibrancy, huge flowers of unimaginable exquisiteness. A loving high-charged energy emanates from the grass, the trees, the flowers, and the sky. Others see grand cityscapes of glittering crystal or skyscapes filled with rainbows. For still others what unfolds before them is an inner space that, like deep space, is full of the rushing movement of stars and galaxies.

THE TIMING OF DEATH

The dying can and do control the day, hour, and even minute of passing, if that control serves an aim. Of course, such fine-tuning is not always possible. But when it is, it shows again that the dying are not passive victims but are actively orchestrating a complex set of events that works in more than one reality.

The dying often take specific dates into consideration, planning to die after a family holiday, an anniversary, a birthday, or any particular time of personal significance. Stories abound about someone spending one last Christmas with the family or waiting for an upcoming birthday before leaving. I remember reading one instance in which a child died from leukemia the day after Mother's Day.[25] Delays of this sort normally carry a double intention: first, to participate one last time in a ritual of familial reunion and goodwill and, second, to avoid darkening that special day for everyone else. Delay occurs most of all because reconciliation is not yet fulfilled. Since fulfilling it nearly always involves a significant other, the dying usually wait until that person is present or can at least be reached.

Dying sooner than expected is not as easy to recognize as dying later than expected. Nor is the earlier departure usually as easy to accept psychologically. My friend Barbara died sooner than expected from lung cancer, and her timing was superb. Barbara lived in Germany. Her son was visiting from the States, full of apprehension about having to go back before she passed. Three days before he was scheduled to go, she slipped away, more than six weeks before her physician's estimate. As a result, she spared her son anguish and gave him and her husband enough time to mourn together and arrange her funeral.

Another mother with lung cancer demonstrates the more usual delay. In this instance the woman was waiting for her son to return from Amsterdam. In the meantime, her lungs had collapsed, and she was no longer able to breathe. She prayed for help and suddenly saw a giant hand come down and lift her up. "The hand kept pushing my back up and then letting it go back down again until I started breathing on my own." She remained stabilized long enough to be with her son.[26] Like anyone preparing for a faraway journey, the dying have a natural wish for a meaningful good-bye. They also know that if their loved ones arrive too late, it will cause distress, if not guilt.

The "right circumstances" in which to die generally require the presence of the immediate family. The dying may also wait for someone to arrive who can help loved ones deal with grief and the many difficult tasks ahead. On the other hand, they may wait until someone leaves, as my father did for his toddler granddaughter. Children often send their parents away to spare them grief and the pain of witnessing the last moments.[27] Some even insist on dying in a hospital or hospice to alleviate their parents' burdens.[28] Since children know that their deaths will break their parents' hearts, they have to find the strength to go against the wishes of their mothers and fathers for recovery. With parents out of the way, the conflict is a little easier to bear.

Regardless of age or condition, the dying are usually quite conscious that they are causing distress and may either die more quickly to spare their loved ones more suffering or delay death to give them time to adjust. Most need to know that their closest and dearest support their passing, and some may need to hear verbal permission to die. If someone around you seems to be delaying death for no identifiable reason, search yourself for attitudes and fears that might be holding the person back. They may need to know that you are willing to let them go. In one case, a man waited until his sister ordered him to die![29]

Unfortunately, I know of some cases when the timing was engineered with less than the best intentions. One concerns a man of ninety-six. With his wife of more than forty years standing next to him, he lay in the arms of his young nurse, looked up into her face smiling, and said quite clearly to the nurse that he had hoped to die in her arms. Without even a glance at his wife, he then closed his eyes and left. This deliberate act of spite was the outcome of a long, dysfunctional marital relationship that neither spouse had made the least attempt to resolve. The second situation has more to do with unconscious beliefs. A woman who felt victimized by neglect knew that her favorite son was on a plane to see her. She died totally alone an hour before he arrived. This was not to spare her son, who is a physician specializing in AIDS and used to death, but a final gesture made in line with old beliefs that her children didn't love her.

THE FINAL PUSH

There is a phenomenon I call the final push. It occurs when people are too weak or, alternatively, too healthy to get out of their bodies and need some sort of stimulus. It might come in the form of mustering a last strength, a surge noticed by medical staff as a spontaneous improvement in vital signs. Without warning, a person might actually get out of bed for the first time in weeks and then fall, to the terror of everyone around. Although he or she may be trying to reach someone we don't normally see, the act itself serves as a final push to passing over.[30]

Mary Ellen, whom we will meet again later, was dying from breast cancer, which had spread into her bones, liver, and brain. She was only thirty-three and otherwise healthy, so death was slow in coming. While I was visiting her in the hospital, she told me quite vehemently that the one thing she would no longer endure was getting "sticked" for blood samples, an everyday occurrence. The next morning, when the blood technician came to take a sample, as soon as that needle poked her skin, she died. I wonder if some people in comas and on mechanical life support continue to live merely because the resources for the final push and the greater process of acceleration are not there.

The final push might also bring on a momentary return to consciousness, as it did for my cousin's wife. There is one remarkable story of a man with Alzheimer's who was unable to speak and had come close to being comatose over the course of ten years.[31] One day when his two sons were with him, his skin color suddenly turned ashen, and he slumped forward in his chair. The one son told the other to call 911. Suddenly, the father spoke after a decade of silence: "Don't call 911, son. Tell your mother I love her. Tell her that I am all right." And he died. The autopsy showed that his brain had been destroyed by the disease.

⍣

We as a society are just beginning to acknowledge the wondrous positive sides of dying. If we were to stand back and carefully watch the process, we would be stunned by the variety of ways passing is accomplished, the sheer creativity of it. We would be dumbfounded by how the dying know their way, how the body works with the psyche to resolve life issues and catapult the soul out of matter. The dying themselves would be more attuned to the deeper levels of the dying process, more prepared for the miraculous, more at ease. Dying opens up the greater dimensions of the self. It is the healthiest thing we can do when going forward in the body is no longer viable or rewarding. It is healthy for our psyches and for the planet. We simply wouldn't be alive without it.

CHAPTER ELEVEN

Going through the Threshold
and the Period of Adjustment

When someone is in that liminal place between life and death, a palpable feeling of sacredness often surrounds the deathbed. We are struck by the preciousness of life, its fragility, its transience, its beauty, and by the grandeur of the moment. Time dilates, so every moment grows longer, larger, and richer in meaning. In this expansion, realities converge, circling round and round into the past, into alternative realities (*if only we had found that cancer sooner, maybe...*) and into the world beyond. In a way, we are all there, gathered around the threshold. Although only one of us will go through, the expanded reality reaches out from the other side to touch us all. We watch as the dying grow ever more still, lambently poised between this world and the next, until it becomes difficult to know which one they are in. Finally, they let go and gently lift off. Once they get through the threshold, the real adventure begins.

GOING THROUGH THE THRESHOLD

Leaving the Body

Liftoff — leaving the body — is of course the great turning point. It is in itself a breathtaking achievement worthy of serious study, especially for researchers in the relatively new field of quantum biology. For now, we can explore it only from more modest perspectives: from the position of an onlooker watching clairvoyantly and from the position of the dying person who is in the act. The inner experience of leaving the body is fortunately well attested from near-death and out-of-body reports and, to a lesser extent, from past-life therapy records and after-death communication research. From all these sources, the accounts are individual and personal. Fortunately, there has been no attempt in the literature to force these experiences into preexistent spiritual frames. By contrast, the outsider's view is poorly attested. What few descriptions we have are drawn almost entirely from esoteric philosophies of the nineteenth century. I have therefore drawn on my own experiences of watching the dying for real eyewitness accounts.

The View from the Outside

Before breathing stops, I make it a practice to shift focus and concentrate on what is going on in those barely perceptible spaces adjacent to the body. It is there that one can best see a person leaving our world. My hope is that more and more of you will learn to watch this process and its aftermath, even in the midst of high emotion, since passing is without a doubt the most dazzling event of a lifetime outside of its counterpart, birth. Again, the experience of each is unique, and my attempts to make generalizations do not do justice to the brilliant creativity on display.

From my standpoint, the energy body or ethereal body simply rises out of the physical one, usually somewhere from the region of the head. A person most often goes from there into a space filled with a creamy or golden living light. At other times, however, leaving the body is slower and looks more like a gentle floating upward through layers of emotion-laden atmospheres, each effervescent with a color that loosely represents a psychological tone or state, like ascendance through various layers of water, some cooler and darker, others warmer and lighter as a person goes slightly upward.

This small step out of the damaged shell, out of the fragile dream called life, is not always accomplished without a struggle. Michael died while intensive-care personnel were trying to jump-start his heart. When he was leaving his body, the first levels he rose through were especially vivid, red streaked with purples and smoky blacks. As I look back on it now, these must have been the levels of his immediate psychological and physical state, colored by the atmosphere of alarm in the intensive-care unit. Above that was a softer stratum of bright yellows, and beyond that were cloudlike whites and grays. He rose up, reaching the yellow zones, only to sink down again into the red whenever the paddles were applied to his chest. The phenomenon, which I saw so clearly with him, also reflected the red alert of the people around him. Trying to come to a decision whether to live or die, he wavered back and forth between returning to his body and leaving it altogether, alternating quickly from full awareness, lifting up and looking down at his body in surprise, to what seemed from the outside like falling asleep. Once he had moved through the denser strata and entered the lighter ones, he seemed to drift momentarily sideways in a kind of billowing peace. His decision was made.

Occasionally, I and others have seen a grayish or silvery mist enveloping the dying in their last hours, especially those who are unconscious or heavily medicated. This atmospheric phenomenon feels like a thick blanket of tender security, inviting the more vulnerable to slowly and safely release into it. More rarely a dead person takes the place of the mist and simply shows up to lift a person's ethereal body out. And finally, I have often had the privilege of watching the dead catch people or animals in their arms as soon as they broke out of the body, just as with a delivery!

There are many exceptions, however. I will never forget someone who died in the middle of a choking fit. With one last heaving effort to get air, she shot upward out of her head in a great whooshing movement, like riding upward on the water spout of a whale. As she came out, she turned around and looked at me with the most astonished expression on her face. A few seconds later, she was met by her closest friend.

The Inside Experience

For the interior experience of leaving the body, the literature on out-of-body experiences and especially near-death experiences affords thousands of accounts that are too various to be summarized here. Nevertheless, I do want to mention a few points. First, near-death experiencers frequently report emerging from the head region and going upward, which corresponds to what I usually see. When they come out and look down on their own bodies, they do so with an unusual degree of emotional detachment.

We past-life therapists encounter this remoteness all the time. Past-life deaths that come up in therapy sessions are nearly always traumatic. The objective then is to get a patient to mentally reenter the body to work through the trauma. Once they have reexperienced death and leaving the body, they turn around and look down on it, typically with compassion, if not pity, but as though the body and the life it lived belonged to someone else. No matter how gruesome the past-life death may have been, immediate relief from fear and suffering and a feeling of floating into a luscious peace are the norm.

Once near-death experiencers are out of the body, they still have a sense of having a body, which is now free of pain and disabilities. Their descriptions of their energy bodies can range anywhere from being a point of consciousness to a colored auralike field, a cloudlike form, or a form shaped similarly to the one they just left but much less dense. These forms have a way of never staying still. A man named Craig said he could still feel the boundaries of his being even when he expanded to what seemed like miles, only to contract again to his former size, which he described as "a two- or three-foot egg-shaped mass of energy."[1] He also added that he never felt better in his life. Interestingly, children often tell us that they are adults when out of the body but are at a loss to explain how they know this.[2]

In the early stages of this experience, people may try to get the attention of someone in the room, either by speaking or touching, which, with few exceptions, goes unnoticed. Raymond Moody tells of a remarkable case in which a woman already out of her body tried to stop him from resuscitating her. She related afterward that when she realized he couldn't hear her, she tried to grab his arm, but her hand passed right through him. She felt something like an electric current running through a substance that had the consistency of "very rarefied gelatin."[3] I have frequently witnessed the newly dead try to get the attention of the living, mostly in situations in which their demise was abrupt or unexpected. In the out-of-body state of the dead and the "near dead," locomotion is accomplished by an act of will. People move freely through walls and ceilings and hover over rooftops. They can travel anywhere simply by putting their attention on a destination and are known to visit people and places sometimes out of pure curiosity. You've already heard a few after-death reports from the scads on record of people fresh out of the body calling in on friends and relatives to let them know they have passed. Sight becomes panoramic, as you know, capable of perceiving in all directions at once, and observations are razor sharp.[4] Sometimes the lingering presence of the dead is felt unintentionally. In an interview of ninety emergency service workers (police officers, firefighters, and emergency medical personnel), 17 percent reported feeling the presence of the dead victims they were attending as well as having contact with them.[5] As in past-life recall and NDEs, the newly deceased frequently stay around to watch the scenes of their own deaths.

The event of getting out of the body is met with joy, sometimes mixed with gravity, usually relief, and, 99.9 percent of the time, awe and wonder. That tiny slip of perspective from inside matter to outside it, that slight movement, no greater than a flick of the wrist or a snap of the fingers, can instantly remove us from the person we were just moments before.

Changing Gears: The Tunnel and Other Phenomena

From my position, out-of-body people who are at least a bit conscious and have no intention of lingering vanish for a second or two before reappearing again in another scene. They seem to shift to an entirely different psychological environment, one that agrees point by point with the exquisite deathbed visions of the afterlife. Alternatively, those who are too sedated or deep in coma and cannot go on by themselves might remain in the secure mist mentioned above or are looked after by others until they come to, sometimes in hospital-like settings. However, I have seen people in artificially induced comas already active and alert on the other side, although their bodies had not yet died. In more typical situations, that instant of vanishing before reappearing in a different environment is a time when rapid shifts are taking place. And it may well correspond to the experience in which near-death survivors feel pulled through a tunnel. I have only rarely witnessed the dead going through tunnels, and few have ever mentioned a tunnel experience to the living. A substantial number of near-death experiencers have never encountered them either.[6] Some have instead reported going up a set of stairs, over a bridge, over a river on a boat, through doorways, or into valleys, fogs, or black spaces with a light at the farthest reaches. There is sometimes a swooshing or humming sound or a sense of vibration that accompanies what is perceived as movement.[7] Others had no impressions of going anywhere.

I view these sensations of passage as spatial interpretations of a transition from one frequency to a much faster frequency. After all, in inner space you don't actually go anywhere, because there is no real distance to cross. This hypothesis is based in part on my own trance experiences in which I suddenly felt as though I were hurtling through space. Although I did not see "space," I could feel the skin on my face being pulled back and flapping as it does when you free-fall from a plane before the parachute opens. The analogy becomes more interesting when considering that at those speeds during free fall from a plane, the earth and its horizon take on a tube or tunnellike appearance.

Tunnel and spiraling experiences occur to people in altered states, in out-of-body trips, and in dreams, where they sometimes meet the dead.[8] In one account, a near-death experiencer found himself in a clockwise spinning vortex, which comes quite close to describing what I have felt.[9] Surely making a jump from one dimension to another requires some kind of adjustment in consciousness, an adjustment that might well be felt like speed or motion.

The Helpers

No matter what stage you are in during death, helpers are standing by right on the other side. They are usually from the immediate family, a departed spouse, parent, grandparent, or sibling. Sometimes, however, who shows up might surprise you. Occasionally you might see someone who is still alive. Or you might be greeted by a person you knew from another life. Pets are common members of the welcome committee, to the absolute delight of their newly dead owners. My cousin Cassandra was met first by her beloved dogs, to her total joy and relief. The dogs were, in turn, wildly happy to have her back.

Then there are times when someone a person would logically expect to come is not there. These absences always occur for good reasons, which may not be discoverable right away. I know of one woman, for instance, who was puzzled because her husband was not there to welcome her, although her mother and her estranged father were. She was soon to realize why. Because her marriage of more than a half a century was not based on a deep and abiding union but on practicality and duty, the emotional ties were just not there.

Sometimes the newly dead will sense the presence of family and friends only as a supportive psychological ambience, allowing more compelling experiences to safely dominate their attention. Unless someone is hallucinating a situation that stimulates feelings of loneliness or is deliberately reviewing episodes of loneliness in the life just exited, loneliness is simply not part of the afterlife picture. Given this steadily purring background of warmth, some feel no need to pause and acknowledge specific greeters but want to charge on to explore the new universe before them. Still others may be immediately engulfed by the Presence.

Specialists

Many types of helpers should be characterized as nonhuman or superhuman, angels being just one type. Some of these seem to be specialized in helping people adjust after death. They help resolve conflicting spiritual beliefs, ease the tortured conscience, and facilitate the release of feelings of unworthiness. In order to best do that, superhuman entities as well as human death workers, *alive or dead*, occasionally take on the guise of a figure important to the belief system of the newly deceased. These figures are often the prophets, saints, and paraphysical beings of a person's personal religion, although once in a while, only a specific historical or mythical figure can get the job done. Alone or with others, the helpers might act out a drama designed to produce a specific cathartic effect. Extreme cases may even involve re-creations of archetypal hells where a person is able to confront the ugliest self-condemnation in graphic terms, much the way nightmares work. The objective in all cases is to usher that person toward cathartic revelation, inner resolution, and liberation.

The Being of Light

Then there is the being of light, a personage of incalculable magnitude to many near-death experiencers. Surveys show that the percentage of survivors who have actually encountered this being range from as low as 16 percent to more than half.[10] Given that the permanently dead do not speak of this splendid entity, I have to conclude that it mostly comes to assist people in the decision-making process of whether to stay or return to their bodies. Logically, however, some people in this process must decide to stay, in which case a few from this group are likely to have met this figure. The being emanates such indescribable love and compassion, often with a good deal of humor, that some people come back with the conviction that they have met God or Jesus. This is understandable, considering the overwhelming power of the experience. But if you have been dipping into otherworldly dimensions for any length of time, you begin to realize that they are populated with no end of the most divinely endowed entities.

There is little doubt that the being of light represents a distinct personality, possessing an intimate knowledge of human nature. I would speculate that many such beings exist. I also suspect that they manifest in different forms in order to meet an individual's psychological needs and preconceptions, and indeed, descriptions vary.

I would further argue that the beings of light are human oversouls. As such they would contain all possible human experience within them. My deepest instinct is that they personify the magnificent potential of the human soul — in other words, what you already are in the future. I have come across some support for this from Mellen-Thomas Benedict.[11] This is the same man we met in chapter 9, whose brain tumor disappeared after an NDE in 1982. In the midst of the experience, he had the presence of mind to say to the being, "I think I understand what you are but I really want to know what you *really* are." At that point the being showed itself as a "matrix" or "mandala of human souls." Benedict understood, and probably quite rightly, that the mandala was a symbolic representation of what he calls "the higher self," which I would identify with the oversoul. If this is so, if it is true that we are already beings of light in some future state, then there can be no greater incentive for the human spirit to expand.

The Life Review

A life review can occur at any time, especially when a person's life is perceived to be at risk or is in great transition. Because the dying often have life reviews or at least superintensified reflection on the past, life reviews should be considered as part of nearing-death awareness. Some people have even described being conducted through their pasts by deceased relatives or angelic beings. For the dying and the aged in general, the review could take the form of time looping, in which immersion in the past can be so total that immediate physical surroundings are no longer acknowledged.

Given the importance of life reviews, I wonder why I have not so far heard a word about them from the dead themselves. Not so long ago, I had several strong, clear, and extensive communications with a man shortly after he had died from drowning. Although he related to me and his wife point by point what he had experienced — what he was thinking about and what he was looking at when he fell into the water, the momentary panic, and then the fascination — the life review, which is strongly associated with drowning, was not part of it. Here again I sense a discrepancy between permanent death and near-death experiences. The impossibly concentrated life review of near-death survivors, including its futuristic aspects, seems to help people decide what kind of spiritual ethics and aims they will follow on return. It's an event of indescribable momentum that compels them to experiential dead honesty.[12] On the other hand, it might be safe to assume that some people who start out in an NDE and go through a life review will decide not to return. A compressed review is not necessary for those not returning, since a great majority of them will end up devoting a big slice of their afterlives to examining their pasts anyway at a more leisurely pace. Unfortunately, a small minority of the newly dead seem to lack any insight about their earthly past, remaining bewildered or stuck in old patterns. Clearly these few at least have not had life reviews, despite common claims in near-death literature that all people have them after death.

THE PERIOD OF ADJUSTMENT

For those who are ready to cross over for good, the focus is more on adjusting to the other side. Trying to describe what people do in the afterlife is about as easy as trying to describe what people do on earth. Obviously comprehensive coverage is impossible, and generalizations that are inevitably distorting are the rule rather than the exception. Yet the alternative is no discussion at all. All I can offer is what I and other researchers have so far uncovered with regard to the dead of the modern West.

Most people seem to take about three days before they are oriented enough to move on. More often than not, they "get it" in one revelatory flash sometime during this period and jubilantly start trying out their unbounded capabilities. Their expanded cognitive abilities take in events unfurling in more than four dimensions. For some this happens immediately after death. Others may go through a gradual process of dawning recognition after the commotion of dying has settled down. A majority go to some idyllic place directly after changing gears, whereas a minority go to a kind of temporary holding place. Still others linger close to this plane mostly to pay reassuring visits to loved ones.

The "Vacation"

In general, people who die from a long-standing medical condition or a traumatic event or were heavily medicated require a break for recovery, what I think of as a vacation. Serious infirmities were all too often the focal points of their lives, and absorption of such intensity may not necessarily dissipate right off. Breathing space may be needed to separate from the imprints of physical infirmity, to clear the mental body from drug effects and sometimes the habits of relentless anguish and fear. Full recuperation is usually rapid, taking place in a deep feeling of safety and a benign, enveloping warmth in which the weighty cares of physical life dissolve.

What a delight to hear their exuberant reports about their return to youthful health and the discovery of newfound freedoms. Unlimited mobility is usually at the top of the list. "Look! I can walk again!" shouted an aunt of mine who had spent the last nine years of her life in a wheelchair. I did look. She was not just walking; she was whizzing between skipping and flying. My artist friend Gabriella, who was bedridden from double breast cancer for two years, was skating along at her own funeral three days after her death, using the blades to skate colors in the sky! This childlike spirit of playfulness is more integral to spiritual expansion than any other mind-set. As far as I know, no one has ever seen the dead adopting saintly or sanctimonious postures.

Normally, by the time of their funerals, the deceased are already operating from a place of greater vision. Yet I have learned not to expect enlightenment, however slight, from everyone. Sometimes lifelong patterns mulishly persist. I remember watching with some amusement a tetchy nonagenarian angrily buzzing around his own funeral service, making sure everyone was doing a proper job. Death had not immediately erased his old habits of control and scornful mistrust, although at some points during the service, he looked quite pleased, especially with the way participants were ranked in order of importance in the church pews.

With great frequency, people — and animals — tumble into idyllic environments for full recuperation. No matter where they go, it will feel like home sweet home. Although landscapes of unearthly beauty are quite common, some may instead remove to a thought construction of a place that was significant in the past. My father, who was greeted by his brother and mother, went to a house by the ocean where the family had spent summer vacations when he was a little boy. Michael went fishing in a large, tranquil lake. He told me he occasionally took a few of his living friends along. They in turn related superreal dreams of lake fishing with Michael in a boat. My brother-in-law Robert was one of those who went on without the assistance of helpers, although he had had a powerful deathbed vision of his mother a month before he passed. From a full year of meditation before his death, he was quite comfortable maneuvering out of body. He went over very quickly and in his characteristic sunny, understated way simply said, "I made it. That wasn't so bad!" Robert emerged into a spacious seascape shimmering with pearly whites and bisques, sea greens and aqua blues, colors that for him signified peace and freedom. It was the sea that had been his source of spiritual renewal. A few days later, he was elatedly skipping along with the boat that carried his ashes. After this respite of a few weeks, he went to work on the analysis of the life he had just left and, being an architect heart and soul, worked a great deal out on a drafting board. It was then that he reunited with his mother.

Those whose deaths were traumatizing, emotionally debilitating, or too sudden for resolving life issues gravitate to custom-made adjustment zones. There they assimilate the past, as a rule, through playful creativity and interaction. After Michael had had enough of fishing, he built a restaurant where people gathered to talk through personal issues. In life he was a restaurateur. Art, who was murdered, appeared to his wife, Pauline, in a dream seven months after his death.[13] He showed her a little two-room house where he was staying until moving to what he called a halfway house, where he would recover from the shock of his death. As part of the healing process, he was working with flowers the size of dinner plates. For most who suffered long-term illnesses, natural environments are the ideal healing agents, although a few will create a cheery hospital setting in which they feel cared for and secure.

Then there are the people with energy to spare who explode into inner space for a thrilling cosmic ride. They seem to soar out of this existence without looking back, just as some hurtle down the birth canal to get in. It's just possible that the inner-space journey is a way of grappling with an unimaginably rapid expansion of consciousness. The relief of getting out of a body and perhaps a life that was as confining as an outgrown carapace can feel explosive and unstoppable.

Merging with the Presence

I have seen others release into a blessed fluidlike ambience. When a priest I knew gently rose out of his body, a soft light diffused through him and around him, turning him golden. He emerged directly into the Presence, no passing through intermediary emotional atmospheres, no entering gardens, no meeting helpers, nothing but this fusion with luminosity. He understood it as the Holy Spirit. A sense of utter peace and release into all-engulfing love was apparent in his attitude. This was what he had spent his entire life preparing for. What he then recognized, however, was that we are always merged with the Divine, effortlessly, whether we work for it or not. The Divine is our natural habitat. The poignant beauty of his passing continued to inspire me for weeks afterward.

The Holding Zone

What I am here calling a holding zone is not really a place but a projection of a suspended mental state in which a person is focused no longer completely in physical reality and not yet in the reality of the afterlife. This betwixt-and-between state looks to me like an area of white to golden luminescence. Frequently, there is an illusion of a border or barrier at its edge, again, a spatial representation of an inner state. Crossing the barrier is tantamount to a full change of focus in the afterworld lying beyond. Near-death experiencers also encounter barriers, manifested as a flowerbed bordering a garden, say, or sensed as a difference in atmospheres, like a curtain of rain seen against a cloudy sky. They instinctively know that if they cross it they will not return to physical life. Holding zones differ from other conditions in several ways. The people in them keep their attention on our side of the veil, whereas those in adjustment phases are already fully engaged in their new lives.

The creative abilities that the great majority of deceased use to fashion their personal locales seem to be deactivated in holding zones. A person is instead suspended.

There are all kinds of reasons someone might stay in a holding zone before going on. A person driven by concerns for people left behind might pause there to stay within range of their physical and emotional circumstances. The parent of a young child is likely to take this path. For the most part, people hang back because they are unable to clear up major personal conflicts or unfinished business. I worked with a woman who was stuck there for six months in our terms because she was unable to release a seventy-year-old repressed memory of child-hood rape. When she did release it, a truly explosive event for her and for me, she was able to move on. Others are in holding zones because they are unable to accept their deaths. Material realists who were ada-mantly opposed to the idea of an afterlife can and do wind up there from sheer denial of survival, even insisting that they are still flesh and blood. Other people stay put because they need to tell their stories. The need is particularly compelling if the living are unaware of the person's pass-ing, such as in instances of disappearance, or if the deceased was mur-dered. Confusion plays a big role in nearly all holding-zone situations.

Occasionally the newly deceased will close themselves off in hold-ing zones, resisting help from the outside. They then remain in isolated suspension, unable to alleviate their confusion and accept their deaths. Some may simply take the next train back and reincarnate without any reflection on the life they just left. When they do, they later describe this in-between place as a blank period or a sleep time. Because they return without separating from their previous existences, their former identi-ties remain dominant in their new lives, at least in their youths. The lack of separation might also leave imprints on their bodies, such as birth defects or birthmarks, which are often residual indicators of a person's past-life physical condition at death.

Holding-zone states are important for us to be aware of, because the dead who find themselves there are the dead who need our help most.

Since they are not focused on the afterlife, they are more responsive to the living. For those who are in delusions, like Joe in chapter 7, it usually takes a mediator from among the living to instigate release. For this reason, I want to walk you through a fairly typical holding-zone situation, should you one day be in the position of mediator.

The young and beautiful Mary Ellen, mentioned in the previous chapter, was in a holding zone because she was not prepared to accept her death. In life, she belonged to a large New Age spiritual community with a strong healing orientation. She was a wife and mother of two small boys. When she was in advanced stages of breast cancer, she came to my then husband, Ron, and me for help. Ron was also part of this group. We were joined by Janet, another member and a registered nurse, who, like Mary Ellen, was somewhere between Catholic and New Age. Encouraged by the cult's expectation of a miracle, Mary Ellen went along with the denial of her own terminal illness. Now I am certainly not rejecting the possibility of miracles, but in Mary Ellen's case she used this expectation to avoid facing the probability of death. Ron and I brought her to our apartment for a few days, where she rested with our sixteen-year-old cat, Squeekie. The cat probably did more than any of us to restore a small measure of peace to a very sick and confused woman.

Neither Ron nor I had the courage to talk to her directly about death. We were both young and inexperienced and, like everybody else, hoped for a miracle. Her illness proceeded predictably. Strangely enough, as she developed a new symptom, it simultaneously appeared in the cat. Eventually Mary Ellen was hospitalized.

Ron, Janet, and I arrived at the hospital a half hour after Mary Ellen had passed away. Meanwhile Squeekie had also just died. From an outsider's point of view, Mary Ellen had resolved what she needed to resolve before her death. When the three of us got back to the apartment, we sat down on the floor to meditate and send her "light." Soon enough that prickling at the back of the neck (and our dog barking furiously at a point over our heads) told us she was in the room. The mood we were picking up was anything but one of joy and peace. We looked at each other sheepishly with that "Uh-oh, here it comes" expression on our faces. Then it started. All three of us instinctively ducked the shadow blows she rained on our heads. At last Mary Ellen was angry. She was not exactly screaming. It was more of a whine: "You didn't tell me this was going to happen" — words that make me cringe to this day.

She specifically accused Janet of lying to her for promising that the Virgin Mary would greet her on the other side, when in fact *no one* was there. Janet admitted red-faced that she had indeed told Mary Ellen that the day before she died. As Janet apologized toward the space just under the living-room ceiling, I remember, I formulated a rule that I have kept ever since: never, ever tell someone who is dying what to expect, unless you have some very explicit and exact foreknowledge that pertains specifically to that person and only that person. Do not promise that a mother or a husband or some other close relative will be there, or Christ, or angels, or anything else we have been taught to expect. Instead, offer them a wide range of possibilities drawn from *personal accounts* rather than religious and spiritual traditions. People passing over have enough to deal with without the added conflict caused by trumped-up expectations.

Mary Ellen told us she had not intended this. She was not prepared to *really* die. No one told her the truth. What about her little boys? What was going to happen to them without her? There was a pause of a few seconds in her harangue as she turned her attention to my stomach. I controlled the reaction to close my legs. I knew what she was thinking, that perhaps if I got pregnant, she could come back as my daughter. Images of her growing up as my daughter flashed through all of our minds. Mary Ellen as a schoolgirl, her sons nearly ready for college. We all watched as she fast-forwarded through this probable future to test its viability. It did not take her long to realize how unworkable such a scheme would be. She then sped off.

I ached with guilt for not having had the guts to be straight with her while she was still alive. There is a fine line between accepting death and thwarting the possibility of a miraculous recovery, a line that I did not help Mary Ellen to walk. Yes, we were all partly to blame, but she knew perfectly well that breast cancer metastasized in the bones and brain was the final stage. Nevertheless, this woman was dear to me. Not just because of her fragile beauty, her childlike helplessness, and her tender heart. She was dear to me also because she was the first person I deliberately attempted to stay with after death. She lingered with me for three days. Much of that time I lay on my bed in a slight trance. We talked telepathically. About life. About death. I tried reasoning with her in order to get her to accept her new circumstances and move on. Although reasoning often works, it was apparently not what she needed. On the third day, she turned up carrying my cat Squeekie in her arms. This was so unexpected and so much in line with my own needs that I began to think I was making it all up. Yet even more unexpected was her rationale for presenting the cat to me. She said, "Look! I can't be dead. Squeekie is here." When I told her Squeekie had also died, she looked crestfallen. Her last defense having failed, she made her first step toward acceptance.

Suddenly a man appeared softly behind her, wearing a simple tunic. He looked to be about forty, tall and well built, light brown hair in a bowl cut, a manly jaw and handsome face that communicated his strength of character. Mary Ellen did not seem to be aware of him, resolutely facing my world rather than his. The man asked me quietly to tell her that he was a friend from another life. He had come to help. After I transmitted the message, Mary Ellen turned slightly toward him. The man reached out his hand, and she took it. I asked her to take Squeekie with her as far as she could, to which she nodded agreement. Carrying the cat and holding her friend's hand, she slowly and sadly walked away. The steady diet of unrealistic expectations was finally wearing off. Although I never saw her again, twenty years later a psychic told me that a "very happy spirit named Mary Ellen" wanted to thank me.

Suicides

The literature of near-death experiences includes a fair number of people who have come back after suicide attempts. Nearly always they report unpleasant if not nightmarish experiences. Those who committed suicide in order to join a deceased beloved never met that person. All had intense feelings of wrong for breaking one of the two greatest laws: not to kill others and not to kill oneself. You might remember that suicide victims who had NDEs never again attempted to take their own lives, whereas a high percentage of suicide survivors who did not have them tried it again.[14] The interviewees had acted out of a combination of uncontrollable despair and feelings of helplessness, an unresolved condition so strong that it is bound to cause unfavorable repercussions after death whether caused by suicide or not.

What happens after a successful suicide depends entirely on the state of mind a person was in at the time of death. The terminally ill who elect assisted suicide in order to sidestep a spiraling degradation of body and spirit are generally well primed for the consequences and have little trouble on the other side. A person who has chosen to give up his or her life to preserve that of another dies in the exalted awareness of the fundamental oneness of humanity, a great advantage to anyone in passing over. In many cultures, suicide was historically either an honorable act or a way to redress personal dishonor. Two famous examples are the Japanese tradition of hara-kiri to preserve honor and the suicides of elite Romans in order to protect their families and property from state punishment. In such instances, people who decide to die by their own hand are usually well prepared. Because they have social support and approval, there is no wading through the shame that act provokes in today's Western cultures. Nor is there fear of having committed a sin so insidious that proper burial rites are denied.

The after-death experiences of most of the suicide victims I have worked with reflect the emotional climate before and at the time of death. Nevertheless, there are substantial differences between "accidental" suicides by drug overdose and intentional suicides. Self-hatred is, of course, only one reason people end up annihilating themselves with drugs. Some people are born to live on the edge and accidentally die because their last adventure went too far. Nonetheless, they knew and accepted the risks they were taking. Others turn to chemically induced altered states believing they will discover wisdom in unknown realities.

One young woman I knew was traveling along a similar route, searching through the distant hazes of drugs and alcohol for her father, dead some fifteen years earlier. It was not the daughter who told me, but her father. He was anxious for his daughter to stop the binges, for he knew all too well that she could and would die in her attempt to find him. This man was particularly active and strong. He spoke insistently and at length, with such clarity I was able to type out what he was saying while he was saying it. Just before leaving, he told me he was going to visit his other daughters. And much to their amazement, he did. Largely because of his deep concern and high degree of participation, his troubled daughter has been drug- and alcohol-free for over ten years.

Drug-induced deaths often lead to angry self-blame, a feeling of being cheated, and sometimes shock. The worst result is when the drugged mental state segues into hallucination after death in which a person does not realize death has occurred. Cindy, an Australian with a history of alcohol abuse and suicide attempts, presents exactly this worst-case scenario. She died at the age of thirty-two from a combination of drugs and alcohol. Although I was not officially informed for nearly a week, my body found out the day she died. In a matter of hours, it blew up so that I felt like a poison-filled blowfish. Mentally, I was incapable of constructing a single clear thought and struggled for a full day against unnamable feelings of doom. Since Cindy was too muddled to send a telepathic message of her death in mental thought patterns, her body sent the message at a cellular level.

I met with Cindy in a series of chaotic dreams. She was still hallucinating and doggedly held on to the pretense that she was alive. Trying to explain to her what had happened was useless. Five years later, she came back. When I once again tried to get through to her that she was no longer corporal, her response was so surprising that to this day it is easy to recall: "Oh, I'm not dead. It's just that my mother keeps telling everybody that." I reminded her quite harshly that her mother was dead too, a full ten years by this time. Not wanting to hear this, she left in a huff.

The whole episode with Cindy is difficult for me to recount, because it offends my own cherished beliefs in the triumph of the human spirit after death. However, it has helped me to remember that what is five years to me may be only moments to the dead. Alternatively, I may have been picking up on just one level of Cindy, the level of her resistance, rather than her core levels. There is nothing particularly otherworldly about this possibility. Each of us operates on more than one psychological plane, some of which are more apparent than others. But when I really look squarely at who Cindy was in life, I see a woman not so very different from the one who visited me after death. If there was one word to describe her, it would be *obstinate*. She was also a loner, depressed, and resistant to help.

If people have an eternity to work out issues, why then should Cindy or anyone for that matter have to change immediately after death? Until she felt ready to go on, why should she not remain much the same as she was before? It seems to me now if she was unable to accept the conditions of life on earth, she would not be able to accept the conditions of life in the afterworld either. Yet I cannot help thinking that if she had died more consciously, her after-death experience would have been radically different.

Conscious suicide, in which people make a definite choice, tends to have different results. In fact, as soon as they discover themselves out of the body, communication can be strikingly clear and detailed, largely from raw need and high emotions, the two factors that make for the best telepathy. Because panic is the rule, communication can come at such a speed that you have to get these suicides to slow down. There is also a strong impulse to try to reverse the situation by immediately reincarnating, which we helpers need to prevent. Nevertheless, conscious suicides generally come to terms with the consequences of their acts rather quickly.

It took Jordi less than a week. Jordi was a handsome twenty-two-year-old, charming to the point of slickness, fun loving, and smart. On the eve of his college graduation, he threw himself in front of a train. Afterward even he was stunned by the brutality he had used against himself. He was only just beginning to put together what his reasons had been when I caught up with him. One of his goals was punishing his parents. Yet from his new standpoint, he saw himself differently, as a person independent of his family's drama. He realized that he had destroyed what could have been a terrific life and that he would probably never again be reborn with the same outstanding advantages.

Conscious Death

Certain people are well prepared to die and even look forward to it. Unlike most who spontaneously find themselves on the other side, in an idyllic scene or with deceased family members, people who die consciously have more control. They decide what they want and where they want to be. So it was with Caroline, a psychologist who died from cancer. Several weeks before her demise, she asked me to help her more fully embrace her own death. I met with her three times a week. One could not help but be inspired by her obvious state of transcendence, which spread an otherworldly luster on her face and bald head. As the time approached, she was moving more and more between planes of existence.

Although I was not present at her death, about an hour afterward I wanted to see if I could find her and help her if she needed it. Rather than staying home to do this, I went to Riverside Park. What I saw there astounded me. It was one of those precious times when phenomena appear so vividly they block out the common realities of day-to-day life. I stood at the top of the park next to a lofty elm tree, looking across at the Hudson River. Suddenly I felt something behind my eyes, as if someone had entered my head and was looking through them. Just as I realized it was Caroline, the sky exploded into action. In one corner it was raining. In another were a rainbow and a brilliant sun that, as I watched, began to set, although it was early afternoon. Gathering around the sun were lofty clouds in pinks, golds, and purples. And finally snow crystals glittered as they sifted down in the sunshine. All the beauty of earth's drama was present at once. I stood there with tears streaming down my face, hardly able to take it all in.

Just then I left my body, specifically out of the right side of my head. I found myself entering a squirrel's nest high up in the elm beside me. Once inside it, I saw it from the squirrel's point of view, overcome by the nest's coziness and warmth, the spicy, woody smell of its leafy lining, the sweet animal scent emanating from the furry baby squirrels that slept snuggled in the leaves. What Caroline wanted was to savor the very essence of earthly existence before she left it. Perhaps experiencing it through my physical body gave it a directness and an intensity that may not have been possible otherwise. Then again, perhaps it was her parting gift to me. When I returned to my body, Caroline shot out of my head and into the sky. The whole episode took only ten minutes, yet it remains to this day one of the most exuberant in my memory. This was a woman who did not just die consciously; she rode on the natural acceleration of her death with rapture.

PHENOMENA AROUND DEATH OCCURRING TO THE LIVING

So far, we have concentrated on what happens to the dying as they move through the final threshold. But a person's last act commonly affects those close to him or her in strange and profound ways. In this final section, I want to point out a few phenomena that are known to occur during and after a significant death. They are included here because they are either poorly recognized or not ordinarily covered in the traditional literature of bereavement.

Simultaneous Experience of Death

Simultaneous death experiences tend to occur between close relatives or friends and when one participant is not consciously aware of the other's imminent demise, the conditions we just encountered in the account of Cindy and me. The death experience is usually shared with someone who had some sort of custodial function with respect to the dying, as I had with Cindy. In effect, the dying person calls out for assistance through his or her sensory perception. Most information comes through via clairsentience and can be so exacting that the receiver takes on the symptoms or mimics the experience kinesthetically. Clairvoyance and clairaudience can also come into play.

Properly, simultaneous experience of death belongs under the rubric of rescue work, in which all of us participate to some degree. Although full clairsentience of a death appears to be somewhat rare, I would not hesitate to say that partial sharing of a dying person's emotional, psychological, or physical condition is common, even though it is seldom consciously identified. Animals also have simultaneous experiences, as Squeekie did with Mary Ellen, which often facilitate the animals' own deaths. To my knowledge, however, the clairsentient projection of symptoms onto humans never leads to fatality, because humans know deep down that the symptoms are not theirs.

On June 16, a woman had come home from her night shift at one in the morning when she suddenly was overcome by chest pains, weakness, and tears.[15] After she dropped to the floor, she began rocking back and forth and found herself repeatedly saying, "I am not ready. I can't die like this. Oh please, please, not like this…" This woman, like myself in similar situations, knew instinctively that the symptoms, thoughts, and feelings were not her own. Consequently, there was no fear, and she let the process take its course. A short time later, it all came to a stop. Drained, she went to bed. On the 17th, a concerned neighbor of this woman's mother broke into the mother's apartment thirty miles away to discover that she had died there alone. She was found sitting on the floor, dead from a heart attack. The coroner estimated the time of death between one and three, the morning of the 16th, the time her daughter had had her experience.

Even more remarkable is the story of Louisa Rhine, who awoke in

California at 4 AM from the sensation of blood pouring from her head. She found herself gasping and choking. She then heard her son's voice call, "Oh Mama, help me." Two days later she learned that her son, a soldier stationed in Germany, had died from a gunshot wound to the head at exactly the same time she had had this experience. Clearly, these women were psychically sharing the deaths of their loved ones. My reason for believing that sharing helps to lighten the load of the dying comes from experiences in which I spontaneously took on symptoms of people on the verge of death who then recovered. I know of others who have rescued people in critical distress the same way.

The Cord

A phenomenon that happens the moment a person becomes aware that a principal other has died has to do with what I call a cord.[16] For me, it occurred at the death of my father. While he was drifting out of his body, I felt an urgent tugging at my solar plexus, from which a cord composed of strands of energy was issuing. The tugging turned into an abrupt and clear snap, as if some unseen force had pulled it out. It then followed my father upward, like streams of billowing smoke, to disappear along with him into thin air. Once he was gone, I felt an aching emptiness in the same spot. I knew intuitively that the part of my father I carried within me had gone with him. This hollow area at the solar plexus was the locus of my deepest mourning. Not the emotional mourning, not the mental or spiritual mourning, but the most profound and intimate mourning of the body.

I have seen this stream since then emerge from others at the death of someone particularly close. Like an umbilical cord, it links one person to a primary other, normally a parent figure. Its function seems to have to do with one person's inner dependence on another for sheer corporal survival. This primal lifeline will attach to anyone suitable, regardless of the biological background, and can be transferred from one person to another. I am not the only one who has seen it. A man I knew was connected to his mother via this cord. The moment he found out about her death, it disconnected from her and shot out in streams from his solar plexus to attach itself to his wife, standing next to him. He and I both saw it happen. Not only did this instant redirection of the cord cause many marital problems, adding, as it does, new meaning to the psychoanalytic term *transference*; it also seemed to inhibit this man's capacity to truly mourn the loss of his mother's physical presence.

Fast-Forwarding to Disaster

After the death of someone who was your source of primary identity, it is not unusual to fast-forward in dreams or daytime altered states to a potential future episode that most closely expresses the intensity of your loss. By primary identity I mean your deepest self-concept with regard to someone else; it may be as a son to his mother, a daughter to her father, or one spouse to the other. It can also be to a group leader from whom a person draws security and identity. I know of people, for instance, who have had what seem like prophetic visions of the end of the world right before or after the loss of their religious leader. Dante had such a terrible vision just as he learned that his beloved Beatrice, his raison d'être, had died. In the metaphoric world of dreams and visions, when someone that important to us dies, the world as we knew it has indeed ended. Such dreams and visions are a way of releasing fears of a future in which the very rock we once stood on has crumbled under our feet.

Dreams and Nightmares

Dreams in which the dead interact with the living are typically so powerful and lucid that there is no denying contact was real. They also fill us with renewed life and break up grief or depression. In chapter 16, on communicating with the dead, you will learn how to make such dreams come about.

Another set of dreams in which the dead appear can be the stuff of horror. If you have had a nightmare concerning someone who has recently passed, know that you are looking into the face of personal inner conflict. You might dream, for instance, that your dead mother is buried alive or comes out of her grave in a corrupted body in search of you. What you are looking at here is the clash of two sets of ideas about death. On the one hand, a person is dead and rotting; on the other hand, that same person is still alive. The inner self uses the appropriate symbols to try to come to terms with the contradiction of being alive and dead at the same time. I am not sure to what extent people on the other side actually participate in these dreams. My private experience has given me the impression that the dreams are triggered by attempts of the departed for contact. The macabre images we use to deal with the contradiction, however, are ours alone and stem from cultural attitudes about death and the body.

The conflict could lie in a different direction altogether. As a demonstration of how complex such dreams can be, I offer a simple one I had shortly after the death of my cat Twyla. It was a nightmare constructed out of human guilt. Even though I loved Twyla, for a combination of reasons she was only second best in the hierarchy of house pets. I had never done anything to hurt her, and her death was natural. Still I felt guilt, as though not giving her the full measure of my love was the direct cause of her death. She came to me in a dream skinned alive, a bloody mass of muscle, sinew, veins, and arteries. I looked at her, horror-struck at what I had done. Given her condition, I could not understand why she seemed perfectly healthy and happy and full of affection for me.

I'm ashamed to admit that it took me over a week to understand what this nightmare was about. The skinning depicted the ugly fate of many animals in human hands. For Twyla, the picture was particularly apt because we used to joke about selling her for her fur, which was gorgeous, like the coat of a gray seal. My subconscious had also incorporated the callous adage "There is more than one way to skin a cat." This multivalent graphic, typical of dreams, brought my feelings of guilt to the surface. But the real meaning was more profound and once discovered assuaged my conscience. Twyla's coat represented her mortal body, her outer shell. What she showed me was more than "skin deep" — the real Twyla underneath, who was quite alive, happier than ever, and still loved me.

Stress, the Great Activator

In the immediate aftermath of a death, most of us are drained physically, psychically, and emotionally. What energy we have is taken up with getting in touch with family and friends and dealing with funeral arrangements and legal necessities. The day-to-day feels surreal, in which the strange and unusual can happen; the rate of events seems to speed up. We negotiate each moment between mourning and relief. In many ways, there is a psychic bruising, similar to the bruising caused by an operation, for just as an organ is cut out of your body, a person is cut out of your life. How can someone we love be here one minute and gone the next? In an effort to convince ourselves of what seems impossible, many of us, in the beginning of the mourning process at least, pronounce internally a litany of things that have disappeared along with the body: "I will never be able to hold your hand again...hear your laugh...look into your eyes...hug you...kiss you..." Such litanies are an important part of the adjustment processes.

So all around, it is a time of maximum stress. But it is also a time of maximum psychic activity, because stress heightens psychic abilities. We have already seen many examples of this, and there are more to come. The time immediately after death is also a time when you as well as the departed are most in need of contact. Pathways between dimensions are the most open and, as a rule, stay wide open for the next three months. On the surface, it seems unfair that just at the time when contact is easiest, those closest to the departed find themselves too overwhelmed to act on it. The truth is, the natural mechanisms of the psyche have set up ideal conditions; the driving need for contact on both sides soon after death and the close proximity between this world and the next, together with strong emotion, all work to your advantage for communication of maximum clarity. Strong emotion will propel contact. It's just a matter of learning how to use it, which you will before you finish reading this book. In the meantime, keep a look out for your loved ones from the corner of your eye. They are around.

PART IV

All about Contact

CHAPTER TWELVE

It's Okay to Talk to the Dead, but What Happens When the Dead Talk Back?

*W*hether or not the personality survives* after death is perhaps life's biggest question. It is no wonder, then, that the first human impulse for making contact with the departed is to find out simply, Are you still there? Even if we get a resounding "Yes!" we are still bound to wonder if that answer is nothing more than wishful thinking. We may be comfortable talking to late friends and relatives in private moments, to pictures, to tombstones, and we may chatter away at mental images that we too often mistake for memories, but the idea that any one of them might talk back is another thing altogether. It shakes our belief systems to the foundations. It slams one reality against another and creates moral, philosophical, and psychological dilemmas. As a society, we simply refuse to believe that real contact is possible, at least for the ordinary individual.

Because one of my projects is to normalize two-way communication, the first part of this chapter is aimed at clearing away beliefs that erode trust in our perceptions of the dead and consequently shut them down. The second part discusses the enormous benefits you as well as your departed loved ones reap when communication is established.

Grief is so important to the discourse of death, especially as a factor in either making contact or blocking it, it has a section of its own toward the end of this chapter.

The dead can hear and see us, shout at us, and send signs, but getting through our layers of social conditioning is so frustrating that most eventually give up. Some rely on dreams, which are not always as effective as direct waking contact. Still others hang around professional mediums. Our job is to get rid of the social sludge so that the dead can get through to us directly when they want to and we can get through to them — one to one.

Many other cultures have long realized that contact makes sense for its members, alive or deceased, while also helping to maintain continuity within any given community. They have therefore integrated communion with the dead into their societies. In many preindustrial cultures worldwide today, the barrier between the two worlds is allowed to remain porous, and individual communities support at least one specialist, the medicine man or woman, the shaman, the priest or priestess, who speaks with the spirit realm.

In many parts of the world, a one- or two-day period is set aside annually for the return of the dead. The famed Mexican celebration of the dead, El Día de los Muertos, is divided into two days: the first for the return of deceased children and infants, and the second for adults. Across the globe (Brazil, Spain, Guatemala, the Philippines, Haiti, Japan, Korea, China, Nepal, and many African groups), such celebrations typically include visits to graves and prayers for the departed.

Similar rites are preserved in Western societies. People go to modern-day shamans, mostly psychics and mediums, to commune with the other side. Many have elaborate rituals around the corpse. Embalming, makeup, and hairdressing are designed to return it to a lifelike appearance. Objects are tucked into the casket for protection and remembrance. We pray officially in churches, synagogues, and mosques for the well-being of the deceased's soul. We tend gravesites. And once we had a yearly three-day period set aside for honoring the dead,

Halloween (Hallow's Eve), All Saints' Day (All Hallows or Hallow-mas), and All Souls' Day.

Halloween has become a mockery of what was once an important Celto-Roman festival that took place before the onset of winter, when this world and the next were believed to be closest. The ancient respect for the dead has been reduced to a parody of death's supposed dark side, personified by stereotypical ghosts and witches, vampires, black cats, and bats, all relegated to child's play. The American Halloween has also given the entertainment industry an opening to manufacture even more horror films revolving around the not-so-dead.

FEAR OF CONTACT

Fear of the dead and of the paranormal in general produces power-ful oppositions to contact. Just think of the traditional words for the appearing deceased — *ghosts, apparitions, specters, phantoms, shades, spooks*. Would any of them describe Uncle Harry smiling at you from the corner of a room? Would you want to witness a "visit from the grave"? Although we claim to be free of the superstitions of the past, some part of us still fears the dead coming back to haunt us or presag-ing the imminent death of the beholder. In the early twentieth century, Freud developed the theory that lurking in the darker corners of the psyche is a death drive, or Thanatos, innate in humankind. Those of us who believe in such an instinct might well fear that communication with the dead will activate a death wish. Even worse, our culture teaches us that communing with the dead marks us as morbid, sinister, and dark, if not just plain crazy.

Some people avoid contact because they were taught that human emotions and need hold the dead back from their celestial progress. The subtext is that communication harms the dead: taints the soul's purity, disturbs its "rest," or pulls it down unwillingly to our level. Desire for contact then is selfish. Christianity has added its own twist: if God wants a person with him in heaven, we have no right to intrude. Does death purify and elevate souls to such an extent that they lose all concern for the living? Can genuine human emotion really be contaminating? Are the deceased afraid that contact with us will shove them off their newly won spiritual heights? All accounts of after-death communication gathered to date say — absolutely *not*. The dead are constantly seeking contact. They know it benefits them as well as the living. Besides, there is no reason to believe they lost their defenses along with their bodies. It seems that the rigid divide between this life and the next was not set up to protect the dead from us but to protect us from our fear of death.

Anxieties about influencing the progress of the soul demonstrate how poorly we gauge the robustness of the self, in or out of the body. It would help to realize that the extent of an individual's influence is always vast, radiating in every direction telepathically, whether or not it is consciously exerted. Personal influence is simply everywhere all the time. Trying to suppress it is like trying to trap wind in a box.

The dead, like the living, can choose what they are willing to expose themselves to and what not. Thinking of contact as a telephone call helps put the problem of influence into perspective. You place the call, it rings on the other end with caller ID, and the person can decide to answer it or record the message. If there's a message, a person chooses whether or not to listen, whether or not to call back. The same options are opened to you as well. You don't have to answer the phone either, metaphorically speaking, and you can permanently disconnect the line with your departed if you want.

We may avoid contact because we don't want the deceased to know what's going on in our hearts and minds. We might want to bury the guilt of not having done enough, whether true or not. Parents who have lost a child are sometimes so plagued by "what ifs" and "if onlys" that they are caught between longing for an encounter and the dread of stirring up more anguish and self-reproach if they have one. We may also be afraid that the dead will chide us for things we did wrong or for ignoring specific requests, like strewing the ashes in a certain place. Or we might be afraid of recrimination for the harm we committed against the deceased in life. Some fear old secrets might be revealed, private grudges, jealousies and unspoken hates, cheating on their spouses, hidden money, and so forth. Or new secrets may be laid bare, such as looking for another sexual partner before the grave is cold, so to speak.

Contact might be avoided because of anger against the deceased, anger we want to hide. It can stem from feelings of abandonment, unsatisfactory wills, or a mess left behind for others to clean up. People also feel anger because a person did not die in the "right" way, died too suddenly to prepare them, didn't "fight" enough, didn't forgive or ask for forgiveness. There may be guilt for having wished a difficult person had died sooner or on somebody else's watch. Resentment for having had to care for someone through a long ordeal might be acute when the dying one had a history of being neglectful or destructive to the caregiver.

When someone has resentment or anger against the deceased, resistance to contact can be paralyzing, even when it is sought. I have seen people reject the experience totally and sit there frozen, attempt to change the subject, or turn on me rather than use the connection as a platform for forgiveness. Such powerful resistance hinders contact and the flow of information.

A while back, a man came to me for help in developing his psychic abilities. As we sat there, his mother, who had died forty years earlier, appeared over his right shoulder. Then I saw that she had brought his brother into the scene. Despite having accurately given this guy their names, physical descriptions, emotional characteristics, and messages, some of which contained details known only to the three of them, he still insisted it couldn't be his mother and brother. Here I am feeling such floods of emotion that it brings me to tears, and he feels nothing. He sidestepped all our joint efforts to engage him by hurling criticisms and doubts and repeatedly interrupted what his mother was trying to say by going off on tangents of the horrifying highlights of his family history. She was there for forgiveness, something he was not prepared to give.

This story has a wonderful epilogue, however. Despite his initial resistance, the man eventually gave in to his mother's twelve-year-long efforts a few months after our session and began communicating with her on his own. Allowing his mother back into his life has set him on a road of true healing. Just as important are the changes I have seen in her. Because she is letting go of the blame, sorrow, and helplessness she had been struggling with since her death, she is brighter and younger and looking forward to helping her son to a better future.

Another common reason behind blocking an encounter is a deep-seated refusal to face someone's death, despite conscious recognition of it. Resistance of this kind is understandable and fortunately only temporary, lifting when the survivor is finally strong enough to fully accept the loss. Until then, reactions are often inconsistent, like patchwork, for a person who refuses to consciously make contact while awake may be dreaming with the departed, acknowledging in sleep that the other is physically gone.

Recently, I received a phone call from my friend Kathleen in Ireland. She began talking to me about her father's death two years earlier from a catastrophic stroke. She was not present, a fact that gnawed at her conscience. Holding on to the last tragic hours of her father's life, trying to imagine over and over again what he had been going through, constantly outraged by the police's ignorant mishandling of the situation, and dwelling on revenge were her way of not letting him go. Kathleen and I had not been in touch for a long time, so she was unaware that I was writing this book. While she was talking, her father came through. Much to my surprise, she refused to acknowledge him and began, instead, to babble and coo at her baby, who was sitting in her lap. Again I tried, "Kathleen, your father is here now. Talk to him." A moment of silence passed. She then told me in a low voice that she didn't want to see him. If she made contact with him, it would mean that he was really dead, a fact she was not yet able to admit.

Many of us, including myself, can accept separation from those most important in our lives only in measured degrees. Despite our being at the bedside while death took place, picking the coffin or urn the next day, organizing the funeral or memorial service, a part of us might expect the departed to physically return. Each person reacts differently to a major death. On the one extreme, a person may blast through, packing away all the personal effects of the deceased directly after death in a now-or-never mode. Others may go so far as to leave everything exactly as it was for years, separating only a little at a time. Respect what you need. If you are not willing to make contact now, don't worry about losing your opportunity. It will come again. If you are trying to make contact but it isn't working, you may be unconsciously avoiding the irrevocability of your loss.

There is a whole other side to this coin, of course. I am referring particularly to the superstition that contact with the dead pulls us over to their side. The deceased are not trying to yank us over the threshold. For one thing, they don't have the power; for another, such a goal is contrary to afterlife ethics. If the old fallacies of the dead pulling us over or being contagious were true, there would be no mediums left alive. The fear that contact will pull you over is about as logical as the notion that if you talk to somebody on the phone in North Dakota, you will be involuntarily teleported there, never to return.

Many regard contact with the dead and, for that matter, any dabbling in the supernatural as perilous and forbidden, even believing that necromancy leads to damnation. The very word conjures up pictures of witches, sorcerers, Satan worship, black magic, voodoo, and the like. Necromancers are imagined as entrapping unwitting souls and using them to do their bidding or calling up the evil denizens of hell.

The conservatively religious frequently consider modern-day seers, meaning psychics and mediums, as "false prophets," conscripting the weak in faith to the left hand of God. How this came about is a mystery to me when I read the letters of Paul, which are the most authentic sources in existence for first-generation Christianity. The charisms — ecstatic visions, prophecy, second sight, speaking in tongues, laying on of hands — were crucial aspects of the new faith. Of all the heavy criticisms the leaders of the movement in Jerusalem (including James, Jesus's own brother) had against Paul's stewardship abroad among the gentiles, the importance of charisms was not one of them. Charisms were originally endorsed as manifestations of divine grace.

Just as some people think that those who exercise their psychic abilities are doing the "work of the devil," others deem them mentally unbalanced or freakish. This is partly the fault of media representation, discussed in chapter 9. There is a third unrealistic view too, that such people are spiritually advanced or chosen by God. That means that unless you are one of the blessed, you will not be able to communicate with those in the next life. The pervasive belief that the "average" person cannot make contact is obviously a stubborn communication blocker. In my years as a professional psychic, whenever I saw a look of reverence in a person's eye, I lit a cigarette. That usually broke the spell. By contrast, my own brother, who became a fanatical born-again Christian in the last year of his troubled life, was convinced I was working for Satan and prayed for my salvation. Since we had lost contact for most of my adult life, his conviction was based purely on the teachings of his religious community. The irony is, I saw more of him *after* he died than before!

The truth is, those who commune with the unseen are not different from anybody else. They do not sit in the upper stratospheres of the earth planes, nor are they in their "last life" of the reincarnational cycle. Because of all the balderdash we have been told about healers, prophets, seers, and the like as spiritually "above" us, we have separated ourselves from our own natural abilities. Again, "paranormal" activity is the very essence of normal. The abilities that allow humans to see the invisible and hear the inaudible belong to us all. You are one big piece of magic, each and every one of you. And never forget it. The dead won't.

The more each of us suspends former beliefs and attitudes about survival and paranormal activity, whether from science, religion, or society in general, the more contact will occur, and the more accurate it will be.

Fear of the "Overactive" Imagination

In our society, fear of contact with the dead is practically inseparable from the anxiety of having a so-called overactive imagination. Not trusting the imagination is part and parcel of not trusting the inner self. If you recall, people (especially men) who have had near-death experiences have been quite hesitant to speak about them for fear of being labeled delusional. At least their clinical deaths and the aftereffects are a matter of record. But people who have had visits from nonmaterial realms, a group at least five times larger, are not so lucky, and up to three-quarters of them hide the fact for fear of ridicule. If they do tell someone about an experience, they usually start with qualifiers like: "I know you won't believe this..." or "You'll probably think I'm crazy..."

Raymond Moody, one of the founders of NDE research, was himself shocked by his colleagues' reactions when he turned to the study of after-death communication. Although scientists and physicians usually commended him for his courageous work with NDEs, when it came to postmortem communication one psychologist quipped, "There goes your career!" Another colleague called the project "stupid and funny" and forbade him to speak of it in her presence. The worst was a doctor who, after reading Moody's summary of his mirror-gazing technique for inducing contact, tersely remarked that it was clear proof Moody had "gone off the deep end." He diagnosed Moody as manic-depressive and prescribed lithium.[1]

It's hard enough to prove to someone that your grandmother, dead some twenty years, just stopped by. But sometimes it's even harder to convince yourself. When contact does occur, it's too easy to pass it off as the product of an overactive imagination. What most reassures people that after-death communication is real is its unpredictability. Whether contact is spontaneous or deliberately induced, how the dead appear and the messages they convey nearly always take us by surprise. Recipients rarely experience what they expected or wanted.

Unpredictability strongly suggests that the dead who come to us are independent of our imaginations.

The other bugbear is the viewpoint that an appearance is just wishful thinking. Well, is it? According to one survey, 82 percent of people who had spontaneous encounters with the departed were neither longing for one nor expecting one.[2] By contrast, many who yearned for contact never had it. Although this provides some evidence that the departed appear independently of our wants, the data can also be interpreted as an indication of self-sabotage. We don't have to wait for the deceased to call all the shots. And desire is one of the surest ways to guide the deceased into range, if we just learn to put our trust in it.

Still, nothing is wrong with a little skepticism. As long as it doesn't stop the process cold, it will challenge you to sharpen your perceptions. Healthy skepticism should not, however, be confused with what Dianne Arcangel calls "dogmatic skepticism," which she characterizes as cynical, arrogant, self-opinionated, dictatorial, and authoritarian.[3]

Before you wonder if people who have seen or heard the dead were really just drunk, on drugs, or at least unhinged, let's look at some facts. As outlined in the introduction, research and polls indicate that between 42 and 72 percent of the American population has had contact with the dead. And that's just from reports of spontaneous communication. Since then, many thousands more have made significant and meaningful contact in induced after-death communication therapy, a number that is likely to skyrocket in the coming decades.[4] Also not factored in are deathbed visits, childhood encounters, and contact through mediums. These statistics represent on average well over half of the good citizens of the United States. Are they all crazy?

Rather than being emotionally upset when an encounter occurs, people are usually relaxed, in the midst of a favorite pastime, daydreaming, or asleep. According to the Guggenheims, a surprising number are driving their cars.[5] They are not, then, in a delusion-causing crisis but in a half-conscious state, which allows receptivity. On the other hand, people can also be excited, bored, or in a panic, happy, or sad. Any time you are in a state of expansion, at a particularly joyful event like a wedding, gazing at the ocean or shooting stars in the night sky, the deceased are likely to wedge themselves into the newly opened corners of your expanded consciousness.

A major survey analyzed which type of person is most likely to have after-death encounters or perhaps, really, which type is willing to *admit it*. Experiencers are socially active and wealthier than the norm. They are also independent thinkers and influential trendsetters.[6] These are the people who have the self-assurance to stand by their experience and say, "Yes, I have met with the dead."

A review of prominent, bold, and brilliant people in the past who openly admitted an interest in making contact with the dead or who actually achieved it should convince you that you are in excellent company as you embark on this quest. They include scientists, inventors, and psychologists, philosophers and religious leaders, artists and writers, politicians, including presidents and prime ministers, military men, and too many celebrities to name. Reportedly, Thomas Edison was working on a telephone to bridge the gap between this life and the next before he died. Other scientists include Guglielmo Marconi, Nobel Prize winner for physics and inventor in the field of wireless telegraphy; the physicists Sir Oliver Lodge, Sir William Crookes, Sir William Barrett, and Nikola Tesla; the inventors Benjamin Franklin and Henry Ford; psychologists and psychiatrists William James, Carl Jung, and Elisabeth Kübler-Ross; the philosophers Socrates and Emanuel Swedenborg; several popes, including Pope Pius XII and Pope John Paul II; writers such as William Shakespeare, Victor Hugo, Oliver Wendell Holmes, Mark Twain, Robert Louis Stevenson, Sir Arthur Conan Doyle, Charles Dickens, and the Nobel Prize winner Thomas Mann; Senator Leland Stanford, founder of Stanford University (who gave a fortune to Stanford for after-death research); English prime ministers Arthur James Balfour and Winston Churchill, and U.S. presidents Abraham Lincoln and Jimmy Carter.

"Real men" admit to seeing the dead too. Sir Hugh Dowding, of the Royal Air Force, who was responsible for the successful defense against the Nazi Luftwaffe in the Battle of Britain, the true turning point of the war, spoke constantly with those pilots who met their deaths under his command. During the same war, General George Patton spent evenings in deep conversations with his dead father in his field tent. The father sat down, talked strategy, and gave encouragement. The list of important personages goes on and on. There are also the researchers, physicians, and psychologists who investigate survival in near-death experiences and facilitate contact with the dead.

Investigators do influence contact, of course, telepathically. Careless ones can either obstruct communication or distort it. I have read of some actually screening their invisible sources with questions like "Do you believe in the Lord Jesus?" Many of those poor souls who make an effort to reach across the great frontier won't even know what such a question means. And what if you were to fish up Einstein?

The movers and shakers mentioned above are generally not afraid of the imagination but depend on it for breakthroughs. If you are not a person bursting with self-confidence, you might well fall prey to the overactive-imagination assumption. The denigrating attitude toward the imagination is an offspring of the Age of Reason mentality. In one way or another, we have all been subjected to this prejudice. Parents and teachers try to curb children's imagination and shape it according to what society deems acceptable. Here is where it all begins. When children tell their parents they have seen their dead grandfather, their experiences are dismissed as imaginary, or they are accused of lying, the same way parents react to children's past-life memories.

As adults, we no longer need our parents to censor experiences. We do it ourselves, mostly by denying them: "There's no one there. I'm just imagining it," or "I must have been dreaming." Censoring can be so instantaneous that it blots out the event almost before it begins. When suppression of the imagination is strong enough, it can clog the pathways that lead to our inner selves, making it hard to distinguish between fantasy and real intuited data.

What we call the imagination is where inner knowledge manifests in waking consciousness. It is the expressive mechanism of the inner self. It possesses the kind of rationality that organizes nearly unlimited amounts of information instantaneously. Once you allow your imagination to lead into the true rationality of the inner self, you will quickly realize that its depth and breadth, its unerring logic, make the rationality of reason look absurdly inadequate by comparison. It takes some discipline to work with the imagination so that the valid data it carries can be retrieved. If we were to live in a more enlightened environment, one that understands and values the imagination for what it really is — a creative tool that funnels information and sets up networks for growth and awareness — it would guide the human race to tremendous advancements.

Fear of the overactive imagination includes the fear of "seeing things." If you have had an encounter but were afraid it was a hallucination, rest assured that those afflicted by hallucinations who also had encounters report that the two are not at all alike. As several researchers have pointed out, they differ in visual and emotional quality. And encounters are orderly; hallucinations tend to be chaotic. Furthermore, hallucinations are usually accompanied by a feeling of helplessness and anxiety, to the point of panic, followed by depression, whereas studies show that encounters typically bring joy and comfort. Lastly, hallucinations don't cure the soul, but contact does.

Can Contact Be Dangerous?

The belief that contact with the dead is dabbling in the dark arts is deep-seated. Although one part of us may hope to see dear Auntie Jean, another part often fears that what will show up will look like something out of Fright Night television. More Americans than you realize dread that when the portal is open they will unwittingly invite in evil rather than good and then become possessed. Popular films like *The Exorcist* and *Carrie* deliver staggeringly false messages about the uncontrollable powers of darkness.

If you feel susceptible to "evil," you've got some soul-searching ahead of you. First, examine yourself for a childhood belief of being bad. If you are trying too hard to be good, you are probably covering up something, a feeling of unworthiness, anger, or shame. Do you try to keep yourself under control? If you were to lose control, what do you envision would happen? Are your religious or spiritual attitudes framed in good-versus-evil dualisms? Ask yourself where you got the notion of evil. Were you taught that evil is ever ready to take over if you relax your vigilance? What is your attitude toward possessing extraordinary powers? If you had them, what would you do with them? Even if you believe in the existence of evil, having faith that the deepest part of you is fundamentally good is enough to begin. Nevertheless, before attempting contact, set your intentions, as chapter 16 explains. They will protect you.

Truthfully, there is nothing out there that can really harm you. Only the fear you bring to an encounter can do that. You are in far greater danger from your everyday interaction with the living. Dr. William Roll, one of the world's leading experts on apparitions, said that he had never once uncovered a case in which harm had come to anyone from an apparition.[7] And Allan Botkin, drawing on thousands of cases from induced after-death communication therapy, states that *all* so far have been positive. Without exception, patients perceive "the deceased as being loving, remorseful, or forgiving, attentive and compassionate. In no instances has the experiencer described an angry, blaming, or harsh message from the deceased. Messages are always loving, insightful, and uplifting."[8] The people involved in the massive after-death communication project founded by the Guggenheims would definitely agree.

Most of you readers are probably geared toward contact with one specific person. If this is true for you, you are not likely to run into discarnates outside your immediate concern. Remember, about 89 percent of the time, people have reported encounters with dead relatives and friends and 10 percent happily with pets!

Bill Guggenheim and Judy Guggenheim, who have collected accounts numbering in the tens of thousands, remark that no one yet has reported contact with someone who committed a malicious crime or an atrocity.[9] Well, that's mostly true, but it depends on the context. There are cases in which the communicating deceased had inflicted great harm on others while alive, such as murder or rape. However, in nearly all of these cases, the offenders were already known to the beholders. They were not anonymous malevolent spirits out to get the vulnerable. Furthermore, to the best of anyone's knowledge, when an offender does make contact, it is driven not by a compulsion to harm but rather by agonizing remorse.

Nonetheless, confronting someone who was greatly feared while alive can be difficult. The following story of Christopher, a Botkin patient, is one of the most moving and courageous I have ever come across.[10] It shows that confronting your worst fear is the surest way to liberation. It also shows the unfathomable power of forgiveness.

Christopher's childhood was true hell. His father was a drinker. He would bring home drunk friends, and together they would physically and sexually abuse his son as well as his two little daughters, Fran and Jill. Christopher remembers one time being locked in a closet, listening to his sisters screaming for hours while they were raped. Even when he was an adult, the fear of his father, by now long dead, continued to be so strong that during a dream involving him, he lost control of his bowels. He lived his life between extreme fear and extreme rage, punctuated by intrusive visions of abuse. Both sisters eventually committed suicide. Christopher sought out Botkin because of his longing to follow them. Since Fran had killed herself only weeks before he began therapy, he and Botkin started with her. After induction, Christopher saw her. He wept because, for the first time, she looked happy. Fran apologized for the pain her suicide had caused him and urged him not to take his own life, not to give up.

Christopher then began having dream encounters with his father, who was begging for forgiveness. Finally, his two sisters appeared with their father in a dream to encourage their brother to forgive, not for the father's sake, but for his own. Sheer terror woke him up.

A few days later he was back in therapy, ready to face his father. Botkin worked to control the fear and anger in order to get to the underlying sadness. When his father appeared, Christopher still pushed him away. Then he saw that his father fully realized the extent of the damage he had done, and Christopher began to forgive. When he met his sisters again in subsequent sessions, they reassured him that the intrusive memories, nightmares, and suicidal longings were over. They turned out to be right.

Many children experience similar maltreatment. But few realize as adults that they can still break the devastating bondage of rage, hatred, and fear. Truthfully, it's easier to work with dead abusers than living ones, because they won't resist taking the blame. Their apparent intense remorse can turn the abused person's life around.

Some readers may believe that heinous acts should not be forgiven, that forgiveness will lead offenders to moral impunity, resulting in social chaos. Hell should be their reward. Critics of near-death experiences scoff at the governing law of forgiveness in the afterlife, calling it "cheap grace." The dead don't agree. They will even forgive their abusers without being asked. They also know that acknowledging harm done morally strengthens the conscience,[11] whether a person is alive or dead, and that true contrition unleashes natural morality. They know that forgiveness liberates, that it enhances the capacity to love. For them, forgiveness is the better part of the Golden Rule.

FEELING FEAR WHEN CONTACT HAPPENS

Surveys show that up to 98 percent of the people who had encounters found them comforting to some degree; most felt elation and enjoyed long-lasting, positive aftereffects. Nevertheless, a handful of those interviewed reported feeling fear or no comfort.[12] I would like to emphasize that no one in this 2 percent group was frightened because they saw something ghoulish. On the contrary, what people perceived were family members and friends who were youthful, healthy, and more beautiful than they were when last seen in the flesh. So why did they feel fear?

First, the encounters reported in surveys were spontaneous; that is, they happened outside the recipients' control. It is no wonder, then, that researchers have mostly attributed fearful responses to a lack of comprehension and familiarity with the phenomenon. We'll fix that soon enough! As understanding of the process grew, fear diminished to a mere 1 percent of this subgroup. The remaining 99 percent were eager for more. Fortunately, over half succeeded in making contact. Subsequent encounters brought tremendous comfort rather than fear.

With intentional contact, as I am proposing, encounters are not outside our control, and we are not taken off guard. Instead we are prepared. If encounters were regarded as a normal occurrence and, better, were *expected*, familiarity and social support would eradicate fear altogether.

A second fear response that surveys uncovered was caused by the arrival of a deceased parent. This experience occurred to a group of respondents in which over half were between the ages of three and seventeen.[13] Apparently, fear occurs when children perceive their parents as disciplinarians coming back to reprimand them. Some adults have had similar reactions when encountering people who were their professional superiors. Conversely, children who were not frightened by encounters with deceased parents regarded them as protectors who had come to aid them.

Although I agree with this explanation of the fear response, I am not wholly satisfied with it. In general, children tend to confuse the physical disappearance of a parent with abandonment, as do adults. And if Mommy or Daddy left them, then they must have done something wrong. Hence, many children feel responsible for the death. Their fear reactions are likely to be fueled by a dread of exposure. Children also telepathically absorb the emotions and thoughts of others. If a child's mother dies, for example, and her death is silently attributed to the heavy burdens of motherhood, that child is likely to feel that he or she actually killed her.

As you know, I was present at my grandmother's death, but no one spoke to me about what was happening. I was expected to disappear. The atmosphere around her deathbed was raw, angry, and filled with unspoken accusations. It was not until I was in my midforties that I finally had a dream that released me from a guilt I didn't even know I had. The whole dream was characterized by the kind of trepidation that brings on a cold sweat. I dreamed I had murdered someone and buried the body behind a brick wall in a basement. Once I had mustered the courage to break the wall open, my grandmother's corpse came tumbling out. At that instant, the realization that I hadn't killed my grandmother after all hit me like a ton of bricks (probably from the wall)! I had finally released a secret I had kept "blocked up" deep down (in the cellar) for some thirty years. The guilt I had been carrying was picked up telepathically from all those unspoken accusations.

Whatever distress children might have would be eased if adults were to bother to really discuss death with them and allow them to participate in the process. A child sees right through dismissive comments like "Daddy went on vacation" and "Mommy went to sleep," or even the slightly more acceptable but usually cursory remarks about the deceased being "in heaven" or "taken by God." The message is: we don't talk about death because death is bad. Children are too often shunted aside during deaths, left to fend for themselves, which considerably adds to their confusion. The exclusion, like the abandonment, is easily interpreted as punishment. The notion that a child should not be exposed to death or will not understand it is really a blind that defends us from our own ill ease and ignorance.

DEALING WITH GRIEF

Research has also investigated why some encounters produced low or no comfort within the 2 percent group that was initially fearful. The reason seems to be grief. A person may be overcome by waves of sorrow while the apparition is taking place. Sometimes these feelings rush in directly after an encounter or come up over days in moments of intense longing for the deceased's return. What is quite unexpected about exacerbated grief in this 2 percent is that it arose most often when contact was made through mediums. People who went to séances felt afterward that they had lost their loved ones twice.[14] A few even reached the same levels of desolation they felt at the time of their loss. This is not pure grief speaking; this is a profound feeling of helplessness.

In the beginning, a successful séance can generate enormous excitement, even transcendence. Participants feel that genuine communication took place. For them, survival was proved. Unfortunately, the high can be followed by a crash. First of all, the dead talk to the mediums, not directly to the participant. This puts the participant in a passive, noninteractive position, experiencing the deceased secondhand, which is not as effective as direct communication. Then when the participant is back in everyday reality, he or she might easily begin to doubt the validity of the séance. This is not to advise you never to go to a medium but to suggest that you think of using our skills as a starting point for developing contact on your own.

One-on-one encounters, in which people *directly* experience the departed, don't present these problems. And there is nothing, absolutely nothing, like a *direct* encounter with the departed for alleviating grief. For most people, the intimacy and emotional depth, the clear detail of what is seen, felt, or heard, leave little doubt that real and meaningful contact was made. Personal, unmediated contact has an impact and vividness that never diminish. In fact, the memory of it grows more precious over time. If we were practiced in reaching the departed whenever we need to, rather than waiting and hoping for a visit, the agony of irretrievable loss that puts such a sharp edge on grief would be curtailed right away. We would also feel less helpless in the face of our loss.

Researchers and therapists who have discovered reliable techniques to bring about contact, such as Moody and Botkin as well as Arthur

Hastings and his colleagues, have been astounded by the swift resolution of grief when the living directly meet the dead.[15] Botkin records that 96 percent of those who participated in his earliest induced after-death-communication trials had *full resolution* of their "core sadness." That also includes the anger, numbness, and guilt used to insulate a person from deep grief.[16] By contrast, traditional bereavement counselors hold that it takes an average of one to two years to get back to normal, if it ever happens, in extreme situations. Grief therapists are now beginning to recognize that maintaining bonds with the deceased helps survivors adjust better to their loss, whereas old-fashioned counseling sought to sever those same bonds. Nevertheless, what Botkin calls secondary feelings of loss can crop up on occasions like a birthday and the anniversary of a death. Since these feelings are no longer anchored in the core sadness, they can be dealt with easily and constructively.

Some people suppress deep grieving because they think it's an indulgence. Those who are ashamed of their emotions or deny feelings of vulnerability will also suppress grief. Allowing ourselves to fully mourn is crucial for assimilating the corporal loss of someone dear in our lives, and that means a pet too. You still have to face that vacant spot at the dinner table or the empty food bowl on the floor. I know a woman who at the death of her dog locked herself up in her apartment for a two-week drunk, shutting out friends and relatives. If you suspect that you are protecting yourself from your own feelings, you are cheating yourself of the healing that grieving can bring. You are also setting up a pattern of emotional dishonesty and probably blocking communication, the very thing that will help most.

Others believe that a sad face is the last thing the dead want to see. Even though the dead are not happy about being the cause of sorrow, it doesn't mean they can't sympathize. More often than not, they are abreast of our emotional states, or rather ahead of them. And sometimes they mourn us too. As a rule, cheering you up is a key motivation for connecting with you in the first place.

Grief is a multifaceted emotion that can be used in many ways. Just as some people avoid it as much as possible, others grieve dramatically. I used to belong to the latter set. After a death, I used obsessive grief to stay close to the one who died. I was sure that if I allowed one jot of cheerfulness to get through, it would break our connection. I can't stress enough that obsessive grief is a kind of *possessiveness*, and it is the one thing that does indeed bother the dead. In some parts of the world, East and West, obsessive or excessive grief is encouraged, even institutionalized. The equation between bereavement and faithfulness is best seen in reverse situations in which a person gets over a death too quickly. A speedy recovery arouses suspicion about the sincerity of the bond and sometimes moral condemnation. Obviously we don't have to use grief as a way of staying connected. Certainly the dead don't.

Strong grief can be used to either block communication or facilitate it. Paradoxically, people often feel a sudden upsurge of grief exactly when the departed arrive to reassure them of their continued presence and undying love. As soon as a person senses the loved one's presence, the habitual association of the deceased with mourning kicks in. The sought-for encounter is then engulfed in uncontrollable emotion. If you find yourself feeling a powerful surge of loss, chances are high it means someone you care about is standing right beside you. The upsurge and the appearance are not that hard to separate. In chapter 16, I'll explain how to work with a grief wave so that it can play out simultaneously with the encounter. In fact, using your grief as a springboard to talk to the departed is an ideal response.

Studies show that the stronger the support for bereavement is, the better a mourner moves through it. The dead can be key facilitators in our support group if we allow them. In fact, they are by far the best bereavement counselors in existence. Grief of any level of strength, if honestly followed, can also lead to breakthroughs in creativity and quantum leaps in psychic abilities. The genuine desire for contact is potentially such a powerful driving force it can propel us onto a fascinating, life-changing path.[17]

Perhaps one day grief will no longer be necessary. In an ideal world, we would accept as fact the unbroken continuity between this world and the next. We would rely on the accessibility of the other side and be able to use interaction to better advantage.

AFTER-DEATH COMMUNICATION THERAPY AND POST-TRAUMATIC STRESS DISORDERS

I want to concentrate a moment on Botkin's work in order to highlight the inconceivable therapeutic value of direct communication with the dead. At the loss of a loved one, his patients frequently report a feeling that a part of them was taken away. They are often depressed and have inexplicable bouts of weeping. After the session in which they reconnected, they feel whole again. Such results are beyond enormous, especially for one to two therapy sessions. But what is really spectacular is that the actual contact time normally lasts a mere five to twenty seconds.

It is important to note that neither the patient nor the therapist is in control of these sessions. Instead, the dead are. Patients cannot make things happen the way they want them to, nor do they experience what they personally expected or wanted. Their beliefs, whether from before treatment or after it, have no effect on the experience or its outcome. The unexpectedness of what happens during contact, combined with the vividness and clarity of the event, quells any doubts that a genuine reunion occurred. The therapists, too, are awestruck and forced to rethink many of their most prized psychoanalytic theories. Because of the strength of communication, some of them are finding to their amazement that they also see and hear what their patients are experiencing.

After a significant death, some people suffer from post-traumatic stress disorder, typically reliving the death scene over and over. We touched on this in chapter 10. This debilitating syndrome can lead to drug or alcohol abuse, depression, severe sleep disorders, repetitive nightmares, and suicide attempts. With induced after-death communication treatment, the traumatic event quickly recedes into the distant past and is replaced by the portraits of happiness, radiant health, and wholeness the departed send us. This total relief from a long-standing torment is a gift without measure, especially for those who witnessed or were responsible for a traumatic death. Botkin relates many accounts of Vietnam vets who were plagued for decades by images of the bloody deaths of comrades, sometimes from friendly fire. Or they can't stop seeing the mutilation and murder of the innocent, women and children raped and killed, babies lying shot in the head or crying on the bodies of their dead mothers. They are haunted by the look of fear in the eyes of the enemy just before they were killed. Some combat veterans came to therapy because they could no longer live with the guilt. Others could no longer live with the rage or the hatred. At the bottom of all these feelings was this core sadness.

A few simple words from the dead — the comrade, the murdered civilian, the enemy — a friendly gesture, a bit of advice, the knowledge that the deceased are themselves doing fine and have forgiven or are asking for forgiveness, eradicate these obsessive, life-destroying emotions. My favorite piece of advice came from a soldier in Vietnam whose body was found in a river with a slit throat. The guy who found him was his combat buddy Barry, a vet who came to Botkin because of relentless guilt and grief. The dead soldier actually chided him: "Why are you still thinking this way? It's not your fault, and it doesn't matter how it happened. We were all kids back then. You need to give this up and take better care of yourself. You can see I'm still living; my body is just gone." That last line deserves a round of applause! It worked for Barry too, for at that moment his sadness and guilt completely resolved.[18]

The stunning success of Botkin-style therapy depends first of all on the brilliant healing abilities of the dead. But it is also aided by two things on our end. First, Botkin makes sure that his patients access their core sadness. If they don't, either communication will not happen or it will abort. As always, sincere emotion leads us to exactly the right place where healing is most needed. As I will later discuss, strong genuine emotion is also the most reliable way to call forth a specific loved one. Second, therapy is tightly focused on curing a specific trauma or condition related to a death. This kind of focus is not easy to maintain on your own in view of the human tendency to avoid painful feelings.

Those of us not in need of a therapist can learn to stay focused despite pain and grief. We can even learn to use these powerful feelings to make contact happen. If we firmly make up our minds for a healing encounter, honestly stay with our emotions, and rely on the dead to know what we need, it may all be over in a minute.

CONTACT — IT'S GREAT FOR THE SOUL, YOURS AND THE DEAD'S

Contact is not just good for you; it's one of the *best* things that can ever happen to you. Several researchers have noted that the experience of contact affects people in ways very much like those of near-death experiences.[19] If you remember, those changes are massive, are always positive, and last a lifetime. Like NDEs, contact works to eliminate the fear of death as well. We have seen that a person dramatically transforms for the better when that fear is out of the way.

Besides alleviating grief, one of the greatest blessings after-death communication grants us is the relief of knowing our loved ones live on. Relief can be overwhelming, particularly at the loss of a child or loss by traumatic death. We also find out how well they're doing. Warnings from the dead save lives and prevent accidents, crimes, and suicides. They give us encouragement, reassurance, and valuable advice from a perspective so wide it includes the future.

Communication helps the dead too. They want to tell us of their gratitude, to convey messages to others, to help us find important things, to conclude unfinished business, to show us how marvelously they have recovered. Sometimes it's even crucial for their well-being. I have seen them go from confusion and anxiety to pure euphoria when their messages get through, especially when death came unexpectedly. Others remain tortured by remorse and want more than anything to confess the wrong they have done. They seek forgiveness for having been abusive or too hard, for not saying I love you or I'm proud of you. Hearing those longed-for words can and has changed lives forever. They want you to know they will always be there for you, at your graduation, your birthday, or wedding, on the day you give birth, and on the day you die.

LIVING RELATIONSHIPS

Allowing relationships with primary others in the afterworld to remain alive and active promotes ongoing growth on all fronts. With continual contact we see the dead change. We get to experience firsthand who our family members really are when the fears and constrictions of physical existence are out of the way. This is far more significant than you may at first realize, because who they are affects who *we* are. Nearly all of us identify with our families, even if we refuse to admit it. Common statements that you are just like your mother or father are either derogatory or complimentary while your parents are alive. But when they are dead, you may take them as the highest praise.

The changes in my own father have amazed me. He is lighter, usually in very high spirits, if not fun-loving, always encouraging, and very at ease with emotions, all the things he was not when alive. And he continues to help me and to care. Recently he showed up at the birth of his first great-grandchild, twenty-five years after his death. Believe it or not, he actually broke down and cried. In my understanding, these changes came about partly because he knows I have forgiven him. He also realizes that I perceive him and accept him for what he is now. What a relief to the dead that their real selves can finally be appreciated by the living who matter most. Being the daughter of such a wonderful father has in turn changed me in more ways than I can name.

As the dead discover their true selves, their newfound openness, their lovingness, their playfulness, their unpretentious wisdom, and profound desire to help are downright infectious. Ongoing contact with them lets us realize we have become a member of a family that is charged with the best qualities of human nature, with more than a few superhuman gifts thrown in. Through their eyes, we see what the world to come is like and from that template begin to recognize the latent potential of a paradise on earth. We also begin to trust, not just ourselves, not just our families, but the true inner nature of reality.

❧

Through meeting those on the other side, we get a precious glimpse of the grandeur and beneficence of the inner universe. More important, contact stimulates inner life and brings us into familiarity with our greater spiritual identities. Our greater identities are living demonstrations of a more inclusive kind of good, the kind that flows from the wellspring of spontaneity and self-trust. So when the dead talk back, listen.

CHAPTER THIRTEEN

Familiarity: The Key to Successful Contact

By now you've read many accounts of communication between the living and the dead and have some idea of what it's like. This chapter will take you deeper into the experience, break it down for you, so that you have a clear picture of what to expect. Some people unfamiliar with after-death communication don't recognize it when it occurs and end up ignoring it. Others are so startled by it that they stop it before it has a chance to unfold. The more you know about the various forms of contact, about what you might see, hear, and feel, the more prepared you will be when it happens. Familiarity is the key. With a little familiarity, you know when an encounter is happening. Identifying the often subtle signs that the departed are nearby will become second nature. Familiarity also settles down confusion. You can then start to relax into an encounter while staying more focused, more receptive to messages. And too, it will help you develop sustained two-way communication. Even better, it will pave the way for initiating contact whenever you need to. Best of all, familiarity will make it much easier for the departed to get through.

Again, let's use a telephone analogy. When the telephone was still a newcomer in the house, it was an object approached with a definite measure of mistrust. When it rang, it set off a wave of alarm. People shouted into the receiver as though their voices had to reach the other end of the earth. Today, of course, nearly all of us use phones with absolute casualness. When it rings, we remain collected and in command, prepared to hear a disembodied voice and to enter into dialogue. The point is — familiarity.

In chapter 4, after-death communication was arranged into two traditional categories: spontaneous and intentional. Any categorization, however, is merely for convenience and displays the current limits of our thinking. Just these two seemingly safe generalizations have a habit of crisscrossing each other in actual practice. Until now, spontaneous communication seems to have made up the great majority of encounters. It also tends to be short, lasting less than a minute, sticking to the crucial message: I'm okay. Be happy. I love you. We'll be together again.

Intentional after-death communication usually lasts longer and is more complex. There are several distinguishable subcategories beyond private one-to-one intentional communication. One, the large subgroup called instrumental transcommunication, was introduced in chapter 4 and includes many different methods. We can confidently name mediumship as another large subgroup. Then there are the smaller, more specialized forms of contact, such as Raymond Moody's mirror techniques and Allan Botkin's induction methods, as well as book tests. Considering that four out of the five subgroups are of fairly recent invention, with mediumship the exception, the ways and means for inducing contact will no doubt proliferate in the coming decades as interest escalates and technologies advance.

WHOM TO EXPECT

As you know, who we meet from the other side is ordinarily a family member: a spouse, a child, a sibling, a parent, or a grandparent being the most common. Occasionally they'll show up together, as a mix of several generations. Half the time your pets will come with a family member in tow. You might meet a friend, perhaps from your childhood, a colleague, a neighbor. Sometimes you will encounter someone who is unknown to you, only to find out later, usually through old photographs, that the person was a relative or family acquaintance you'd never met in life. A person you either don't know or barely know may show up to give you a message for someone else among the living. If that happens to you, congratulations! You've become a medium!

You might also encounter someone who seems familiar but whom you can't place. In this instance, the person is liable to be from what could be called your spiritual family, most likely from one or more incarnations in which you two knew each other. Rarely, a person who seems to be unrelated to you or totally foreign might appear to act as an introductory mediator between you and someone else. You might even meet a historical figure or famous person. And then again, you might see a ghost. After all, many people have. Ghosts, however, are *not* discarnate humans. In the next chapter, I will tell you why.

The group made up of historical and famous people is a mixed bag. Most of them are not who they seem to be but are guides or helpers who adopt the personas of iconic figures in order to more effectively help you. Napoleon, for instance, may be your inner icon for power, leadership, courage, and will. He may also stand as the little guy who made it, despite the odds. If you need an injection of any of these qualities, your spirit helper may indeed appear to you as Napoleon. Still, sometimes the famous personality is just that, a celebrity who feels a connection with you.

When to Expect It

Studies show that from 39.4 to 53 percent of spontaneous encounters occur in the first year after death. In one sample of 350 cases, a significant percentage, 10.5, occurred within the first twenty-four hours.[1] In that same sample, spontaneous contact decreased in frequency over time: to 16.1 percent between one and five years and to 6.8 percent from six to ten years. After a ten-year lapse up to the time that this survey was taken, an undefined but generally longer period of time, it rose only 13.9 percent. The percentages are hefty enough, but why not a future in which percentages are closer to 100, especially directly after death?

This profile, which is based on spontaneous communication, is similar to that of any long-distance relationship. Typically communication is high the first year when someone you're close to moves far away. Although it fades over time, the bond endures even after decades of silence. When you do finally get in touch, it will seem as though the two of you had never lost contact. Why? Well, the truth is, on the inner waves you never have. Then you have what we idiotically call a coincidence. The phone rings. You pick it up. It's your old friend you haven't heard from in years, and you blurt out, "I can't believe you just called me! I was just thinking about you!" Who actually called whom? It's the same with the dead. This is where spontaneous communication and intentional communication crisscross.

Contact may be delayed for months or years for a variety of reasons. If, for instance, there is no unfinished business, the deceased may not feel any urgency to communicate right away. Sometimes direct communication is delayed because the departed don't feel separated from those they love on our side. Alternatively, a survivor may be too raw from mourning to take in direct contact. The deceased may also need "time" and "distance" to change old, unwanted habits before communicating. Delayed contact often occurs between deceased parent and adult child when their relationship was troubled, because the dead parent needs time to come to terms with the problems before attempting communication. When communication does start, it can last for months, if not longer, until the dilemma has been sorted out. I had delayed contact with both my parents. By contrast, contact with people with whom I have had less problematic histories usually occurs within a few days of their deaths.

While Asleep and Dreaming

Untold numbers of encounters occur in dreams while we are asleep. The dead use dreams to reach us more than any other means, because dreams are the natural crossroads of inner and outer realities. In dreams, the dead have more latitude, and we have less resistance. Whether remembered or forgotten, dream encounters will affect you. You may feel charged with inspiration the next day or find yourself humming a tune with lyrics that convey an important message. Unlike contact made while we are awake, most sleep-state encounters are not as tightly structured. They are not necessarily realistic, either. I know of one man whose father whirled in as a ball of light and swept him up to the sky. Although this man did not see his father in human form or hear words, the dream marked the greatest turning point of his life. The dead also break into dreams. The Guggenheim authors of *Hello from Heaven!* describe the intrusion as akin to watching a TV show when a voice suddenly says, "We interrupt this program to bring you a special announcement!"[2] In dreams when both the dead and the living are present, usually only the dreamer is aware of the deceased; the other living participants don't seem to notice.

While Awake

Spontaneous communication while we are awake is most likely to occur when we are in an open relaxed state, perhaps daydreaming or driving a car, as already mentioned. Nevertheless, it can crop up while people are in the midst of just about any activity, eating in a restaurant, doing taxes, walking the dog. It is quite likely to happen during major family events, such as births, graduations, weddings, deaths, and funerals. All these are markers of significant transitions that tend to expand awareness. The dead will come in times of critical distress as well as delirious joy, while you're energized, cruising in neutral, or just plain bored. And they are there at the end of your days to bring you home to their world.

THE SIGNS: HELLO, IS ANYBODY THERE?

If you haven't already been bowled over by one of your discarnate loved ones, you may have had contact without realizing it. The signs can be subtle, so how do you know? The more informed you are about what to be on the lookout for, the more you will notice. The means by which the dead make their presence known are too diverse to fully cover here. And how they appear to us may come as a surprise to them as well. They don't necessarily *choose* to show up as a ball of light, as a familiar smell, or as a vaporous form.

Many people feel brushed by a cool mass, as though an open window had just let in a breeze. This phenomenon may develop into a full and unmistakable body sensation of tingling. I'll give you more on that later. Also extremely common is just knowing all of a sudden that you are not alone. This kind of awareness is closely related to the documented human ability to sense the presence of a living person outside the visual range. Typical, too, is seeing something from the corner of your eye, a cloudiness or stirring in a vacant area of space around you. Or a tiny light might appear, perhaps a spark of color. A block of space might start to look like a cubist had painted it or like a digital television image breaking up when the signal is failing. Such visual disruptions can also appear superimposed on just about anything, on the sky, for instance, or a piece of cloth, and show up quite readily on reflective surfaces.

You might feel specific physical sensations, a caress of some kind, like a hug or a kiss. As a rule, tactile approaches occur only between people who were very close. Since the manner of touch was characteristic of the deceased while alive, it will be familiar and comforting rather than frightening. My father's favorite was an affectionate finger tapping on the crown of my head.

Animals might pick up the presence of the dead even if you don't. Dogs might bark at a specific point in space or suddenly start running around in excitement. Your dead pets will do all sorts of things, jump against you, lick you, and bounce onto your bed. You might feel your cat settle into your lap.

Smells coming from nowhere are far from uncommon. Floral scents have been known to flood up to announce a person's death or to wish you a happy birthday. You might get wafts of the perfume your wife favored or the aftershave your husband used or smell the aromas of the dish your mother cooked on special occasions. My sister smelled my father's distinctive cherry pipe tobacco a few years after he died. Odors can be anywhere from faint to truly overwhelming, literally filling up a room. In nearly all instances in which olfactory phenomena were reported, there was seldom any other kind of communication, no visions, no words, just the smell.[3] That's because very few know how to work with an olfactory sign to get to real communication.

A remarkable instance of an acrid ammonia odor happened in my home. My two friends Alexandra and Jean-Pierre were visiting. Suddenly they both started shouting, coughing, and gagging. Their hands flew up to shield their eyes, which were actually tearing. One fled the room, while the other just ran around in panic. I stood there dumbfounded because I didn't smell anything. Instead I saw and heard Alexandra's dead father. I guess I just didn't need the smell to know he was there. As soon as his presence was acknowledged, the smell disappeared. Alexandra and I withdrew to talk to him. And did he talk, passionately, for over an hour. Apparently she and her mother had smelled ammonia several times in the years before. They were both sure that it was connected to the father's last days in an old-fashioned hospital in Scotland, where ammonia was lavishly used for cleaning. Not knowing what to do, they never got past the olfactory overload to start communicating.

Sounds are also part of the repertoire of subtle signs. The familiar sounds of a certain person's footsteps, a way of coughing, blowing the nose, or laughing are sometimes clear enough to make us snap to attention. Occasionally a person might hear the auditory equivalent of disturbed space mentioned above in the form of a momentary humming, whirring, or clicking within the white noise of our busy lives. A few phrases might drift by, sung or played by someone on the other side. Your name might be called. Such auditory "intrusions" into our reality generally dissipate very quickly.

The dead frequently use inanimate objects to get our attention, and are particularly successful with electrical and electronic devices. Unexplained power surges happen. Brand new lightbulbs burn out. Lights, radios, and television sets flicker, grow dim or bright, or blink on and off. I had eleven days of the telephone ringing, the fax twittering, and the answering machine switching to record, among other phenomena, after Michael died. It all stopped as soon as real communication began. The stove can heat up and the mixer whir. Music boxes suddenly start to play, even though they have been broken for years. The same thing quite frequently occurs with clocks and watches. Or clocks may suddenly stop working, as can anything else. The exact time these events happen often has some significance to the dead. Sally Jones returned home the night her husband died to realize that two of her clocks had stopped at 3:45, the moment of his death.[4] And again like "disturbed space," the picture on your TV or computer screen might get scrambled or turn into the face of someone you know on the other side. Radios have turned themselves on precisely when that special song is playing. Not infrequently, people hear their loved one's favorite song blaring from the speakers of a public place, such as a restaurant, the moment they walk in. One dead person revved up a parked car that was turned off and locked!

In the middle of the night, a husband and wife witnessed the lights and electrical appliances, including the stereo and the TV, turn on from the top floor to the basement and even outside the house. This extravagant display started when the woman could not convince her husband that her dead Granny was sitting at the foot of their bed.[5] Well, Granny took care of that. One person was able to communicate with the dead right away and therefore did not need physical phenomena, whereas the other person needed a real stunner.

Similarly, the dead will make things fall, pictures from walls and mantelpieces, books out of bookcases, papers off desks, plates off shelves. And other things rise or move or appear out of nowhere. I know of three cases in which a recently bereaved widow found her favorite flower tucked under the windshield wiper of her car. Right before their eyes, witnesses have seen books open and turn to a page that contains a message for the living.[6] The dead often use pictures to signal their presence. Glenda, her husband, Alec, and their friend Lilly all watched as the picture of Glenda's daughter, dead for two years, started glowing. The glow lasted for nearly four minutes.[7] Pictures can easily lead to full contact. For me, the face of the deceased emerges right out of the frame and begins to communicate. All in all, the range of physical phenomena is limitless.

Equally limitless are indirect encounters. According to reports, butterflies play a strong role here, flittering right into the room or alighting on your shoulder at a meaningful moment. The appearance of a rainbow has also been interpreted as a sign of an indirect encounter. Wildlife, small birds and such, seem also to help the dead get our attention. People help too, usually without knowing it. They show up on impulse with just the thing your loved one would have given you, a bouquet of particular flowers, something in the departed's favorite color, a CD of music with special significance or whose lyrics turn out to be a message.

Any of the above phenomena represent contact of some sort, but a type that is one-sided and often frustrating for the dead. It's as though they make a phone call, and even though you hear ringing, you haven't figured out how to answer it. Nonetheless, even the briefest sign can be beyond thrilling and more than reassuring.

WHAT TO EXPECT

When contact progresses beyond the signs just described that herald the arrival of the dead, more senses come into play. Typically a person will feel, see, and hear the dead at the same time. Two senses are at the top of the list, one conventionally called sentience, and the other vision. Hearing comes third.

Feeling

Sentience

Sentience is a physical-emotional perception that someone is there, a kind of all-over-your-body knowing that uses protobiological and parabiological mechanisms not yet officially acknowledged. Because each person has a certain identifiable quality you might call an energy signature or vibration, you usually know who it is despite not seeing or hearing anything. Communication takes place osmotically, often through feelings, many of which cannot be precisely named. There is the sense of being psychologically touched by the departed, stirred by love and mutual understanding. In sentient after-death communications, the feelings *are* the message, wordless yet so engulfing that a person may often dwell in a state of wonder for a long time afterward.

The Tingling

The presence of the dead comes to me most often as a sensation I call tingling. Although tingling obviously falls under the category of feeling, it differs from the more common, more ambiguous sentience in intensity and focus. Tingling is as extraordinarily pleasurable as it is jam-packed with information. The sensation feels almost as though something sparkling and electrical is pouring down over me. It usually starts at my head, then streams into my neck, shoulders, and arms, occasionally coursing into my feet, all the while flowing over my skin, causing a sensation akin to goose bumps. It is always wonderfully energizing and sometimes so strong it makes me sway on my feet. Tingling is highly effective in calling one's attention to the mysterious and the revelatory. Many people feel it when struck by inspiration. And since unseen spirits are often behind inspirations, the tingling may be doing double duty as a signal of their presence.

I like to think of this scintillating streaming as caused by the high-voltage presence of the out-of-body. But it is more than this, for it follows the ebbs and flows of the dead's intensity. It surges exactly when contact is strengthened and emotions are coming through in force and dwindles when contact is wavering or becomes more intellectual. As such, it belongs properly to telepathy, to the thought intention of the departed, despite its physicalized characteristics. People unfamiliar with the sensation are often slightly alarmed the first time they feel it, partly because of its strength and surprise effect. It also tends to make the eyes well up with tears. The second time it happens, however, people usually love it. Tingling is something for which an increasing sensitivity is easily acquired. The more you notice it, the more responsive to it you become.

Seeing

The second main vehicle for communication is sight. Most visual encounters carry quite an emotional punch, even if they are only fleeting. First, I want to address what not to expect. Popular beliefs and media representation have fed us an awful lot of tripe about clairvoyance. The entertainment industry's obligation to physically objectify what is essentially mental activity, to show it visually on the screen, has resulted in the dead appearing as clear and solid. Those "gifted" with second sight are depicted as barely able to distinguish between the dead and the living. Were this actually true, which it isn't, it would certainly complicate day-to-day living. Besides, a lot of this "seeing" in real life goes on in pitch darkness or with the eyes closed. If you are still not convinced that this sight is coming from a pair of eyes other than the ones in your head, consider that the blind as well as people in out-of-body states also "see" the departed without the use of their physical eyes.

Having said that, I'll also add that instances do occur in which our visual experience of the dead approximates or even exceeds the clarity of our physical world. Superreal experiences seem to happen with more frequency when the recipient is working with an after-death-communication facilitator. One reason for this has to do with the techniques used, which are designed to induce highly targeted altered states. Consequently, a person goes deeper and stays more focused. Second, facilitators encourage altered states to come about by making deliberate attempts to suspend everyday reality beforehand. Third, the dedicated intention and energy of the facilitator amplify and focus electromagnetic energy, resulting in boosted clarity. Facilitators are in effect performing a kind of mediumship.

Because children are not so schooled in what is real and what isn't, they too sometimes see the deceased as present in the flesh. At the same time they may perceive them without having to translate them into human form, as whirling light, for example. For the more mature, lifelike manifestations do happen, but very seldom. There are some stupendous reports, however, of people lying all night in the arms of their deceased beloveds, who stroke them and speak to them.[8] The recipients have insisted that the deceased were exactly as real and as solid as they were when alive.

What you are most likely to see is subtle, resembling what you see in your mind's eye. Like people in visual memories, visitors usually display form and color, although colors are somewhat washed out. A lot of my visual experiences come in tinted silvers. Visions are also transparent to some degree, being, as they are, mental thoughts projected by the deceased, not objects reflecting light. I have seen transparency so extreme that some areas of the bodies look empty. Unlike memories, which are usually stationary, visions of the dead are fluid. You can watch their features changing as well as their movements and activities. The mental pictures might be compared to holograms in motion. They have also been compared to images from films, television, and videos, realistic but less than three-dimensional and somewhat transparent.

Internalization

Sometimes the dead appear like images projected externally onto an invisible screen in space. The majority of people, however, see them internally, that is, mentally. If I perceive the dead as an outside projection, after a brief pause, I will automatically turn it off and switch to inner mental pictures. I call this process of switching from exterior images to inner mental ones internalization, an extremely important step for maximizing communication, as further explained in chapter 16. Internalization seems to draw the dead into closer range, where communication is faster, more comprehensive, and more enduring.[9] This is because external visions don't usually last long, so if you don't transfer them quickly, you might lose the connection. Also, telepathy is more efficient when information is exchanged internally.

How the Dead See Us

Sometimes the dead see us as others in the physical world do, and sometimes they don't. It depends on their depth of focus. If the focus is superficial, they may even be fooled by appearances, surprising as it may seem. When my dead friend Al came for a visit while my cat Twyla was in the room, he mistook her for his cat Peaches. In defense of Al, these two cats were nearly identical, and as Al knew, Peaches did occasionally live with me. I have had the extraordinary privilege of viewing myself through the vision of Peter, whom you met in chapter 8. It was an invitation on his part, which I jumped at, of course. Much to my shock, I did not see a human body, nor was any of my physical environment apparent. What I did see was a white pointed arc with regularized flamelike edges in a black space. The arc enclosed a smaller white flame-form, which expanded and contracted ever so slightly. It was like looking at some kind of electrical version of myself. No doubt the dead perceive us in a countless variety of ways, many of them exotic indeed. In general, however, we can infer from the mass of after-death-communication accounts that the deceased usually see us the way we see ourselves, only less dense and with patterns of light that change according to emotions.

Hearing

All the quotations of the dead you have read by now might give you the impression that they speak in much the same way as they did while embodied. Not really. Pure auditory after-death communication is comparatively rare. If you do hear a voice distinctly as though its source were outside you, the message will typically be short, such as your name or a brief sentence, and almost always without images. The speaker's voice characteristics — accents, pronunciation, timbre, impediments — are preserved. The startling words from out of nowhere can be delivered in a shout or a whisper; even whispers, though, can be quite emphatic. Instances in which voices are truly audible are on the rise, reaching up to 15 percent when communication is facilitated by a third-person specialist,[10] indicating again the amplification that facilitators unknowingly provide. As with visual encounters, an auditory encounter endures longer and is more complex once it is internalized. People flounder trying to explain what internal hearing is actually like. Statements like "I didn't hear real words; I just knew" are attempts to describe what people currently understand as telepathy.

To all of the above, there are exceptions. Once in a while, people will have extended conversations with the deceased, on telephones, for example, in which the deceased's voice is strong and coherent. Or a person might have a mixed auditory and visual encounter in which the deceased seems to be external. There are riveting stories of children sitting side by side with a discarnate parent in heart-to-heart talks. We heard one in chapter 4. In most of my extended communications, what the deceased are saying wavers back and forth from nonverbal information, which is still quite understandable, to passages in which speech is clear enough to pick out word for word. If I miss something, I ask the deceased to slow down, repeat it, or say it louder. Sometimes words appear spelled out in midair. With spontaneous after-death communication, the living rarely have enough time and control to influence speed and clarity. What recipients often "hear" then tends to be quick, wordless bursts, which are later translated into words.

Light, Atmospheres, and Color

The dead often appear illuminated. People report seeing them sparkling, shining, glowing, radiating, and lit up from within. Light surrounds their forms, emanates from their bodies, faces, or heads, or streams from behind, like Steven Spielberg's famous backlighting effects. As in near-death experiences, the light can have unimaginable intensity. Although most perceptions are internal, occasionally the departed will show up in an external sighting so charged with light that the whole room fills with a dazzling luminescence, even in the middle of the night. In other external visions, the brilliance is concentrated solely on the form of the dead and does not affect space.

Most people see a golden or white light, yet silver whites are also common, as is iridescence. Other colors issuing from the body, clothing, jewelry, and landscape features are usually infused with a glimmering quality, as though a piece of clothing or a ring were radiating unbounded vivacity. In all cases I am aware of, these colors realistically match the ones to which we are accustomed. You won't see green skin, for instance, or pink grass. Colors around the body are telling. The troubled dead might display darker light, perhaps in grays or deep, brownish reds. But once the reconciliation they seek is achieved, the atmosphere around the dead will transform instantly. Relief can be explosive and can set off sparks. In fact, most emotions and shifts in states of mind will find visual expression in light and color.

Bodies and Touch

As you know, the energy bodies of the dead appear in exuberant health. Disabilities vanish, and all functions are restored. If a dead person shows up still bearing the signs of an illness, a wound, or anything less than perfect well-being, consider it as part of the message, a sign for something they want you to know. Professionals frequently see the fatal damage imprinted on the body, such as a red area of constriction around the heart of someone who died from cardiac arrest. But we know that this is part of the information packet meant to help us identify that person to the living. Bodies always appear clothed, which seems to be a hard-and-fast rule of the afterlife.

Rarely do people see the full head-to-toe form of the dead. The head and upper body are privileged. The lower half, if seen at all, usually tapers off somewhere between the hip and the ankle. Nothing about partial bodies causes distress. In fact, people are usually too involved to notice. Contact with a face alone is bracing enough and full of surprises.

It is also not unusual for the dead or parts of them to appear larger than life. In addition to this expanded quality, their forms can be characteristically soft and uncontracted. I sometimes have the impression of seeing the dead from the spread-out multiple perspective of a fly's eye and so closely that their forms whirl in a blur, from which an arm or a head can be made out. I understand expanded appearances as demonstrations of the dead's expanded inner states.

The sensation of being touched by the dead is normally realistic, and the intent behind it quickly understood. A few recipients, however, feel touch as heat or describe it as a vibration. For unknown reasons, in some accounts of after-death communication and near-death and out-of-body experiences, the discarnates specifically forbid touch or pull back when the living reach out to them.

Changes in Age

One of the most consistent things you will ever hear about after-death communication is that the old appear younger and the young appear older. Psychics will tell you, as will just about anyone who has had visual contact, that after passing, people spontaneously adopt a condition of maximum potential. Appearance is also pure information, for radiant youthfulness is an accurate expression of their inner states. In this sense, bodies are symbolic. Infants and young children frequently appear as older children or teenagers, and teenagers as young adults. The old usually appear in youngish middle age. But if your grandmother wants to convey "grandmotherliness," showing up as a thirty-year-old simply won't do. She will probably appear looking like the grandmother you knew, although slightly younger and in perfect health. Most of the time, parents see their adult children as younger. Less often, grown children appear as they were in childhood in order to emphasize their relationship with their parents and grandparents. When young children appear as adults, take it as a visual message that they have not just survived death but also continued to grow. When parents perceive their young children at the age they were when they died, this usually happens for the purpose of reassurance. A deeply distressed mother may well feel bewilderment rather than comfort if she sees her recently deceased six-year-old boy as a young man. Nevertheless, infants and children will communicate with the maturity of an adult.

Clothing, Grooming, and Adornments

How the dead look in terms of clothing, hairstyles, accessories, and adornments also conveys information. It would be safe to say that what they wear, including hairstyles, is an outward expression of what they value in the afterlife. Most show up in the same kind of clothing they wore while still in the body, primarily casual wear. To my knowledge, today's Western deceased never appear in anything that connotes high status or formality. The keynote idea here seems to be no frills. Many times they wear something that was one of their favorite items or was essential to their identities, such as a uniform.

Clothing can also identify the dead. If you don't know who appeared, you may later find a photograph of that person wearing the same thing. Some have discovered what they saw in their vision packed away in a trunk among other belongings of the deceased. People picking up messages for others might see the deceased in something that grabs their attention, say, ceremonial attire or a distinctive pin or hat. When the message is delivered and the apparel described, you are likely to see a look of shocked recognition on the face of the person for whom the message was meant.

Items of dress can also include cherished gifts. If a watch was a gift, it will convey an ongoing connectedness with the giver. If it is a wedding ring, take it as a sign that the wearer is telling you he or she still feels a marital connectedness. The dead want to look their best for you, and we hear of accounts in which they appear neatly dressed, with their hair perfectly coiffed and even wearing makeup!

There are other layers to the clothing issue, if you'll excuse the pun. Occasionally people see their loved ones wearing robes, usually in a shimmering white. This ideological heavenly garb may have been donned to signal spiritual well-being. Or it is worn because that's what you need to see. It may also signify that the deceased has let go of the circumstances of time, place, sex, and social status of their last life. Most often, however, we see robes because they are the easiest for the dead to project.

Landscapes and Activities

Of all the things that most fascinate me about after-death communication, it is those precious glimpses of the dead's immediate environments. Their environments, as you know by now, are mostly gardens and other scenes of preternatural splendor. Then there are the vacation spots, those places where the dead felt happiest on earth, which they recreate in their new life. What you are not likely to see are features that make up conventional pictures of heaven or hell, such as pearly gates. Snippets of landscape might also appear as settings for specific activities. A luscious green field may open up before you, where you see your loved one alone or joined by others in front of an easel, holding a palette and a paintbrush. Yes, people paint in the afterlife; in fact, it's rather common. They also make music, garden, and do other little things, like learning to speak in mathematical languages! What is given here is only typical for Western societies of the past few generations and reflects the cultural values people take with them to the other side. When you get deeper in and make contact with those who have long been on the other side, landscapes and activities become much harder to describe.

Reincarnational Cues

Lastly, I want to mention that the dead may want to tell you of other reincarnations. From the togas of privileged Roman men to the rags of Victorian street beggars, clothing is an effective means for isolating the time and place of a past life. Reincarnational material might also come in the form of environments, such as an icy landscape or an ancient city. Typically, something in the background, a building or people dressed in period clothing, will mark time and place. Images such as these, and there might be a whole chain of them, are projected by the deceased in order to tell you something about themselves and what they are exploring and possibly about your relationship with them in those other lives.

SOUL-TO-SOUL COMMUNICATION

After scrolling through what can be expected from after-death communication, you might find yourself wishing for a clearly audible, involved conversation with a departed loved one you can see and feel outside yourself as solid flesh. You might even be fantasizing that the departed will bend a few spoons while they're at it. Well, think again. Although objectified experiences are eminently persuasive, another way communication happens is unrivaled in power and intensity. I call it soul-to-soul communication. In soul-to-soul, the psychological buffers used in more typical contact are utterly absent. Nothing is filtered. You meet the person raw. You are so up close, so intimate, you may not even see a form. If you do, it is more likely to look like a mass of color and light in ceaseless motion. In soul-to-soul, you are no longer able to distinguish yourself as separate from the other. Instead you merge with your loved one or feel engulfed by him or her. Information is passed through merging, in huge chunks, rather than strung out logically in a wordy telepathy. Revelations can come in long, rolling waves. Many levels of information, the spiritual, the psychological, the futuristic, occur at once. In soul-to-soul communication, the intensity of the love and compassion and the tidal flood of intimate knowledge are without parallel. The soul-to-soul experience seems to happen primarily between spouses or between an adult child and a late parent, as it has with my mother and me.

⋘⋙

No matter how communication between us and our departed loved ones is achieved, contact never fails to deeply touch us. Even for those of us who are most familiar with after-death communication, it never becomes routine. The merest hint of a presence leaves us with profound feelings of wonder, joy, and gratitude, not just for the appearance itself, but also because the dead open us up to the magic and magnificence of the greater universe we all inhabit.

CHAPTER FOURTEEN

Ghosts, Thought Forms, and "Earthbound Spirits"

In this chapter I want to draw distinctions between the deceased and other energy personalities that are habitually confused with them. We will primarily look at ghosts and so-called earthbound spirits. Because both have been historically misrepresented as deranged or frightening, confusing them with the dead has only added to our fear and darkened our view of what happens after death.

GHOSTS, SPIN-OFFS, AND FRAGMENT PERSONALITIES

Ghost sightings have a long-standing reputation for raising the hair on your head, unless of course you are at Hogwarts School with Harry Potter. But what is the difference between dear dead Auntie Jean and a ghost? The short answer is — lots. Auntie Jean will appear wherever your mind is, because she is coming expressly to communicate with you. Ghosts, on the other hand, are associated with a specific place. They are also characterized by repetitious movements, much like reruns of a video clip. For example, a ghost might be seen going up the same staircase, as though caught in a permanent trance. Some habitually go through walls at specific places where doorways once were. Ghosts are compulsive and self-involved. Lacking any real intention to interact, most remain mute and unresponsive to the people and events around them. Unlike the dead, they do not appear to tell you they love you, to say they're all right, or to give advice. They don't appear for your sake at all. When you do see them, they tend to be close to colorless, wispy, and often lacking feet, and they don't emit light.

Why? Because ghosts are not all there, literally speaking. A ghost is only a portion of the core self. It is an electromagnetic imprint created by a human and is perceptible (to some) under certain atmospheric and emotional conditions. Laboratory experiments have shown that certain talented people can deliberately impress mental images, say, of the Eiffel Tower, onto unprocessed film and the like. The imprints are the by-products of strong bursts of focused mental energy. What makes a ghost imprint is usually a combination of a person's extreme emotion and obsessive-compulsive thought. Ghosts, then, are castoffs of human thoughts and emotions. They can be so power packed that they affect the atmosphere, resulting in phenomena like the well-known column of cold air. Ghosts can also affect matter — I worked with one who raised beds — although this is an exception and more random than purposeful.

As mentioned earlier, many emotions and thoughts, especially habitual ones we call beliefs, don't simply dissipate once we have them. The intense ones, traditionally called thought forms, go on to have a life of their own. The stronger they are, the longer they endure and the more agency they have. They can semimaterialize, aggregate compatible thoughts and feelings drifting around, and cast off parts of themselves. In short, strong thoughts and emotions have a kind of consciousness. Although they are fragments of the core personality who created them, they live and grow independently. Ghosts are such fragment personalities. Yet some are so exceptionally developed that little distinguishes them outwardly from their creators. I follow a policy of approaching ghosts as though they were core personalities. They deserve as much respect and compassion as we are capable of giving them.

I've worked a lot with ghosts and love doing it. My objective is not to destroy the ghost, as the term *ghost busting* implies, but to liberate it. Although the fixated, self-involved nature of ghosts can be difficult to penetrate, the process, which I explain elsewhere, is similar to working with the troubled dead.[1] Both processes come under the rubric of "rescue work." There are differences, of course. For one, ghosts have to be channeled out of our dimension, which they find themselves trapped in, whereas the dead are already out of it. A second difference is that, unlike the newly deceased, ghosts are much less responsive to human intervention and almost never seek help. You have to work hard to get their attention. The dead are very responsive, even to reasoning, although at first they can sometimes be in too high an emotional state, too preoccupied or confused, to let anyone in. Core personalities get help from dead relatives and friends waiting in the wings. So far, I have never seen helpers show up for ghosts, unless it's a specialist like myself. With a ghost, reasoning will not do a thing to loosen its fixation, because a ghost is its fixation. Characteristically no facet of its personality is developed enough to look at its situation from the outside, let alone evaluate it.

Fragment personalities of one degree or another are everywhere and people never cease creating them. In fact, you might be making one now. Few, however, are directly perceptible. Spin-offs of living people, which are fragment personalities as well, are also everywhere but harder to pinpoint. You may, for instance, sit down in a chair that was recently vacated by someone absorbed in sorrow and suddenly feel great sadness without knowing why. You've sat in that person's cheerless spin-off, an emotional fragment the core personality wants to separate from. I've noticed a tendency among the aged residing in nursing homes, especially those who have Alzheimer's and other forms of deregulated consciousness, to throw off fragments strong enough to get picked up by others as ghosts. As I understand them, ghosts are highly developed thought forms made and shed by the living at critical turning points. Their growth continues whether their creator is alive or dead.

I have tried to clarify what a ghost is to the best of my ability, not because I'm worried that when you make contact with the deceased your living room will suddenly be crowded with moaning specters gliding in the air, but because we cannot understand the dead without some distinctions. I'm also not worried, because ghosts are, after all, harmless, and sightings are quite rare in comparison to visits from the dead.

"EARTHBOUND SPIRITS"

Many investigators of the paranormal and intuitives will not share my view that ghosts and the dead are different sorts of entities altogether. Instead they regard ghosts as a special category of the human dead, what is known in the literature as earthbound spirits. Most define earthbound spirits as dead people who cling to the earth plane.

Too often, researchers in the paranormal, psychics, and spiritual counselors are themselves stuck in simplistic, outdated interpretations. It hardly dawns on them that they are passing off as truth socially influenced subjective conceptions. The earthbound-spirit interpretation is one of these unexamined "truths." It is modeled on the ideas of hell and purgatory, a dualistic and unsafe universe, and finally spiritual evolution.

The claim is that because these tortured souls cannot or will not move on to the afterlife, they are imprisoned in a hell-like "astral realm," a place very near to earth but "lower." The assumption that the inner dimensions are like a layer cake, in which our world is between a lower plane at the bottom and a heavenly kingdom at the top, is just that — an assumption. There is no end to other dimensions, which are largely interactive and without borders. As far as I know, no experiential accounts exist from the living or the dead describing an encounter with a dimension so rigid that it works like a holding pen for an astronomical number of literally "lost souls." This is merely a spiritualized version of hell and purgatory and great fun for the entertainment industry.

These "unevolved" souls supposedly remain in "detention" because of their powerful negative feelings. Another theory is that some are stuck because they died without believing in an afterlife. They are able to see and hear those in our reality but can't understand why they can no longer communicate. Yet another is that a quick, violent death can throw the spirit body out of the physical body with such speed that a person fails to notice the body is no longer there.

I want to explore for a moment the extremes some supporters of the earthbound-spirit interpretation go to in order to illustrate the kind of mind-set that could first visualize and then invest in such a ghoulish version of the afterlife. Harold Sherman, a strict spiritualist who rejects reincarnation and holds a barely disguised belief in heaven and hell, asserts that these discarnates, unaware they have died, wander around, returning to familiar places, trying to get our attention. These are the relatively harmless ones. The author goes on to cite another investigator who seems to have encountered only those earthbound spirits who harbor "hatred and other destructive thoughts."[2] Both claim that there are earthbound spirits who influence people of the impulsive and easily aroused kind to kill other human beings. There is no real motivation for manipulating the living other than the discarnate's malicious nature. We are expected to believe that particularly virulent earthbound spirits can gain control over us when we are at the height of some passion or another and turn us into mass murderers. They also supposedly attach themselves to us when we are, and I quote Sherman here, "open to possession through use of the Ouija board, automatic writing, excessive indulgence in alcohol or drugs, or as the result of nervous breakdowns and sordid misuse of sex."[3]

These moralistic advocates of the earthbound-spirit hypothesis are not satisfied with just turning us into mass murderers. According to them, when we die we can ourselves become earthbound spirits by entrapment.[4] They deliver all this nonsense with pulpit-level gravitas. Rescue weighs heavily on their broad shoulders, but — unbelievably — all these authorities have to do to bring these deranged and often treacherous souls to salvation is inform them they are dead. How can earthbound spirits be so dangerous if all it takes to dispel them is a few firm words?

The earthbound-spirit hypothesis is not at all consistent with the findings of so many others who are either researching after-death communication or practicing it. In the thousands upon thousands of incidents collected, not one mention is made of encountering an earthbound spirit. Nor have any of us seen harm done to any living individual by the dead. In addition, most people involved in after-death research have by now encountered dead people who had excessively indulged in alcohol, drugs, and "sordid" sex while in the body, but what became of them after death has little to do with earthbound spirits. They did not become one, nor were they entrapped by one. Here I want to remind you of the story given in chapter 12, of Christopher's father, a drunkard who raped his son and daughters in orgies with his drunken buddies. After his death, he did not possess the living, drive them mad, and force them to commit heinous acts; rather, he felt powerful remorse and sought forgiveness.

Sherman and others like him are staunch supporters of spiritual evolution and the notion of an unsafe universe. He claims that in our world today, "mass humanity is pretty low in the scale of spiritual growth — that on every side, in every country — in every class of citizenry — we are confronted by lawless, criminal, murderous — even bestial conduct, which has opened the door to possible possession."[5] It troubles me that anyone can hold such poor opinions of the human species, designating whole populations as mentally and morally inferior. The supposed criminality of some earthbound spirits also presupposes that some human souls have no redeeming sides.

Descriptions of earthbound spirits are so utterly mindless and one-dimensional that they cannot be applied to that most miraculous and complex life-form we call a human being. Those who have ever probed the deeper portions of the human spirit will tell you that no matter how simpleminded some people may seem to be on the surface, their inner lives are the stuff of genius. Sherman and his colleagues also seem to be unaware of the powerfully transformative effects of death. Furthermore, they seem to have missed one very crucial fact: that the human core is cut from the greater divine cloth of good.

Yes, some people have trapped themselves in a delusion after death, but a delusion of their own making rather than a prefabricated "lower region," or low astral plane. Nearly all of us are caught up in one delusion or another. We can cripple ourselves with a delusion that we are worthless or unlovable, for instance, or go seriously off course with the delusion that revenge will set things straight. For the most part, death is the greatest delusion breaker there is, even for psychiatric patients and sociopaths. Those comparatively few who remain in a dream or nightmare after death seem to be going through some necessary process of their own design, a private program of atonement or a plan for discharging old hatreds, before going on. In all the stuck cases I and others have come across so far, none of the deceased turned into ghosts, haunted the earth, or preyed on the living.

It seems clear to me that if there are entities akin to earthbound spirits, they are really fragment personalities, perhaps sometimes nothing more than stray thoughts picked up telepathically or through instruments. One reason I would argue that earthbound spirits are not the human dead is their anonymity. They have virtually no identity, no history. We hear neither their individual voices nor their personal stories. If they are fragment personalities or thought forms, then whose thoughts are they? Well, anyone's. If we could keep track of all the thoughts that run through our minds in a five-minute period, we would probably catch a few that are pretty worrisome.

Certainly our world would be a better place if we were to learn to free troubling fragment personalities and thought forms wherever we sense them. Even more effective would be learning how to prevent their formation in the first place; after all, they are our own creations. This unacknowledged mess pollutes the body, the mind, and the atmosphere. We can live with it, like air pollution, but we would live better if it were cleaned up.

If you sense that certain areas in your home or workplace have collected uncomfortable energies, there are many things you can do. First, ask yourself why in that specific spot. It may be a place where an unhappy fragment personality or troubled thought form is lingering. On the other hand, it may be that an object put there was a gift from somebody you simply don't like. Or it might remind you of an unsettling event. Get rid of it. Allow free space to circulate around furniture and things. Weed out clutter. Bring order to drawers, closets, and basement areas, all spatial metaphors for the subconscious. Simply washing the floor is one of the most effective ways to exorcise a house. Let scented candles burn in places that seem to need clearing. But above all, play music, big, gorgeous, vigorous music like Vivaldi's court pieces, Handel's *Resurrection*, or Respighi's "Birth of Venus." Put a speaker right in the spot that bothers you and let it blast away until that area feels airy and light. There is nothing like the power of music to transmute unwanted thought forms.

Then again there are massacre zones, battle zones, anyplace where mass death has occurred, that are filled with fragment personalities, violent psychic turbulence, and sometimes lingering curses. They are all over this planet but mercifully seldom palpable. Many I have come across were wholly unsuspected. It would never have occurred to me, for instance, that galleons from the Spanish Armada brought the war between England and Spain as far as the western coast of Cornwall. But I saw them. I witnessed the bloodshed. Only later did I learn that fighting had indeed gotten that far. There was a massacre even on our property in Germany. What I picked up occurred around 700 CE, when the local pagans rose up against a group of newly baptized Christians. No one told me this, although the spring in front of our house is hailed for being the first baptismal site in all of ancient Saxony. So far, the visions I have of those bleached bones lying deep within the unconsecrated soil of our front yard have inspired little more than curiosity. I feel much more ill at ease when I am near a slaughterhouse or a pig farm. In some areas of the world, concentrated violence is too pronounced to escape detection. It might take centuries before settlement of such places of unspeakable inhumanity as Auschwitz is attempted, if ever. What remain for the most part in such zones of negative intensity are not earthbound spirits but mindless gestalts of terror, hatred, and suffering. Even they can be cleaned out with teamwork.

Many more things than mentioned here that cross the spaces of the human psyche cannot be explained as the by-products of human thoughts and emotions. An infinite number of entities are not — and have never been — part of this world. I have seen some of them, and I know others who have. Many are indescribably beautiful; others, not much more than a speck of light. One of my most cherished examples is an energy personality that I think of as a being of solid-state emotion. It crossed my bedroom one night when I was half asleep, a stocky golden entity carved out of pure, solid love, a love so powerful, certain, and condensed, so compacted, there was no room for the more vulnerable aspects of human love, like compassion. An entity of this caliber is so far beyond human capacity that we cannot really form a conception of it, let alone describe it. If only we had the cultural values that would promote investigation on this front, it would expand our consciousness immeasurably. I wonder how many species of entities are out there that will never interact with us, not even in the deepest regions of human inner space, because they are simply too different.

CHAPTER FIFTEEN

Telepathy:
Your Tool for After-Death Communication

If making contact with the departed is your first foray into the "paranormal," you are bound to feel a few uncertainties. Telepathy is your main tool for after-death communication, and you'll find it in that toolbox you were born with. So relax. Working with telepathy is a matter not really of learning a foreign skill but of boosting the efficiency of something you are already using every single day. In order to get the maximum use out of telepathy, it helps to become more aware of what it is and how it works.

The most common example of telepathy again concerns the telephone. If you have ever known who is calling before you answered the phone or were thinking about the caller just before it rang, you've got evidence of your telepathic ability. Everyone has it to a greater or lesser extent. Without telepathy, we would not be able to survive. An infant could not communicate with its mother, or the mother with her infant. Nor could cells communicate with one another. Without telepathy, prayer would be meaningless. On a grander scale, telepathy is the medium of mass consciousness, which regulates us and other animals so that we can live together on one planet. For humans, it is the foundation stone of civilizations, which are brought into being by the synthesis of conscious and unconscious mass agreements.

Telepathy is the lingua franca of the dead. They can therefore sustain it for any length of time. It is also the native language of our inner selves. So when we brush up on it, the short communication we currently have with the dead will evolve into lengthier exchanges.

WHAT IS TELEPATHY?

I would love to be able to give a definition of telepathy with a quasi-scientific flourish, such as "telepathy involves the movement of units of consciousness (or maybe we should call them c-particles), just as electricity involves the movement of electrons." In this model, a unit of consciousness would be so infinitesimal that it would make an electron look like the *Hindenburg*. But honestly, there is no such scientific-sounding definition, so you will have to be satisfied with a descriptive one. No one is 100 percent sure what electricity is, anyway, scientifically speaking, or how it works, but we know how to use it. Similarly, despite not knowing the physics behind telepathy, we know how to use it. Telepathy has been tested over and over again in laboratory experiments, so its existence has been proved beyond doubt.

I take telepathy to be the use of *any* extrasensory perception for the transmission and reception of thoughts, feelings, and images. As such, telepathy encompasses much more than our usual understanding of it as a mental communication following the logic of a verbal thought process. As the Prince of Wales will tell you, people have telepathic relationships with their plants. As far as I know, plants don't send messages in the King's English, although evidently they like to hear it when it is spoken to them lovingly. Instead, telepathy often takes the form of a delicate two-way probing for information on an extrasensory level.

Returning to human-to-human telepathy, imagine a scenario like this: just as you are thinking about ordering in pizza for dinner, your spouse comes in with the pizzeria's take-out menu. Coincidence? But when you thought about pizza, you weren't just thinking in abstract words or mentally verbalizing; you were also thinking in images, say, of a round, flat pie. At the same time, you were probably conjuring up both taste and tactility while remembering how the hot cheese and crusty dough feel in your mouth. Most likely you were running through some probable future events as well. Cheese and pepperoni or cheese and mushrooms? Ray's Pizza or Pizza Hut? So thinking about getting a pizza is actually quite complex. What part of the constellation of thoughts was telepathically picked up? And was it you who transmitted it to your spouse, or your spouse to you? Before you try to decide, consider the possibility that the two of you had pizza thoughts at the same time, that somewhere in the back of your minds you instantaneously agreed to put pizza in your immediate future.

For people in our visually oriented society, thought is transmitted more often in images than in words, although images and words are not easy to delineate. Imagery can be converted into words, just as words carry peripheral pictures. In fact, in the earliest writing systems known, from Mesopotamia and Egypt, each written sign derived from a picture. The peripheral images around a word can be captured and then analyzed to tweeze out embedded telepathic connotations. Telepathic transmissions frequently involve other senses as well: smell, touch, impressions combining color and temperature, and so forth, which are not easy to interpret as strictly image-word transmissions.

Let's go back to the pizza. Let's suppose that your spouse was drinking a cup of scalding coffee somewhere away from home. At that moment, you're at home and suddenly remember a time when the tomato sauce on a pizza burned the roof of your mouth. You can't imagine why that memory came to you out of the blue. What happened was, when you telepathically picked up your spouse's experience with scalding coffee, you unconsciously tried to make sense out of it by drawing on your own bank of associations with the sensation. You then settled on the memory of biting into a piece of pizza while it was too hot. Ouch, the pizza thought cluster goes into orbit.

Cellular Telepathy

If you momentarily experience the inside of your mouth burning before having any thoughts or memories of that sensation, you are picking up information through your body rather than your mind. For want of a better term, I call this cellular telepathy. Many healers work this way, sensing someone's physical problems in their own bodies or through their hands. Cellular telepathy is one reason some people can see auras. And it emphatically occurs between the living and the dead. I want to remind you here of the most common mode of perceiving the dead, sentient after-death communication — feeling an unseen, unheard presence. More common for me personally is that tingling sensation described in chapter 13. Our bodies pick up the presence before our minds do. It's not that the energy bodies of the dead have cells, but they do have electrical charges that can be palpable to the bodies of humans and animals, in particular to nerve cells.

Direct Knowing

Once in a very special while, transmissions come without words, images, or any sensory packaging. In a flash, a whole block of information bursts through as a revelation. This spectacular phenomenon was called "direct knowing" in the metaphysical literature of the nineteenth century. If it hasn't already happened to you, I guarantee you'll know it when it does.

Telepathy as Consciousness in Interaction

All words and images start out as thought before they come into perceptible manifestation. By thought I don't mean logic or intellectual thought here, although both could be components. I mean something deeper and broader that is anchored in consciousness. Beliefs are ultimately thoughts; so are feelings and emotions if you track them to their origins. In fact, it seems impossible to name anything that is not to some degree thought or clusters of thought consciousness. As previously described, consciousness amasses to create form, whether as thoughts, words, images, or objects. Our bodies are essentially thought forms, projections of inner consciousness that are made at such high speeds that they appear to be solid. Recall from the discussion on the illusion of solidity in chapter 2 that the amount of matter in an atom in ratio to the overall size of the atom is approximately equivalent to a pea in a football field. So when you are looking at your own hand, almost all of it is just a light show projected by the master illusionist, consciousness. That knowledge alone should make you feel more comfortable about seeing the projections of the dead. You can put aside any doubts that a physical you can perceive a nonphysical someone else, since the divide between the two of you is slender indeed. You are both projections of the same stuff — consciousness — and you share the same native tongue of telepathy.

I would argue that the projections themselves are telepathy. I would further argue that telepathy is consciousness in interaction with something else, such as another consciousness. That's huge. Since your consciousness is always in interaction with its inner and outer environments, some form of telepathy would be in constant operation, say, between you and your plants. So why aren't we more aware of it?

TELEPATHY AND MASS AGREEMENTS

Mass consciousness reaches agreement through mass telepathy, which also operates during dreaming. That means that people of the same civilization are in an overall telepathic agreement about how to think, how to perceive, what is possible and what is not, and, most important, what is normal and what is abnormal or paranormal. For the moment, let's take sight as an example. Since you were a newborn, you have been conditioned to perceive in ways that agree with the mass consciousness of your time and place. You have unknowingly conformed to seeing the pattern of energy — the radiation of subatomic activity, oscillations and vibrations, electromagnetic attraction and repulsion — not as it really is (i.e., constant motion) but as substance. A woman I regressed to the age of three months saw the sofa she was lying on as undulating waves of color. Before social conditioning she saw movement and light, not solids.

We all have learned how to perceive in culturally approved, codified ways. That also means we have learned to turn off other types of perception not used or condoned by our society. Some people show perceptual capabilities of stellar magnitude because they were raised outside this conditioning. I am thinking here of documented accounts of babies brought up by wolves. The one I remember best was written by two missionaries in India. They had adopted a child who had lived with wolves for over a decade. Although they tried to teach him human ways, he refused to walk upright and scrambled at incredible speeds on all fours, for which his knees and feet had adapted by growing horny skin. He snatched food and ran off with it to eat in hiding. But more to the point, he had extraordinary night vision as well as senses of smell and hearing that went far beyond what we believe the human capacity to be. This child, who did not live long in captivity, possessed such abilities because in his wolf society they were standard issue for everyday use.

Sometimes whole cultures have perceptual abilities that are so foreign to ours that we dismiss them as fictions of primitive minds. The ancient Greeks, for example, believed a person could hear the voices of the gods. For thousands of years, the peoples of ancient Mesopotamia wrote about a light radiating from certain people and objects. These shining auras, called in cuneiform languages hi.li (Sumerian) or *kuẓbu* (Akkadian), had the ability to attract as well as to radiate; they were the visible expression of charisma. Most academics of the ancient Near East dismiss these descriptions as nonsense. Are they? Leaders of the Special Air Service, the British special forces (equivalent to the American Delta Force), don't think so. They train their soldiers in how to diminish their auras so that when they are in hiding, behind a door, for example, and retract their auras, detection by the enemy is close to impossible.[1]

Perceptual agreements can also hinder rather than help. Hypothetically speaking, let's say you were brought up in a society in which all members were isolated in an empty, small, white room with bare walls. Your depth perception would not have developed, because your eyes would have lacked opportunities to focus on objects against a background and especially on distances. Since your society had no experience of depth perception, for you, it would not exist. When it comes to telepathy, the industrial West is like the White Box Society, under too many restrictions to use this inborn capacity. It then remains undeveloped or perhaps even atrophies. When we come across someone who has kept it intact, we assume that he or she has paranormal gifts or, worse, is making up the whole idea of telepathy.

This may have a biological correlation as well. In readings, during routine body scans, I began noticing two parallel tracks of tiny unidentified glands that start just inside the base of the skull and descend the spinal column. As part of the old brain, they seem to control altered states, including sleep. Because they are visible only in clients who are psychically active, they may be atrophied or retracted in the less active.

Why Some People Seem More Psychic Than Others

It is true that some people have stronger psychic abilities than others, just as all people can sing, but some sing better than others. Part of the reason for the disparity is that different people value different skills. Unfortunately, in the cultures of the modern West, telepathic skills are at the bottom of the value barrel. Another part of the reason has to do with a person's overall life plan, which usually sets his or her natural aptitudes. A final part is just plain training.

We are always in some kind of psychic activity, consciously or not. Sometimes those extrasensory probes don't extend very far. For instance, when a cook is roasting meat in the oven without the use of a meat thermometer, unconsciously the cook will mentally project into the roast to "see" if it's done. This is called guessing in everyday parlance, but it is a "guess" educated by telepathy. Great cooks use this ability more consciously, in which case it is called not guessing but rather instinct, talent, or experience. At other times those probes pop way out and start feeling further afield.

I will never forget this one girl who came to me for a reading. She and her family were part of a Latino community in northern New Jersey. When I met her, she was not yet out of high school but already street smart. She wore heavy makeup, had dyed jet-black hair and a row of nose rings, and chewed gum while smoking Newport Longs. During the reading, while I was describing her high psychic energy, she began to follow what I was saying telepathically and to see the thoughts shifting in the air before I spoke them. Other clients have also noticed this. So far, no big deal.

What was a big deal happened the following day when she called me in a state of great excitement. Since the reading, she had been experimenting with her abilities. "Guess what," she said breathlessly, "all I have to do is look at a Coke machine and a can comes out!" I sighed. How effortless it all was for some. How many times have I tried to influence objects like this and failed? She did leave me with a lesson, though: different people have different aptitudes, so go with your strengths.

Where you were geographically brought up plays the broadest role in determining the extent of your psychic abilities. If you were brought up in Naples, Wales, or Estonia, you more likely sing better than people from other regions, because your social environment regards singing as worthy and important. In such places there are many singers to learn from who also set high standards for you to reach. At the same time, the ability to sing is taken for granted. Similarly, certain cultures take the paranormal for granted or are at least more used to it. Social conditioning operates to a lesser extent in subcultures, such as religious communities. One may value mystical experiences, for example, while another may condemn them, and a third may say they do not exist.

An influence just as strong as geography is personal upbringing. Two examples illustrate how American families have promoted clairvoyance in their children, accidentally or not. In both cases, the children grew up to have natural, healthy psychic abilities that were integrated with daily life. The first is Sascha Feinstein. Sascha was brought up to believe in creativity as the greatest gift to humankind. His father was an abstract artist of unusual depth, whereas his mother painted pictures that were more representational and leaned toward aesthetic treatments of nature. Both parents believed that the imagination leads to deeper truths. Although Sascha scrupulously left painting to his parents, his love of the arts is boundless. His creativity has found expression in photography, music, and especially writing, all of which he does with an unusual combination of buoyant joyfulness and critical thinking. Creativity flows from him, in his speech, in his everyday approach to life, and in his chosen fields, out of his bedrock trust in his inner self. This trust, together with training since early childhood to look inward, to probe deep for meaning and inspiration, led to the development of his psychic gifts. Sascha was not aware of his extrasensory aptitudes; he simply used them.

The second is Stefanie Nagorka, a professional psychic of the first order. Stefanie is the daughter of two excellent professional psychics who raised her to recognize clairvoyance as a distinct tool. She and her sister began formal training at the age of thirteen. This majestic woman is the first professional psychic I ever met. I was bowled over by my reading with her and afterward vowed to learn how she knew what she knew, even if it took the rest of my life. What to me then was the most exalted thing in the world, the most extraordinary breakthrough in the advancement of knowledge, was to her just a casual extension of the everyday, employed with impartiality. What Stefanie knows consciously and Sascha knows instinctively is that psychic ability and creativity not only are allies of each other but also spring from the same source.

The third family situation that promotes psychic abilities in children is regrettably much more common than the above two. This is the one to which I belong. Quite simply, expanded awareness develops because children need to protect themselves from their home environment. Although Brian de Palma's famous film *Carrie* (1976), based on a Stephen King novel, is a wild exaggeration, it does capture the psychological conditions of oppression, powerlessness, and desperation that can lead a child to strong psychic activity, including telekinesis. There were two main drives in my childhood. One was the defensive strategy to know what my parents were thinking, which alone fostered telepathic skills. The other was to get out of the living nightmare by leaving my body. I remember once trying to squeeze myself into Jim Dear and Darling's old-fashioned living room in Disney's book *Lady and the Tramp*. For help, I turned especially to the unseen, including saints and angels. Lastly, I strove for the common and infinitely tragic childhood notion of self-protection — making yourself invisible.

Parental maltreatment may not inspire a 180-degree personality shift in a child, but it does force children to temporarily vacate their bodies, as does almost any traumatic abuse. Out-of-body experiences, reading minds, trying to disappear into another dimension or become invisible are just some of the psychic ploys that make up the arsenal of damaged children.

The fact that stress is a producer of paranormal phenomena is widely recognized. Near-death experiences in which a person exits a body stressed to the maximum are the most extreme example. Interestingly, research shows that people who have had NDEs usually had a history of childhood trauma as well.[2] Many religions ritualize stress in order to evoke revelations; witness the old biblical formula of fasting "forty days and forty nights" in harsh desert conditions. Various Native American rituals push the body to the brink of human endurance to receive visions. Many rites around the globe are known to apply psychological and physical stress, including lying in a grave overnight and self-mutilation. As with the damaged child, if the danger is perceived as strong enough, the psyche goes into overdrive. It may choose to sidestep impossible levels of pain or fear by temporarily vacating the body, which can then result in a mystical experience. Or it may go into a hyperalert, adrenaline-flooded state in which the senses, including the protobiological ones, become ultrasharp, and thoughts, actions, and reflexes acquire supernormal speeds and strengths. We have already seen a number of examples. From them we get a better idea of what humans are really capable of. Both Sascha and Stefanie would tell us, of course, that we don't have to wait for traumatic conditions to find out. A safe environment that supports the validity of the imagination, creativity, and inner knowing is by far the better teacher.

LOOKING AT COMMUNICATION FROM THE OTHER SIDE

I have probably given the impression that success with after-death communication depends entirely on you and your abilities. It doesn't. Success also depends on the ability of the dead to communicate from their end. Generally, this is not about their telepathic skills so much as it is about other factors, namely, emotional and climatic, which affect the clarity and strength of telepathy. Desire, of course, is the crucial factor. Certain psychological conditions between you and the dead, as well as meteorological, seasonal, and circadian atmospheric conditions and a host of other preconditions, will promote contact or deter it. The same happens right here and now. People are generally moved to interact more in the spring than in winter. Meditations go best at certain times of the day or night. Individual biorhythms come into play too. You may be a morning person or a night person, for example, which also influences after-death communication.

It must be said that some people on the other side don't have the least interest in making contact with us earthlings. A rare few who chose physical existence as a one-time experiment or who could not adapt to it may, after death, simply reject all memory of earth life and move on as quickly as possible to more compatible dimensions. There are also those who have used their various reincarnations to explore all they had set out for themselves and are ready for a whole new set of experiences outside the sphere of our immediate understanding. They have little enough desire to keep their attachments to our world, and even if they did, their experiences would probably be too alien for us to comprehend.

Some dead people are just poor at communicating or lack significant enough relationships with the living to make the attempt. Others may be so locked in a self-made delusion that they forget the world they once inhabited. More often than not, the dead will stay silent because they are out of our psychological range, absorbed in some exploration or in a level of activity too unfamiliar to us to bridge telepathically.

In other cases, silence may serve a specific purpose, such as helping you become more independent. Ordinarily, when we do not hear from our departed loved ones, we jump to a lot of wrong conclusions: they don't love me anymore; they forgot me; I'm not worth it; they have better things to do; I can't communicate with the dead. The truth is, they may be silent precisely because they do love you.

Peter took this route. He was my ultimate inspiration, a man who by the age of twenty-four had a string of achievements behind him that very few ever attain in a lifetime. The last time I heard from him was in 1975, in a letter from England, where he lived. I had always hoped that one day we would reunite once I had caught up to his level — well, at least almost his level. For twenty-three years I dreamed about him, frightening dreams about trying to find him. I never could. In 1998, a friend of mine invited me to visit her in England. Now was the time for that long-awaited reunion. Just two days before I got on the plane, after-death communication with him began. His visits (described in chapter 8) shook me, and I fought hard against the knowledge that he was dead. Once I got to London, old colleagues of his confirmed that he had indeed passed, way back in 1975. I was devastated. Why hadn't I intuitively known all those years?

About a month later I found out. In an after-death communication that stands as one of the most fascinating I have yet experienced, I asked him why I didn't know. His answer was simple: "Because I didn't tell you." I understood immediately that he had long realized the role he played in my life. If I had known he had died, it would have seriously eroded my drive for self-improvement.

Fortunately, many on the other side in the supercommunicator class have no intention of keeping silent. They belong to a group I call loud minds. Alive or dead, loud minds seem to share certain characteristics, namely, an intellect powered by strong emotion and tons of desire. That all adds up to great telepathy. The most tenacious afterlife communicators are those who were unable to deliver important messages before dying or left something undone. The man in chapter 13 who showed up with an ammonia smell strong enough to knock out an elephant was one of these. Urgency tends to result in loud and insistent transmissions to anyone who will pick them up, what I think of as broadcasts. Murder victims usually belong to the broadcaster set, that is, murder victims whose homicides have not been solved or for which the wrong person was accused. In order to tell their stories, they might even emerge out of pictures shown of them in TV newscasts and documentaries.

The vast majority of our loved ones fall between the two extremes of the taciturn and the loud minds. When the desire or the need is there, they will eventually find a way to get through.

ALTERED STATES

In order for telepathic communication to be sustained, some kind of altered state is necessary. Recent research at the University of Wisconsin led by Dr. Giulio Tononi is looking at and measuring consciousness in new ways. Now it is believed that the brain can be in a "trillion" different states.[3] I agree. For me, an altered state is hardly different from deep concentration. When you read a book, vacuum, talk on the phone, take a shower, fall asleep, jog, make love, close a business deal, or look into firelight, you instantly alter your state to meet each of these acts. You can't read, for instance, if you're not in an altered state; otherwise, you would not be able to block out enough sensory data to concentrate. In fact, it is fair to say that an altered state basically involves concentrating in one specific area, which you already do spontaneously, day in and day out. Not only are we in a particular altered state at every given moment; other states as well continue to roll along just under the surface. And no matter what we are doing, our subconscious is also involved in some kind of dreaming. The undercurrent of images never stops. Since the subconscious is the most used crossroads for contact with other dimensions, whether awake or asleep, we are in constant communication with something not of this world.

When you are deep in a novel you screen out the world around you; nonetheless, while you are sitting in your living-room chair reading, a part of your awareness may be in the kitchen, waiting for the soup to boil. At the same time, you may be aware of certain things going on outside the house or in your body, like hunger pangs. While you're reading, the subconscious self is making connections between what you are reading and your own personal experience. Many other inner processes from the psychological and sensory levels are at work too, as are projections into future possibilities, including the author's plot!

Once you appreciate the variety of altered states you pass through on any given day, you can more easily locate the ones that best suit after-death communication. They become your reference points. A radio analogy works here. For the sake of simplicity, I am the transmitter of a specific radio station, let's call it WBGX FM, and you are the receiver or the actual radio. I send you signals, which in radio technology would be sound waves, for you to pick up. In order to do that, you must use your inbuilt tuner to find my station, which comes in best at 96.8. If you don't find it, you won't get the right frequencies, and you will hear nothing but noise. In this same way, you use your inbuilt tuner to find the right altered state for reception of telepathy with the least interference. Once you know where that station is calibrated on your inner radio dial, you can preset it to 96.8 FM so that you can return to it again and again without effort to catch WBGX transmissions. The process is automatic. You can press the preset button even in the middle of chaos, and it will still tune in just fine.

TELEPATHY OUTSIDE THE SPACETIME MATRIX

Unlike mechanical transmitters and receivers, telepathic transmitters and receivers work together to establish the right frequencies. In deep-trance mediumship, the discarnate entity (formerly called the control) might take months or years to build the necessary psychological bridges before it and the medium are sufficiently attuned. The analogy further falls apart in the differences between the transmitter and the receiver in telepathy, which are not clear-cut. In some cases transmission and reception occur simultaneously, in which case distinguishing the receiver from the transmitter is impossible.

The notion of a transmitter and receiver depends on the notion of sequential time. And since the inner universe barely acknowledges sequential time, to claim that telepathic transmission happens *before* telepathic reception is inaccurate. Furthermore, thought, unlike sound waves, is everywhere at once; it does not go from point A to point B. And too, you may not be picking up a "live" broadcast. What you might take to be happening in real time may actually be an old recording or even a future recording, which has been thought by someone you know from another point outside our spacetime. It is let out to roam the waves, carrying the signature of its creator.

Let's suppose your now-dead mother had a persistent wish that you would one day live in a nice house. Although she may no longer be hoping for it as she moves deeper into her afterlife experiences, that wish is still active in the spheres of consciousness and will indeed put opportunities in your way for an unusually good buy. Because the wish carries your mother's signature, you know instinctively that she is help-ing behind the scenes.

Constellations of thoughts, feelings, or images, or any combina-tion of these, are driven by intent. As such, they are alive; they grow and have the capacity to respond. Free-floating telepathy spawned by someone you have never known will find you only if you and it are on the same wavelength, so to speak. Most likely it will have come from someone with whom you have a strong mental, emotional, or psycho-logical resonance. And when it arrives, it usually has the impact of an inspiration.

THE PEEL-OFF

So far I have given many reasons why we should abandon the old idea of telepathy as strictly mind-to-mind communication. I have one more, saved till last because it so beautifully illustrates the idea of telepathy as consciousness in interaction. You might have noticed that people who have had after-death communication pepper their testimonies with com-ments of experiencing giant weights lifted off them. This may not be as metaphorical as it seems. Although mostly what they are describing is the release of something burdensome or repressed, a form of activity that takes place telepathically can produce such an effect. It is when the dead literally remove from your person a harmful thought form, created from a set of less-than-ideal mulish beliefs. The thought form appears as a symbol. I call this event a peel-off, because when I watch it happening, it reminds me of the shadow that peeled off Peter Pan. For example, a woman experienced a peel-off when she encountered her dead mother-in-law, someone she hated with a vengeance. During the encounter, the daughter-in-law felt all her hatred and negativity lift off her like taking off a "heavy coat."[4]

I know someone who woke up in the middle of the night to see the shadow of her dead husband kneeling over her as she lay in her bed. To her total mystification, she saw that he was removing shackles from her wrists. They were not real shackles, of course, but phantom ones. He was freeing her from a whole complex of thoughts and beliefs that kept her enslaved to others. It's as though he somehow compressed them into a symbolic form that truly said it all. He peeled them off, and her life made an abrupt change toward emancipation. From then on she quickly got over the morbid grief of his death and began for the first time to live for herself.

A peel-off once happened to me. For most of my early life there was a background feeling of mournfulness, transferred to me by my mother while in the womb. I was conceived within a year of the death of my infant brother, an event that caused my mother inconsolable sorrow. Consequently, I was given to excessive grief at the death of anything innocent, especially animals. In my adulthood, a dear friend appeared. Like the husband in the above account, he hardly bothered to acknowledge me but simply got to work. He leaned over my body and reached into my side to extract a dead infant, the embodiment of the grief I had been carrying for my mother from the death of her baby boy. At that moment, the wild remorse I felt at a death and the dread of its happening to anyone around me left me for good.

Peel-offs are breathtaking demonstrations of the complexity and depth of thought interaction. But more than this, they demonstrate the wisdom and compassion of the dead and the power inherent in telepathy itself.

Chapter Sixteen

How to Make Contact

*N**ow that you know communication with the departed** is* good for you, now that you have some idea of what to expect and what tools you'll be using, it's time to get ready, take action, and make contact. First, we are going to look at spontaneous encounters and how to work with those subtle signs the dead give us to announce their presence. You can then use these signs to launch full communication. After that, we will explore different ways you can initiate contact on your own. I recommend that you read this chapter a few times before attempting contact. You'll see that there are several techniques given for reaching the departed, so you can choose which one suits you best. It doesn't matter if you forget some or most of what is suggested. After a few readings, what works for you will be in your mind somewhere to come springing back when you need it. Besides, I will repeat over and over again what is essential. If you still feel uncertain, there are a lot of tips to help you and a quick review of the steps for easy reference at the end of this chapter. In the meantime, I'm going to give you four little rules that lie at the core of all types of successful encounters. I will explain each one more fully later on.

THE FOUR LITTLE RULES

1. *Stay with your truest emotion.*
2. *Talk out loud.*
   Talk out loud in the direction you sense or imagine your departed to be. Describe everything you think, see, feel, or hear. Don't stop talking.
3. *Internalize.*
   No matter what phenomena seem to be happening outside you, switch from perceiving them as exterior phenomena and start searching for them internally. That means, start looking with your mind's eye and listening with your mind's ear for mental images and messages. If you recall from chapter 13, internalization leads to fuller communication.
4. *Ask the deceased questions.*
   Ask the deceased questions directly. Pause, look, and listen internally for answers. Answers are likely to arrive as images or thoughts.

Remember above all that no matter what happens, you are never helpless. If the dead want to communicate with you, they will do everything they can to accommodate your needs and limitations. The second thing to remember is to proceed as though the departed are the same as the ones you have always known — no more and no less. They will show you what changes they have made.

PREPARING FOR CONTACT

With a little preparation, as soon as you sense a subtle sign that a spontaneous encounter is about to happen, you'll be ready to seize the opportunity. Knowing what to do is usually all it takes to open up a slightly felt presence so that it expands into two-way communication. Preparation will not only help you become more receptive to the dead but will also carry you along when you are in the midst of contact and help you sustain it. This section on preparation applies to intentional communication as well.

Working with the Inner Senses

When we work with the inner senses it's good to keep in mind that they are not biological, although many correspond to the biological senses. Each extrasensory perception of "seeing," "hearing," and so forth might be regarded as an individual language group used for the purpose of translating telepathic projections. As with any language group, the senses are somewhat mixed in the way French and German are mixed into English. We are used to regarding the five physical senses as distinct faculties. But recall the onion tests of our childhoods. With eyes blindfolded and nose pinched closed, a person is given a piece of onion and a piece of apple and asked to identify each by taste. Surprisingly, the onion and apple are hard to distinguish because what we thought was taste was really smell. In the same vein, most of us have impressions of color and form when we listen to music; the artist Kandinsky actually painted what he saw as he listened to music. In short, there is slippage between the senses.

Your inner senses do the same thing. Protobiological senses are primary; they are the formative consciousness of the physical senses. Without them, your physical senses would not be able to function. A blind person can still see when out of body by using the inner, protobiological sense of sight. The inner senses are what you take with you when you die, which means they are what the dead use. When you are interpreting what comes during contact, you will notice that even nonvisual senses carry light and color at times, just as light and color carry elements of other inner senses as well as emotion. Under the main five inner senses are even subtler ones, a little like a smell or sound, for instance, which are difficult to put into words. I call them parabiological senses. The more sensitized you become to the exquisite functioning of the inner senses, the more you will be able to perceive from the other side.

Sharpening Your Inner Visual Sense

What you will see during an encounter usually comes in the form of interior images. So let's work on sharpening your inner visual sense. It will only take a minute. Think about the way you concentrate on any mental picture, throwing your energy into the area of your brow, like Rodin's *Thinker*, forcing your attention inward. Experiment right now. Sit down and close your eyes. In your mind's eye, locate an object in another room of your house or office; it can be anything, a vase, a painting, a chair. Bring the image of that object into your mental focus. If you find yourself trying to scan it with another set of eyes just above your eyebrows, you have just stumbled onto remote viewing. Describe the object to yourself in as much detail as possible, its size, color, and so on. If you discover your descriptions were inaccurate, pick another object and try again until you learn to faithfully capture the object in mental images. Once you have achieved this, congratulations! You are already seeing the nonphysical.

The Snapshot: The mental picture you just took of an object outside your range of vision is no small step. The ability to take accurate mental "snapshots" is second in importance to emotion for maximizing communication. The instant you get a mental image of someone or something from beyond, memorize it. That memorized picture, your snapshot, goes into your memory file as a fixed visual document, which you can pull out and refer to whenever you want. Your aim here is to get a snapshot of the mental image in its *most original* form, with as few distortions as possible, even if you don't understand it.

When receiving an image imprint, the psychological tendency is to try to make sense of it. We usually do this by altering the image so that it looks more like something we would expect. The altering happens so fast, we don't know we're doing it. In the process, the original image is skipped over and lost to memory. A classic example comes from one of my psychic development classes. I had asked my sister to go somewhere in New York City at a specific time to pick a building or some other site. She was to mentally send the image of her chosen destination to my students while standing in front of it. A few in the group reported picking up a post office. When my sister returned to tell the class what she was looking at, it was not a post office. But it was something close to it: a red brick building with a two-story-tall white post in front. What these students did was convert an unidentifiable building into something familiar. They transformed the post into a flagpole and added the American flag, which waves in front of post offices all across the country. This unconscious remaking, called analytic overlay, takes the original image and then searches through our memory banks for near matches with which to interpret it. It is the most common cause of inaccuracy in psychic work.

The only way to head off analytic overlay is to stay open, very alert, and snap, snap, snap as much and as fast as you can. It is perfectly fine to describe a red brick building with a post in front by saying it *reminds* you of a post office, while keeping in mind that the snapshot in your head is not telling you that. Don't worry about understanding what you see at first, although understanding is likely to be immediate. Just "save" the picture so that you can analyze it in the following moments or return to it for more analysis days, months, or even years later. If the picture begins to change or move before your mental eyes, watch it and take as many stills as you can. Because I am such a visually oriented person, I never stop looking for images during an encounter. While I'm doing it, my head tends to swivel around slightly, like a small-range searchlight.

The Tingling

The tingling described in chapter 13 belongs to the inner sense of touch. It is one of the most common signs of the dead's presence. You don't have to do anything to develop a sensitivity to it other than be aware of its significance. Most people don't know what it means and find themselves confused the first time they feel it. Fortunately, this energy streaming usually occurs in context, most often when we have some kind of recognition of the dead. It can come immediately after a dying person leaves the body and tries to approach you. It typically arises the moment you make contact in intentional after-death communication. It may come the second you first hear of someone's demise. And it frequently interrupts conversations in which you are talking about a particular deceased. Sometimes you'll start feeling it only after you have acknowledged one of the other more subtle signs. Its miraculous energizing effects make it easier to be hyperalert to any internalized images and thoughts.

Deep Listening

You may recall that most of what you hear during an encounter will come not in the form of actual sounds or words but as thought. Nevertheless, you will still be using your inner senses to listen, the process I refer to here as deep listening or inward listening. Deep listening comes naturally and is similar to the concentrated and somewhat strained listening a person automatically uses when trying to hear a low whisper.

Mental Intrusions

Mental intrusions are often related to the inner sense of hearing. They are without a doubt the most common way the dead connect with us. They are surprising, uplifting, often funny, but regrettably also the easiest to miss. Most intrusions take the form of a mental thought or image. Although they may not be consciously noted, a person might feel one as a sudden inspiration, a boost in self-confidence, or a solution to a problem that comes out of the blue. Many people do notice, however, and give a quick thanks to the sender. Once you get used to the idea that intrusions occur regularly, learning how to spot them is rather easy. For instance, you may be worrying about how to tell your daughter you don't like her new boyfriend, when suddenly you somehow know that the relationship won't last anyway and there is no need to interfere.

Then there is inner prompting. How many times have you heard yourself say, "Something just told me...," as in "Something just told me I would meet you here," or "not to buy that house," or "I should change doctors." So many mysterious coincidences are set up by those on the other side. Of course not all "coincidences," insights, and hunches are gifts from the dead, but many of them are.

You can also spot an intrusion when your train of thought takes a sharp turn or a new thought appears out of context. Take special notice if your thoughts begin to run like a dialogue. Occasionally words will pop right out of your mouth, and then you wonder, Where did that come from? Well, now you know. Once you recognize an intrusion, you can either simply acknowledge it, giving credit where it's due, or try to open it up for lengthier communication.

For me, the most trustworthy intrusions come in the form of music. Nearly every one of my dead friends and relatives has their personal signature song. When I start to hear one in my head or realize I'm humming it, I know who is trying to get through. Michael's song is the one played at his funeral. My father's is the tune of the music box my sister and I gave him for his last birthday. My mother gave me hers in a gorgeous dream about a month after she died, so aptly titled "I'll Be Seeing You." She soon fulfilled that promise.

Sometimes you'll hear a signature song. Other times, you'll be singing along with a mental tune only to realize that the lyrics are telling you something. Musical intrusions will persist (occasionally for days) until you acknowledge them or the dead finally give up. Once you recognize a musical intrusion, announce your awareness of that person's arrival — I hear you, Mama! — and begin the internalization process.

Thickening the EM Field

Just as you have inner senses for perceiving subtle energies, you also have another parabiological mechanism that generates an atmosphere around you. This personal force is constantly adjusting to your inner climate. Its visible manifestation is the aura. It is a type of electromagnetic (EM) field, one of the four fundamental forces of nature, although I sense many other components, such as ghost hormones and also negative ions. People feel another person's energy field quite easily when it is deliberately directed, somewhat like heat or a mild pleasurable electrical current. The EM field can greatly extend itself, in which case the person is usually considered charismatic and often perceived as physically larger than he or she actually is. Great entertainers know how to magnify their fields to enfold an audience of hundreds, if not thousands; the audience's individual fields expand in response, bonding with the entertainer's and hence feeding it yet more energy. By contrast, this field can retract to practically nothing when a person sharply withdraws for self-protection or is ready for death, as we have seen.

Among many other functions of this personal atmosphere, the two most pertinent to after-death communication are, first, that it can thicken and, second, that it can display information. The thicker it gets, the more information is available. When it is thick enough, it works like a screen upon which the invisible becomes visible. If two psychically active people are together in this thickened state, its power and capacity to contain and pass information grow exponentially. The EM field can then significantly alter reality. Miracles happen. Healings occur. Voices are audibly heard. Future events are witnessed. Revelations are received. And visions of discarnates arrive with a superreal clarity. On a more mundane scale, bonding of two heightened fields is at the base of that magical "chemistry" new lovers experience — talk about ghost hormones! Sadly, this exponential increase in power has been neither harnessed nor studied, at least to my knowledge.

When you sense the presence of the departed, what you want is to thicken your own field so that you and your departed work better together, like the two psychically active people just mentioned. When the dead appear, thickening happens spontaneously to some degree, but since I will call on you to "thicken your energy" from time to time, you may as well try it out beforehand. It's done with the imagination. Sit for a moment feeling the boundaries of yourself, where your skin intermingles with the atmosphere. Imagine that there is a sheath of energy emanating from your skin. You can give it a color if you like. Look at it in your mind's eye to estimate its thickness. If you don't see or feel anything, just use your imagination. Now visualize the sheath growing thicker, expanding like a layer of dense air. Pump energy into it. Keep doing this, pumping and intensifying, with the intention of filling up the room. Sometimes during this exercise people see a smokiness or cloudiness in the room. Keep going until your imagination tells you that the atmosphere in the room has become denser. Now that you have set up your own personal screen, picture it catching telepathic projections made onto it from the departed. Most of them will be visual.

Thickening your energy is not a process of effort and force but rather a releasing of energy from your own endless inner reserves. If a person habitually uses a special place for sitting in meditation, prayer, or any intense inner work, the atmosphere in that area generally remains thicker.

Heart-Speak

Nothing improves receptivity in after-death communication more than opening your heart. Try opening your heart with a trusted friend, not as a preparatory exercise but as a way to find out how well it works. Sit with a willing partner and soften your heart area by stimulating a feeling of compassion or love in your chest for that person. I know this sounds strange. Don't worry if you don't feel any real compassion or love. Believe it or not, faking it is just as effective! The heart chakra, as it is sometimes called, is, like the brain, a major information-gathering center, which is no doubt why the ancients considered it the seat of the mind. It is the threshold to another kind of thinking, the intuitive, holistic thinking talked about in chapter 7, which combines emotion and intellect with information gleaned from the psyche. We unconsciously recognize the wisdom and depth of the heart in expressions like "speaking from the heart," "knowing in your heart," and "following your heart."

Once you have softened your heart area, focus on the heart area of the friend sitting in front of you. You might imagine streams of connective energy passing from your heart to your partner's. Once you feel a heart-to-heart connection, ask yourself, What's the most important issue in this person's life? You might be quite surprised at the answer you get. If you think that what you are getting is only what you already knew, try it on someone you barely know or go out to a public place like a café and try it on a stranger. Sit somewhere and soften your heart for someone nearby. Ask the question and see what happens. When you are getting ready to meet with the dead, softening your heart will make you more receptive to them. It will also make you more emotionally honest, which the dead find irresistible. Heart-speak is just about the only way they know how to communicate.

Talk, Talk, Talk

More often than I can count, a late loved one arrives just when you're talking about that person. It happens all the time, and it happens anywhere, in public or in private venues. That's because, without realizing it, the living routinely invoke the dead just by talking about them. So talk! Talk to someone you trust about the person you want to contact, but stay aware the whole time that a third party might show up. Talking allows you to stimulate the atmosphere with your desire for an encounter. It often leads to revelations about your real beliefs and concerns. And finally, it allows you to take advantage of the added energy of a second person, even if you are only talking on the phone.

GETTING THE MOST OUT OF A SPONTANEOUS ENCOUNTER

Now that chapter 13 has familiarized you with what happens during an unprompted encounter, you won't be off guard when one occurs. The few simple skills just described will help you maximize it. But first, we have to consider what to do when you are confronted with one of those subtle signs that heralds the presence of the dead. If you remember from that chapter, they are atmospheric shifts, spatial disturbances, smells, sounds, or voices and physical sensations, such as a touch or the tingling. Or you may feel grief waves. Add to that list the most subtle of all, mental intrusions.

All too often contact stops short because of counterproductive reactions. The uninformed, the fearful, and the disbelieving might simply ignore the signs or immediately shut down when they begin to perceive them. Others become too involved with the phenomenon, as Alexandra did with the ammonia odor. And still others are too startled to take advantage of the situation. You, however, are not going to do any of these things. You are going to react by helping the dead emerge.

The aim is to open up those subtle signs, including the grief-wave response, for real contact. Occasionally, though, a sign is all you will get, because the deceased's objective is only to let you know they're around. And too, if a sign falls under the category of physical phenomena, such as a flower tucked under your windshield wiper, and you were not there to witness it, you can do little if anything at that point other than cherish it.

Using Subtle Signs as a Starting Point

No matter what signs the dead manage to use, the process of opening them up is more or less the same. Let's say you are suddenly struck by the scent of your dead mother's cologne. Don't waste time wondering whether you are imagining it — act! Since you already know what this phenomenon means, you can immediately engage with it.

I am going to give you *five little steps* to use as soon as you perceive a sign of the dead's presence. Every one of them is extremely easy to do.

1. *Go still.*
    As soon as you perceive a sign, go still. Stay inwardly poised and alert, even if you are shouting with excitement

or crying with grief. Believe me, you can do both at the same time. This inner stillness will give your inner mechanisms the space they need to function clearly.

2. *Thicken your energy.*
   Pump up your energy and let it flow in the direction where you feel a presence in order to send the dead an energy boost for clearer transmission.

3. *Start talking out loud.*
   Announce to the deceased out loud that you recognize his or her presence and welcome it. This is an important reassurance to the dead. It will also give them the permission they need to come forth, and it lets them know that you can meet them halfway. Throughout, continue to talk out loud directly to where you most sense a presence, describing all that you experience. When you feel a connection, begin asking questions.

4. *Start the internalization process.*
   Search inwardly for any mental images — you might want to close your eyes — throwing your concentration a little above your eyebrows, as though you were looking with a second, higher pair of eyes. Listen inwardly.

5. *Record what you see and hear.*
   Take mental snapshots. Record any thoughts or messages that might be coming from the deceased.

SUMMARY — *Using Subtle Signs, the Five Little Steps: When you perceive a sign, go on inward alert, send the deceased energy, start talking to the deceased out loud and ask questions, look for mental images and listen for messages, and, finally, record what you see and hear.*

It's really rather simple, isn't it? You can use this same procedure for most of the subtle signs, as long as you can identify the sender. The same techniques work for fleeting apparitions, although your first task will be holding their attention. Confirm that you can see them and then start the process of internalization. If there are no distinguishable signs, but you simply know all of a sudden that someone is there, focus your energy where you most feel something. Guess if you have to, just to get started. If it is a sound or a touch, focus where the source seems to be.

There is also empathic telepathy, in which you pick up an emotional or physical impression from the dead. You might suddenly start giggling, for example. Acknowledge the impressions out loud and then get busy internalizing. Relying too heavily on sensing through the body is a problem, though. People often get too wrapped up in their own physical sensations, making it difficult to redirect their attention to a mental search for images and information.

If you can't immediately identify the sender, you have a few additional steps to take. As an example, let's use the feeling of a cool mass, which tends to appear more anonymously than other signs. Since this is the one most featured in films about dangerous ghosts or "evil" entities, in which mediums grope around with their hands, feeling for an atmospheric anomaly, its popular association with something sinister is strong. Don't believe it! And don't waste time looking for a source of a draft. The point is to coax that cool mass into communication. You will do that largely by asking it questions and loaning it enough energy for it to be more operative in our reality.

PREPARING FOR INTENTIONAL COMMUNICATION

Finally we've come to what to do when *you* decide it's time for a reunion. You can choose from a variety of techniques, depending on what best suits your inclinations and comfort needs. You can work with a friend or alone, use photographs and other objects to establish a link, or set up a dream encounter. And you can use a combination of techniques or discover new ones. Before you launch into contact, some thoughtful preparation, all explained below, will boost your effectiveness. A crucial part of that preparation is setting your intentions, so that what happens during your session works for the good of everyone involved.

Making Lists

Knowing what you want out of contact can help you get it. The more precise you are about what you need to say and to hear, the more aware you will become of your real feelings. Write two lists one or two days before you make your first attempt.

In the first list set down all the things you most want to say to the departed, no matter how momentous and no matter how trivial. You can make the list in letter form. If the letter seems to ramble or go in circles, organize the contents so that what you want to say becomes sharp and clear. If you had the chance to say only one thing, what would it be?

In the second list put down all the questions you have for the departed. Later on, we'll explore how to work with questions and answers during contact so that you know when a question has really been answered. Since working on these lists stimulates your connection to the departed, don't be surprised if you're already feeling someone around. Take your time thinking about what questions to ask. At this point, insights and answers are likely to start popping up in the back of your mind.

While you are in the list-making process, try to keep the outside world at bay. Take a walk on your own. Contemplate. You will probably find that you are already talking to the dead, at least in your mind. If you are, take note of what you are mentally saying and feeling. During this preparatory period, which need not last more than an hour, you might want to go through some of the deceased's belongings if they're available. Just by holding them, you will pick up your loved one's "scent" or vibration. If you have photos, pull them out and go through them thoughtfully. Indulge yourself in a few memories, happy times, sad times, poignant times, and times of maximum intimacy. Out of the photos and belongings, select one or two that speak to you most and put them aside. You may want to use them later.

In your mind or out loud, tell the departed that you are preparing yourself for contact in the next day or two. Meanwhile, stay on the alert for anything out of the ordinary that might indicate your loved one is able to hear you and act on your request.

Picking the Right Time for Contact

Although no one can do much about atmospheric conditions that help or hinder communication, working in harmony with your own personal circadian rhythms will help. Once you are familiar with them, you'll have some idea when you are likely to be the most receptive during the course of any twenty-four-hour period. I have three times: mid-morning, after I've been through my most concentrated busy work; late afternoon, when my biological clock is slowing down; and especially late at night, when the world is quieted and I can best hear my inner self.

So take a moment to review the past twenty-four hours. Pull back and watch yourself in your mind's eye as though you were looking at a video of your entire day. Watch what you did, what you were thinking, and when you felt the most energetic or fell into reverie. Also take note of emotional highs and lows, especially grief waves. As you look back, was there a time when you sensed that communication might have been possible? And if so, why? Was it because of your state of mind? The time of day? Atmospheric conditions? Or was it triggered by outside circumstances, such as finding your loved one's old shoes under the bed? If you can't find anything in the past twenty-four hours, scroll back in time until you do find that bump in everyday reality. That's your contact window.

Creating Sacred Space

Whether you are planning to work alone or with a friend, prepare a space in your home where you can shut out the rest of the world.

Mentally roam around your house for the best possible room or corner. Arrange the privacy you need for whatever comes up.

Small, closed-off areas are more favorable to deep concentration than large, open spaces. Some amount of darkness also helps you focus better on your inner senses. Darkness also begs to be filled up, with thoughts, inner pictures, and presences. If you are uncomfortable without some light, keep a small lamp on or light a candle.

Before you begin, you might light a few candles or play music in the room to clear it of any residual thought forms. Bring in some belongings or a picture of the individual you are planning to reach for that person to home in on. Have your lists on hand and keep pen and paper nearby for writing notes after the session is over. Make the room ready with ritual deliberateness.

In the place where I do inner work, I have a special chair. This is my chair, carrying no one's imprints but my own. If you don't have a personal chair, pick one that will be comfortable for about an hour, and if you are working with a partner, pick two. The chair or chairs should not remind you too strongly of someone other than the departed. Using the favorite chair of the departed will often enhance contact as long as your feelings and memories associated with it do not interfere with your ability to concentrate. If there are two of you, set the chairs so they are directly facing each other. When you are ready, make sure other members of your household know to leave you undisturbed, no interruptions, no phone calls, until you tell them otherwise.

Burial Sites

Some people feel that where the departed's remains are buried or housed is the most appropriate place for communication. If you are one of them, your space is already ritually prepared. The cemetery is a natural location for after-death communication. With just a few minor adjustments, the procedures set out below for encounters at home will serve you at a burial site equally well. If the urn containing ashes is not in a cemetery but at home, bring it into the space you have prepared.

Setting Intentions

At the beginning of every session, whether you are working alone or with a friend, or before going to sleep for a dream encounter, you must set your intentions. Setting your intentions is much the same as saying an opening prayer. Verbalizing intentions impresses the ethers more forcefully than silently reciting intentions. Setting them establishes your overall goal for the coming session. *That goal is always and above all an overarching good.* Not just for you or your session partner. Not just for the departed. But for all things that exist in the universe. In order to reach this goal, you must enlist divine help. With as much heartfelt conviction as you can muster, ask a divine power to ensure that whatever transpires will be for the best and fullest good for everyone and everything involved.

Begin at the top. I invoke All That Is. Others may use different names for the Supreme Being: God, Lord, Divine Light, the Holy Spirit, the Creator, Our Father in Heaven, Mother-Father God. If you are uncomfortable with the idea of a godhood, consider the more abstract Universe or the Presence. Whichever name draws you closest to your own greater being is the name you want. You may then call on intermediary figures to assist you: personal guides, angels, saints, dead relatives, and, certainly if you are Christian, Jesus or Mary.

Although the words should be your own, your intention may sound something like this: "I ask All That Is that whatever transpires be for the best and fullest good for me, for the departed, and for all things in the universe."

At this point, anticipate that help is at hand. Then, speaking to those you have invoked, state your more specific purpose: that you are here at this moment to make contact with a certain person, giving that person's name. Again, request aid from the spirit world, those guides and deceased relatives who are so happy to assist. Here's an example of what you might say: "I am here at this moment to make contact with _____. I ask all my guides and helpers to come to my assistance now." Pause for a moment and check for any indications of accelerated energy, such as heightened concentration on your part.

Setting intentions is no little thing. If you have made a committed prayer for good, you have built a beneficial frame around the coming events. Then whatever comes is easier to accept, because you know it's for the best. It also calls in help and protects you, the departed, and the session itself from taking an unproductive turn. It helps alleviate fear and encourage faith in the process. Last and most important, it aligns you with the beneficence that underlies all creation, seen and unseen.

After you have set the general intention of good and the more specific intention of meeting with a certain deceased, you are going to turn to the person on the other side to set the second part of your intentions. Make your mind up to establish *real* contact. Talk directly to the person as though he or she were already before you. Be strong, even commanding. Clearly state that person's name as frequently as possible in order to send its unique frequencies out into the interdimensional "radio" waves. Use a personal epithet, nickname, pet name, whichever carries the most power. If you are calling on your father, you might want to use what you called him as a child, Daddy, for instance, instead of the more adult Dad or Pop. Similarly, Mother and Mom might become Mommy. The names you used in childhood tend to carry more emotional force. What you say now may sound something like this: "I call on you, _____, to be present with me now. I call on you, _____, to reveal yourself to me. May all that transpires between us be for the best and fullest good for you, for me, and for the universe."

These last words, which are crucial to pronounce with the utmost conviction, are a restatement of your general intentions but made this time directly to the deceased. With them, you reassure him or her that no matter what happens, your greater purpose is the most beneficial outcome for all. Trust in these words, and the deceased will too. Speak them with such certainty that you forget your doubts and fears. Now that your intentions are clearly set, we'll look at the two main ways to conduct a session, alone in sitting vigil or with a friend.

SUMMARY — *A Model for Setting Intentions: "I ask All That Is that whatever transpires be for the best and fullest good for me, for the departed, and for all things in the universe. I am here at this moment to make contact with _____. I ask all my guides and help-ers to come to my assistance now. I call on you, _____, to be pres-ent with me now. I call on you, _____, to reveal yourself to me. May all that transpires between us be for the best and fullest good for you, for me, and for the universe."*

SITTING VIGIL ALONE

The most private and usually the most powerful way to initiate contact is what many call sitting vigil. I generally sit vigil late at night, when the world around me is at rest. I keep the exact time of the sitting open, letting a heightened feeling of energy and alertness determine when to begin. So far, we have concentrated on how to open up those signs the dead send of their presence. When you initiate contact on your own, you won't have those subtle signs. So you have to create your own starting point. And that starting point will of course be your genuine desire to communicate, powered by emotion. I have stressed over and over how critical desire is for making contact. Desire combines focused intention with emotional interest. Without it, little happens. This holds true even with professional psychics, who, by and large, are responding to the real need of their clients whether they are in this world or the next.

The Power of Emotion

Contact can be made in nearly every mood you can name. You can be euphoric, confused, hurt, ecstatic, enraged, silly, frightened, in anguish, in turmoil, or full of love. You can even be sarcastic. If you are feeling sheer frustration, you can just order the person to appear. They often will. It does *not* matter what emotion your mood is riding on, as long as it's sincere and as long as you keep directing it to the departed. Ostensibly negative emotions like anger work as your launchpad for contact as well as positive ones do. Genuine need and emotion carry enough energy to explode into the inner realms with a sharpness difficult for the dead to ignore. They will locate a person beyond the veil more surely than half-baked niceties or skirting around what is really weighing on your heart.

Four things should keep you emotionally honest. First, hiding your feelings doesn't work. If you're feeling rage, a sugar-coated show will only scramble your efforts. Second, there is no point whatsoever in being anything other than honest. Doing so will not bring you resolution or further your awareness. Third, you can't hide feelings from the dead anyway. Last, if you are busy hiding your feelings, you will not be open to catharsis and the euphoria contact usually brings.

Speaking Out Loud

Working alone means you have to find ways to keep momentum going before you make contact as well as during it. One of the best ways to stay on track is by talking out loud, and that means directly to the departed, whether you sense someone there or not. Talking works like an interdimensional slide for the dead to glide in on. Verbalizing questions as well as whatever answers occur to you not only keeps the flow going but also maintains focus and adds structure to your sitting.

The Procedure

The steps described below are not rules but recommendations. They should be taken as a model or case scenario. Let your own intuition be your strongest guide, and don't forget to ask the dead for help in establishing a connection. Stay open for some surprises.

The First Step — Invoking the Departed

First, prepare your space. Make sure you have your lists within reach and something to write with. Sit down and compose yourself, but *do not meditate*. The associations commonly held around meditation will only sidetrack you at this point, and the last thing you want to do now is dampen your emotions. With as much sincerity and power as you can manage, set your overall intentions, as explained above. Thicken your energy, and begin the second part of setting intentions, calling on that particular person to appear. Don't be timid. Be firm. Repeat the person's name often.

Pause and look for any indication of a presence outwardly and inwardly. You may experience only a heightened sense of expectation or a feeling that the energy around you is quickening. As you go through the sitting-vigil sequence, you are to keep that inner searchlight on high beam, checking and rechecking for mental images and messages.

What is really motivating you to seek contact? To find out how the departed is doing? Or are you so full of feelings that you are a dam about to break? Whichever one is uppermost, go with it. Address that number one concern to that person now, out loud.

If you most want to know how the departed is doing, then let loose the emotional element to propel that question forward. After all, it's doubtful that your wanting to know is just intellectual curiosity. It's a real *need*, so express it that way. "I *need* to know how you are." What's driving that need? Love? Fear? Grief? Find it and proceed from there. If you are bursting with feelings, it's time to start pouring them out. If you miss the departed, say so. If you are furious with the departed or with yourself, spit it out. If you can't stand the grief, talk about it. If you feel abandoned or scared, tell them. Then again, you might be in that place in which you feel overcome by love for the departed, and all you want is to share it.

Whatever the case, begin with your most potent emotion and verbally propel your feelings out to the person you want to contact. While doing this, form an image of that person in your mind. Speak to the heart of it, literally and figuratively. As you speak, the sense that you are not alone should grow stronger.

SUMMARY — *Sitting Vigil, Invoking the Departed: In your prepared space, set your general intentions, then the specific intentions to the departed you want to reach, and start talking to a mental image of that person from your deepest emotion.*

The Next Step — Engaging with the Departed

Once you begin to sense a presence, direct your energy toward the area where you most feel it, soften your heart, and search inwardly for images and messages, as described above.

Sometimes you can feel the moment your wavelength and the wavelength of the departed come into sync, the moment you are "in," so to speak. It can come like a hit of energy or emotion, a stream of tingling, or a pop, as though two lenses have suddenly clicked into place. The sensation of being "in" is something you already know. Think back to a time when you were trying to get someone's attention. You might have been speaking to the person and realized he or she was not actually listening. You were on different wavelengths. What lets you know people are not really paying attention? It's not strictly body language, for they may be looking straight at you with their eyes trained on your face. What lets you know the moment you finally do get their attention? If you can recall the split second when someone's focus finally clicked into sync with yours, then you know what it feels like to be in sync with a person without a body.

Start engaging the departed. Here's where your lists come in. Tell him or her all the things you most want to say. Then involve the deceased more deeply by asking questions. I don't know about you, but my first question is usually rhetorical: "Is that really *you*?" Go along with the responses and answers you are mentally receiving *without censuring*. As you proceed, you will find the dialogue growing stronger. Energy picks up, especially as you let go emotionally and become more engrossed. Doubts may crop up, but they generally stay in the background when an encounter has come this far.

It is important here to continue describing out loud to the departed what impressions you are getting. If you've asked how he or she is doing, and you either sense happiness or see your beloved's smiling face, you might respond with something like, "I feel like you are saying you are happy." Ask for confirmation by repeating it as a question: "Are you happy?" It is surprising how often you will get a clear answer. In a yes response, the departed might grin all the harder or nod his or her head vigorously, or you might "hear" something like, "Happy? I'm ecstatic!" If you are not sure you heard it right, repeat it, "You're ecstatic?" You might see the departed jumping, running, or dancing to show you how overjoyed he or she is. If your beloved is not happy, you will probably see his or her head shake no. Ask for confirmation. "Are you sad?" Usually you'll grasp the reasons for sadness right away. If not, ask the deceased. Watch and deep listen for visual or verbal answers.

No matter what you are getting, do not stop describing your impressions out loud to the deceased and checking with him or her for confirmation. Because events can happen swiftly, articulating them helps form markers in your memory line while making subtleties more concrete. It also lets the dead know what's coming through, which strengthens the connection. Keeping up a dialogue with the departed will encourage a back-and-forth, ongoing flow that keeps you from dead-ending yourself. It's a discipline. And take snapshots. Whatever you see, immediately take as many as you can, describing all the while what you are seeing. If it is all going too fast for you, tell the departed to slow down. Remember you can always ask him or her to repeat what's been said or shown to you.

In addition to actions, everything else that appears contains information too — facial expressions, movement, color, clothing, and all else listed in chapter 13. The dead might also show you symbols or objects, which are usually immediately understandable. If you don't get it right away, say so and ask for clarification. Sometimes the meaning will come clear only later. In any case, you have your snapshots that you can take out of your mental file whenever you want to examine them for more information.

If at any point you feel the connection weakening, tell the departed. Pause and build up intensity again by thickening your energy. Send it his or her way. Sharpen your senses. Heighten your expectations. Restimulate your need. Make efforts to keep the departed's attention focused on you. You can impose a little here, instructing him or her to stay put until you're finished. Again, talking and asking questions are effective in maintaining the connection. Be as precise as possible. You might ask about the dead's present experiences or seek advice. No matter what it is, try to be specific. A lot of times communication will peter out because it becomes too vague.

As you continue to speak, to listen, and to watch, you will discover more and more about how the deceased is doing, even *what* he or she is doing, such as meeting family and friends on the other side, pursuing specific activities and interests, and exploring certain issues. You will especially learn what lingering earthly concerns are left to work out. Heartfelt apologies typically arise in the early stages of communication too. In fact, they may be the very first topics addressed.

Keep going with it until you feel you are reaching the end. You might simply run out of questions, at least for the first session. Or it might feel as though the connection is getting too thin to follow or that nothing new is happening. A good question at this point is: "Do you have anything more to tell me before we come to a stop?" At the end of the session, thank the departed. And if you want to, ask if he or she is willing to meet with you again.

When the sitting has come to an end, start writing down everything that happened. This is your documentation, so include the date and time of the sitting.

SUMMARY — *Sitting Vigil, Engaging with the Departed: Direct energy toward where you most feel it and start the internalization process of searching inwardly for images and messages. Out loud, begin telling the deceased what you need to say. Ask questions. Ask for confirmation and clarification wherever needed. Describe everything you experience and take snapshots. At the end of the session, thank the departed. Then write down everything that occurred.*

What to Do When You're Not Sure

If you are not sure if anybody is around, thicken your electromagnetic field. Build up the intensity of the atmosphere around you by pumping more energy and even more intent into it. You might imagine a heart-to-heart link between you and the person on the other side growing stronger and thicker.

Keep telling yourself, *I can do it!* Restate your goal to make contact with a no-nonsense conviction. Holding a picture of your loved one in your mind, call on that person again, using his or her name frequently.

And *keep talking.* You are literally going to talk yourself and the dead into communication. Describe out loud any thoughts occurring to you, no matter how inconsequential they may seem. Posing some of them as questions will reinforce the feeling that someone is on the other end of the line. Let's say you are trying to reach a person named Jim. You think, but are not sure, that you felt a tiny spark of joy or an itsy-bitsy thrill. First state what you're feeling. "I am feeling joy." Then ask Jim as though he were right before you if that joy is coming from him. Pause for the answer. If you get an internal yes, you have the answer.

Go on by saying something like, "I'm getting the impression you are happy, Jim. Is that right?" If you pick up a yes or see Jim's happy face in your mind's eye, you have your answer. You are "in," so to speak.

If you are still too suspicious that what you are picking up is just wishful thinking, shake your head vigorously and reset your intentions again with renewed determination for real, no-fooling-around contact. Use words with conviction: "I set my intention to make real contact with you, Jim. All else I put aside." Then try again. Pose the question again or, as just suggested, restate the impression you are getting as a question. Decide that this time it will be *clearly* answered. Pause. Listen. And look inwardly. If you get the same answer or image or both, you are definitely in. If you get a different one, follow it. Jim might not be happy. Or you may have contacted not Jim but someone else.

It helps to bear in mind that when you talk to someone on the telephone, even though that person is bodiless from your point of view, you have no trouble accepting his or her validity as real. What's more, you carry an image of the person on the other end of the line quite easily, habitually giving visual substance to the voice. This is similar to what you want to be doing now. Don't worry if the conversation seems at first one-sided. It will gradually evolve into more.

Tips for When Nothing Seems to Work

If nothing you do seems to be working, it's time to turn to the imagination, the gateway between worlds. Just as talking works as a slide on which the dead can come in at any point, an imaginary encounter in which you act as though you were already in communication presents fresh possibilities for the dead to grab on to. Ask out loud, "Jim, if you were here, what would you say?" Then listen intently to your inner voice. Look inside for a mental picture of the departed and imagine him speaking. Keep doing this, verbally posing questions as well as giving the answers, until you get the impression that your thoughts are not yours alone. For example, you might have the feeling that one of your answers is a little off the mark, as though something or someone independent of you is letting you know you're off course. Ask the departed for clarification.

If you are simply floundering, it may be an indication that you are avoiding something. Releasing it will pull out the stopper, allowing emotional energy to flow.

If still nothing works, go to the "Troubleshooting" section below.

The Buddy System

Some people are more comfortable doing their first sessions with a friend. That second person is your witness to the encounter. He or she also adds energy to the session. This approach has a few drawbacks, though, mainly the tendency to hold back deeply personal information and strong emotion while in front of someone else. Be careful whom you choose. If your friend is not comfortable with strong emotion, pick another person. Find someone with a track record of being supportive. Stay away from anyone who has denigrated you in any way, undermined your past efforts, or considered you flaky. Unless your friend is able to stay focused, he or she may be more of a distraction than a help. Most of all, choose a person who respects your intention to communicate with the dead without being afraid of it. What you don't want is someone who bursts out laughing from discomfort in the middle of setting intentions or just when your loved one is coming in.

Before you begin, go over the questions you want to ask with your partner. Together, read over the procedures recommended in this chapter and discuss how you want to handle them. What you are going to do is similar to the sitting-vigil prototype above. Take your places face-to-face in the sacred space you have created, and synchronize your energies by softening your hearts for each other. Set your intentions out loud. You might want to hold hands while doing this. Now begin releasing your electromagnetic energies. Fill the room up, channeling your joint fund of desire. While your partner remains actively observant, begin pouring out your main concerns, shaping them eventually in the form of questions posed directly to the deceased.

An ideal use of partners is to get them to ask you questions, not necessarily ones from your list, but some that are more about what you are thinking, seeing, hearing, and feeling, just to keep you moving forward. Your partner's probing questions will push you into articulating your inner experiences. If you have difficulty getting started, a smart friend will try to stimulate communication by employing your imagination. He or she might ask, for example, "What would you say to Jim if he were here right now? What would Jim say to you? If you were seeing Jim now, how would he look? What is he wearing?" And then give a range of possibilities for you to select from: Happy? Sad? Younger? Older? Many of the answers that come to mind are likely to surprise even you.

All the while you are going through this question period, both of you should stay on the lookout for subtle signs and especially internal images and messages. Once one of you senses the departed, you should both focus entirely on the new arrival. The perceiver should keep the other informed about what is seen, heard, or felt by describing it out loud directly to the deceased. If both of you sense a presence, all the better. If you and your partner sense different things, don't assume one of you is wrong or that you are both making it all up. Remember the story about Alexandra's father announcing himself with the ammonia smell? She smelled it and I didn't, because we were each tuned in to a different level of his appearance. One of you might have a nonvisual experience while the other has a visual one. Or both of you might see something but not the same thing. Say one of you sees Jim more or less the way he was at his death, and the other sees him as healthy; you are picking up different areas of information. Compile them afterward to get a more complete picture. As your engagement grows and you and your partner become more synchronized, differences in perception will lessen.

As in sitting vigil, thank the departed at the end and write everything down.

SUMMARY — *The Buddy System: Review the questions you have for the deceased together. Then read this chapter to familiarize yourselves with the general flow and decide how you want to proceed. In your sacred space, sit facing each other and establish a heart-to-heart connection. Set your intentions and thicken your energies.*

Start talking about your main concerns, following your strongest emotion. Your partner might ask you questions about anything you are experiencing, especially if you are having difficulty getting going. Both of you should go into search mode for internal images and messages. Whatever is picked up — thoughts, feelings, images, or messages — should be described out loud directly to the deceased while keeping the session partner informed.

At the end thank the departed. Then compare your experiences.

OTHER TECHNIQUES FOR INTENTIONAL COMMUNICATION

Over the millennia, people have used a multitude of other ways to commune with the dead, such as rituals involving fire, smoke, water, blood, body fluids, crystals, special ointments, psychedelics, and other substances; dreams; live burial; animal sacrifice; and self-mutilation. Added to these are mirror gazing, letter writing, table rapping, and, more recently, using Ouija boards and eye movement desensitization and reprocessing (EMDR), to name some. In this section, I describe only a few techniques, picked from among the many because of their psychological familiarity. Still, they'll give you a glimpse of the range of ways after-death communication can be achieved.

Using Pictures

An effective way of initiating communication is to talk to a picture of the deceased. This is a common, time-honored method, which comes quite naturally to most people. We have all heard of the living giving a good-night kiss to a picture of the deceased on the bedside table or having regular discussions with a picture on a mantelpiece. Many who speak to pictures report that they feel the deceased listening, sometimes even answering, and that what transpires is helpful and comforting. Because talking to a picture is grounding, it is especially useful if you're experiencing a grief wave.

Photographs are not just gateways into the past; they carry vital information. Psychics routinely rattle off a great deal about people and animals, about their personality, state of health, and future, just by looking at a photo. In a way, photographs carry adjacent realities that can be read just off the page. That's something you can tap into.

Using images for launching contact can help maintain focus. And it easily fits into the sitting-vigil procedures. The only difference is that instead of talking to what you see in your mind's eye or sense outside yourself, you will be talking to a picture. If you feel you are getting lost in the picture, you are going into trance and will have some kind of meaningful contact. On the other hand, if you begin to sense the presence of your loved one independent of his or her likeness, switch to internalized images in order to get the most out of the encounter.

Setting Up a Dream Encounter

You will most likely have a dream encounter whether you are planning to or not. Remembering it when awake is another matter. Since the dead consider dream reality just as legitimate as physical reality, dream encounters are as valid as waking ones.

There is a difference between dreaming *with* someone and dreaming *about* someone. A dream of the deceased might not be a contact dream but rather an exploration of some facet of your relationship. True dream encounters tend to be vivid and intense. They also follow sequences that are ordered more in line with our waking reality. Dreaming *about* someone, by contrast, is usually jumbled, fragmented, and full of symbols and metaphors.

For me, the big dreams occur most often during afternoon naps, when sleep is lighter and less involved with body repair. Short naps of about twenty minutes seem to be the most beneficial. Dream retrieval is more difficult from deep sleep. A few swallows of coffee or tea before sleep will help you maintain a level of internal alertness that facilitates recall.

Keep a pen and notepad by the bed for recording the dream as soon as you wake up. If you want, tuck your lists under the pillow. To stimulate the emotional climate, you might take a belonging of the departed to bed with you. Put a picture of that person within eyeshot, next to a low light. Lying down, stare at it, dwelling on the features of the face. While doing this, begin to slowly relax your body from head to toe.

Once you feel relaxed, set your general intentions for the best possible good. You are going to set the more specific intentions of meeting your loved one as a hypnotic suggestion. Falling asleep usually comes about by hypnotic suggestion anyway, although we don't normally catch ourselves doing it. The moment just before slipping into sleep is when the command to meet the departed goes in the deepest. Using a picture or mentally focusing on the person you want to contact, tell yourself of your intention to meet that person right now during this very sleep time. Then say it again directly to the departed, using his or her name. Say it hypnotically over and over in synchronization with your breathing. "In my dreams, I am meeting you," giving the departed's name. Notice here that I am using the present tense. This is a hypnospeak technique. Saying "I *am* meeting you," rather than "I *will* meet you," is a more definitive command. Also tell yourself that it is easy to remember the dream because you *want* to remember it. Relax into the suggestion rather than forcing it. If you find yourself mentally saying at the same time that it won't work, you will probably follow that suggestion instead.

Sleep-state encounters usually wake us up. If yours does, lie there without moving and quickly review all the sequences, mentally taking as many snapshots of key points as you can. Start writing as soon as the initial review is over; more will come back. Write down everything: images, feeling tones, events, words, sounds, colors, emotional atmosphere, and so on. The details, which often carry layers of meaning, work like doorways opening into fresh insight or a forgotten sequence.

If you did make the suggestions but don't remember anything when you wake up, stay still. Try not to come fully awake. Let your mind drift back into a state of reverie and begin searching around in your dream memory bank. Follow whatever feeling or image comes to you most prominently. Dwell on it until it opens up and reveals the dream or at least the face of the person involved. If you see a face, probe the emotion associated with it until the dream context surfaces. Reentering the original dream and working through it by memory rather than entering into a new dream will take a certain amount of discipline.

If you get nothing, take comfort in knowing that the dream you want will often come one or two nights after making the suggestions. If you don't have a dream encounter after two nights, repeat the process.

Automatic Writing

Some people have been successful using automatic writing as a technique for initiating contact. If you are so inclined, the process is rather simple. Sit down with pen and paper in a quiet spot and think of the person you want to contact. Set your intentions. Hold the pen in your hand lightly against the paper, poised to write. Keep your writing arm and hand relaxed, as detached as possible from the rest of your body. Whatever physical impulse comes, let your hand follow it. Try not to influence the direction your hand is taking; just let it happen. You may get a word or a drawing. Spontaneous writing can look a little wild and loopy, with large letters. Some automatic writers write reams without pause, so have a big stack of paper available. Many also telepathically hear the words as they are writing them down.

Instrumental Transcommunication

As intriguing as instrumental transcommunication is, experimenting with it in the current state of our knowledge is a tedious process requiring long-term commitment for results. You also need equipment. If your sole interest is contacting a specific person, this method is probably not the way to go. Communication is usually extremely brief and one-sided, and the sender most often anonymous. The upside of using equipment is of course that you may be able to get material evidence for postmortem survival. If you are interested in experimenting with instrumental transcommunication, search the Internet for instrumental transcommunication or electronic voice phenomena. You will find a good range of websites (mostly in English.) The quality of information is uneven. Some of the sites intend only to entertain or shock. So discriminate.

Troubleshooting

What do you do if you've tried to make contact but haven't been successful so far? Sometimes the dead cannot or will not connect with you at the time of your choice. If this is your intuition, clearly restate your wish for contact. Tell the departed as though he or she were right there with you that you have done all that you know how to do to meet him or her. Then leave it to the departed to initiate contact. In the meantime, you might ask for a sign or a message that gives you some idea why your attempts have failed. You might also consider going to a professional medium.

If the problem is on your side, there's a lot you can do. First, make sure you picked a time of day that suited your inner needs rather than the convenience of others. Then make sure you created a space in which you felt safe. After that, go to the "Quick Review of Procedures" section (see page 363), and make a mental checklist. Which steps did you feel confident in doing and which caused you discomfort? Did you omit any of them? Did you avoid anything, such as talking out loud? Build on those steps that inspired confidence. For the ones that made you uncomfortable or that you omitted altogether, before you attempt contact again practice them until whatever bothered you is rooted out.

Another thing to consider is whether you have been too timid in letting the dead know what you want. Initiating after-death communication can require a certain amount of aggression. I don't mean belligerence but, rather, aggressive determination.

You might try working with a friend, especially if you've had trouble keeping momentum on your own. Or use a picture to help you maintain focus. You may be more successful turning to dreams for an encounter.

Then again, you might be trying too hard, a common enough problem. Trying too hard is usually a sign of self-doubt. You may believe, for example, that you are not worthy of having an encounter. If you are trying too hard, give it a rest for a week or two. In the meantime, work on building your trust. You might design some affirmations for yourself, such as, "I deserve to have an encounter," which you repeat over and over until you really do believe it. It's best (and hardest) to be looking at yourself in a mirror when doing affirmations. Just as important is saving some time for recreation. Do something playful and completely disconnected from the person you want to reach.

Resistance

Some people really don't want to communicate with the dead, even though they say they do. Given our current attitudes, resistance is more often the rule than the exception. As you know, the main reason for this is almost always fear. Resistance to after-death communication often produces symptoms that are fortunately easy to recognize. If any of the following apply to you, ask yourself right away, "What am I most afraid of?" The very first thing that comes to mind is usually the one most on target. Rereading chapter 12 will help you work through resistance.

Symptoms of resistance occur more frequently with spontaneous encounters than with intentional ones. You are already aware of many of these symptoms, such as the phone ringing and other electrical and electronic anomalies the dead bring about when you don't acknowledge them. Then there is the distracting outburst of grief just as your loved one appears. Flashes of anger that are really cover-ups for unwanted feelings of vulnerability are also quite common. In addition, a person might suddenly get a headache, have a sneezing fit, get an annoying itch, or feel a wave of nausea. Many people turn off with abrupt changes of activity. A person may be quietly reading when the departed make an approach, for example, and instead of moving into the experience, he or she might impulsively jump up and start cleaning the house. If you are in a conversation with someone about the departed and the invisible subject joins in, unconscious resistance is likely to cause an immediate change of subject. Minor accidents like cutting your finger or dropping something also serve to divert your attention from the dead.

The good thing is, if you notice a symptom and truly want to over-come your reluctance, you can use it as a sign of the departed's arrival. Then you can let the symptom play out while launching the search for a presence. You can have a headache, for instance, experience grief, sweep up the debris from dropping your glass, and at the same time still look for internal images and messages.

One symptom, however, seems to be irremediable — numbness. Numbness is associated more with intentional after-death communica-tion than with spontaneous encounters. Because the nature of numbness won't permit activity on any level, psychologically or physically, break-ing out of it is difficult. If you have experienced numbness, work toward preventing it from happening again by investigating its source.

Getting Messages for Others

Many people perceive the deceased around their friends and relatives. Now that you are more sensitized to communication with the departed, this may happen to you. Although I usually encourage people to deliver the messages they pick up for others, in some situations, it might be better if you don't. If a person is not psychologically prepared to accept the message or the fact of after-death communication, your efforts may bring on anger or distress rather than insight. Find another way to get the message across. If you can't without revealing your source, ask the dead person to get through in dreams. Rest assured, the living will get the message when they are ready, with or without your help.

If you sense that the person is open to after-death communication, go ahead and relate the message. What is important is using compassion and the utmost discretion in delivering what is likely to be very private information. Don't be afraid to describe how you got the message. Many times the details the deceased show you of their environment, clothing, and choice of words are deliberate pointers to their identity. Just as often they have personal meaning to the third-party recipient.

If you get information about when someone is going to die, *never*, and I repeat this, *never*, tell that person. The moment and means of death are not written in stone; they are an ongoing, ever-changing individual choice. Prophesying imminent death or an early death works like a hypnotic suggestion, which serves to fix the time and means in our reality. Instead, engage that person in a discussion about survival and the afterlife, about his or her fears, beliefs, hopes. Without imposing your own ideas, help him or her to move toward the most constructive views. Sometimes discussion alone will actually change a person's direction, so that those who intended to die young, for instance, may instead live to an old age. On the other hand, if the information pertains to a person already in terminal stages, suggesting a time frame can be helpful for caregivers.

As you grow more practiced and consequently more accurate about what the dead are trying to convey, your level of confidence in them will rise. On the basis of long experience, the very best mediums follow a simple policy — the dead are always right.

QUICK REVIEW OF PROCEDURES
FOR AFTER-DEATH COMMUNICATION

THE FOUR LITTLE RULES:

1. Stay with your truest emotion.
2. Talk out loud.
3. Internalize.
4. Ask questions.

FOR SPONTANEOUS ENCOUNTERS:

- Go still at the first indication of a subtle sign of the deceased's presence.
- Thicken your energy and let it flow in the direction where you noticed the sign.
- Start talking out loud, acknowledging to the deceased that you have recognized the sign. Keep talking to the deceased and asking questions throughout.
- Start the internalization process.
- Take snapshots and listen inwardly.

FOR INTENTIONAL AFTER-DEATH COMMUNICATION:

- Write two lists.
- Prepare a sacred space.
- Set general intentions for the ultimate good.
- Thicken your energy.
- Set personal intentions for an encounter, directing them at the person you want to reach. Frequently repeat the deceased's name.
- Start talking directly to a mental image of the deceased from your most sincere emotion.

- Go into search mode and stay there throughout.
- When you sense a presence, direct energy toward it.
- Talk and ask questions.
- Internalize whatever you see, taking snapshots and listening inwardly for any messages.
- Verbally describe your impressions directly to the departed and ask for confirmation.
- At the end of the sitting, thank the departed.

CONCLUSION

What Would the World Be Like without the Fear of Death?

I n these pages, we have heard from just a few of the many millions of people who have encountered death, whether in clinical death, in past-life therapy, or through direct communication with the departed. From their testimonies, some conclusions can be drawn. The first is perhaps the most astonishing — we are never more dead than we are right now. It bears repeating what one dead person said to his friend: "You can see I'm still living; my body is just gone."[1] Backing up this astounding statement are the demonstrations from near-death experiences in which identity, perceptions, thought, and memory can and do operate without the physical body.

Science steps in to inform us that the divide between the physical and the nonphysical is extremely narrow, irregular, and even bridged at certain subatomic points. Whether on the quantum level or on the grander multiverse level, the two realms are much closer than we are accustomed to think. By extension, the difference between us and the dead is also slighter than we think. In fact, it's literally infinitesimal, since the atoms that make up our physical bodies are 99.99999999999999 percent empty space. We and the dead are made from largely the same stuff

— consciousness. We speak the same language of telepathy, we share the same memories, and we both use the inner parabiological senses. Death is not what separates us from the departed; fear is.

Communicating with the dead is an inborn drive, a natural part of the human makeup. It is also among the handful of universals known for the human species. Contact between the living and the dead is actually a regular event, taking place subconsciously in dreams and in the privacy of our minds. Although nearly all of us commune with the other side in one way or another, it remains one of the world's best-kept secrets.

These many millions who have encountered death and the dead are presenting us with a wholly new view of the afterlife, built on composite individual experiences rather than on social constructions and religious traditions. They consistently explain the afterlife as a reality or a state of mind where the ineffable is met, where impossible levels of love, forgiveness, understanding, safety, freedom, creativity, and wisdom are claimed as humanity's God-given rights. Finally, they have demonstrated that we can know something real about the afterlife. It is our last frontier to explore, the final destination in the life of every creature on earth.

What would the world be like if our fear of death were extinguished? What would the world be like if conscious contact with the dead were a normal part of everyday life? Just as a diminished fear of death leads to more contact with the dead, more contact with the dead leads to less fear of death. It's a feedback loop.

Chapters 9 and 12 furnish some data on the changes that take place in people when that fear is out of the way. Mental, intellectual, and psychic capacities measurably increase. People become more reflective, more philosophical, more spiritual, more aware of their reincarnations. They also develop a hunger for knowledge. The desire for success and material gain wanes, as does the impulse to compete. Instead there is a stronger tendency toward service and a boosted sense of personal life purpose. Old dualistic beliefs that instigate prejudice, exclusivism, and a them-versus-us mentality give way to concern and compassion for others. A greater sensitivity to nature and the environment quickly develops. Reverence for all life and love itself become uppermost in the spectrum of new values.

What would the world be like if we were all like this? Would we invest in dualisms that pit one sex against the other, one race against another, one nation against another, the young against the old, the rich against the poor, especially when reincarnation becomes fact and more past lives as different sexes, different races, and different social and economic statuses are remembered? Would we be one global family, caring for one another, for all the creatures of the earth, and for the planet itself? How would our attitudes toward dying change? Would grief still exist, or would we regard death as cause for celebrating a birth into the next world? What would it mean to the dying to know that they can continue to communicate with their loved ones, that it's never too late, because relationships still live and continue to grow? That they will face not judgment but compassion and expanded awareness? What would it mean to the dead if their existence were finally validated instead of dismissed?

If we were to truly grasp our immortality, how would it affect our attitudes about health and the body? If we were no longer to fear aging, what would happen? Would we be more like other animals, living life to the last in a high state of health until that time comes? How many more spontaneous cures would occur if we were to let go of fear and rediscover our natural body trust?

How would morality change, our judicial systems,[2] our religious institutions? Would punishment or the threat of punishment still be the rule? Church leaders have criticized the afterlife rule of forgiveness as "cheap grace," and many others feel there can be no morality without punishment. Yet the facts are that punishment is at the root of immorality in the first place. Ask any prison warden about the childhoods of inmates. Criminality springs from an inculcated belief of being bad, of being wrong, of being weak, unlovable, unwanted, from childhoods spent in chastisement, physical abuse, and hatred. Punishment does not rehabilitate; true forgiveness does. True forgiveness and inner reconciliation strengthen the conscience and lead us back to our native morality.

Since the punishment we inflict here on earth and the threat of it we imagine in the world to come have not raised the mean level of morality for the past five millennia, they are unlikely to do so in the near future.

If we were to lose our fear of death and understand the universe for what it is, how would our explanations of reality change? How would the narratives of history change, for instance, or the narratives of biology, of psychology, anthropology, and archaeology, which purport to tell us what it means to be human? How would we revise them, and how would we teach them? What would happen to the belief of "man and aggression," of "kill or be killed"? Would war become obsolete?[3]

The dead are potentially a bottomless resource for knowledge. With after-death communication normalized, how much more inspiration and knowledge would reach people in the hard sciences and in the social sciences, in psychology, medicine, history, and the arts?

We have seen many developments in the past century that promote a kinder, fairer world. They are appearing for the first time in humanity's history. Among them are human rights, women's rights, gay rights, and the slowly dawning animal rights. The first two movements have managed to penetrate even the most sequestered, the most resistant societies, largely through the globalizing power of the Internet but also through the faster, greater power of mass telepathic communication, the true force for change in mass consciousness. Technology not only has given us the means for instant worldwide communication but also seems to serve as a training ground for telepathic communication, whether from one person to another or from one dimension to another. Telepathy spreads quickly and, like the Internet, crosses all barriers. We know this for a fact. We see it in animals separated by great distances, even in certain species of trees, and computers in universities all over the world have monitored the simultaneous activity of telepathic, even precognitive, mass consciousness in humans. There is no doubt that mass consciousness is already changing with regard to death, the afterlife, and communication with other dimensions, at least in the West. The striking similarities between the two systems of telepathic communication and technological communication allow them to easily ally and work together to effect global change.

What would it be like to really practice interdimensional communication? To experience firsthand the expanded states it offers? To consciously use our parabiological senses? How far could humanity go? I guarantee you that if we, as a society, learn to normalize communication with the other side, the outcome in the not-too-distant future, within the next two hundred years, will be spectacular. People in the centuries to come may well look back on us and wonder how we managed to survive without it.

What would it be like to finally know that the physical universe is but one mode in which reality emerges? To know that we are not alone? How would mass consciousness change with respect to our position in the universe and the nature of the universe itself? We would no doubt find ourselves heading into a true revolution. As with all revolutions, a revolution in consciousness will come with hardships, difficulties, and confusion, yet the end results are more than worth the attempt. Ironically, it will be the dead in the end who can teach us how to live, how to be happy, how to play, to love, to be ourselves. It is also the dead who have the blueprints for a heaven on earth.

As we move deeper into interdimensional communication, humanity will begin to get glimpses of even greater, more exalted states of being. What would it be like, for instance, to commune with the being of light, with your oversoul, and with others yet more extraordinary who inhabit the nonphysical dimensions? To know that some future version of your own restless soul is already going in those directions, that these unimaginable transfigurations are what await us? And especially, to live day by day with a palpable awareness of the Presence on earth, enfolded as it is in the heart of All That Is? From all that we know so far from the dead and the clinically dead, the exquisite sharpness of the material realm is to be cherished, playfully explored, and enjoyed. No doubt more of us would if we could just stop trying so hard to stay alive. We are alive. And we will always be alive.

Acknowledgments

I owe a great debt to my sister, Paula Johnson. Her close critical reading of the manuscript, her invaluable gut-felt but savvy recommendations for improvement, and fervent commitment to its message are far beyond what any sister could hope for. This book would not be where it is without her. No one could be more blessed than I was to have had Dr. Larry Dossey as my first outside reader. His bedrock belief in this book, his words of encouragement, and unstinting (and successful!) efforts to find it a home made all the difference. Larry, you are a godsend! And big thanks go to the marvelous Georgia Hughes, a truly gifted editor and a joy to work with, and to the entire New World Library team, especially Kristen Cashman, Kim Corbin, and freelance copy editor Robin Whitaker, for their expertise, warmth, and enthusiasm. You have all been a joy to work with.

Grateful acknowledgment goes to those generous friends who read all or parts of the draft. Above all is Timothy Thorson, my sole supporter at the inception of this material and its first reader. Timothy, what would I have done without you? Anne Dehne teamed up with

Timothy to coax the manuscript through its final stages. The engagement I felt from both, their suggestions, and trust in this project were gifts beyond measure. Wally Ballach and Frances Duncan read early versions of the manuscript and offered thoughtful advice. And thanks, Frances, for your whole-hearted support and the hilarious brainstorming sessions we had together. My appreciation for Suzanne McCleod is without bounds for her endless caring and help. Her quick-witted intelligence led to so many provocative discussions. Very special thanks go to Mark Coles, whose fabulous job on creating *The Last Frontier*'s website was a true act of friendship; and to the wonder boy, Gernot Haas, for spreading the word.

No words could adequately convey my gratitude to my husband, Professor Walter Mayer, for tirelessly holding my hand through every up and down phase of this book's development. As he is a writer of books himself, his advice, his insider's understanding of the writing process, and his remarkably steadfast belief in the book's message gave me the courage to continue. Lastly, this book could not have been written without the priceless help of the many departed who shared their experiences and knowledge of the dazzlingly miraculous reality they live in.

Notes

FOREWORD

1. Arthur Koestler, *Janus: A Summing Up* (New York: Random House, 1978), 282.
2. Emily Dickinson, *The Complete Poems of Emily Dickinson*, ed. Thomas H. Johnson, (Boston: Little, Brown, 1960), no. 324, stanza 3.
3. St. Teresa of Avila, attributed.
4. Henry David Thoreau, quoted in Carlos Baker, *Emerson among the Eccentrics* (New York: Penguin, 1996), 435.
5. Larry Dossey, *The One Mind* (forthcoming, 2013).
6. Henry P. Stapp, quoted in Menas Kafatos and Robert Nadeau, *The Conscious Universe: Parts and Wholes in Physical Reality* (New York: Springer, 2000), 70.
7. Robert Nadeau and Menas Kafatos, *The Non-local Universe: The New Physics and Matters of the Mind* (New York: Oxford University Press, 1999), 5.
8. Erwin Schrödinger, *What Is Life? and Mind and Matter* (London: Cambridge University Press, 1969), 139, 145.
9. David Bohm, quoted in Renée Weber, *Dialogues with Scientists and Sages* (New York: Routledge & Kegan Paul, 1986), 41.
10. Donald Hoffman, "Conscious Realism and the Mind-Body Problem," *Mind and Matter* 6, no. 1 (2008): 90.
11. Gerald Feinberg, "Precognition — a Memory of Things Future," *Quantum Physics and Parapsychology*, ed. Laura Oteri (New York: Parapsychology Foundation, 1975), 54–73.

12. O. Costa de Beauregard, "Wavelike Coherence and CPT Invariance: Sesames of the Paranormal," *Journal of Scientific Exploration* 16, no. 4 (2002): 653 (italics mine).

13. O. Costa de Beauregard, "The Paranormal Is Not Excluded from Physics," *Journal of Scientific Exploration*. 12, no. 2 (1998): 315, 316.

14. James Glanz, "Physics' Big Puzzle Has Big Question: What Is Time?" *New York Times*, June 19, 2001.

15. Richard Feynman, quoted in John Boslough, "The Enigma of Time," *National Geographic*, March 1990, 109–32.

16. Paul Davies, *Space and Time in the Modern Universe* (New York: Cambridge University Press, 1977), 221.

17. Robert G. Jahn and Brenda J. Dunne, *Margins of Reality: The Role of Consciousness in the Physical World* (New York: Harcourt Brace & Co., 1987), 280–81.

18. Henry P. Stapp, "Harnessing Science and Religion: Implications of the New Scientific Conception of Human Beings," *Science & Theology News*, February 2001, 8.

19. David Darling, *Soul Search* (New York: Villard, 1995), 188.

20. Larry Dossey, *The One Mind* (forthcoming 2013).

21. Voltaire, "La princesse de babylone," *Romans et contes* (Paris: Editions Garnier Frères, 1960), 366.

INTRODUCTION

1. For the United States, 42 percent was found by Andrew M. Greeley, *Religious Change in America* (Cambridge, MA: Harvard University Press, 1989); 66 percent was found by L. Vargas et al., "Exploring the Multidimensional Aspects of Grief Reactions," *American Journal of Psychiatry* 146, no. 11 (1989): 1484–89. The five-year project, the Afterlife Encounter Survey, recorded the highest incidence, at 72 percent; for discussion, see Dianne Arcangel, *Afterlife Encounters: Ordinary People, Extraordinary Experiences* (Charlottesville, VA: Hampton Roads, 2005), 277–300. For the results of a British Gallup poll from 1987 (= 48 percent), see D. Hay, "The Spirituality of the Unchurched," *British and Irish Association for Mission Studies*, March 12, 2007, www.martynmission.cam.ac.uk/BIAMSHay.htm.

2. Raymond Moody, *Reunions: Visionary Encounters with Departed Loved Ones* (New York: Ivy Books, 1994), viii.

3. David Lester, *Is There Life after Death? An Examination of the Empirical Evidence* (Jefferson, NC: McFarland, 2005), 176.

4. According to Kenneth Ring and Evelyn Elsaesser Valarino (*Lessons from the Light* [2000; repr., Needham, MA: Moment Point Press, 2006]), just reading about NDEs can cause similar effects.

5. See Allan L. Botkin, *Induced After-Death Communication: A New Therapy for Healing Grief and Trauma*, with R. Craig Hogan (Charlottesville, VA: Hampton Roads, 2005).

6. Hospice nurses Maggie Callanan and Patricia Kelley first coined the term in their book *Final Gifts: Understanding the Special Awareness, Needs, and Communications of the Dying* (New York: Bantam Books, 1992).

7. Polls come from Lester, *Is There Life after Death?*, 23 and 24, and from George Gallup Jr., *Adventures in Immortality* (New York: McGraw-Hill, 1982). The results of other polls were published by Greeley in *Religious Change in America*. They include the American Institute of Public Opinion (AIPO) Survey, conducted almost yearly since 1944; the General Social Survey (GSS) of the University of Chicago (NORC), information collected from 1944 to 1985; and the Survey Research Center (SRC) at the University of Michigan, conducted less regularly with regard to afterlife opinions since 1950. See also the survey in Richard Morin, "Do Americans Believe in God?" *Washington Post*, April 24, 2000, www.washingtonpost.com/wp-srv/politics/polls /wat/archive/wat042400.htm. The 1994 Gallup poll shows 75 percent for Americans.

8. With the 1975 Mockingbird edition (Atlanta) of *Life after Life*.

9. The 1982 Gallup survey (Gallup, *Adventures in Immortality*) shows 16 percent of scientists believing in survival after death as opposed to 67 percent in the general population. Among members of the National Academy of Sciences, all in the hard sciences, 79 percent around the end of the past century did not believe in God. See E. G. Larson and L. Witham, "Leading Scientists Still Reject God," *Nature* 394 (1998): 3313.

10. It is probably no coincidence that John Logie Baird, inventor of the television as well as the infrared camera (commonly used in paranormal research), claimed that he had made contact with Thomas Edison through a medium. See Baird's 1988 publication, *Sermons, Soup and Television — Autobiographical Notes* (London: Royal Television Society). Edison is purported to have been working on a telephone bridging our world and the world of the hereafter before he died.

11. Ring and Valarino, *Lessons from the Light*, 46.

CHAPTER ONE. CAN SURVIVAL AFTER DEATH BE PROVED?

1. Quoted from Heinz Pagels, *The Cosmic Code* (New York: Bantam, 1982), in John Gribbin, *In Search of the Multiverse* (London and New York: Allen Lane, Penguin, 2009), 20.

2. For the many-worlds interpretation and the quantum computer, see John Gribbin's *In Search of the Multiverse*.

3. See, for instance, the works of the quantum physicist Amit Goswami.

CHAPTER TWO. HOW REAL IS REAL?

1. Although the idea of a blinking universe seems to stem primarily from the Seth material channeled by Jane Roberts, quantum physicists of great stature, such as David Bohm, a member of the Manhattan Project team, which developed the atomic bomb, have considered it a possibility. The blinking universe is implicit in the fact

that a subatomic particle is there and not there, depending on whether or not it is observed. Until it is observed, scientists regard it as in a superposition, which means anywhere in the universe or nonexistent. Not only do subatomic entities go from particles to waves and back again, but they also change in other equally significant ways. For instance, a photon converts itself into a pair of one electron and one positron. Because an electron is negative, and its antimatter, the positron, is positive, they annihilate each other and become a photon again. More important perhaps is quantum fluctuation, which speaks of particles such as an electron-positron pair that appear out of nothing and disappear back into nothing. The fluctuation lasts for only about 10–21 seconds. These "virtual" particles are not hypothetical but have been detected as forming clouds around other charged particles. The blinking universe also underlies some interpretations of zero-point field theory. Deepak Chopra explores it in some depth in his book *Life after Death: The Burden of Proof* (New York: Harmony Books, 2006), 211–13.

2. The smallest increment of time is called Planck time, named after the quantum physicist Max Planck. Planck time is 10^{-43} second, a decimal point followed by forty-two zeroes with a 1 at the end.

3. 100,000,000,000,000,000,000,000,000,000,000 atoms; see John Gribbin, *In Search of the Multiverse* (London and New York: Allen Lane, Penguin, 2009).

4. These statistics are from R. Craig Hogan, *Your Eternal Self* (n.p.: Greater Reality Publications, 2008), 1.

5. From R. Craig Hogan's discussion on the brain in chapter 1 of his book *Your Eternal Self*, 7.

6. Ibid.

7. See especially E. F. Kelly, E. W. Kelley, A. Crabtree, and A. Gauld, *The Irreducible Mind: Toward a Psychology for the 21st Century* (Lanham, MD: Rowman and Littlefield, 2006). The notion of the extended mind or the mind as a supraphysical entity has spawned an ever-growing body of scientific and philosophical literature.

8. For the telepathic parrot N'kisi and other psychic pets, see the works of Rupert Sheldrake: *Dogs That Know When Their Owners Are Coming Home: And Other Unexplained Powers of Animals* (New York: Crown, 1999); and *The Sense of Being Stared At: And Other Unexplained Powers of the Human Mind* (New York: Crown, 2003).

9. C. Choi, "Strange but True: When Half a Brain Is Better Than a Whole One," ScientificAmerican.com, May 24, 2007; and Hogan, *Your Eternal Self*, 9.

10. Reported by Reuters, July 19, 2007. The article "Brain of a White-Collar Worker," *Lancet* 370, no. 9583 (July 21, 2007), is available on the Internet at www.thelancet .com/journals/lancet/article/PIIS0140-6736(07)61127-1/fulltext. It includes excerpts from Dr. Lionel Feuillet in Marseille and commentary from Dr. Max Muenke, a brain-defect specialist at the National Human Genome Research Institute.

11. See Joseph McMoneagle, *Remote Viewing Secrets: A Handbook* (Charlottesville, VA: Hampton Roads, 2000). McMoneagle is a veteran of Project Stargate, the U.S.

military's secret remote-viewing program. He also instructs readers on how to develop the skill. See also Courtney Brown, *Remote Viewing: The Science and Theory of Nonphysical Perception* (Atlanta: Farsight Press, 2005).

12. The reports were compiled and studied by Dr. Charles Honorton and his colleagues at the Division of Parapsychology and Psychophysics, Maimonides Medical Center, in New York. The compilation represented two million trials. See C. Honorton and D. C. Ferrari, "Future Telling: A Meta-analysis of Forced-Choice Precognition Experiments, 1935–1987," *Journal of Parapsychology* 53 (1989): 281–308. Subsequent research at the University of Edinburgh and Cornell has produced the same results. For more examples and an excellent overview of the scientific backup of parapsychological research, see Dean Radin, *The Conscious Universe: The Scientific Truth of Psychic Phenomena* (New York: Harper and Row, 2009).

13. Chopra, *Life after Death*, 225.

14. See the works of Joseph Chilton Pearce on savant syndrome: *Evolution's End: Claiming the Full Potential of Our Intelligence* (New York: HarperCollins, 1992); for the "automobile savant," see his book *The Biology of Transcendence: A Blueprint of the Human Spirit* (South Paris, ME: Park Street Press, 2002), 82, also reviewed in Chopra, *Life after Death*, 226.

15. The story of Jay Greenberg was reported on *60 Minutes*, a CBS news production, in 2004. For those interested, look up www.cbsnews.com/stories/2004/11/24 /60minutes/main657713.shtml; also see Hogan, *Your Eternal Self*, 43. The relationship between savant syndrome and genius is explored in "The Key to Genius," www.wired.com/wired/archive/11.12/genius_pr.html.

16. Benjamin Libet, "Subjective Antedating of a Sensory Experience and Mind-Brain Theories: Reply to Honderich," *Journal of Theoretical Biology* 155 (1984): 563–70. In the same vein, see especially Sheldrake, *The Sense of Being Stared At*.

17. The same results were replicated at the University of Amsterdam and the University of Utrecht. See Dick Bierman and Dean Radin, "Anomalous Anticipatory Response on Randomized Future Conditions," *Perceptual and Motor Skills* 84 (1997): 689–90; and Radin, *The Conscious Universe*.

CHAPTER THREE. NEAR-DEATH EXPERIENCES

1. Among the many published sources for these two accounts is the more technical by the research specialists Kenneth Ring and Madelaine Lawrence, "Further Evidence for Veridical Perception during Near-Death Experiences," *Journal of Near-Death Studies* 11, no. 4 (1993): 223–29. See also Kenneth Ring and Evelyn Elsaesser Valarino, *Lessons from the Light* (2000; repr., Needham, MA: Moment Point Press, 2006), 65–68.

2. This story, which rocked the world of NDE research, has been published by various authors. For the full account, see Kimberly Clark Sharp, *After the Light* (New York:

William Morrow, 1995), 3–16. Also see her original write-up, "Clinical Interventions with Near-Death Experiencers," in *The Near-Death Experience: Problems, Prospects, Perspectives*, ed. B. Grayson and C. P. Flynn (Springfield, IL: Charles C. Thomas, 1984), 242–55.

3. See L. L. Morris and K. Knafl, "The Nature and Meaning of the Near-Death Experience for Patients and Critical Care Nurses," *Journal of Near-Death Studies* 21 (2003): 139–67.

4. This is one instance taken from Sabom's study of thirty-two near-death survivors. In all thirty-two cases, the survivors recalled events taking place during resuscitation in perfect detail. By contrast, all those who were resuscitated but did not have an out-of-body experience made significant errors. See Sabom's *Recollections of Death: A Medical Investigation* (New York: Harper and Row, 1982).

5. This is described in Raymond Moody, *The Light Beyond* (New York: Bantam Books, 1988), 141–43.

6. For more examples, see Barbara Rommer, *Blessing in Disguise* (St. Paul, MN: Llewellyn, 2000); and Ring and Valarino, *Lessons from the Light*, 60–64.

7. Kenneth Ring and Sharon Cooper, *Mindsight: Near-Death and Out-of-Body Experiences in the Blind* (Palo Alto, CA: Institute of Transpersonal Psychology, 1999).

8. The Gallup poll of 1982 estimated that over eight million Americans had had near-death experiences, not all caused by imminent-death situations, representing about 5 percent of the adult population, or one person in every twenty. A later poll, from 1992, estimated thirteen million Americans have had them. See Rommer, *Blessing in Disguise*, 3.

9. The term for unpleasant near-death experiences was coined by Barbara Rommer (*Blessing in Disguise*). Of Rommer's study group, 17.7 percent had had less-than-positive experiences (twenty-four). P. M. H. Atwater estimated about 14 percent of her subjects had had that type (*Beyond the Light* [New York: Avon, 1995]). Many prominent researchers, such as Raymond Moody, Michael Sabom, and Kenneth Ring, did not report negative experiences other than occasional moments of uncertainty or confusion.

10. When Moody and Ring combined their data with research from Evergreen State College, in Olympia, Washington, they found that only 0.3 percent of the respondents described hellish near-death experiences (Moody, *The Light Beyond*, 27). Gallup found only 1 percent.

11. For discussion on a more plausible identity of this being, see chapter 11.

12. See chapter 8 for simultaneous time and nontime experiences, especially during life reviews.

13. Rommer, *Blessing in Disguise*, 11.

14. S. K. Pasricha and Ian Stevenson, "Near-Death Experiences in India: A Preliminary Report," *Journal of Nervous and Mental Disease* 175 (1986): 165–70; S. K. Pasricha,

"A Systematic Survey of Near-Death Experiences in South India," *Journal of Scientific Exploration* 7 (1993): 161–71.

15. And see Raymond Moody's rebuttal in *The Light Beyond*, 109–27.

16. B. Greyson, "Near Death Experiences in a Psychiatric Outpatient Clinic Population," *Psychiatric Services* 54 (2003): 1649–51.

17. For a review of these studies, see David Lester, *Is There Life after Death? An Examination of the Empirical Evidence* (Jefferson, NC: McFarland, 2005), 57–58.

18. These inexplicable changes have been charted since the mid-1960s. See R. G. Druss and D. S. Kornfeld, "The Survivors of Cardiac Arrest," *Journal of the American Medical Association* 201 (1967): 291–96.

19. For several cases of severe illnesses disappearing, see Melvin Morse, *Transformed by the Light: The Powerful Effect of Near-Death Experiences on People's Lives* (New York: Villard Books, 1992).

CHAPTER FOUR. AFTER-DEATH COMMUNICATION

1. See n. 1 of the Introduction; and Dianne Arcangel, *Afterlife Encounters: Ordinary People, Extraordinary Experiences* (Charlottesville, VA: Hampton Roads, 2005), 277–300.

2. Judy Guggenheim and Bill Guggenheim founded the ADC Project, which resulted in their book *Hello from Heaven!* (New York: Bantam Books, 1997) based on thirty-three hundred accounts.

3. The Afterlife Encounter Survey, in Arcangel, *Afterlife Encounters*, 284.

4. For this and more, see Guggenheim and Guggenheim, *Hello from Heaven!*, 248–50.

5. Raymond Moody, *The Light Beyond* (New York: Bantam Books, 1988), 173–74.

6. Arcangel, *Afterlife Encounters*, 22.

7. Guggenheim and Guggenheim, *Hello from Heaven!*, 249.

8. Ibid., 252–54; and Emma Heathcote-James, *After-Death Communication* (London: Metro Publishing, 2004), 47–49.

9. Guggenheim and Guggenheim, *Hello from Heaven!*, 244.

10. Ibid., 257.

11. Ibid., 274.

12. Ibid., 267–68, 293–305.

13. Ibid., 50–51, 293–94.

14. Arcangel, *Afterlife Encounters*, 111–12.

15. Guggenheim and Guggenheim, *Hello from Heaven!*; Arcangel, *Afterlife Encounters*, 157–60.

16. Guggenheim and Guggenheim, *Hello from Heaven!*, 286–87.

17. Ibid., 275–85, for these and other similar reports.

18. Ibid., 334.

19. Kenneth Ring and Evelyn Elsaesser Valarino, *Lessons from the Light* (2000; repr., Needham, MA: Moment Point Press, 2006), 267.

20. Arcangel, *Afterlife Encounters*, 39.

21. D. Scott Rogo and Raymond Bayless, *Phone Calls from the Dead* (Englewood Cliffs, NJ: Prentice Hall, 1979).

22. John Lerma, *Into the Light: Real Life Stories about Angelic Visits, Visions of the After-life, and Other Pre-death Experiences* (Franklin Lakes, NJ: New Page Books, 2007), 172–73.

23. Guggenheim and Guggenheim, *Hello from Heaven!*, 193–94.

24. The story has many sources. This account is from Arcangel, *Afterlife Encounters*, 106–7.

25. In particular, these ways of conjuring include Allan Botkin's induction therapy and Raymond Moody's mirror-gazing techniques.

26. Carl Gustave Jung, *Memories, Dreams, Reflections*, trans. Richard Winston and Clara Winston (New York: Random House, 1963), 312–14.

27. I was unaware of the cross-relics phenomenon until I read about it in the entertaining and informative book *The Survival Files: The Most Convincing Evidence Yet Compiled for the Survival of Your Soul*, by Miles Edward Allen (Henryville, IN: Momentpoint Media, 2007), 98–114. See also *The Mystery of the Buried Crosses: A Narrative of Psychic Exploration*, by the Pulitzer Prize–winner Hammlin Garland (New York: E. P. Dutton, 1939). Garland found sixteen more crosses through a medium channeling the already-deceased Violet Parent.

28. I have omitted much, including the vastly important Cross Correspondences: snippets of obscure verse and prose delivered by the dead to various mediums. They were put together like puzzle pieces, resulting in some three thousand manuscripts. For coverage of all phenomena bearing on the survival issue as well as a bibliography, see David Fontana's thoughtful book *Is There an Afterlife?* (Alresford, Hampshire, U.K.: O Books, 2005), 175–85 and passim.

29. Readers interested in physical mediumship might want to start with the Scole experiments. See again Fontana, *Is There an Afterlife?*, for many full accounts or search the Internet.

30. Hereward Carrington, *The World of Psychic Research* (North Hollywood, CA: Wilshire Book Co., 1974), 54.

31. Shirley Bray, *A Guide for the Spiritual Traveler* (Cleveland, Queensland, Australia: Scroll, 1990), 15; also cited in R. Craig Hogan, *Your Eternal Self* (n.p.: Greater Reality Publications, 2008), 116.

32. Charles H. Hapgood, *Voices of Spirit: Through the Psychic Experience of Elwood Babbitt* (New York: Delacorte, 1975), 224–27; also cited in Hogan, *Your Eternal Self*, 116–17.

33. Fontana, *Is There an Afterlife?*, 232.

34. See Gary E. Schwartz, *The Afterlife Experiments: Breakthrough Scientific Evidence*

of Life after Death (New York: Atria Books, 2002). The mediums included some of the very best America has to offer, Suzanne Northrop, John Edwards, and George Anderson, with Laurie Campbell and the minister Anne Gehman.

35. This famous séance has been published in several sources. For the best review of the reams and reams of astoundingly detailed, complicated information delivered by the dead concerned, as well as background on the amazing Garrett herself, see Fontana, *Is There an Afterlife?*, 144–56.

36. Ibid., 312–18; and the website "Helen Duncan: The Official Pardon Site," www.helenduncan.org.uk/.

37. See Erlendur Haraldsson and Ian Stevenson, "A Communicator of the 'Drop-In' Type in Iceland: The Case of Runolfur Runolfsson," *Journal of the American Society for Psychical Research* 69 (1979): 33–59, reviewed in Fontana, *Is There an Afterlife?*, 164–66.

CHAPTER FIVE. REINCARNATION

1. A Gallup poll taken in 1969 showed 20 percent of the American population as believers in reincarnation, 18 percent for England, 25 percent for Germany, 26 percent for Canada, and 23 percent for France. By the time of the 1982 poll, Americans were up to 23 percent, and in 2001, 25 percent. The dip indicated in the 2005 poll (20 percent) is already on the rise.

2. See Thorwald Dethlefsen, *Voices from Other Lives* (New York: M. Evans and Co., 1970); Edith Fiore, *You Have Been Here Before* (New York: Coward, McCann, and Geoghegan, 1978); Bruce Goldberg, *Past Lives, Future Lives* (North Hollywood, CA: Newcastle Publishing, 1982); Denys Kelsey and Joan Grant, *Many Lifetimes* (New York: Doubleday, 1967); and Dick Sutphen, *Past Lives, Future Loves* (New York: Pocket Books, 1978).

3. Alexander Cannon, *The Power Within: The Re-examination of Certain Psychological and Philosophical Concepts in the Light of Recent Investigations and Discoveries* (New York: E. P. Dutton, 1950), 170.

4. Joe Fisher, *The Case for Reincarnation* (London: Diamond Books, 1993), 41.

5. Ibid., 39.

6. R. Kampmann, "Hypnotically-Induced Multiple Personality," *International Journal of Clinical and Experimental Hypnosis* 24 (1976): 215–17.

7. Unlike most other regression therapies, the Netherton method does not use hypnosis or relaxation techniques. Instead the patient is reminded that he or she already knows what point in the past the problem stems from and is in fact already there. Usually without delay, the patient locates the moment the fear or problem is anchored in and begins to reexperience it. It is just as likely to be in the patient's present life as in a past one. As a complement to psychic work, I became a certified past-life therapist in the mid-1980s. I was trained at the AAPLE center in California, founded by Morris

Netherton. Part of the course was to undergo the therapy as a patient. I can honestly say, it very quickly changed my life. One inadvertent side effect of regression therapy is the emergence of natural psychic abilities, no doubt because on the couch we have finally learned to listen to our inner selves.

8. Morris Netherton and Nancy Shiffrin, *Past Life Therapy* (New York: Ace Books, 1978), 197–99.

9. See the web page www.centrodifusao.hpg.ig.com.br/morris.htm for Morris Netherton, *The Psychology of Past-Life Regression*; and Miles Edward Allen, *The Survival Files: The Most Convincing Evidence Yet Compiled for the Survival of Your Soul* (Henryville, IN: Momentpoint Media, 2007), 175–76.

10. See Bruce Goldberg, *Past Lives, Future Lives Revealed* (Franklin Lakes, NJ: Career Press, 2004), 101–17.

11. Netherton and Shiffrin, *Past Life Therapy*, 7.

12. Guirdham's main works on reincarnation are available in reprints: *The Cathars and Reincarnation* (London: C. W. Daniel, 2004); *A Foot in Both Worlds* (Wappingers Falls, NY: Beekman, 1991); *We Are One Another* (London: C. W. Daniel, 2004); *The Lake and the Castle* (London: C. W. Daniel, 2004); and *The Great Heresy* (London: C. W. Daniel, 1993).

13. Rieder wrote three fascinating books on the Millboro phenomenon: *Mission to Millboro* (1991), *Return to Millboro* (1996), and *Millboro and More* (2003), all by Blue Dolphin Press (Grass Valley, CA).

14. See Jenny Cockell: *Yesterday's Children* (London: Piatkus Books, 1993); and *Across Time and Death: A Mother's Search for Her Past-Life Children* (Whitby, ON: Fireside, 1996).

15. The story of James Leininger broke on ABC's *Primetime* show in 2004. See Ian Lawton's website www.ianlawton.com/cp13.htm, "The Past Life Memories of James Leininger."

16. See Ian Stevenson's works: *Twenty Cases Suggestive of Reincarnation* (1966); *Cases of the Reincarnation Type*, 4 vols. (1975–83); *Unlearned Language: New Studies in Xenoglossy* (1984), all from the University of Virginia Press; and *European Cases of the Reincarnation Type* (Jefferson, NC: McFarland, 2003), among others. Psychiatrist Jim B. Tucker, who is currently carrying on Stevenson's work, has reviewed twenty-five hundred cases and forty years of research at the University of Virginia in *Life before Life: A Scientific Investigation of Children's Memories of Previous Lives* (New York: St. Martin's Press, 2005).

17. Ian Stevenson, *Cases of the Reincarnation Type*, vol. 1: *Ten Cases in India* (Charlottesville: University of Virginia Press, 1975), 176–78.

18. Fisher, *The Case for Reincarnation*, 5–8.

19. Ian Stevenson, "Birthmarks and Birth Defects Corresponding to Wounds on Deceased Persons," *Journal of Scientific Exploration* 7 (1993): 403–16.

, trans. A. E. J. Wils (New York:

nation (1966; repr., Charlottesville:
, *Exploring Reincarnation*, 247.
nlearned Languages: New Studies
ginia Press, 1984); also see Sylvia
sadena, CA: Theosophical Univer-

st (New York: Penguin, 1981), 169.

on: Psychic Press, 1970), 126.

f northern Palestine, primarily the
ew pockets of the Near East. The
ia Cranston and Joseph Head, eds.,
ego, CA: Point Loma Publications,
soulproof.com.

THE AFTERLIFE

as been published in various places
d F. Wente, *Letters from Ancient*
49; and R. B. Parkinson, *Voices from*
142.
Revised Standard Version.
Greek of "fallen asleep" rather than
ised Standard Version.
ed by the Council of Nice in 533 CE.
Sukie Miller's book *After Death:*
fter Life (New York: Simon and

from Heaven! (New York: Bantam

ENESIS OF SIN

e representation of sin in the story of
uch as the development of the ego,

den," is a Sumerian word several
thousand years older than the earliest biblical writings. Its original meaning is

"steppe," the grassy area between waterways and desert. Its use throws the action into the most remote past known in antiquity. This fairly common literary device is here calculated to convey the impression that the story itself has been passed down from the first humans, possibly through Abraham, who came from Sumer.

3. In all of Asherah's representations and rites, trees or treelike objects are involved. She could be represented by a living tree that people planted and that Deuteronomy 16:21 forbids, a stylized or sacred tree, a lopped trunk, or an aniconic piece of wood sometimes planted in the ground; her image was also carved into a living tree. Passages condemning her worship are found in Exodus, Deuteronomy, Kings, Judges, Isaiah, Jeremiah, and Micah. That she was originally Yahweh's wife or "consort" is no longer disputed.

4. The doctrine was formulated after Pelagius, the champion of human innocence, was declared a heretic. According to it, the Virgin Mary is the only mortal born without original sin, for which she is named the Immaculate Conception.

5. Once in a while relationships between people, often parent and child or siblings, are so binding that one is actually incomplete without the other. Such relationships usually arise in very strong family constellations in which each member works out a different side of the same issue, as I see it here. Once the work is finished, dying is the appropriate next step.

Chapter Eight.
"Spiritual Evolution," Nontime, and the Ego

1. Ronald C. Finucane, *Appearances of the Dead: A Cultural History of Ghosts* (Amherst, NY: Prometheus Books, 1984), 223.

2. In addition to individual regression therapists and hypnotists who have come to this conclusion based on their own practices, Hans TenDam canvasses the results of many practitioners in *Exploring Reincarnation*, trans. A. E. J. Wils (New York: Penguin Arkana, 1990).

3. We are already close to discovering that a species' consciousness engineers genetic change, as Rupert Sheldrake's work suggests. (See especially *The Presence of the Past: Morphic Resonance and the Habits of Nature* [Rochester, VT: Park Street Press, 1995].) More important are the findings of quantum biology that show intelligent, efficient, and purposeful change at the most miniscule level of organic life. Last is the research at MIT on frogs that show unequivocally that growth, such as the formation of eyes in this study, is engineered by electrical signals rather than genes. I have little doubt that Darwin's vision of a hit-or-miss adaptation will eventually be proved wrong.

4. Ian Stevenson, *Cases of the Reincarnation Type*, vol. 1 (Charlottesville: University of Virginia Press, 1975), 34, 65.

5. Helen Wambach, *Life before Life* (New York: Bantam, 1978), 42, 75.

6. See Ian Stevenson and E. W. Cook, "Involuntary Memories during Severe Physical Illness or Injury," *Journal of Nervous and Mental Disease* 183 (1995): 452–58.

7. See J. M. Holden, "Unexpected Findings in a Study of Visual Perception during Naturalistic Near-Death Out-of-Body Experience," *Journal of Near-Death Studies* 7 (1989): 155–63.

8. Raymond Moody, *The Light Beyond* (New York: Bantam Books, 1988), 30–32.

9. For life reviews, see Kenneth Ring and Evelyn Elsaesser Valarino, *Lessons from the Light* (2000; repr., Needham, MA: Moment Point Press, 2006).

10. Harold Sherman, *The Dead Are Alive: They Can and Do Communicate with You* (New York: Ballantine, Fawcett Gold Medal, 1981), 111–13.

11. I first learned about this life during my only session with a hypnotist in 1974, in which my full name in that former existence was uncovered. Through a subsequent series of paranormal events and dreams in 1998, I was conducted to a tiny abandoned churchyard in rural southern England, where I found the tombstone of my past-life personality.

12. Jenny Randles and Peter Hough, *The Afterlife: An Investigation into the Mysteries of Life after Death* (London: Piatkus Books, 1993), 190.

13. David Lester, *Is There Life after Death? An Examination of the Empirical Evidence* (Jefferson, NC: McFarland, 2005), 103.

14. See C. R. Lundahl, "Near-Death Visions of Unborn Children," *Journal of Near-Death Studies* 11 (1992): 123–28.

15. See John Gribbin, *In Search of the Multiverse* (London and New York: Allen Lane, Penguin, 2009).

CHAPTER NINE. THE FEAR OF DEATH

1. Genetic similarities between humans and certain apes are so strong that some scientists advocate moving chimpanzees and bonobos into the genus *Homo*, to which we *Homo sapiens* and Neanderthals belong. See news.bbc.co.uk/2/hi/science/nature/3042781.stm for discussion.

2. Of course, not all physicians ignore nonmedical routes to health and healing, but a great majority of them do. Physician Larry Dossey offers a number of surprising nonmedical remedies, such as humming and forgetting, in his book *The Extraordinary Healing Power of Ordinary Things* (New York: Random House, Three Rivers Press, 2006).

3. For studies on tears eliminating toxic waste, see ibid., 58–71.

4. In addition to the research cited in this section, the following discussion is also drawn from M. Bauer, "Near-Death Experiences and Attitude Change," *Anabiosis* 5 (1985): 39–47; C. P. Flynn, "Meetings and Implications of NDEr Transformations," *Anabiosis* 2 (1982): 3–14; B. Greyson, "Near-Death Experiences and Personal Values," *American Journal of Psychiatry* 140 (1983): 618–20; B. Greyson and I. Stevenson,

"The Phenomenology of Near-Death Experiences," *American Journal of Psychiatry* 137 (1980): 193–96; R. Moody, *Life after Life* (Atlanta: Mockingbird Books, 1975); C. Musgrave, "The Near-Death Experience," *Journal of Near-Death Studies* 15 (1997): 187–201; R. Noyes, "The Human Experience of Death, or What Can We Learn from Near-Death Experiences?" *Omega* 13 (1982–83): 251–59; K. Ring, *Heading toward Omega* (New York: Harper Perennial, 1984); Barbara Rommer, *Blessing in Disguise* (St. Paul, MN: Llewellyn, 2000); and C. Sutherland, "Changes in Religious Beliefs, Attitudes, and Practices following Near-Death Experiences," *Journal of Near-Death Studies* 9 (1990): 21–31.

5. Rommer, *Blessing in Disguise*; Melvin Morse, *Transformed by the Light: The Powerful Effect of Near-Death Experiences on People's Lives* (New York: Villard Books, 1992).

6. Benedict's near-death experience is recounted in many publications. For the story and medical commentary, see Deepak Chopra, *Life after Death: The Burden of Proof* (New York: Harmony Books, 2006), 122–25.

7. For expanded mental awareness, electrical sensitivity, and other physiological changes, see Kenneth Ring, *The Omega Project: Near-Death Experiences, UFO Encounters and Mind at Large* (New York: William Morrow, 1992); Morse, *Transformed by the Light*; and P. M. H. Atwater, *Beyond the Light* (New York: Avon, 1995). For neurological changes in particular, see the *Journal of Near-Death Studies* 12, no. 1 (1994). For hypersensitivity to environmental stimuli, see especially Michael Shallis, *The Electrical Connection: Its Effects on Mind and Body* (New York: New Amsterdam Books, 1998); Hilary Evans, *The SLI Effect* (London: Association for the Scientific Study of Anomalous Phenomena, 1993); and Albert Budden, *Allergies and Aliens: The Visitation Experience, an Environmental Health Issue* (New York: Discovery Times Press, 1994). See also Dannion Brinkley, *Saved by the Light: The True Story of a Man Who Died Twice and the Profound Revelations He Received* (New York: HarperOne, 2000).

8. Pim van Lommel, Ruud van Wees, Vincent Meyers, and Ingrid Elfferich, "Near-Death Experience in Survivors of Cardiac Arrest: A Prospective Study in the Netherlands," *Lancet* 358 (December 15, 2001): 2039–42.

9. For paranormal sensitivities, see Ring, *The Omega Project*; Morse, *Transformed by the Light*; Atwater, *Beyond the Light*; and Cherie Sutherland, *Transformed by the Light: Life after Near-Death Experiences* (Sydney and New York: Bantam, 1993).

CHAPTER TEN. PREPARING TO DIE

1. Many dead people have reported leaving their bodies before impact in after-death communications. Bill Guggenheim and Judy Guggenheim have found many instances of the same reports in their files. See *Hello from Heaven!* (New York: Bantam Books, 1997), 149–50.

2. The physiological aspects of dying are drawn from my own experience and especially from Maggie Callanan and Patricia Kelley's book, *Final Gifts: Understanding the Special Awareness, Needs, and Communications of the Dying* (New York: Bantam Books, 1992), 33–34.

3. Melvin Morse, *Closer to the Light: Learning from the Near-Death Experiences of Children* (New York: Ivy Books, 1993).

4. Carla Wills-Brandon, *One Last Hug before I Go* (Deerfield Beach, FL: Health Communications, 2000), 188–89.

5. Ward Hill Lamon, *Recollections of Abraham Lincoln 1847–1865* (Lincoln: University of Nebraska Press, 1994), 116–17.

6. Dianne Arcangel, *Afterlife Encounters: Ordinary People, Extraordinary Experiences* (Charlottesville, VA: Hampton Roads, 2005), 110.

7. See the Princeton Engineering Anomalies Research Laboratory on the Princeton University website or Dean Radin, *The Conscious Universe: The Scientific Truth of Psychic Phenomena* (New York: Harper and Row, 2009), for scientific analyses of this and other anomaly research.

8. Larry Dossey, *The Power of Premonitions: How Knowing the Future Can Shape Our Lives* (New York: Dutton Adult, 2009).

9. For many fascinating examples, see Dossey, *The Power of Premonitions*, which also discusses the problems of validating premonitions as well as the thornier dilemma of whether or not to act on them.

10. See the excerpt by Robert Sullivan in Raymond Moody, *The Light Beyond* (New York: Bantam Books, 1988), 165.

11. Callanan and Kelley, *Final Gifts*, 196.

12. Ibid., 173.

13. Karlis B. Osis, *Deathbed Observations by Physicians and Nurses* (New York: Parapsychology Foundation, 1961); see also the more popular Karlis B. Osis and Erlendur Haraldsson, *At the Hour of Death: A New Look at the Evidence for Life after Death* (New York: Hastings House, 1977).

14. See John Lerma, *Into the Light: Real Life Stories about Angelic Visits, Visions of the Afterlife, and Other Pre-death Experiences* (Franklin Lakes, NJ: Career Press, 2007).

15. See Wills-Brandon, *One Last Hug before I Go*, 121–24.

16. Ibid., 119–20.

17. The idea of flying divine beings and protective spirits is very old. To the peoples of antiquity, whatever was considered airborne must have wings. There were many winged figures in ancient Mesopotamia, Egypt, Canaan, and Greece, yet none bears much similarity to the modern notion of angels. Perhaps the most impressive was the Assyrian *lamassu*, a colossal guardian figure sculpted in the form of a winged bull with the divinely crowned head of a virile bearded man (examples are housed in the Metropolitan Museum of Art, the British Museum, and the Louvre). *Lamassus* must have made an unforgettable impression on the peoples of antiquity. I

suspect that the giant *lamassu* contributed to Ezekiel's vision of cherubim, with their bovine hooves, four heads, and four sets of wings. As discussed in chapter 6, angels came rather late to Judaism, appearing predominantly in more mystical strains. The Hebrew seraphim and cherubim were among the highest known beings, and images of cherubim were fixed to the four corners of the Ark of the Covenant. The conception of angels as winged human adults may have originated from the esoteric belief in angelmorphism, also discussed in chapter 6, for the truly holy. The modern baby cherub is an adaptation of the Roman *putto*, a supernatural chubby male infant. Sometime around the Renaissance *putti* were depicted with wings and acquired the rank of angels, now called cherubs.

18. In the Osis and Haraldsson study, 25 percent died within the hour, 20 percent within six hours, and 62 percent within the day. For these findings and discussion, see chapter 3, pp. 16–33, in *At the Hour of Death*. There are also many known instances in which visits occurred daily for weeks before the actual demise.

19. Arcangel, *Afterlife Encounters*, 120.

20. Callanan and Kelley, *Final Gifts*, 173.

21. Bill Guggenheim and Judy Guggenheim found that nurses have more after-death communication than members of any other profession. The patients of nurses working with the terminally ill frequently come back after passing to thank them or offer aid (*Hello from Heaven!*, 174).

22. Callanan and Kelley, *Final Gifts*, 84–85.

23. Lerma, *Into the Light*, 154.

24. Callanan and Kelley, *Final Gifts*, 101–5.

25. The story of this child and his contact with his mother three weeks after death is quite a stunner. See Guggenheim and Guggenheim, *Hello from Heaven!*, 325.

26. Arcangel, *Afterlife Encounters*, 120–21.

27. On the sparing of grief, see Callanan and Kelley, *Final Gifts*, 207.

28. See, for example, the story of the nine-year-old Matthew, in Lerma, *Into the Light*, 21–29.

29. Callanan and Kelley, *Final Gifts*, 221.

30. Ibid., 183.

31. Amit Goswami, *Physics of the Soul: The Quantum Book of Living, Dying, Reincarnation, and Immortality* (Charlottesville, VA: Hampton Roads, 2001), 73; originally in Rachel Naomi Remen, *Kitchen Table Wisdom: Stories That Heal* (New York: Riverhead Books, 1996).

CHAPTER ELEVEN. GOING THROUGH THE THRESHOLD
AND THE PERIOD OF ADJUSTMENT

1. Kenneth Ring and Evelyn Elsaesser Valarino, *Lessons from the Light* (2000; repr., Needham, MA: Moment Point Press, 2006), 14.

2. Raymond Moody, *The Light Beyond* (New York: Bantam Books, 1988), 74.

3. Ibid., 9.

4. See Ring and Valarino, *Lessons from the Light*, 63; and chapter 3 herein.

5. See R. E. Kelly, "Post-mortem Contact by Fatal Injury Victims with Emergency Service Workers at the Scenes of Their Death," *Journal of Near-Death Studies* 21 (2002): 23–33.

6. P. M. H. Atwater's research of 3,000 adults and 277 children found few reported tunnels (*Beyond the Light* [New York: Avon, 1995]). In addition, tunnels were almost nonexistent for survivors interviewed from Southeast Asia (David Lester, *Is There Life after Death? An Examination of the Empirical Evidence* [Jefferson, NC: McFarland, 2005], 51).

7. Moody, *The Light Beyond*, 11.

8. Bill Guggenheim and Judy Guggenheim, *Hello from Heaven!* (New York: Bantam Books, 1997), 181.

9. For this and other variations of the tunnel experience, see W. J. Serdahely, "Variations from the Prototypic Near-Death Experience," *Journal of Near-Death Studies* 13 (1995): 185–96.

10. Moody, *The Light Beyond*, 17.

11. From Ring and Valarino, *Lessons from the Light*, 286.

12. For life reviews, see Ring and Valarino, *Lessons from the Light*.

13. Guggenheim and Guggenheim, *Hello from Heaven!*, 175.

14. See Moody's synopsis of Dr. Bruce Greyson's research in *The Light Beyond*, 99.

15. The two accounts that follow are from Carla Wills-Brandon, *One Last Hug before I Go* (Deerfield Beach, FL: Health Communications, 2000), 150–53.

16. This is not to be confused with the "silver cord," which Spiritualists claim connects the physical body to the astral body.

CHAPTER TWELVE. IT'S OKAY TO TALK TO THE DEAD, BUT WHAT HAPPENS WHEN THE DEAD TALK BACK?

1. Raymond Moody, *Reunions: Visionary Encounters with Departed Loved Ones* (New York: Ivy Books, 1994), 35–36.

2. See Dianne Arcangel, *Afterlife Encounters: Ordinary People, Extraordinary Experiences* (Charlottesville, VA: Hampton Roads, 2005), 288.

3. Ibid., 98–99.

4. See Allan Botkin, *Induced After-Death Communication: A New Therapy for Healing Grief and Trauma*, with R. Craig Hogan (Charlottesville, VA: Hampton Roads, 2005).

5. Bill Guggenheim and Judy Guggenheim, *Hello from Heaven!* (New York: Bantam Books, 1997). See also Arcangel, *Afterlife Encounters*, 115.

6. Arcangel, *Afterlife Encounters*, 105–6.
7. Moody, *Reunions*, 65.
8. Botkin, *Induced After-Death Communication*, 54.
9. Guggenheim and Guggenheim, *Hello from Heaven!*, 239.
10. Botkin, *Induced After-Death Communication*, 117–19.
11. See ibid., 115–16.
12. For example, those in Arcangel, *Afterlife Encounters*, 284–85; and others.
13. Ibid., 285.
14. Ibid., 287–88.
15. Arthur Hastings et al., "Psychomanteum Research," *Omega* 45 (2002): 211–28.
16. Botkin, *Induced After-Death Communication*, 197, and discussion on 26–34.
17. See, for example, the story of A. J. Plimpton, whose deep grief over the death of his wife, Wilma, led to developing entirely new interests and creative abilities as well as the skills to communicate with her on a daily basis. See Harold Sherman, *The Dead Are Alive: They Can and Do Communicate with You!* (New York: Ballantine, Fawcett Gold Medal, 1981).
18. Botkin, *Induced After-Death Communication*, 76.
19. See, for example, Raymond Moody, Dianne Arcangel, and Allan Botkin, among others.

CHAPTER THIRTEEN. FAMILIARITY

1. See Dianne Arcangel, *Afterlife Encounters: Ordinary People, Extraordinary Experiences* (Charlottesville, VA: Hampton Roads, 2005), 103. In one poll of 1,200 people from nineteen countries, 53 percent of the 1,978 accounts of contact reported had occurred in the first year, and 47 percent had occurred well after that.
2. Bill Guggenheim and Judy Guggenheim, *Hello from Heaven!* (New York: Bantam Books, 1997), 144.
3. Emma Heathcote-James, *After-Death Communication* (London: Metro Publishing, 2004), 131.
4. Ibid., 102.
5. Guggenheim and Guggenheim, *Hello from Heaven!*, 198–99.
6. See ibid., 206, for one example among many.
7. Ibid., 205.
8. Almost any compilation of after-death communication will offer at least one physicalized encounter.
9. Bill Guggenheim and Judy Guggenheim have come to the same conclusion (*Hello from Heaven!*, 112).
10. As found by Raymond Moody; see his *Reunions: Visionary Encounters with Departed Loved Ones* (New York: Ivy Books, 1994), 85.

Chapter Fourteen. Ghosts, Thought Forms, and "Earthbound Spirits"

1. See my website, www.juliaassante.com, for a blog series on ghosts and ghost liberating.
2. Harold Sherman, *The Dead Are Alive: They Can and Do Communicate with You* (New York: Ballantine, Fawcett Gold Medal, 1981), 118. Sherman has authored several books on the paranormal.
3. Ibid., 314.
4. Sherman and his colleague P. Kaluaratchi began writing a book with the alarming title *The Great Drama of Earthbound Spirits — How to Escape Afterlife Entrapment* (ibid., 117); however, Sherman died in 1987, before the book was completed.
5. Sherman, *The Dead Are Alive*, 314.

Chapter Fifteen. Telepathy

1. Personal communication from an ex-SAS soldier who does not want to be named.
2. David Lester, *Is There Life after Death? An Examination of the Empirical Evidence* (Jefferson, NC: McFarland, 2005), 43.
3. See Carl Zimmer's article, "Sizing Up Consciousness by Its Bits," *New York Times*, Science section, September 20, 2010. My thanks to Paula Johnson for drawing my attention to this article.
4. Dianne Arcangel, *Afterlife Encounters: Ordinary People, Extraordinary Experiences* (Charlottesville, VA: Hampton Roads, 2005), 128.

Conclusion

1. Allan Botkin, *Induced After-Death Communication: A New Therapy for Healing Grief and Trauma*, with R. Craig Hogan (Charlottesville, VA: Hampton Roads, 2005), 76; and chapter 12 herein (p. 275).
2. See Gary Schwartz's sensitive and realistic speculations on this subject and about the vast changes in general that would take place if we were to believe in what he calls the "living-soul hypothesis," in his book *The Afterlife Experiments: Breakthrough Scientific Evidence of Life after Death* (New York: Atria Books, 2002), chapters 18 and 19.
3. As Raymond Moody suggests in *Reunions: Visionary Encounters with Departed Loved Ones* (New York: Ivy Books, 1994), 102.

Index

A

Abraham (Old Testament figure), 127–28, 135

Adam (Old Testament figure), 127, 129

Adapa (Mesopotamian wise man), 112

ADC (After-Death Communication) Project, 54, 379n2

Aeneid (Virgil), 106

after-death communication, 25
    ancient beliefs, 96–97, 99–101, 108–10
    backwards, 73, 156–57
    base elements of, 54
    benefits of, 2, 3, 7–13, 64, 253, 274–77
    book tests, 66–67
    as dangerous, 265–68
    death preparations and, 206
    as direct afterlife experience, 8
    discussions about, 171
    documentation of, 351, 357–58
    evidence of, 28, 53–54, 61, 66
    expectations of, 279, 280–83, 287–97
    familiarity with, 279–80
    famous people admitting, 263–64, 375n10
    fear during, 268–70
    fear of, 255–60, 265–68
    fear of death and, 167–68, 183
    forms of, 279
    grief and, 270–74
    as inborn drive, 366
    increased belief in, 13

    information given during, 55–56, 59–60, 67, 298, 361–62
    instrumental transcommunication, 64–66, 209, 358–59
    intentional encounters, 63–76, 269, 271, 280, 282, 290, 339–45, 355–59, 363–64
    intentions in, 266, 340–41, 343–45
    mediumship, 67–76, 140–42
    need for, 248–49
    normalization of, 368–69
    numbers of encounters, 53, 262, 390n1
    ongoing contact, 12–13, 277–78
    personal accounts of, 1–2, 36–37
    physical phenomena associated with, 61–63
    receptive occasions for, 262–63
    research studies on, 222
    sensory types, 55
    sequential encounters, 61
    shared witnessing of, 60–61
    signs of, 279, 284–87, 327, 337–39
    skepticism about, 53–54, 64, 262
    soul-to-soul, 297–98
    spirit communication, 139–40
    spontaneous encounters, 54–63, 262, 269, 271, 280, 281–82, 336–39, 363
    as telephone call, 256, 279–80
    timing of, 55, 56–58, 341
    unpredictability of, 261–62

About the Author

Julia Assante is both a mystic and a scholar. She has been a professional intuitive and medium for over four decades. She is also an active past-life therapist and All-Faith minister. Julia gives workshops in the United States and Europe, focused on unleashing the full range of people's natural psychic capacities, from remote viewing and healing to reincarnational recall and after-death communication. Her accuracy in telepathy has been clinically tested at Columbia University (1987), which scored her high above other professional psychics. As a scholar (PhD, Columbia University), her landmark publications on ancient Near Eastern magic, cult, and religion have revised many long-standing assumptions in the study of antiquity in general. She has taught at Columbia, Bryn Mawr, and the University of Münster (Germany) and given talks at many major universities around the world. Currently she divides her time between the United States (Northern California) and Europe (France and Germany). Her official website is www.juliaassante.com.

NEW WORLD LIBRARY is dedicated to publishing books and other media that inspire and challenge us to improve the quality of our lives and the world.

We are a socially and environmentally aware company, and we strive to embody the ideals presented in our publications. We recognize that we have an ethical responsibility to our customers, our staff members, and our planet.

We serve our customers by creating the finest publications possible on personal growth, creativity, spirituality, wellness, and other areas of emerging importance. We serve New World Library employees with generous benefits, significant profit sharing, and constant encouragement to pursue their most expansive dreams.

As a member of the Green Press Initiative, we print an increasing number of books with soy-based ink on 100 percent postconsumer-waste recycled paper. Also, we power our offices with solar energy and contribute to nonprofit organizations working to make the world a better place for us all.

Our products are available
in bookstores everywhere.
For our catalog, please contact:

New World Library
14 Pamaron Way
Novato, California 94949

Phone: 415-884-2100 or 800-972-6657
Catalog requests: Ext. 50
Orders: Ext. 52
Fax: 415-884-2199
Email: escort@newworldlibrary.com

To subscribe to our electronic newsletter, visit
www.newworldlibrary.com

HELPING TO PRESERVE OUR ENVIRONMENT

3,147
trees were saved

New World Library uses 100% postconsumer-waste recycled paper for our books whenever possible, even if it costs more. During 2011 this choice saved the following precious resources:

	ENERGY	WASTEWATER	GREENHOUSE GASES	SOLID WASTE
www.newworldlibrary.com	22 MILLION BTU	600,000 GAL.	770,000 LB.	225,000 LB.

Environmental impact estimates were made using the Environmental Defense Fund Paper Calculator @ www.papercalculator.org.